Organizational Culture and Behavioral Shifts in the Green Economy

Violeta Sima
Petroleum-Gas University of Ploiesti, Romania

A volume in the Advances in
Human Resources Management
and Organizational Development
(AHRMOD) Book Series

Published in the United States of America by
    IGI Global
    Business Science Reference (an imprint of IGI Global)
    701 E. Chocolate Avenue
    Hershey PA, USA 17033
    Tel: 717-533-8845
    Fax: 717-533-8661
    E-mail: cust@igi-global.com
    Web site: http://www.igi-global.com

Library of Congress Cataloging-in-Publication Data

Names: Sima, Violeta, 1968- editor.
Title: Organizational culture and behavioral shifts in the green economy /
  Violeta Sima, editor.
Description: Hershey, PA : Business Science Reference, [2018]
Identifiers: LCCN 2017013422| ISBN 9781522529651 (hardcover) | ISBN
  9781522529668 (ebook)
Subjects: LCSH: Corporate culture--Environmental aspects. | Organizational
  behavior--Cross-cultural studies. | Organizational behavior--Environmental
  aspects.
Classification: LCC HD58.7 .O736156 2018 | DDC 302.3/5--dc23 LC record available at https://
lccn.loc.gov/2017013422

British Cataloguing in Publication Data
A Cataloguing in Publication record for this book is available from the British Library.

All work contributed to this book is new, previously-unpublished material.
The views expressed in this book are those of the authors, but not necessarily of the publisher.

For electronic access to this publication, please contact: eresources@igi-global.com.

Advances in Human Resources Management and Organizational Development (AHRMOD) Book Series

ISSN:2327-3372
EISSN:2327-3380

Editor-in-Chief: Patricia Ordóñez de Pablos, Universidad de Oviedo, Spain

MISSION

A solid foundation is essential to the development and success of any organization and can be accomplished through the effective and careful management of an organization's human capital. Research in human resources management and organizational development is necessary in providing business leaders with the tools and methodologies which will assist in the development and maintenance of their organizational structure.

The **Advances in Human Resources Management and Organizational Development (AHRMOD) Book Series** aims to publish the latest research on all aspects of human resources as well as the latest methodologies, tools, and theories regarding organizational development and sustainability. The **AHRMOD Book Series** intends to provide business professionals, managers, researchers, and students with the necessary resources to effectively develop and implement organizational strategies.

COVERAGE

- Entrepreneurialism
- Upward Feedback
- Organizational Development
- Personnel Retention
- Job Enrichment
- Recruitment Process
- Organizational behavior
- Work-Life Balance
- Human Resources Development
- Disputes Resolution

IGI Global is currently accepting manuscripts for publication within this series. To submit a proposal for a volume in this series, please contact our Acquisition Editors at Acquisitions@igi-global.com or visit: http://www.igi-global.com/publish/.

Titles in this Series

For a list of additional titles in this series, please visit:
https://www.igi-global.com/book-series/advances-human-resources-management-organizational/73670

Management Strategies and Technology Fluidity in the Asian Business Sector
Patricia Ordóñez de Pablos (University of Oviedo, Spain)
Business Science Reference • ©2018 • 338pp • H/C (ISBN: 9781522540564) • US $225.00

Arab Women and Their Evolving Roles in the Global Business Landscape
Ebtihaj Al-A'ali (University of Bahrain, Bahrain) Minwir M. Al-Shammari (University of Bahrain, Bahrain) and Hatem Masri (University of Bahrain, Bahrain)
Business Science Reference • ©2018 • 321pp • H/C (ISBN: 9781522537106) • US $200.00

Creativity in Workforce Development and Innovation Emerging Research and Opportunities
Sally Blake (Flagler College, USA) and Candice M. Burkett (University of Illinois at Chicago, USA)
Business Science Reference • ©2018 • 152pp • H/C (ISBN: 9781522549529) • US $145.00

Evaluating Media Richness in Organizational Learning
Albert Gyamfi (Aalborg University Copenhagen, Denmark) and Idongesit Williams (Aalborg University Copenhagen, Denmark)
Business Science Reference • ©2018 • 328pp • H/C (ISBN: 9781522529569) • US $185.00

Teaching Human Resources and Organizational Behavior at the College Level
John Mendy (University of Lincoln, UK)
Business Science Reference • ©2018 • 305pp • H/C (ISBN: 9781522528203) • US $195.00

Handbook of Research on Organizational Culture and Diversity in the Modern Workforce
Bryan Christiansen (PryMarke LLC, USA) and Harish C. Chandan (Argosy University, USA)
Business Science Reference • ©2017 • 506pp • H/C (ISBN: 9781522522508) • US $255.00

Handbook of Research on Human Factors in Contemporary Workforce Development
Bryan Christiansen (PryMarke LLC, USA) and Harish C. Chandan (Argosy University, USA)
Business Science Reference • ©2017 • 563pp • H/C (ISBN: 9781522525684) • US $255.00

For an entire list of titles in this series, please visit:
https://www.igi-global.com/book-series/advances-human-resources-management-organizational/73670

701 East Chocolate Avenue, Hershey, PA 17033, USA
Tel: 717-533-8845 x100 • Fax: 717-533-8661
E-Mail: cust@igi-global.com • www.igi-global.com

Table of Contents

Detailed Table of Contents

Chapter 1

Ecological Responsibility and Sustainable Development as Preconditions for
Development of the Concept of Circular Economy 1
Olja Munitlak Ivanovic, Institute of Economic Sciences, Serbia

Ethical and ecological responsibility represent the root of sustainable development taking into account intergenerational justice. Mass production and consumption have left negative effects on the environment. Disregarding ecological responsibility, production processes were mainly based on uncontrollable use of raw materials and non-renewable energy sources. Taking into account limitation of raw materials, economic and ecological disasters, a concept of resilience has been developed to make all elements of society flexible in terms of unwanted shocks. This chapter describes two conceptual economic models: linear and circular. The linear model is based on the principle "take, produce, consume, and throw," meaning that usability of waste is reduced and that waste is simply thrown out after consumption. Circular economic model takes into account environmental responsibility, but it also makes companies more competitive. Waste is treated and processed adequately and used as raw material in production, thus increasing competitiveness. Waste that cannot be processed is disposed permanently.

Chapter 2

Valuing Sustainability: How National Culture Influences Attributions
Towards Green Advertising 21
Daniela Rojas Morales, University of Amsterdam, The Netherlands
Lars Moratis, Antwerp Management School, Belgium & NHTV Breda
University of Applied Sciences, Belgium

Consumers' low awareness and negative attributions remain critical impediments to companies' attempts to reap the potential benefits of CSR. Addressing the gap of how and under which conditions what type of attributions arise and the role of stakeholder factors in CSR communication strategies, the aim of this chapter is to assess to what extent national culture influences the attributions that arise towards green advertising. Preceded by a pre-test, a survey was conducted in Colombia, The Netherlands and USA. With a total of 248 responses, a multiple regression analysis was performed to analyze the data. Results show main effects of national culture on the attribution of negative motives. Specifically, the cultural dimensions power distance and uncertainty avoidance have a negative effect on negative attributions. On the other hand, results indicated that positive attributions are not influenced by national culture. The research stresses the relevance of national culture as a stakeholder-factor, influencing the effectiveness of green advertising.

Chapter 3

Tamer Baran, Pamukkale University, Turkey
Mehmet Kiziloglu, Pamukkale University, Turkey

Firms have an unfavourable effect on environmental problems that severely threatens the ecological balance. In this context, firms' responsibility must be heavy on environmental problems. In the last two decades an approach guiding firms' socially beneficial activity as well as profitably activity has emerged. Accordingly, many firms launched marketing campaigns in order to claim themselves environment friendly. But it is not possible to say all of these campaigns reflect the facts. Some firms conduct greenwashing campaigns, which means misleading activity in order to persuade external stakeholders and consumers to appear more environmentally friendly than they actually are. In this chapter, the authors explain the effect of greenwashing advertisements on organizational culture using findings of previous studies as evidence. Organizational image, greenwashing concepts, and factors that drive firms' greenwashing activities are explained and then the effect of green advertisements on organizational image is revealed through previous studies' findings.

Chapter 4

Augustin Constantin Mitu, Petroleum-Gas University of Ploiesti,
Romania
Daniela Steluta Uta, Petroleum-Gas University of Ploiesti, Romania

Following the development of marketing theory concerning the policies in general, promotional policy has known an impressive development. Today, the practice fields professionals operating with relatively sophisticated notions and concepts, which are fine-tuned and pragmatic in terms of results. For example, it is significant that concepts such as rating and market share have already entered into ordinary language, including being properly understood by consumers covered. Annually large amounts of money for advertising are spent; almost all large companies allocate non-negligible amounts for such purposes. The launch of new brands is accompanied by consistent advertising and promotional campaigns conducted on multiple levels to cater to potential consumers with tangible and intangible components associated with the various products, services, or brands.

Organizational culture is one of the determinants of a company's competitiveness, and consequently, realistic analysis of the link between these two elements can provide relevant information to optimize it and, on this basis, to increase the company performance. The direct implications of organizational culture are important in business efficiency. Increasing the quality of human resources, efficient exploitation of material resources, and financial mean the achievement of provisioned levels of turnover, market share, or value added. Organizational culture, through its forms and manifestations (symbols, rules of behavior, customs, ceremonies, history, prestige, and authority of managers and employees), influences and leads to a series of behaviors and attitudes so that employees can tap the full potential for achieving goals. Eliminating fear in an organization is an essential requirement, as it encourages people to take more risks, responsibilities, and initiatives. Remarkable results can be achieved if performance will be measured properly and if a direct reward is chosen.

Local and organic food is of global importance and benefits our health, community, and environment. Today, people come together and build a food community to access local and organic food directly from the farmers under a chain of trust. It is an amazing opportunity to support small farmers and reach fresh produce. Organic markets, participatory guarantee systems, farm shares or community supported agriculture, work exchange, and other co-operatives allow us to connect with one another and perpetuate social and ecological sustainability. This chapter analyzes these direct organic marketing mechanisms and community building ways towards green economy. It demonstrates these cultures and gives some best practices in the creation of sustainable food community networks around the world. The chapter concludes with emphasizing the significance on the sociality and locality, thus contributing to the long-term goal of sustainable development and resilience.

Chapter 7

Georgiana-Raluca Ladaru, Bucharest University of Economic Studies,
Romania

In current economies, the organic agrifood markets have started to gain more proactive dimensions by volume, revenue, and demand. Analysing the trends, constraints, and transformations of Romanian organic agrifood market represents an actual research subject, which should be understood as a growing part of agricultural economics and marketing research. Starting from the general assumption that organic agrifood market represents a share of one percent and growing, the main aim of this chapter is to reveal the primary transformation and constraints from a multiperspective approach.

Chapter 8

Alfredo J. Escribano, Independent Researcher, Spain

Livestock production requires important amounts of resources, which are limited. Therefore, the feed industry is under pressure to combine food security and sustainability. Hence, it is going through an important process of remodeling (both in focus and in practice). The feed industry should make good use of this context as a way to evolve towards a more sustainable future, and constitute itself as a player in global sustainability efforts. The present chapter reviews the concept of quality (using meat products as model) and gives examples of how to modulate animal products healthiness/safety and reduce the environmental impact of the sector through animal feeding practices. Finally, it provides an overview of the main research areas and ongoing projects that the main global organizations involved in the feed sector are currently running in order to successfully overcome sustainability challenges.

Chapter 9

Predrag Vuković, Institute of Agricultural Economics, Serbia
Svetlana Milorad Roljević-Nikolić, Institute of Agricultural Economics,
Serbia

Practice has shown that the best results in solving problems that burden rural areas give mechanisms which coordinate development of agriculture with other economic activities on the principles of sustainable development. Partnership in the development of rural tourism and organic agriculture represent a logical sequence of things. People today are aware of the complex problem of burdening the global food chain and natural resources with the remains of persistent pesticides, nitrates, and the worsening of organoleptic properties and nutrient-like food. The concept of organic farming insists on the natural balance of interests. For this reason, tourists who come to the rural areas expect that they will be able to consume organically produced healthy food. The chapter analyzes the concept of rural tourism and organic farming, their dynamic development in the world and in Serbia. It points out the importance of its connectivity to eliminate existing negative trends which burden life in rural areas and possibilities to implement the goals of the green economy.

Chapter 10
The Role of the Educational System in Promoting Local Culture Within
    Cristina Iridon, Petroleum-Gas University of Ploiesti, Romania
    Cristina Gafu, Petroleum-Gas University of Ploiesti, Romania

The present chapter presents the results of a research developed within a series of rural schools in Romania (Prahova and Buzău County) regarding the role of the educational system in preserving the individuals' cultural identity and in promoting the local culture within the rural areas. Schools, be they urban or rural, are meant to contribute to capitalizing, reevaluating, and valuing the local cultural identity. The present analysis takes into account both the formal activities (included in the study programs or in the units of study planning: topics of discussion, study themes, optional courses, etc.) and non-formal events (traditional local festivals, school feasts, religious/folk celebrations, etc.) organized with the support of the local community projects, workshops conceived by the teachers in order to preserve the local culture and to make the young generation aware of their identity values.

Foreword

During the recent years numerous researches were addressed to understanding and highlighting the role of culture in contemporary economies. Starting from the assumption already existed in literature which defines culture as a state of intellectual evolution of people, a state of social development that includes values, in this book the contributors have taken into consideration the norms which may be based on an economic activity and are useful in modelling behaviours on an organization and its members in a particular economy. In this context it is more than necessary to identify the features of a specific area. It is necessary to understand, apply and develop management models reflecting the culture as well. Culture affects business outcomes both positive and negative. The transition to a green economy requires policies and investments to link economic development, biodiversity, the ecosystem, climate change, health and well-being of the population over the medium and long-term. These premises must be interconnected to achieve sustainable development - considered as the basis for the resumption of global economic growth. Moving towards the Green Economy implies a proper focus on knowledge, research, and innovation that creates a favourable framework to foster sustainable long-term development. A solution for adapting the economy and the evolution of new global challenges can be the transition to Green Economy, integrating the environment into the sustainable development paradigm.

A key component of an organization's way to success involves incorporating sustainability into the organizational culture.

There is a relevant literature on organizational behaviour from a strategic perspective as well as on specific kinds change building cultures of health and safety or building cultures of compliance.

This book brings together culture - Hofstede's dimensions of cultural values, organizational behaviour, and green economy. The interaction of culture and organizational behaviour describes how culture affects ethical behaviour, leadership, and motivation of employees in organizations. From another point of view, the principles of green economy should be taken into consideration to highlight the new organizational changes. Highlighting how culture can affect business outcomes both positive and negative, this book could be considered as a reference for professionals, researchers, practitioners, and students. The overall objective of this book is to highlight the changes in the green economy and the transformations they bring in organizational behaviour, aiming at studying cross-cultural differences. These differences have an impact on communication among people from different cultures.

Exploring these issues could offer new exciting perspectives for a better understanding of these differences, improving, finally, the organizational performances. This book provides valuable insight for researchers, policymakers, economists, scientists, practitioners working in the field of management, economics, marketing and general readers into the parallels between theory and practice in organizational behaviour from a cross-cultural perspective of the green economy.

Jean Vasile Andrei
Petroleum-Gas University of Ploiesti, Romania

Andrei Jean-Vasile, *PhD, is associate professor at Petroleum-Gas University of Ploiesti, Department of Business Administration and PhD mento in economics at Bucharest University of Economic Studies. He holds a PhD in Economics from the National Institute of Economics Research – Romanian Academy of Sciences. He has earned a BA degree in Administrative Sciences (2005) and in Banks and Finances (2007) from the Petroleum-Gas University of Ploiesti. He has an MA degree in Economics, Administrative and Business Management (2007) earned at the same university. Jean Andrei is Editor-in-Chief of International Journal of Sustainable Economies Management (USA), Associate Editor of Economics of Agriculture (Ekonomika poljoprivrede) published by Institute of Agricultural Economics (Serbia), scientific reviewer for International Business Information Management Association Conferences – IBIMA. He is also member of scientific organizations: The Balkan Scientific Association of Agrarian Economists, Serbia (December 2008). Issues like business investments process, economic efficiency, agricultural and resources economics, business administration, and valuing economic and human potential are among his research and scientific interests, where he has published articles (over 50), scientific books (8), and numerous conferences presentations.*

Preface

Business development in the contemporary world takes place in an economically, politically and socially complex environment, defined on two essential coordinates: on the one hand, the national-international relationship, and the cultural dimension, on the other. Regarding the first coordinate, a multi-secular trend led to the progressive expansion of the field of action of the companies, due to the process of internationalization and globalization of economic and social life. On the other hand, it is now necessary to recognize the tremendous cultural diversity of the world, and it is essential to take into account the specific cultural values in managerial strategy and business practice worldwide.

Knowing the characteristics of the different regions is increasingly important for scientists and, especially for managers and marketers as well. Successful management approaches are no longer generally valid (Hofstede, 2001). Relationships between organizations—firms, institutions, states, regional bodies, etc.—involve the interference and interaction of different cultures. For example, for a company, the set of core values (change or conservatism, production orientation or market orientation, a hierarchical structure or a functional one, etc.) defines its "cultural profile". In business relations, the company's culture comes into contact with the cultures of other entities (clients, competitors), so that the management activity is carried out in an environment characterized by cultural diversity. When the company's business is on a global scale, there are several ways: globally, internationally, and corporate to highlight the importance of culture for management conception and practice. The study of cultural differences in management starts from the definition of the term culture and the relationship between national culture and organizational culture. Organizational culture is a concept introduced in 1979 (Pettigrew, 1979), which has developed rapidly. Thus, Peters and Waterman (1982) have demonstrated that there is a close link between the dimensions of organizational culture and the performance of leading corporations.

Culture is one of the most challenging elements in the international environment. To deal with these factors, a manager must realize a factual and interpretative knowledge of the culture. The facts can be learned, but the interpretation comes from experience.

The significance of concepts such as culture, organizational culture, individual culture, or style of leadership has been the concern of many scholars in the sphere of management literature. As these studies have illustrated, the culture-to-individual dilemma manifests itself at the organizational level. Thus, managers have to decide whether they remain tributaries to their values – which, for reasons of pride or convenience, they are willing to impose upon others, or recognize and act following the rules already in place in the environment in which they operate. The goal is to be accepted by a group (Shaw, 2006).

We must admit that both individual and group (regardless of the criteria it is constituted: profession, education, gender, demographic characteristics, religion, etc.) are the bearers of their values, skills, and beliefs. It opens the way to identifying methods and tools designed to put these values, skills, and ideas in place to create and preserve the competitive edge of the enterprise. An efficient modern management must be transcultural. Managers must first make an effort to recognize cultural diversity without judging it (Miroshnik, 2002, p. 524). The culture of an enterprise confers its identity, giving it a set of unique characteristics that distinguish it from other organizations (Collins, 2005). The conclusion of these approaches illustrates the difficulty of the diversity issues faced by today's companies and only emphasizes the usefulness of intercultural management in the contemporary business environment.

The degradation of the environment has led to the need to consider green economic policies as critical and useful environmental management tools. The current situation has generated extensive research and debates among researchers around the world, leading to an increasingly growing volume of literature focused on the best measures that affect the establishment of the green economy - including its development and results.

Green economy means a paradigm shift for achieving sustainable development. In the business environment, the green economy allows the movement towards models which integrate the sustainable development, thus defining a new way for development (Jackson, 2015). For an efficient transformation to take place, supportive policies, institutional and governance reforms and targeted investment at the local, national and global levels need to be put in place. At the microeconomic level, fundamental changes in attitudes and behaviors are necessary. Education should promote the values and knowledge required to help people to cope with change, to adopt new consumption patterns, and to transform mindsets and behaviours.

A shift toward a culture of sustainability presents some unique challenges. The motivation for a sustainability change initiative can often be driven by external forces, like culture, and, at times, the benefits may not appear to enhance value directly. A culture of sustainability is one in which organizational members hold shared assumptions and beliefs about the importance of balancing economic efficiency, social equity, and environmental accountability. Organizations with active cultures of sustainability strive to support a healthy environment and improve the lives of others while continuing to operate successfully over the long term. What differentiates sustainability from other culture change initiatives regarding organizational behavior?

This book put together culture, organizational behavior, and consumer behavior in the context of green economy, highlighting how culture can affect business outcomes, both positive and negative. The primary objective of this book is to point the transformations the green economy determines in organizational behavior, aiming at studying cross-cultural differences, to offer new perspectives for a better understanding of these differences, improving, finally, the regulatory performances. Firstly, it analyzes the recent developments in the green economy about sustainability valuation. Secondly, the impacts on organizational behavior are discussed. Thirdly, it shows effects on the green market, achieving results and identifying causal effects.

ORGANIZATION OF THE BOOK

The book is organized into 10 chapters. A brief description of each of the chapters follows:

Chapter 1 describes two conceptual economic models: linear and circular. The linear model is based on the principle "take, produce, consume, and throw," meaning that usability of waste is reduced and that waste is simply thrown out after consumption. Circular economic model takes into account environmental responsibility, but it also makes companies more competitive. Waste is treated and processed adequately and used as raw material in production, thus increasing competitiveness. Waste that cannot be processed is disposed of permanently.

Chapter 2 aims to assess to what extent national culture influences the attributions that arise towards green advertising, addressing the gap of how and under which conditions what type of attributions arise and the role of stakeholder factors in CSR communication strategies. The research stresses the relevance of national culture as a stakeholder-factor, influencing the effectiveness of green advertising.

Chapter 3 tries to explain the effect of greenwashing advertisements on organizational culture using findings of previous studies as evidence. In this direction, concepts and factors that driver firms' greenwashing activities were explained and therefore the effect of Green Advertisements on Organizational Image revealed throughout previous studies' findings.

Chapter 4 brings to the attention of specialists an integrative approach to promotion policy, insisting on the advantages anchoring promotional policy in the context of all green marketing activities, an aspect often ignored the practice field. This chapter will highlight the fact that, at present, on the Romanian market advertising put too much emphasis on grounding more rigorous approaches in terms of quantity of messages that are conveyed through various media, to the detriment of measuring the effects of these efforts in the consumer or end user of goods and services.

Chapter 5 aims to assess the competitiveness at company level, shaping organizational culture, competitive relationship and outlining possible ways to improve it. This chapter shows a study on the impact of organizational culture on the competitiveness of firms has highlighted the need to raise awareness of the importance of organizational culture in order to obtain components for superior performance.

Chapter 6 analyzes direct organic marketing mechanisms and community building ways towards the green economy. It demonstrates these cultures and gives some best practices in the creation of sustainable food community networks around the world. The chapter concludes with emphasizing the significance of this sociality and locality thus contributing to the long-term goal of sustainable development and resilience.

Chapter 7 aims to reveal the primary transformation and constraints from a multiperspective approach, starting from the general assumption that organic agrifood market represents a share of one.

Chapter 8 reviews the concept of quality (using meat products as model) and give examples of how to modulate animal products healthiness/safety and reduce the environmental impact of the sector through animal feeding practices. Finally, it provides an overview of the main research areas and on-going projects that the main global organizations involved in the feed sector are currently running in order to successfully overcome sustainability challenges.

Chapter 9 analyzes concept of rural tourism and organic farming, their dynamic of development in the World and in Serbia. Point out the importance of its connectivity to eliminate existing negative trends which burdened life in rural areas and possibilities to implement the goals of the green economy.

Chapter 10 presents the results of a research developed within a series of rural schools in Romania regarding the role of the educational system in preserving the individuals' cultural identity and in promoting the local culture within the rural areas. The analysis takes into account both the formal activities and non-formal events organized with the support of the local community projects, workshops conceived by the teachers in order to preserve the local culture and to make the young generation aware of their identity values.

Violeta Sima
Petroleum-Gas University of Ploiesti, Romania

REFERENCES

Collins, J. M. (2005). *Preventing Identity Theft in Your Business – How to Protect Your Business, Customers, and Employees.* Hoboken, NJ: John Wiley & Sons, Inc.

Hofstede, G. (2001). *Culture's consequences: Comparing values, behaviors, institutions, and organizations across cultures* (2nd ed.). London: Sage.

Jackson, T. (2015). A New Philosophical Approach to Social Transformation for a "Green Economy" in Technology and Innovation for Sustainable Development. New York: Bloomsbury Academic.

Miroshnik, V. (2002). Culture and international management: A review. *Journal of Management Development, 21*(7), 521–544. doi:10.1108/02621710210434647

Peters, T. J., Waterman, R. H., & Jones, I. (1982). *In search of excellence: Lessons from America's best-run companies.* Academic Press.

Pettigrew, A. M. (1979). On studying organizational cultures. *Administrative Science Quarterly, 24*(4), 570–581.

Pettigrew, A. M. (1979). On studying organizational cultures. *Administrative Science Quarterly, 24*(4), 570–581. doi:10.2307/2392363

Shaw, P. (2006). *The Four Vs of Leadership – Vision, Values, Value-Added, Vitality.* Chichester, UK: Capstone Publishing Ltd.

Acknowledgment

The editor would like to acknowledge the help of all the people involved in this project and, more specifically, to the authors and reviewers that took part in the review process. Without their support, this book would not have become a reality. Our sincere gratitude goes to the chapter's authors who contributed their time and expertise to this book. The editor wishes to acknowledge the valuable contributions of the reviewers regarding the improvement of quality, coherence, and content presentation of chapters. Most of the authors also served as referees; we highly appreciate their double involvement.

The editor further gratefully acknowledges to Ph.D. Andrei Jean Vasile for checking the manuscripts for originality, and to Mrs. Ileana Georgiana Gheorghe for all the insightful comments, ideas and criticism in drafting the book.

Finally, but not least, the editor wishes to thank also to the entire IGI Global staff involved in developing the current book project for their warm support and recommendations.

Violeta Sima
Petroleum-Gas University of Ploiesti, Romania

Chapter 1
Ecological Responsibility and Sustainable Development as Preconditions for Development of the Concept of Circular Economy

Olja Munitlak Ivanovic
Institute of Economic Sciences, Serbia

ABSTRACT

Ethical and ecological responsibility represent the root of sustainable development taking into account intergenerational justice. Mass production and consumption have left negative effects on the environment. Disregarding ecological responsibility, production processes were mainly based on uncontrollable use of raw materials and non-renewable energy sources. Taking into account limitation of raw materials, economic and ecological disasters, a concept of resilience has been developed to make all elements of society flexible in terms of unwanted shocks. This chapter describes two conceptual economic models: linear and circular. The linear model is based on the principle "take, produce, consume, and throw," meaning that usability of waste is reduced and that waste is simply thrown out after consumption. Circular economic model takes into account environmental responsibility, but it also makes companies more competitive. Waste is treated and processed adequately and used as raw material in production, thus increasing competitiveness. Waste that cannot be processed is disposed permanently.

DOI: 10.4018/978-1-5225-2965-1.ch001

INTRODUCTION

Sustainable development, in the essence of numerous definitions, has a common denominator – intragenerational and intergenerational justice. The most popular definition of sustainable development from report Our Common Future points out that development should satisfy the needs of present generation without questioning the possibility of future generations to satisfy their needs (World Commission on Environment and Development, 1987). Such perception of the concept of sustainable development imposes ethics review, especially ecological ethics review (Cifric, 2000). Cifric defines ecological ethics as needs for different pragmatical approach to development and environment. Ecological ethics became a part of the concept of sustainable development as a result of long-term inadequate treatment of the environment in the post-industrial society.

The issue of ecological ethics or ethical responsibility on micro and macro level refers to facing dilemmas on socially responsible behaviour and therefore, ecological responsibility (Krivokapic, Vujovic & Jovanovic, 2014). The issue of social responsibility and socially responsible behaviour shifted over time from the domain of voluntary philanthropic activities to conscious ethical behaviour and ethical responsibility or ecological legal frame that affect ecological behavior.

Disrupted relationship between people and natural resources resulting from mass production and consumption affects a modern man's behavior. Not only does he exploit nature, but he also destroys it. Nobel laureate Bertrand Russel thought that raising human consciousness about the necessity of changing the relationship towards nature is important for their existence (Russel, 2009). Mass production and consumption logics resulted in ecological crises, energetic crises, unsustainable treatment of natural resources and the value of the product itself. Modern issues of environmental protection are the consequence of the so-called linear economic model. The essence of such economy is exploitation of resources for production of products/services that is followed by consumption and throwing of unused parts representing the waste in this model.

Intensification of production and consumption in consumer society resulted in economic, ecological and social crisis. The response to these challenges was development of a new, essentially different economic model – circular economic model. Simply speaking, circular economy follows circular movement of production and brings it to a higher level. The essence of this model is reuse of waste and remaining byproducts in production. In this way, greater energetic efficiency is achieved, and consumption remains are brought back in the reproduction process. Therefore, unwanted waste coming from production and consumption becomes raw material and production is continued with less externalities (Lacy & Rutqvist,

2015) directly increasing GDP, especially in transition economies (Mitic, Munitlak Ivanovic & Zdravkovic, 2017).

BACKGROUND ON ECOLOGICAL RESPONSIBILITY

Ethical or ecological responsibility is not a new discipline, but the approach to interpreting of producer and consumer's behavior towards nature and environment has changed. A new ethical approach emphasizes the significance of components making the concept of ecological ethics itself. Many of these components are the result of high industrialization of society: economic and social justice, value pluralism, modern moral standards with regard to the environment, new forms of multiculturalism etc. (Cifric, 2000).

The question up to what level it is ecologically justified to use natural resources is an ethical question relating to intragenerational and intergenerational justice of sustainable development (Munitlak Ivanovic, 2017). This question is a basis for formulating of an adequate economic model (circular economy) that respects the concept of resilience as well (with a special emphasis to ecological and economic resilience) (Munitlak Ivanovic, & Zubovic, 2017). Speaking of ethical and ecological considerations, two conceptual bases are predominant in literature (Jost, 1996), namely (1) Perception of the concept of sustainable development based on science and (2) Perception of the concept of sustainable development based on human will.

The concept of sustainability that is based on science starts from scientific researches and thus obtained results relating to natural capacities of the Earth. This concept formulates political and technical conditions and indicators needed for implementation of thus understood concept of sustainable development. There are two models of sustainability that are based on this concept and they are related to the possibility of substitution of the natural and physical capital. Two extreme attitudes are determined within this model: "pessimistic" (neoclassical) approach to sustainability and "optimistic" approach to perspective of sustainability (Jost, 1996). Natural capital implies stocks of natural renewable and non-renewable resources and usability stocks result from work and represent physical capital.

The essence of pessimistic theory of sustainability refers to possibilities of substitution of the most important resources and ecological capacities. In this way, the attitude that selective and restrictive approach to exploitation of natural resources is needed for implementation of the concept of sustainable development is emphasized. This enables "natural" survival of resources over a longer period of time (Munitlak Ivanovic, 2007). The arguments the theoreticians of pessimistic variant of sustainable development refer to are reflected in the fact that there is no optimal way for solving of majority of ecological problems caused by accelerated economic development.

Pollution problem is solved mainly by transferring of pollution from one medium to another (Munitlak Ivanovic, 2009). The activity of paper industry can be taken as an example. In order to solve the problem of water pollution, factories use water filters. However, large amounts of toxic sludge are produced during filtration. This residual has to be burnt in special furnaces or disposed in specially protected areas. In this way, the problem of water pollution as the first medium is transformed in the problem of air pollution or soil pollution as the second, i.e. third medium (Golusin et al., 2011). The need for abandoning of linear economic model and accepting circular economic model is perceived already in this perception of the concept of sustainable development.

Theoreticians of an optimistic approach start from an undefined time horizon for realization of economic activities. The essence of optimistic theory is that majority of natural functions that are important for performing of economic activities (receiver of externality and supplier of natural resources) can be replaced (substituted) with physical capital. Theoreticians who advocate this approach refer to previous historical experience. Namely, optimists advocate the attitude that each developed society always finds an adequate substitute in case of a lack of resources (Munitlak Ivanovic, Mitic, & Popovic, 2015). A lack of wood as raw material in England in the 18th century, which resulted in substitution of the insufficient forest resource with available coal, is usually taken as an example. Such activities caused positive subsequent reactions resulting in new discoveries and innovations. In the first place, this refers to construction of the steam engine that marked first revolution, i.e, had an effect on many other discoveries and innovations and led to general technical progress (Landes, 1999).

Both theories are of extreme character, but it is still possible to find elements which can be implemented adequately in practice. What is common for both theories is that sustainable development, among other things, can also be defined as a responsibility for (Sachs, 2015):

1. Nature and environment.
2. Future generations (intergenerational justice).
3. Intensity of satisfaction of needs.

Pessimistic theory of sustainable development advocates proper perception with regard to ecological capacities for absorption of waste and waste materials, in cases when substitution is not possible at all. Optimistic theory of sustainable development advocates proper perception with regard to renewable natural resources.

Ethical responsibility and all forms of ethical considerations are the essence of different perception of the concept of sustainable development. Market mechanism cannot implement the concept of sustainability without the help of the state and its institutions and this developed a real need for identification of ethical responsibility and new ethical basis for perception of sustainable development. Perception of the market as an automatic instrument for timely adjustment to pollution and exploitation of natural resources has failed. This raised the issue of organization of economy in a new – sustainable way. Therefore, the analysis of ethical and ecological responsibility for realization of the concept of sustainable development stems from the theory and practice at the same time (Stiglitz, 2004). In order to realize the concept of sustainability that is understood in this way, it is necessary to change human standards and activities thus enabling undisturbed long-term life functioning. However, a basic condition for such changes is a clear and conscious will to change behaviour and this will have to be articulated (Viscuci, 1983).

Basic ethical question is whether selfish attitude should be used to raise the present generation's standard of living if this reduces any form of richness of the future generations. This is the essence of intergenerational justice which is integrated in the definition of sustainable development from Brundtland Report. In addition to intergenerational justice, the report "Our Common Future" also insists on intergenerational justice, i.e. on as fair distribution of natural wealth during one, present generation as possible. The question that arises from this is if the present generation should have and if it has rights to satisfy all its needs, even luxurious ones, or only some of them. The issue "our present needs - needs of future generations" distinguishes two basic ethical approaches: anthropocentric and biocentric ethical approach (Max-Neef, Elizalde, & Hopenhayn, 1989).

The possibility of future generations to satisfy all their needs or the level of satisfying of the needs of present generations is an ethical issue that has become the issue of ecological responsibility over time. This results in various relationships and perception of the purpose of the nature. Is the nature only an "inexhaustible" resource or a condition of the survival of mankind (Jost, 1996)?

According to Human Development Theory, basic human needs have to be satisfied. These needs include:

- Need for socialization.
- Need for education.
- Need for culture, expression, information and other social needs that are not of existential nature. As a role of economic science is to help people live better and easier, human development theoreticians advocate an intensive economic development that is sustainable. Such development is a human development at the same time.

5

Traditional perception of needs depending on the culture, environment, historical period, economic and technical and technological development denies the existence of difference between the needs that have to be satisfied and those that don't have to be satisfied. In effect, the main question is: does the existence of a need expresses the right to satisfy that need? This issue was not essential before the period of mass production and consumption. There were enough raw materials and fuels and waste disposal was not problematic as it is today. In the post-industrial society, this is not only ethical and ecological issue, but also the issue of survival and quality life both of this generation and of future ones.

The subject of the following chapters is representation and comparison of two concepts of economy: linear and circular model. Transition from linear to circular model in the European Union is growing faster as a result of development of new business models and new technologies. Ellen MacArthur Foundation was established in 2010 with the aim of making the transition to circular economy faster by its reports (Ellen MacArthur Foundation, 2012; Ellen MacArthur Foundation, 2013; Ellen MacArthur Foundation, 2014; Ellen MacArthur Foundation, 2015; Ellen MacArthur Foundation, 2016; Ellen MacArthur Foundation, 2017). The report from 2015 indicates that the value chain changes and that households in the European Union spend 60% of the average budget for rents and food, as well as that 80% of the total resources is exhausted in this way. This opens the space for more intensive application of circular economic model, which would result in the improvement of economic performance of the European Union.

THE CONCEPT OF LINEAR ECONOMY

So far, economy developed based on the simple principle: "take, produce, consume and throw". This is a basis of the so-called "linear" model implying unlimited and easy access to resources. This way of functioning of economy is characteristic from previous accumulation of capital to the present form of neoliberalism.

The perception that natural resources, especially ores and petroleum, are inexhaustible have been abandoned recently. At the end of the eighteenth century, in his "Essay on the principle of population", Thomas Robert Malthus questions an uncontrollable population growth rate from the point of view of survival funds (Malthus, 1798). Malthus states that population grows by geometric progression and funds needed for life, especially food, grow by arithmetic progression. Furthermore, the capacity of the Earth as a planet is limited, not only with regard to resources, but also to acceptance of industrial waste. Uncontrollable growth of world population and industrial growth are not possible as such processes require even bigger consumption of material resources.

Some other authors also pointed out to unsustainability of such growth. The Report of the Club of Rome from 1972, named "The limits of growth" was not accepted well by economists and therefore it did not have an influence on economic and ecological policy (Donella, Meadows, Randers, & Behrens III, 1974). According to critics of this report, an emphasis was on the significance of redistribution.

The Three Limitations Representing Real Limits of Growth

1.   Soil as a source of non-renewable natural resources and food.
2.   Ability of the environment to accept waste and other negative externalities of production and consumption processes.
3.   Life in cities that incites consumption as a way of life and one of its values.

It is interesting that Brundtland's commission started from the similar postulates in the report as in "The limits of growth". While the report of the Club of Rome was sharply criticized, the report "Our Common Nature" was accepted well and understood as a desirable continuation of economic growth and a condition for sustainable growth and development.

The principle of linear economy "take, produce, consume and throw" treats waste as a residual of production that finishes its life cycle as a trash in the environment. Waste is a material or an object which is not usable and which its owner plans to dispose permanently. According to Stevanovic (2003) waste is divided into solid and hazardous waste. According to the same source, solid waste is further classified into:

•   **Municipal Waste:** It occurs in populated, mainly urban areas and it consists of residential and commercial waste.
•   **Industrial Waste:** It occurs during production. Speaking of impacts on the environment, it can be hazardous and non-hazardous.
•   **Internal Industrial Waste:** It occurs during production, but it is not dangerous for people's health and the environment according to its characteristics.
•   **Medical Waste:** It occurs in health institutions. It can be hazardous and non-hazardous.

In linear economy, all waste will be permanently disposed after consumption, regardless which group of waste it belongs to, whether it is hazardous or not, whether it can be recycled or not. Such attitude towards the nature and production is unsustainable and it has to be abandoned. Figure 1 shows a linear economic model indicating that waste is the end of the life cycle of that production process.

Current period is characterized by the concept of linear economy, as ecological crises are not understood seriously enough. Due to advanced technology, raw materials

Figure 1. Production process in linear economic model
Source: Authors own design.

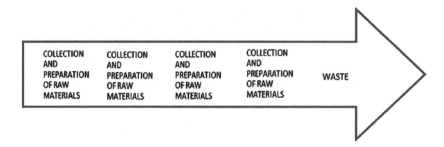

are more available and cheaper and therefore, the concept of linear economy is accepted as an optimal model of growth as it is reflected in the growth of production and employment, profit and standard of living, but also in the growth of cities and demand for all kinds of products and services. Hyper production and consumerism are the bases of such perception of production.

However, the question is when linear economic model is not adequate, i.e. when it can and should be replaced by a new, circular model. Linear model of production was acceptable in the twentieth century. The advent of the next century has brought different demographic motions, from densely populated industrial centers to new growing markets and economies, and therefore the existing methods of production have to adjust to these changes. Growing consumerism requires bigger and bigger quantity of raw materials in order to satisfy growing demand and puts pressure on the prices of raw materials and energy products. Therefore, the model of reuse of waste could be a solution in terms of a new input. The future shifts to a new economic model – circular economy. This is confirmed by the numerical datum published by the Sustainable Europe Research Institute (SERI, n.d.), that 21 billion tons of materials, which were used in production, were not installed in the end products (losses incurred in production as unsuitable, inefficiency, storage problems, unnecessary loss of energy etc.). Although the transition in a wider sense implies processes through which states and people try to achieve economic growth and development as well as social welfare of developed countries, namely North America and Western Europe (Jovanovic, & Eskinja, 2008), this concept can be perceived differently. Transition can be perceived as a process of overall improvement of economy, i.e. abandoning the previous concept of linear economy and accepting another concept that has more modern perception of social responsibility, especially with regard to concretization of the concept of sustainable development.

Exploitation of natural resources in production during which a new usability is created and the remaining resources (waste) are not processed, i.e. are thrown out, is unsustainable in the long run due to limitation of resources. The economic crisis in 2008 and a sequence of frequent ecological crises caused by climate changes intensified the need for application of the existing concept of circular economy. In circular economy, products have longer expiration date and they are upgraded, repaired or recycled at the end of their life cycle, i.e. they are used again. In this way, less waste is disposed in large water areas, less food is thrown, and biodegradable waste is used more intensely, for example, for compost or energy production. All this has positive effects on opening of new jobs locally (Drljaca, 2015).

MODERN ECONOMIC MODEL: CIRCULAR ECONOMY

Based on all above mentioned, it could be said that the concept of circular economy follows circular motion of substance in the nature. The approach to relationship between production and consumption is different, as byproducts of production and consumption are used again in the new production process. The use of non-hazardous waste as an output of one production cycle and as an input for another production cycle results in distinguishing trash and waste. Waste no longer has the role of trash that pollutes the environment, but it becomes a raw material and material resource that reduces the price of the end product (Milanovic, Radovic, & Vucic, 2002). Therefore, circular economy can have an effect on competitiveness on the market. In circular economy, value-added product is used longer before it becomes waste meaning that material resources are used longer and more rationally.

Circular economic model is needed not only for environmental protection, but also for cost savings. The benefits of circular economy can be felt both on micro and macro level. Reduction of needs for new raw materials can save millions or billions of dollars depending on the size and intensity of economy. According to the assessments of the Ellen MacArthur Foundation, the European Union could save 400-600 billion dollars per year, primarily in automated and machine industry (Sariatli, 2017). Apart from the limitations listed below, this model should be used wherever production and technical requirements enable it (e.g. when the waste is toxic or dangerous, this model cannot be applied). However, likewise in all fields of business, managers and policy makers must have (in addition to developed ecological conscience), excellent knowledge on production processes in order to know when and how linear model can be replaced by a circular model. This is especially important if we take into account the lack of standardization in this field of business and that the decisions of this type depend on good knowledge of technology and processes. These exact data indicate the need of transition from one economic model to another only when and if it is possible.

As a new concept, circular economy is one of the reactions to economic crisis from 2008, as it represents a new concept of waste management. Waste is collected and processed, it does not have a negative impact on the environment and it is used again as a raw material in the production process. Each process enabling recycling, regeneration, using of valuable properties of waste as an input or energy source, direct reuse, reduction of quantity and volume of waste before permanent disposal is considered as waste processing. This means that recycling and processing are not the same terms, i.e. that recycling is a method of processing of waste (Stevanovic, 2003). The part of waste that cannot be processed is disposed permanently and safely. This process is shown in the scheme below.

Circular economy keeps some elements of the concept of linear economy. The path of the raw material from a resource through production, distribution, consumption and occurrence of waste is identical in both concepts. If the expiry date of a product is not only considered through the lifetime but also through the further life cycle (following motion of waste occurring from the product), the concept of circular economy is perceived completely. Phases of circular economic model are shown in Figure 2. Basic premise of circular economy is that there is a feedback bringing collected, processed and recycled waste back in production as a raw material.

Figure 2. Production process in circular economic model
Source: Authors own design.

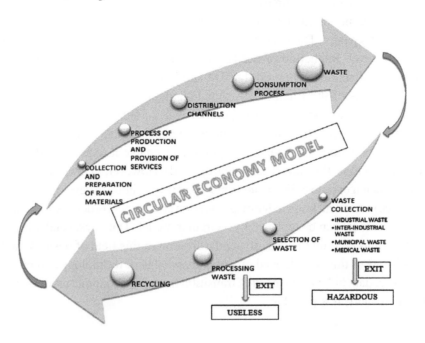

In order for this system to function it is necessary to establish an integrated system of waste management. The idea of creating of such system is minimizing of unusable waste. In this respect, we can arrange phases in the following order (Figure 3):

1. Minimizing of solid waste at the place of its occurrence (end of production or consumption).
2. Recycling.
3. Transformation of solid waste.
4. Sanitary disposal.

Recycling is considered only when all possibilities of minimizing waste at the place of its occurrence are exhausted. Transformation is applied after achieving a maximum recycling level. Recycling is most important in the process of waste processing, as these activities reduce consumption of new raw materials and quantity of waste that has to be disposed permanently. The same waste material or some its parts can be used once or more than once as a substitute for a new raw material or commercial products. In effect, the process of recycling is done in two ways: 1. Separating useful and usable parts from the integral solid waste and processing them or 2. Removing components that pollute the environment from waste and enabling their reuse. All above mentioned phases and processes being a part of water management system are necessary as they are a condition for transition to circular economic model.

On a global scale, transition to circular model should be intensified. Some highly developed countries, such as Japan, achieved great results in this area. Until 2020, Japan plans to organize such production in the city of Kamikatsu that will leave

Figure 3. Phases of minimizing unusable waste
Source: Authors own design.

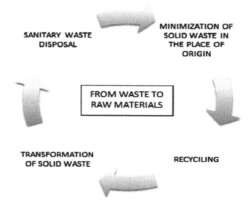

no waste, i.e. Kamikatsu will become the first zero waste city (Medlock, 2017). In its report from 2013, Ellen MacArthur Foundation (Ellen MacArthur Foundation, 2013) points out that only 35% of waste, 75% of which is municipal waste, is used as material inputs in the economy.

Likewise, any other concept, there are certain disadvantages and challenges with which circular economy faces. These disadvantages indicate that there are production processes, technology and/or situations that should function according to linear economic model. Essentially, all disadvantages can be classified in three groups (Circular Academy, 2017): (1) Achievability and desirability; (2) Social dimension and (3) Lack of standardization and strategic guidelines.

Achievability and desirability refer to certain production processes (such as paper recycling), materials and technological processes in which there are limits to which waste can be processed into raw material. As it is shown in Scheme 2, there are materials, such as dangerous waste, that cannot be processed further and therefore they cannot be covered by circular economic model. If dangerous waste remains after a production process, circular economic model cannot be applied, but only linear economic model. Insisting on recycling of waste in terms of production of new raw material at the level of 100% does not make sense if costs of waste recycling are higher than the value of the raw material obtained. Also in this case, economic logic suggests that in such cases linear economy is a better choice than circular economy.

Being focused on recycling the remains from production, circular economy pays less attention to social dimension. Work of employees is harder to standardize and recycling and re-processing require more work. This can have negative impacts on the employees' creativity, as well as on the loss of local jobs if recycling is not done locally, but it is centralized and shifted to areas where labour is cheaper. (Ellen MacArthur Foundation, 2013). This jeopardizes human rights in the developed countries and indirectly supports poor economies.

Lack of standardization and strategic guidelines indicates the disadvantage of circular economy in terms of non-existence of accurately identified criteria, activities or guidelines for implementation of this concept in all situations (such as ISO). The application of circular economic model varies greatly depending on the market and products and therefore any generalization and standardization is imprecise. Although there are no guidelines covering these issues (Ellen MacArthur Foundation, 2014), it still cannot be said that there is an internationally recognized standardization referring to recycling and circular economy for all products and processes.

As researchers from the Republic of Serbia deal with this issue as well, although on a limited scale, we will mention the results of present application of circular economic model, which is still in the initial phase in Serbia. It mainly refers to industrial production. The examples of good practice mainly refer to recycling of:

Tetra Pak, water proof eco boards, plastics, multy-layer packaging for beverages and liquid food, waste tires, used antifreeze, then ash processing and heating by means of briquettes made of coffee beans. Development of circular economy strategy in the Republic of Serbia, together with the action plan for tools for full application is planned for 2017.

Over 70 companies with more than 40.000 employees in total participated in cleaner production and chemical leasing projects in Serbia in the last nine years. Average savings amount to cca. 100.000 € per year together with (Circular economy as a chance for development of Serbia, 2016):

- **Average Reduction of Water Consumption:** 50.000 m3/year.
- **Average Reduction of Electricity Consumption:** 500 MWh/year.
- **Average Reduction of CO2 Emissions:** 500t/year.

It is estimated that 30.000 new jobs can be opened and competitiveness of the economy increased by introduction of the circular economy in Serbia. The Republic of Serbia follows the processes of adoption and introduction of the circular economy in the European Union and it reacted promptly by accepting the recommendations of the European Union on the circular economy. The Ministry of Agriculture and environmental protection has recognized the needs for amendment of the law and suggested amendments to the law on environmental protection in cooperation with the Chamber of Commerce and Industry of Serbia and other relevant institutions. The amendments from February 2016 created legal basis for introduction of circular economy.

CONCLUSION

Development of consciousness, ethical and ecological responsibility resulted in creation of various concepts: sustainable development, resilience, linear and circular economy. Ethical issues and issues relating to ecological responsibility and sustainable development are observed from various aspects in this paper: Human development theory, perception of the concept of sustainable development based on science ("pessimistic attitude") and perception of the concept of sustainable development based on human will ("optimistic attitude").

Sustainable development is based on three pillars: economic, ecological and social. The essence of this concept is in the attempt to distribute natural wealth to all generations, minimize pollution, minimize global warming and solve other issues that are important for environmental protection.

Resilience is a step further to creation of an optimal model of functioning of global society in unstable and unpredictable conditions. It is based on the idea of as much flexibility of four pillars – economic, social, environmental and institutional – as possible. Speaking of this concept, flexibility implies readiness of each pillar to adjust to unwanted situation (shock) and returning of all pillars in the state before shock as soon as possible. In this respect, various strategies (scenario models) are developed in advance within strategic management.

Linear economy, being based on the principle "take, produce, consume and throw", does not treat waste adequately. Due to application of modern technologies, the price of raw materials falls resulting in the attitude that linear economy is an optimal model of growth which is characterized by: employment growth, production growth, profit growth and growth of a standard of living, i.e. hyperproduction and mass consumerism. However, such attitude towards the environment is not sustainable in the long run due to limitation of resources.

In addition to the above-mentioned disadvantages: achievability and desirability, social dimension and lack of standardization and strategic guidelines, circular economic model is the economic model of the future. In order to make a transition from linear to circular economy, it is necessary to define guidelines for each production sector on how to implement a circular economic model and establish an internationally recognized institution for standardization of the circular economic model that would define regulations, standards and necessary activities for each field of business. Unlike linear economic model, audience and consumers are still not familiar enough with the circular economic model. In this respect, social marketing campaigns should be intensified in order to familiarize general public with the advantages of circular economic model. All above mentioned points to the need for larger investments in order to make circular economic model a dominant production model. Manager and policy makers need to know production processes, i.e. characteristics of production sectors very well, so that they could standardize the steps for implementation of circular economy first, and then raise it to the national and international level by forming an official organization for standards related to this model. This means that general theoretical knowledge in economics is not enough and that continuous specialization and collection of new information and knowledge is needed. Lifelong learning and continuous education on higher levels of top management is a precondition for application of circular economy.

Circular economy is a new global response to ecological crisis and climate changes on one hand and economic crisis on the other hand. This new concept of economy of the twenty-first century has a different approach to all economic processes, not only from the aspect of sustainable development, but also from the aspect of social responsibility and therefore ethical and ecological responsibility. In this economic model, waste that occurs after consumption is used again after processing. There is a feedback bringing selected and processed waste back in the new production cycle as a raw material. Speaking of the described characteristics of different concepts, i.e. economic models, it can be perceived that circular economic model is sustainable in the long run. This model is economically justified as it has a positive effect on competitiveness and takes care that economic development is humane at the same time. It is economically justified as it reduces the use of raw materials and quantity of waste. Circular economic model, i.e. its elaboration on micro and macro level, is close to the concept of sustainable development. This model is also a response to ethical and ecological responsibility which each generation and society should implement in practice as intensely as possible.

REFERENCES

Cifric, I., (2000). Bioetika i ekologija. *Socijalna ekologija: casopis za ekolosku misao i sociologijska istrazivanja okoline, 9*(1-2), 143-146.

Circular Academy. (2017). *How can we bridge the circularity gap?* Retrieved from http://www.circular.academy/circular-economy-critics-and-challenges/

Cirkularna ekonomija kao šansa za razvoj Srbije. (2017). Retrieved from http://aarhusns.rs/aarhus/wp-content/uploads/2016/12/Cirkularna-ekonomija-Web.pdf

Donella, C., H., Meadows, D.L., Randers, J., & Behrens III, V.W. (1974). *Granice rasta*. Zagreb: Stvarnost.

Drljaca, M. (2015). Koncept kruzne ekonomije. *Kvalitet & izvrsnost, 4*(9-10), 18-22.

Ellen MacArthur Foundation. (2012). *Towards the Circular Economy: Vol. 1. An economic and business rationale for an accelerated transition.* Retrieved from https://www.ellenmacarthurfoundation.org/publications/towards-the-circular-economy-vol-1-an-economic-and-business-rationale-for-an-accelerated-transition

Ellen MacArthur Foundation. (2013). *Towards the Circular Economy: Vol. 2. Opportunities for the consumer goods sector.* Retrieved from https://www.ellenmacarthurfoundation.org/publications/towards-the-circular-economy-vol-2-opportunities-for-the-consumer-goods-sector

Ellen MacArthur Foundation. (2014). *Towards the Circular Economy: Vol. 3. Accelerating the scale-up across global supply chains.* Retrieved from https://www.ellenmacarthurfoundation.org/publications/towards-the-circular-economy-vol-3-accelerating-the-scale-up-across-global-supply-chains

Ellen MacArthur Foundation. (2015). *Growth Within: a circular economy vision for a competitive Europe*. Retrieved from https://www.ellenmacarthurfoundation. org/publications/growth-within-a-circular-economy-vision-for-a-competitive-europe

Ellen MacArthur Foundation. (2016). *Intelligent Assets: Unlocking the circular economy potential*. Retrieved from https://www.ellenmacarthurfoundation.org/ publications/intelligent-assets

Ellen MacArthur Foundation. (2017). *Achieving "Growth Within"*. Retrieved from https://www.ellenmacarthurfoundation.org/assets/downloads/publications/ Achieving-Growth-Within-20-01-17.pdf

Golusin, M., MunitlakIvanovic, O., Domazet, S., Dodic, S., & Vucurovic, D. (2011). Assessment of the effectiveness of policy implementation for sustainable energy development in South East Europe. *Journal of Renewable and Sustainable Energy, 3*.

Jost, F. A. (1996). *Sustainable Development: The Roles of Science and Ethics*. London, UK: Edvard Elgar.

Jovanovic, M., & Eskinja, I. (2008). Neki aspekti neoliberalizma u svetskom gospodarstvu. *Zbornik Pravnog Fakulteta Sveucilista u Rijeci, 29*(2), 941–985.

Krivokapic, Z., Vujovic, A., & Jovanovic, J. (2014). *Ekoloska inovativnost u funkcji drustvene odgovornosit*. Paper presented at the 41. Nacionalna konferencija o kvalitetu, 9. Nacionalna konferencija o kvalitetu zivota, 5. Konferencija studenata industrijskog inzenjerstva i menadzmenta, Fakultet inzenjerskih nauka, Kragujevac.

Lacy, P., & Rutqvist, J. (2015). *Waste to Wealth, The Circular Economy Advantage*. Palgrave Macmillan.

Landes, D. (1999). *The Wealth and Poverty of Nations: Why Some Are So Rich and Some So Poor*. New York: W.W. Norton & Company.

Malthus, T. J. (n.d.). *An Essay on the Principle of Population*. Available from http:// www.esp.org/books/malthus/population/malthus.pdf

Max-Neef, M., Elizalde, A., & Hopenhayn, M. (1989). Human Scale Development: An Option for Future Development. *Dialogue*, 5–80.

Medlock, K. (2017, January 1). This Japanese town will produce absolutely zero waste by 2020 [Web log comment]. Retrieved from http://inhabitat.com/this-japanese-town-will-produce-absolutely-zero-waste-by-2020/

Milanovic, C.Z., Radovic, S., & Vucic, V. (2002). *Otpad nije smece*. Zagreb, Republika Hrvatska: Gospodarstvo i okolis.

Mitic, P., Munitlak Ivanovic, O., & Zdravkovic, A. (2017). A Cointegration Analysis of Real GDP and CO2 Emissions in Transitional Countries. *Sustainability*, *9*(4), 1–18. doi:10.3390/su9040568

Munitlak Ivanovic, O. (2007). Uloga drzave u primeni ekonomskih instrumenata u funkciji realizacije koncepta odrzivog razvoja. *Poslovna ekonomija*, *1*(1), 135-149.

Munitlak Ivanovic, O. (2009). Ekoloski menadzment kao model upravljanja rizikom. *Poslovna ekonomija, 3*(4), 155-160.

Munitlak Ivanovic O., Mitic, P., & Popovic, S. (2015). Globalizacija i tehnicko-tehnoloske promene – savremenije drustvo i/ili globalna ekoloska propast. *Poslovna ekonomija*, *16*(9), 263-276.

MunitlakIvanovic, O. (2017, April). *Pokusaji redukcije emisija CO2 analizom Kuznetzovekrive i medjunarodnih protokola –instrumenti za realizaciju odrzivog razvoja.* Paper presented on Medjunarodna naucna konferencija: Ciljevi odrzivog razvoja u III milenijumu, knjiga apstrakata, Beograd, Srbija.

MunitlakIvanovic, O., & Zubovic, J. (2017). From the Millennium Development Goals to the Resilience Concept – Theoretical Similarities and Differences. In The State and the Market in Economic Development: In Pursuit of Milennium Development Goals (pp. 7-29). The IIDS Australia Inc.

Russell, B. A. (2009). *The Basic Writings of Bertrand Russell.* London, UK: Routledge.

Sachs, J. A. (2015). *The Age of Sustainable Development.* New York: Columbia University Press. doi:10.7312/sach17314

Sariatli, F. (2017). Linear economy versus Circular economy: A comparative and analyzer study for optimization of Economy for Sustainability. *Visegrad Journal of Bioeconomy and Sustainable Development*, *1*, 31–34.

SERI. (n.d.). Retrieved from http://www.seri.de/home/themes/resource-efficiency-and-demateralisation/

Stevanovic, B. (2003). Cvrsti i opasni otpad. In EnciklopedijaZivotnasredina i odrzivirazvoj (pp. 239-249). Beograd, RepublikaSrbija: Ecolibri.

Stiglitz, J. (2004). *Ekonomija javnog sektora.* Beograd, Republika Srbija: Ekonomski fakultet u Beogradu.

Viscusi, K. A. (1983). *Risk by Choice: Regulating Gealth and Safety in Workplace.* Harvard University Press. doi:10.4159/harvard.9780674186217

World Commission on Environment and Development. (1987). *Our common future.* New York: Oxford University Press.

ADDITIONAL READING

Bazilian, M., Rogner, H., Howells, M., Hermann, S., Arent, D., Gielen, D., ... Yumkella, K. K. (2011). Considering the energy, water and food nexus: Toward an integrated modeling approach. *Energy Policy*, *39*(12), 7896–7906. doi:10.1016/j. enpol.2011.09.039

Drljaca, M. (2015).Tranzicija linearne u kruznu ekonomiju, Association for Quality and Standardization of Serbia, 35-44.

Gabriela-Cornelia, P., Indith, I., & Alexandru, B. (2015). New Theoretical and Practical Approaches of Implementing the Circular Economy for Preservation of Natural Resources. *Procedia Economics and Finance*, *22*, 124–130. doi:10.1016/ S2212-5671(15)00235-X

Gamon, A.R. (2016). Emplotting Virtue: A Narrative Approach to Environmental Virtue Ethics. *Environmental Ethics*, 38(3), United States: Environmental Philosophy.

George, A. R. D., Lin, B. Ch., & Chen, Y. (2015). A circular economy model of economic growth. *Environmental Modelling & Software*, *73*, 60–63. doi:10.1016/j. envsoft.2015.06.014

Ghisellini, P., Cialani, C., & Ulgiati, S. (2016). A review on circular economy: The extended transition to a balanced interplay of environmental and economic systems. *Journal of Cleaner Production*, *114*, 11–32. doi:10.1016/j.jclepro.2015.09.007

Hartwick, J. (1977). Intergenerational Equity and the Investing of Rents from Exhaustible Resources. *The American Economic Review*, *66*, 972–974.

Hartwick, J. (1990). Natural Resources, National Accounting and Economic Depreciation. *Journal of Public Economics*, *43*(3), 291–304. doi:10.1016/0047-2727(90)90002-Y

Jiao, W., & Boons, F. (2017). Policy durability of Circular Economy in China: A process analysis of policy translation. *Resources, Conservation and Recycling*, *117*, 12–24. doi:10.1016/j.resconrec.2015.10.010

Kates, R. W., Parris, T. M., & Leiservitz, A. A. (2005). What is Sustainable development? Goals, Indicators, Values, and Practice. *Environment*, *47*(3), 8–21. doi:10.1080/00139157.2005.10524444

Klein, N. A. (2014). *This Changes Every Thing*. New York, USA: Simon & Shuster.

Kristo, M. (1984). Kruzna ekonomija za brzi razvoj. *Gospodarstvo i okolis, Hrvatski poslovni savjet za odrzivi razvoj.* 11(41), 9-19.

Lieder, M., & Rashid, A. (2016). Towards circular economy implementation: A comprehensive review in context of manufacturing industry. *Journal of Cleaner Production, 115*, 36–51. doi:10.1016/j.jclepro.2015.12.042

Munitlak Ivanovic, O. (2007). *Odrzivi razvoj kao redefinisan pristup ekonomskom razvoju.* Beograd: Zaduzbina Andrejevic.

Norton, B. (1984). Environmental Ethics and Weak Anthropocentrism. *Environmental Ethics, 6*(5), 131–148. doi:10.5840/enviroethics19846233

Prekajac, Z. & Josifidis, K. (1999). Ekonomija i ekologija-ekoloska ekonomija i/ili koncep todrzivog razvoja, *Privrednaizgradnja*, 125-139.

Repetto, R., McGrath, W., Wells, M., Beer, C., & Rossini, F. Authors. (1989). Wasting Assets: Natural Resources in the National Income Accounts, Washington D.C., USA: World Resources Institute.

Sachs, J. (1982). The Current Account in the Macroeconomic Adjustment Process. *The Scandinavian Journal of Economics, 84*(2), 147–159. doi:10.2307/3439631

Sauve, S., Bernard, S., & Sloan, P. (2016). Environmental sciences, sustainable development and circular economy: Alternative concepts for trans-disciplinary research. *Environmental Development, 17*, 48–55. doi:10.1016/j.envdev.2015.09.002

Singh, J., & Ordonez, I. (2016). Resource recovery from post-consumer waste: Important lessons for the upcoming circular economy. *Journal of Cleaner Production, 134*, 342–353. doi:10.1016/j.jclepro.2015.12.020

Solow, R. (1974). Intergenerational Equity and Exhaustible Resources. *The Review of Economic Studies, 41*, 29–45. doi:10.2307/2296370

Solow, R. (1986). On the Intergenerational Allocation of Natural Resources. *The Scandinavian Journal of Economics, 88*(1), 141–149. doi:10.2307/3440280

Szabo, A., & Durkop, C. (Eds.). (2016). *SMEs and Green Economy.* Ankara, Turkey: Konrad-Adenauer-Stiftung.

Weitzman, M. (1976). On the Welfare Significance of National Product in a Dynamic Economy. *The Quarterly Journal of Economics, 90*(1), 156–162. doi:10.2307/1886092

Williams, E. F. A. (2015). *Green Giants: How Smart Companies Turn Sustainability into Billion-Dollar Businesses.* USA: Amacom.

KEY TERMS AND DEFINITIONS

Circular Economy: A desirable concept of the economic model, as non-hazardous waste is processed in various ways and returned in production. Raw materials are used less which increases competitiveness of the company over competition as usability of waste is prolonged.

Ecological Responsibility: A concept which implies socially responsible behavior towards nature. It is an ethical attitude to natural resources during their exploitation and during waste disposal.

Environment: A precondition for the existence of all (economic and other) processes and creatures. It is divided into non-living nature (water, air, soil, minerals, and similar) and living nature (plants, animals, bacteria in ecosystems). Briefly, no system could survive without the environment.

Intergenerational Justice: One of the principles on which the concept of sustainable development is based. The essence of this justice is in intra-generational and intergenerational justice. This means that, within the same generation (i.e., among generations), the principle of equal right to similar quantities of natural resources is respected.

Linear Economy: Still, a predominant form of production that treats waste after product consumption as the end of the life cycle of production and consumption, disposing of it permanently.

Raw Materials: Various natural resources that are used as an input in production. Production of goods or services would be impossible without raw materials.

Resilience: A concept representing the "upgraded" concept of sustainable development. It is based on four pillars, three of which are the same as in the concept of sustainable development and the fourth pillar being institutions. The concept of resilience insists on flexibility of all four pillars in case of an unwanted situation (shock), fast adjustment of pillars to new situation (i.e., returning the whole system in the state before shock).

Sustainable Development: A concept that is based on three pillars: economic, ecological, and social. The main idea of this concept is that economic processes take place on an optimal level, satisfying social needs without prejudice to environmental protection.

Waste: A residual of production (i.e., consumption). It is a material or an object that is not suitable for further use and therefore, it is permanently disposed or thrown. Depending on the category or determined class which it belongs to, waste is treated in the process of waste processing (in circular economy) or rejected immediately as unusable without previous processing (in linear economy).

Chapter 2

Valuing Sustainability:
How National Culture Influences Attributions Towards Green Advertising

Daniela Rojas Morales
University of Amsterdam, The Netherlands

Lars Moratis
Antwerp Management School, Belgium & NHTV Breda University of Applied Sciences, Belgium

ABSTRACT

Consumers' low awareness and negative attributions remain critical impediments to companies' attempts to reap the potential benefits of CSR. Addressing the gap of how and under which conditions what type of attributions arise and the role of stakeholder factors in CSR communication strategies, the aim of this chapter is to assess to what extent national culture influences the attributions that arise towards green advertising. Preceded by a pre-test, a survey was conducted in Colombia, The Netherlands and USA. With a total of 248 responses, a multiple regression analysis was performed to analyze the data. Results show main effects of national culture on the attribution of negative motives. Specifically, the cultural dimensions power distance and uncertainty avoidance have a negative effect on negative attributions. On the other hand, results indicated that positive attributions are not influenced by national culture. The research stresses the relevance of national culture as a stakeholder-factor, influencing the effectiveness of green advertising.

DOI: 10.4018/978-1-5225-2965-1.ch002

INTRODUCTION

Corporate social responsibility (CSR) is playing a key role in today's business world and society. More companies than ever before are engaging in initiatives such as philanthropy and cause-related marketing. One of the dimensions of CSR is environmental commitment comprising, among others, the development of environmentally friendly products, management of hazardous waste and recycling (Bhattacharya & Sen, 2001). In the last decades, especially environmental concern has increased considerably as there is increasing concern about the misuse and scarcity of natural resources and its consequences for future generations. As such, governments, activists and the media work towards encouraging and forcing companies to account for the social and environmental impacts of their actions and consumers worry about more than just the purchase and the consumption processes (Zinkhan & Carlson, 1995).

By engaging in CSR, companies may generate positive consumer attitudes and behaviors, such as favorable stakeholder attribution and behavior, better brand image, better stakeholder relationships and enhanced stakeholder advocacy behavior (Du, Bhattacharya, & Sen, 2010). Driven by these benefits, the public concern and the increased demand towards green products, CSR has entered the realm of marketing and corporate strategy (Cronin, Smith, Gleim, Ramirez, & Martinez, 2011; Gao, 2009; Porter & Kramer, 2006). As consumer awareness is necessary to obtain the benefits, companies are also increasingly communicating their engagements (Cronin et al., 2011; Do Paço & Reis, 2013; Gao, 2009). Green advertising is one of the most commonly employed channels for the communication of environmental efforts (Nyilasy, Gangadharbatla & Paladino, 2014).

With this increase in green marketing, there has also been an increase in greenwashing. Companies are pretending to care and advertise incomplete or false information to improve their image (Parguel, Benoît-Moreau, & Larceneux, 2011). Due to low awareness and the increase of greenwashing, consumers have difficulty in distinguishing between, or even naming, socially responsible and irresponsible companies. They express a desire to know more about what companies do and how they behave, but often react in a skeptical manner when these advertise their sustainability efforts (Nyilasy et al., 2014; cf. Globescan, 2012).

Even though green advertising has increased in the last two decades (Campbell, 2015), marketers generally lack the adequate tools for evaluating its effectiveness, nor do they have sufficient tools for determining consumers' environmental attitudes, intentions, and behaviors (Haytko & Matulich, 2008; Do Paço & Reis, 2013; Peattie, 2001). Not communicating the green efforts effectively and consumers' low awareness are impediments for companies to benefit from the favorable attitudes and behaviors (Du et al., 2010).

How individuals evaluate the motives of others, which is called the attribution process, has appeared to mediate the impact of CSR advertising on attitude and purchase intention (Ellen, Webb, & Mohr, 2006; Folkes, 1988). This indicates that consumers may care more about why companies are doing something than what they are doing (Gilbert & Malone, 1995). If consumers attribute negative motives to the companies' actions, CSR communication can backfire (Cui, Trent, Sullivan, & Matiru, 2003; Yoon, Gürhan-Canli, & Schwarz, 2006). The question of how consumers attribute the motives and under which conditions they attribute negative motives remains however partially unaddressed (Gao, 2009; Nyilasy et al., 2014, Yoon et al., 2006). Understanding consumer skepticism and the attributions that arise with green advertising is crucial to communicate CSR effectively (Nyilasy et al., 2014).

Previous literature has identified various aspects that influence the conveying of favorable attributions and the effectiveness of CSR communication. Azevedo (2004) suggests that companies should communicate informative and educational information, avoid the use of emotional tone and provide a source to corroborate information (as cited by Wanderley, Lucian, Farache, & de Sousa Filho, 2008: 372). Furthermore, Du et al. (2010) list four factors that influence the effectiveness of communication and convey favorable attributions, namely, message content, message channel, stakeholder-specific factors and company factors. Concerning stakeholder factors, these scholars stated that different audiences may vary in terms of expectations and information needs resulting in different outcomes of attitude and purchase intentions. Accordingly, companies should adapt the CSR communication to the audience.

Due to globalization, companies have to compete in markets that are geographically and culturally distant (Franke & Nadler, 2007). As several researchers have stated, international business must analyze and adapt their strategies to the cultural behaviors and values of their consumer base (Brфnn & Vrioni, 2001). This also applies for advertising (Zhang & Gelb, 1996).

In recent years, the relationship between culture and CSR has emerged as a research topic. There is now ample evidence that CSR differs among national cultures (Gao, 2009; Matten & Moon, 2008; Visser & Tolhurst, 2010). Most studies have focused on the perceptions and actions of organizations and practitioners (Burton, Farh, & Hegarty, 2000; Pfau, Haigh, Sims, & Wigley, 2008), concluding that perceptions differ between national cultures. Apparently, this is also the case for green marketing and advertising (Leonidou & Leonidou, 2011). These scholars concluded that green marketing could reflect the differences in demand by stakeholders. This coincides with the literature focused on the consumer side, stating that consumers have different perceptions and expectations of CSR between cultures (Maignan, 2001; Quazi & O'Brien, 2000).

23

Different scholars have researched the relation between culture and communication (Samovar, Porter, McDaniel, & Roy, 2014). Consumers seem to respond to advertising that fit their culture and reward advertisers who understand and adapt the advertising to their cultures and values (Zhang & Gelb, 1996). Additionally, attribution processes also appear differ across cultures (Choi, Nisbett, & Norenzayan, 1999) and attributions mediate the impact of CSR advertising on attitude and purchase intention (Ellen et al., 2006).

The cross-cultural difference of consumer's CSR perceptions, attributions processes and responses to advertising may indicate that national culture is a stakeholder-specific factor that may influence the effectiveness of green advertising. Building on the literature research of the factors influencing the attribution of negative motives and consequently, the effectiveness of CSR communication, this research addresses to what extent national culture influences the motives attributed towards green advertisement. Understanding this influence may help companies convey favorable attributions when communicating environmental efforts to different national cultures. This chapter hence researches the extent to which the attributions that mediate the impact of green advertisement on consumer attitudes and purchase intention are influenced by national culture. The research addresses the environmental dimension of CSR, the channel of advertising and national culture, defined as "values, beliefs, norms and behavioral patterns of a national group" (Leung, Bhagat, Buchan, Erez, & Gilbson, 2005: 357). It focuses on the national cultures of Colombia, the Netherlands and the USA, since these cultures vary on several cultural dimensions.

The chapter starts with an overview of literature. Then, it turns to the methodology and results and finally, the discussion and conclusion are presented.

BACKGROUND

Corporate Social Responsibility

The increasing literature about CSR has led to multiple definitions and a broad conceptualization by different researchers (Bhattacharya & Sen, 2001). A traditional definition of CSR is: "the managerial obligation to take action to protect and improve both the welfare of society as a whole and the interest of the organization" (Keith & Blomstrom, 1975: 6). Aguinis & Glavas (2012) conducted a literature review of CSR based on 588 journal articles and 102 books and defined it as a context-specific organizational actions and policies that take into account stakeholders' expectations and the triple bottom line of economic, social and environmental performance (p. 933). Furthermore, Dahlsrud (2008) conducted an overview of the concepts and definitions of CSR. In the analysis the scholar provided a table of cited definitions and frequency counts from Google. The source with the highest frequency count is from the Commission of the European Communities (2001) with the definition a concept whereby companies integrate social and environmental concerns in their business operations and in their interaction with their stakeholders on a voluntary basis (p. 7). The World Business Council for Sustainable development (1999) follows, with the definition the commitment of business to contribute to sustainable economic development, working with employees, their families, the local community and society at large to improve their quality of life (World Business Council for Sustainable Development, 1999).

Research has shown that the different stakeholders, including consumers, are not aware of companies' CSR activities, making it difficult for the companies to benefit from the stated above favorable attitudes and behaviors (Bhattacharya & Sen, 2001; Du et al., 2010; Pomering & Dolnicar, 2009). Only a few companies such as Unilever and Patagonia have successfully positioned themselves as environmentally responsible (Globescan, 2014). Pomering and Dolnicar (2009) studied consumers' awareness of CSR activities when facing real consumption decisions and concluded that the effect of CSR initiatives on purchasing behavior is not relevant if awareness is low.

Consequently, companies are required to make changes in their marketing strategy (Kotler, 2011). Companies use a wide range of channels for CSR communication but the three most commonly used are social reports, websites and advertising (Birth et al., 2008). According to Zinkhan and Carlson (1995), the most common mechanism companies use to respond to the increasing concern about the environment is green advertising and accordingly, in the last two decades it has grown exponentially (Campbell, 2015). Green advertising can be defined as an explicit or implicit link between a product / service to the environment, a green lifestyle by highlighting a product / service to promote an image of environmental responsibility, the company can offer (Banerjee, Gulas, & Iyer, 1995, p. 22). For its relevance today, literature has paid limited attention to green marketing and advertising and its effectiveness (Cronin et al., 2011; Fowler III & Close, 2012). While traditional advertising has the function to inform, remind, and persuade, green advertising aims to create awareness and favorable attitudes toward the company (D'Souza & Taghian, 2005). Literature suggests that consumers respond positively to CSR communication in general, but in particular to green communication (Nyilasy et al., 2014; Montoro et al., 2006).

With the increase of green advertising there has also been an increase of greenwashing, which can be defined as a company's communication that misleads consumers regarding its environmental practices or the environmental benefits of its products or serv*ices* (Parguel et al., 2011: 16-17). Companies are communicating incomplete or even false claim in order to appeal green consumers and improve their image (Carlson, Grove, Kangun, & Polonsky, 1996; Parguel et al., 2011). Perceiving social responsibility as shared value rather than PR campaign will require dramatically different thinking in business but companies ought to understand that greenwashing has negative consequences for the environment, the consumers and the businesses, as it backfires, hurting the company's reputation and sales (Porter & Kramer, 2006; Furlow, 2010).

With the increase of greenwashing, consumers have become skeptical, doubting the truth or the motive of green advertising. Consumers state they want to know more about what the companies do and how they behave, but often react skeptical when these advertise their sustainability efforts (Nyilasy et al., 2014). In a research project spanning ten countries over the past decade, Globescan (2012) found that fewer than two people in five believe companies communicate honestly about their CSR performance. However, almost four in five say they are "very interested" in wanting to know more about what companies are doing to be responsible.

Specifically, with the communication of the environmental dimension of CSR, people are becoming increasingly skeptical (Pfanner, 2008). According to Leonidou and Leonidou (2011), the increased skepticism is due to the increasing amount of companies promoting their environmental efforts, the growing complaints of consumers and activists on misleading statements and concerns about how ads and facts and presented. Forehand & Grier (2003) argue that consumer skepticism in general is driven by the perception that the firm is being dishonest about its true motives and this has a negative impact on the company's credibility and performance (Mohr, Webb, & Harris, 2001; Vanhamme & Grobben; 2009; Webb & Mohr, 1998).

Accordingly, CSR communication can also harm companies and some firms are better off not communicating their sustainability and environmental efforts (Nyilasy et al., 2014). Some examples that show that CSR campaign can hurt the company are Avon, Philip and Morris (Yoon et al., 2006). On the other hand, as aforementioned, reducing the skepticism, companies engaging in CSR initiatives can exploit several benefits communicating their efforts. Consequently, it is crucial for companies to know how to minimize this skepticism by conveying positive attributions (Du et al., 2010).

Mediating Attributions

There is strong evidence that attributional processes mediate the relationship between green advertisement and attitudes and purchase intention (Nyilasy et al., 2014). Attribution theory investigates the causal explanations people give of others' behaviour. These processes of attribution are fundamental to many aspects of consumer cognitions and behaviours (Folkes, 1988) and have been used to understand how marketers shape consumer response (Friestad & Wright, 1994). Parguel et al. (2011) present two types of motives that consumers attribute towards green advertising, intrinsic motive indicating genuine environmental consciousness and extrinsic motive indicating taking advantage of the trends.

Ellen et al. (2006) stated that the consumer attributions towards CSR are more complex and identified for different types. Shortly, stakeholder-driven, defined as the support of social causes because of pressure from stakeholders. Egoistic-driven relates to exploiting the cause rather than helping it. Strategic-driven motives relates to attaining business goals while benefiting the cause. Values-driven motives relate to benevolence-motivated giving and Win-Win relating to strategic-driven and value driven motive (Vlachos et al., 2009). Depending on the effect on consumers' purchase intentions, Ellen et al. (2006) divided the motive in two groups, namely, positive attributions (values and strategic-driven) and negative attributions (egoistic and stakeholder-driven).

As previously mentioned, Forehand and Grier (2003) argued that the perception of being dishonest about the true motives is what has a negative impact. Sometimes even when companies are communicating their true motives, the wrong motive may be attributed, creating disadvantageous attitudes and behaviors. To obtain CSR strategic benefits, it is key to create awareness while understanding and incorporating consumer attributions in the CSR communication strategy. Communication should be designed in a way to reduce skepticism and convey favorable true motives to the company's' actions (Bhattacharya & Sen, 2010; Nysilaly et al., 2014).

Communication Effectiveness

Increasing literature has researched the factors that lead to favorable attributions and influence the effectiveness of CSR and green communication. However, more research is needed to find all the factors (Turkel et al., 2015). In general, Azevedo (2004) suggests that companies should communicate informative and educational information, avoid the use of emotional tone and provide a source to corroborate information (as cited in Wanderley et al., 2008: 372).

Du et al. (2010) presented a framework in light of the challenge of companies to communicate the CSR efforts increasing awareness while minimizing skepticism and generating positive attributions. The framework reviews four key aspects that have an impact on the effectiveness of the communication, namely, message content, message channel, stakeholder-specific factors and company factors. First, the scholars state the relevance of the message content. A company can communicate its specific involvement or the cause itself, its commitment to the cause, the impact it has on the cause, why it engages in a specific cause and the fit between the company and the cause. For instance, emphasizing the importance of the social issue can reduce the skepticism of the advertising (Menon & Kahn, 2003) and the type of cause that the company supports may increase the attribution of negative motives (Forehand

& Grier, 2003). According to the scholars, firms should sometimes acknowledge the presence of self-serving motives, depending on how the motives are attributed. Marín, Cuestas & Roman (2015) concluded that some of the key aspects that influence the attributions are corporate ability, company-cause fit, interpersonal trust and corporate hypocrisy.

Du et al. (2010) present the influence of the message channel including the extent to which it is controllable by the company, the credibility of the channel and the importance of more informal channels like word-of-mouth. As moderators of the communication effectiveness, Du et al. (2010) pointed two company-specific factors, corporate reputation and CSR positioning. For instance, companies with good reputations have higher source credibility, while for companies with poor reputations CSR communication often backfires (Yoon et al., 2006). Finally, three stakeholder-specific factors are pointed, stakeholder type, issue support and social value orientation. According to Bögel (2015), the role of stakeholders' specific characteristics has not been thoroughly researched and might determine the CSR communication strategy.

Du et al. (2007) argue that it is essential for a company to tailor its CSR communication to the specific needs of different stakeholder groups. They may vary in terms of expectations of businesses and information needs, and thus respond differently to the various communications. As a future research, they included the need to investigate how a company can best communicate its CSR initiatives to different target audiences. This coincides with the literature stating that international businesses must analyze and adapt their strategies based on the cultural behaviors and values their consumers (Brønn & Vrioni, 2001). Accordingly, this study contributes by researching national culture as a stakeholder-specific factor influencing the effectiveness of CSR communication.

National Culture

Culture entails the science of human societies, it deals with how people act, feel, think and behave (Hofstede, 1984). National culture may be defined as "values, beliefs, norms and behavioral patterns of a national group" (Leung, Bhagat, Buchan, Erez, & Gibson, 2005: 357). In this research, the label "national" is applied to culture to distinguish from other forms of culture that are not addressed here. However, because of the globalization and the integration of the world, cultural differences within countries are increasing (Fukuyama, 1995). Accordingly, in this research national culture is defined as a large number of people conditioned by similar background, education, and life experiences.

Culture has been identified as one of the most important differentiators in ethics, ethical attitudes (Franke & Nadler, 2008) and ethical perception (Vitell & Paolillo, 2004). Furthermore, scholars have researched the influence of national culture on CSR and its different aspects, pointing CSR self as nationally contingent (Matten & Moon, 2008; Gao, 2009).

Most of the research is focused on the perceptions and actions of the organizations and practitioners (Burton, Farh, & Hegarty, 2000). For instance, Kim & Kim (2010) investigated the influence of cultural values on the perceptions of practitioners of CSR and found significant relation. Furthermore, Christie, Kwon, Stoeberl & Baumhart (2003) found a strong influence of national culture on business managers' ethical attitudes in India, Korea, and the USA. In accordance with the acknowledgment of Du et al., (2010) about different targets and different needs, Leonidou & Leonidou (2011) performed a literature analysis about green marketing and advertising, found cross-cultural differences and concluded that this could reflect differences in demand by stakeholders.

Research about the consumer's cross-cultural CSR perceptions, expectations and responses instead of the practitioners is limited (Burton et al., 2000; Pfau et al., 2008). Nevertheless, it has indicated that their perceptions differ based on norms and values (Gjølberg, 2009; Leonidou, Leonidou, & Kvasova, 2010; Maignan, 2001). As Leonidou & Leonidou (2011), Gjølberg (2009) stated that as societies differ in culture, context and traditions so do their perceptions of CSR. Maignan (2001) confirmed this in a cross-cultural comparison between France, Germany and USA. The scholar acknowledged in the paper that future research could attempt to investigate whether the differences in perceptions are linked to cultural values.

Although the impact of culture on advertising has been broadly researched among scholars, more research is needed for conclusions and a comprehensive framework (Taylor, 2005). What is concluded so far is that consumers respond to advertising messages that fit their culture and reward advertisers who understand and adapt the advertising to the cultures and values (Zhang & Gelb, 1996). Accordingly, it is essential to understand the cultural differences for successful international advertising (Keegan, 1996). For this, Zinkhan (1994) identified Hofstede's (1980) cultural dimensions as useful. Finally, literature research suggests that attribution processes also differ across cultures. For instance, the perception of dishonesty or inauthenticity diverges between countries (Choi et al., 1999) and as said above, attributional processes mediate the relationship between green advertisement and attitudes and purchase intention (Nyilasy et al., 2014).

Cultural Dimensions

In line with Zinkman (1994), Katz, Swanson, & Nelson (2001) also stated that the cultural differences in CSR perceptions might be based on Hofstede's cultural dimensions. The work of Hofstede (1980, 2001) has been used and validated by several studies to understand differences in national culture. Based on surveys of more than 116,000 IBM employees in 72 countries, Hofstede classified countries in terms of their relative standings on cultural dimensions. He proposed different dimensions to differentiate culture: power-distance, individualism, masculinity, uncertainty-avoidance, and later indulgence and long-term orientation were added. Among them, the first four dimensions have generated a huge number of replications, citations, and discussions (Fang, 2003), and will be therefore the ones used for this research. Hofstede's dimensions capture societal differences and have been proved useful in marketing and consumer behavior research (Soares, Farhangmehr, & Shoham, 2007).

Hofstede's framework has also been broadly criticized. Critics have stated that the research is outdated, for which Hofstede argued that culture change to invalidate the country index scores should not be recognizable for a long period, perhaps until 2100 (Hofstede & Hofstede, 2001). Additionally, using data from one single corporation has been considered a limitation, questioning the applicability of the dimensions to all cultures, Hofstede's response to this criticism is that what was measured were differences between national cultures and "any set of functionally equivalent samples from national populations can supply information about such differences" (Hofstede & Hofstede, 2001, p.73; Soares et al., 2007).

National Cultures Researched

The rationale behind the choice of the national cultures researched is the cultural difference. Colombia is a developing country in South America and it lies amongst the most collectivistic cultures of the world. Combined with a high score in power distance, groups often have identities tied to class distinctions. Furthermore, Colombia scores high in masculinity and uncertainty avoidance. The Netherlands scores high on uncertainty avoidance but is more of a feminine society with a high score on individualism and a low score on power distance. USA is one of the most individualistic cultures in the world, with a low score on power distance and uncertainty avoidance and a high score on masculinity (Hofstede & Hofstede, 2001).

HYPOTHESES DEVELOPMENT

No specific hypotheses related to the countries were developed. The cultural differences among the chosen countries support their inclusion in the research. Based on the literature, the expectation is that, if national culture has an impact on the motives attributed to green advertisement, it will also differ based on each cultural dimension. As the countries differ with regards to these cultural dimensions and this influences the individual's perception of ethical situations, norms for behavior and ethical judgments, among others, so will the various components of their CSR attributions and attitudes towards them. Accordingly, four hypotheses were developed based on the four first Hofstede's dimensions: individualism, power distance, masculinity and uncertainty avoidance. Following the explanation of each dimension together with its corresponding hypothesis.

Individualism vs. Collectivism

Individualism vs. collectivism is the extent to which people in a society are integrated into groups. Individualistic societies pursue self-interests and prefer to have loose ties between individuals. People are expected to take care of themselves and goals and identity of the individual are given priority. Collectivism describes a society in which people view themselves as part of a group, with sense of belonging and support for each other (Hofstede, 1984; Triandis, 1989). People in individualistic organizations tend to be less ethical than in collectivistic organizations (Akaah, 1990) and less friendly to the environment (Triandis, 1993).

In such conditions, this could indicate that as consumers in countries with a high level of individualism put their own goals first, they also expect the companies to be concerned with the interest of the company. Moreover, they are more likely to expect companies to act less ethical and less friendly to the environment in order to achieve their goals. Accordingly, we can expect that negative motives like profit or fiscal advantage are more likely to be attributed in high individualistic cultures. On the contrary, consumers in collectivistic countries consider themselves part of group. This could indicate that they expect the companies to act in there and the environment's benefit, as they feel part of a group where companies should be concerned with the society as a whole.

This is also supported by the study of Mangleberg & Bristol (1998) that states that peer group conformity is negatively related to advertisement skepticism. As such, national cultures with a high level of collectivism are expected to be more likely to believe that companies have a positive motive behind CSR and green advertisement. Accordingly, the following hypothesis is proposed:

Hypothesis One: Individualism has a negative effect on positive CSR attributions (value and strategic-driven) or a positive effect on negative attributions (egoistic and stakeholder-driven).

Power Distance

Power distance is defined as 'the extent to which the less powerful members of institutions and organizations accept the power is distributed equally' (Hofstede, 1984: 419). Individuals from cultures with high power distance usually accept the inequality of power between superiors and subordinates and are unwilling to disagree with superiors, as they believe that superiors are entitled to privileges (Hofstede, 1984).

Research has found that people from countries that score high on power distance are more likely to accept unethical actions (Cohen, Pant, & Sharp, 1996), however, they also expect the 'power' to be doing the correct thing (Javidan, House, Dorfman, Hanges, & De luque, 2006).

On the other hand, cultures with a low level of power distance do not expect this, they tend to have a high degree of consumer activism and are more likely to search for more information than what the organizations claim (Ramasamy & Yeung, 2009).

In such conditions, this could indicate that national cultures with a low level of power distance are more likely to be skeptical about the motives of the organizations behind CSR. They don't expect companies to be acting out of intrinsic motives and are more likely to attribute negative motives and look for further information from other sources. On the other hand, for national cultures with a high level of power distance this could indicate than people expect the organization to act in the benefit of the society and are more likely to believe what the companies communicate and thus less likely to attribute negative motives. Accordingly, the following hypothesis is proposed:

Hypothesis Two: Increasing power distance has a negative effect on negative CSR attributions (egoistic and stakeholder-driven) or a positive effect on positive attributions (value and strategic-driven).

Uncertainty Avoidance

Uncertainty avoidance is the extent to which individuals in a group or culture have tolerance for ambiguity and uncertainty and try to avoid these situations. In cultures with high uncertainty avoidance there is a need for rules and formality to structure life. People are less open for change and believe more in 'expert' figures than people from low uncertainty avoidance cultures. Cultures with a high level of uncertainty avoidance generally rely on absolute truth and are less likely to deviate from the norms. Furthermore, research has found that cultures with low uncertainty avoidance are more likely to take risks (Hofstede 1984), and this risk taking is highly correlated with unethical actions (Rallapalli, Vitell, Wiebe, & Barnes, 1994).

In such conditions, this could indicate that due to the higher risk perception, national cultures with a high uncertainty level are more likely to trust and rely on what the companies communicate, as they expect predictability in the behaviors of the members of the society. Furthermore, it can indicate that national cultures with a low uncertainty avoidance level are more likely to distrust more and believe that companies are taking the risk to communicate out of negative motives. Correspondingly, national cultures with high uncertainty avoidance are expected to be less likely to attribute negatives motives to green advertising. Accordingly, the following hypothesis is proposed:

Hypothesis Three: Increasing uncertainty avoidance has a negative effect on negative CSR attributions (egoistic and stakeholder-driven) or a positive effect on positive attributions (value and strategic-driven).

Masculinity vs. Femininity

Masculinity is the extent of preference in society for achievement, heroism, assertiveness and material rewards for success. In masculine societies, performance is highly valued. Femininity represents a preference for cooperation, responsibility, modesty and caring for the weak (Hofstede, 1980). Masculine cultures are more likely to behave unethically because of greed and competitiveness for personal gains (Vitell & Festervand, 1987). Furthermore, they are also more likely to favor economic achievements than environmental protection (Hofstede, 1980).

In such conditions, this could indicate that people in masculine cultures are more likely to behave in an autonomous way and put relevance on being successful and competitive. Thus, are more likely to behave in an unethical way and also be more skeptical about the companies not doing the same. On the other hand, feminine cultures are more likely to behave in a consensual way; they value responsibility and caring for the weak and the environment. This could indicate that feminine cultures are more likely to attribute positive motives to CSR advertisement and masculine cultures more likely to attribute negative motives. According, the following hypothesis is proposed:

Hypothesis Four: Increasing masculinity has a positive effect on negative CSR attributions (egoistic and stakeholder-driven) or a negative effect on positive attributions (value and strategic driven).

33

CONCEPTUAL MODEL

Based on the literature review and the hypotheses, the conceptual model in figure 1 is proposed. Negative attributions and positive attributions are the dependent variables. Individualism, power distance, masculinity and uncertainty avoidance are the independent variables. We expect the independent variables to have a direct effect on the dependent variables.

RESEARCH METHODOLOGY

The main research question was developed as follows: "to what extent are the attributions that mediate the impact of green advertisement on consumer attitudes and purchase intention influenced by national culture?"

In order to answer this question, a quantitative cross-cultural research method was conducted with an online self-administered survey. The survey was conducted in the languages of the three countries: Dutch, English and Spanish. The Values Survey Module 2008 from Hofstede, Hofstede & Minkov (2010), used in this study to assess the national culture was already translated in the desirable three languages in Hofstede's database. For the rest of the survey, standard procedures to forward- and back-translate were used in order to have linguistic validity.

Figure 1. National culture
Source: Proposed by the Authors.

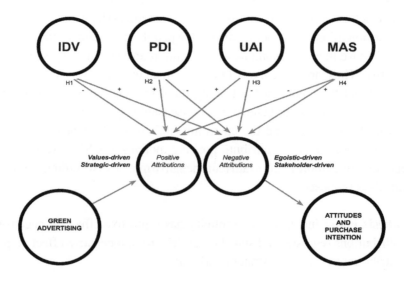

The survey was built with the Qualtrics Web Tool and distributed through Facebook, where people were invited to participate and were asked to send invitations to members of their own networks to participate. In accordance with the definition of national culture taken in this research, the condition to fill in the survey was to be 'born and bred' in the cultures of interest. The invitation contained a short introduction and the link to the survey. In the survey, the introduction described the context of the research, the approximate amount of time it took to fill in the survey (15 minutes) and an anonymity statement, emphasizing the confidentiality of the answers. Respondents were informed that the research was to understand their attitudes and beliefs towards green advertising; there was no mention of cultural values in order to avoid response bias.

The procedure was the same for all participants. The survey consisted of different sections. First, respondents were instructed to answer general questions in order assess the national cultural dimensions and sustainability involvement. Subsequently, three green advertisements, of Coca Cola, Nestle and Toyota, were shown and respondents were instructed to indicate the likelihood of what they thought is the motive of the companies to engage in the correspondingly green advertisement. Lastly, age, gender and education were asked.

Pre-Test

Before conducting the main research, a pre-test was conducted in order to choose which companies' green advertisements were going to be used. The aim of the pre-test was to use multinational companies in the main research that were known and for which consumers had a similar attitude in the three countries. This is because the existing attitude towards the company is used in the attribution process to process the new messages (Bae & Cameron, 2006).

The companies used in the pretest were Coca Cola, Toyota, General Electric, Fujifilm, Phillips, Ford, Starbucks and Nestle. The rationale behind the choice of companies was that they are known companies, not from industries for which negative motives are particularly attributed such as tobacco, alcohol, weapons and pornography (Morsing & Schultz, 2006) and green advertisements where available through the Internet.

With the aid of SPSS, one-way ANOVA tests were conducted to compare the means of the three countries and use the companies in the research for which there were no significant differences of attitude between the countries. The results indicated that Coca Cola ($F(2, 42) = 1.82$, $p > 0.05$), Toyota ($F(2, 42) = 1.47$, $p > 0.05$), Fujifilm ($F(2, 42)= 0.845$, $p > 0.05$), Phillips ($F(2, 42) = 2.54$, $p > 0.05$) and Nestle ($F(2, 42)= 1.41$, $p > 0.05$) were statistically not different between the countries. Because of the lengthiness of the questionnaire the decision was made to use only three green advertisements in the survey. Fujifilm was discarded because many respondents were not familiar with this company and Phillips because of the lower p-value and lower quality of the green advertisement. Accordingly, the companies used in the main research were Coca Cola, Nestle and Toyota.

Sample

Participants were recruited from the population of Colombia, The Netherlands and USA. =Before collecting the responses, the sample size was determined. The minimum necessary number of respondents recommended by Hofstede et al. (2010) to be able to compare the cultures was 50 per country and 30 by Saunders et al. (2009) to have a normal distribution. The sample size had to be thus at least 150.

An advantage of using a survey as research method is the usefulness in describing the characteristics of a large population (Saunders et al., 2009). The survey was purposefully spread within the three countries via Facebook; thence estimating response rate is difficult. Additionally, it should be acknowledged that this non-probability sampling procedure decreases the generalizability of findings (Saunders et al., 2009).

Measurement of the Variables

Validated statements and scales from previous research were used to measure the different constructs in this research. The survey consisted of twenty-one questions and a total of 10 variables. Individualism, power distance, uncertainty avoidance and masculinity are the four independent variables, negative and positive attributions are the two dependent variables and age, gender, education and sustainability involvement are the control variables.

Cultural Dimensions

Hofstede's dimensions have been validated by several studies in international business, marketing and consumer behavior (Soares et al., 2007) and are still the most widely used measures when it comes to cross-national culture research (Kirkman, Lowe, & Gibson, 2006). Some of the studies where this framework is used are by Vitell & Paolillo (2004), Scholtens & Dam (2007), Simga-Mugan, Daly, Onkal & Kavut (2005). As previously mentioned, in this study national culture is measured along four of the dimensions: individualism, power distance, uncertainty avoidance and masculinity. The dimensions were estimated using the Values Survey Module 2008 from Hofstede et al. (2010), a twenty-eight-item questionnaire with questions that relate to each dimension. Example items are: for individualism "In choosing an ideal job, how important would it be to you to have sufficient time for your personal or home life", for power distance "How often, in your experience, are subordinates afraid to contradict their boss (or students their teacher)", for uncertainty avoidance "All in all, how would you describe your state of health these days" and for masculinity "In choosing an ideal job, how important would it be to you to get recognition for good performance".

The value of each dimension is calculated with a linear combination of items derived from the mean scores. Table 1 presents the formulas used, whereby m01 is the mean score of question 01, m02 the mean of question 02 etc. The c (x) is a constant to put the values in the perspective of 0 till 100; it does not affect the comparison between countries (Hofstede et al., 2010) and is not used in this research.

CSR Attributions

Values-driven, strategic-driven, egoistic-driven and stakeholder-driven attributions were measured following Ellen et al. (2006) and the statements were constructed following Vlachos et al. (2009). Two additional statements were included as they

Table 1. Protest one-way ANOVA attitude towards companies

Company	Colombia Mean (SD)	Netherlands Mean (SD)	USA Mean (SD)	p-value
Coca Cola	3.40 (1.55)	4.46 (1.64)	4.13 (1.51)	0.174
Toyota	4.27 (1.28)	3.93 (0.70)	4.60 (1.21)	0.240
General Electric	4.47 (1.19)	3.53 (0.81)	4.6 (0.73)	0.0059*
Fujifilm	3.93 (1.28)	3.47 (0.83)	3.80 (0.86)	0.436
Phillips	4.73 (1.03)	4.73 (1.03)	4.06 (0.71)	0.0912
Ford	3.60 (1.81)	4.87 (0.64)	4.53 (0.99)	0.022*
Starbucks	4.267 (1.39)	3.40 (1.92)	5.00 (1.07)	0.020*
Nestle	4.40 (1.50)	5.00 (0.76)	5.00 (1.00)	0.2554

Note: N =45 *. Mean difference is significant at the 0.05 level

Source: Processed by the Authors.

could also be motives attributed to green advertising: 'They want to enhance their relation with the government" as egoistic motive and 'They will attract more talented employees" as strategic motive.

In total, for the three green advertisements forty-three items were used, rated on a 5 point Likert-scales from strongly disagree to strongly agree. Example items are: for values-driven attribution "They have a long-term interest in the community", for strategic-driven attribution "They will get more customers", for egoistic-driven attribution "They are taking advantage of the cause to help their own business" and for stakeholder-driven attribution "They feel their customers expect it".

Covariates

The research was controlled for age, gender, education and sustainability involvement. The latter was measured following Maignan (2001) in order to assess the consumer's readiness to support socially responsible organizations, what may have an influence on the motives attributed. The statements were rated on a 5-point Likert-scale from strongly disagree to strongly agree. An example item is "I consider the ethical reputation of businesses when I shop".

Statistical Procedure

After checking scale reliabilities, descriptive statistics, normality tests and correlation tests were computed. To test the hypotheses, two multiple regression analyses were used to measure the strength of association between the national cultural dimensions and CSR attributions and to determine the percentage of variance in the national cultural dimensions, which can significantly explain consumers' CSR attributions towards green advertising. This method was also used by Marín et al. (2015) in order to test variables influencing CSR attributions. The regression was run for the two dependent variables (1) negative attributions and (2) positive attributions. Different assumptions needed to be met: non-zero variance, normality of all the variables, homogeneity of variance and no or little multicollinearity between the independent variables (Saunders et al., 2009). Statistical significance for the tests and analyses was established at a level of 0.05.

RESULTS

Description of Respondents

In the end, 342 surveys were opened and 212 were fully completed. During the gathering of responses, despite the incentive, the lengthiness of the survey proved to be an obstacle as 38% of the respondents did not complete it. A Hotdeck imputation was conducted for all the cases where less than 10% were missing (Field, 2009). This approach leads to better results than list-wise, pair-wise deletion or mean substitution (Myers, 2011). The surveys with cases were more than 10% missed, were deleted. In the end, 248 responses were available for the analysis.

The final sample consisted of 96 respondents from Colombia, 96 from The Netherlands and 56 from USA. Both the conditions of Hofstede et al. (2010) and Saunders et al. (2009) were met. Overall, the sample was represented by 48.8% female and 51.2% male. The age of the respondents varied from the categories 'under 20' to 'above 60' with 8 respondents were under 20 years old, 167 respondents between 20 and 24 years old, 25 respondents between 25 and 29 years old, 21 between 30 and 39 years old, 15 between 40 and 49, 11 between 50 and 59 and 1 respondents above 60. Accordingly, a total 80.6% of the respondents was between 'under 20' and 29 years old. The sample was overall well educated with 76.7% of the respondents having 15 or more years of education equivalent to university or applied sciences degree, while only 2.8% had less than 10 years of education. The result of a younger and higher educated sample could have been caused by the sampling method. For a full description, the respondents see Table 2.

DATA CHECK AND MANIPULATION

Reliability Analysis

Data was prepared and analyzed with the aid of SPSS. First, the data was checked for counter-indicative items, but there were not any. Subsequently, a reliability analysis was run to examine the consistency of the measurements. The four CSR attributions and sustainability involvement had a Cronbach's alpha over 0.7 indicating internal consistency. For the cultural dimensions, the reliability test should be based on country mean scores instead of individual scores. The Cronbach's alphas were for this reason based on the IBM database across 40 countries (Hofstede, 1980). For the list of the Cronbach's alpha for all the variables, see Table 3.

Table 2. Index formulas for the calculation of Hofstede's cultural dimensions

$$PDI = 35 \quad (m07 - m02) + 25 \quad (m23 - m26) + C(x)$$

$$IDV = 35 \quad (m04 - m01) + 35 \quad (m09 - m06) + C(x)$$

$$MAS = 35 \quad (m05 - m03) + 35 \quad (m08 - m10) + C(x)$$

$$UAI = 40 \quad (m20 - m16) + 25 \quad (m24 - m27) + C(x)$$

Source: Hofstede et al. (2010); Processed by the authors.

Descriptive Analysis

Means, Standard Deviations

New variables as a function of the items were created for the analysis. For the CSR attributions and the sustainability involvement, the means of the items were calculated. Following Ellen et al. (2006), the CSR attributions were divided into positive (values-driven & strategic-driven) and negative (egoistic-driven and stakeholder-driven) attributions. For the national cultural dimensions, the indexes were calculated with the formulas presented in Table 1 provided by Hofstede et al. (2010). For the means and standard deviations of all the variables, see Table 3.

In the end, there were two dependent variables: negative attributions and positive attributions, four independent variables: individualism, power distance, uncertainty avoidance and masculinity and four control variables: age, education, gender and sustainability involvement.

Comparison of Countries

Although no specific hypotheses related to the countries were developed, it was analyzed if there were any differences between the researched countries. Gender, age and education seemed similarly distributed between the three researched countries. However, to control for statistical differences, one-way ANOVA tests were conducted. There were no statistical significant differences found for age (F $(2, 245) = 0.175$), $p > 0.05$, education (F $(2, 245) = 2.111$, $p > 0.05$) and gender (F $(2, 245) = 0.90$, $p > 0.05$).

Contrarily, results showed a significant difference of sustainability involvement between the countries (F $(2, 245) = 7.655$, $p < 0.01$). Tukey post-hoc tests revealed that the sustainability involvement in The Netherlands was significantly lower compared to Colombia and USA ($p = 0.000$, $p = 0.082$) and there was no significant difference between Colombia and USA ($p = 0.468$).

Subsequently, the cultural dimensions of the three countries were calculated. Contrary to the expectations, the dimensions for USA differed from assumptions based on Hofstede, with a low score for individualism and a higher score on uncertainty avoidance than the Netherlands.

Normality Test

The distribution of the data was tested to check if it deviated from normal distribution. Because of the sample size (>200), skewness does not make a fundamental difference and the risk of kurtosis is reduced (Field, 2013). Accordingly, the shape of the distribution and the values of the skewness and kurtosis I1I were checked rather than the significance. All variables had a normal distribution, so no variables needed to be transformed. By means of a scatter-plot, linearity and homoscedasticity were also assumed.

Correlation Matrix

A general procedure for Pearson bivariate correlation analysis was conducted to check for any significant correlation between the dependent, independent and control variables. The correlation matrix is presented in Table 3 containing an overview of the means, standard deviations, correlations and reliabilities for all the variables.

Correlation analysis gives no indication of the causality, but indicates the presence and direction of the relationship between the variables at a significance level of 5 percent and 1 percent (Field, 2009). The results indicated that the negative attributions were significantly correlated with gender ($r = -0.143$, $p < 0.05$) power distance ($r = -0.178$, $p < 0.01$), uncertainty avoidance ($r = -0.201$, $p < 0.01$) and positive attributions ($r = 0.422$, $p < 0.01$). Positive attributions were significantly correlated with age ($r = 0 - .153$, $p < 0.05$), gender ($r = 0 - .188$, $p < 0.01$) and education ($r = 0.132$, $p < 0.05$). Contrarily to expectations, positive attributions were not correlated with any of the cultural dimensions. Additionally, individualism was significantly correlated with power distance ($r = -0.155$, $p < 0.05$) and masculinity ($r = 0 - .263$, $p < 0.01$). However, these correlations were below 0.8, so a multicollinearity test was not needed.

Hypotheses Testing

The four hypotheses developed were analyzed with multiple regressions. As previously mentioned, this analysis measures the strength of association between independent and dependent variable and determines the percentage of variance explained by the independent variables. The regression was conducted for the two dependent variables: positive attributions and negative attributions.

First, as Table 4 presents, the regression was run for the dependent variable positive attributions. In the first model of the regression, the control variables were entered. Results indicated that the model was statistically significant ($F_{(4, 243)} = 4.282$; $p < 0.05$) and explained 6.6% of the variance of positive attributions.

After entering the cultural dimensions at model 2 the total variance explained by the model only increased to 8.3%. The introduction of the cultural dimensions only adds an additional 1.7% variance in negative attributions, after controlling for gender, age, education and sustainability involvement. This change was statistically not significant ($F_{(4, 239)} = 1.12$; $p > 0.005$). Accordingly, in the final model none of the cultural dimensions were statistically significant.

Subsequently, as Table 5 shows, the regression was run for the dependent variable negative attributions. In the first model of the hierarchical multiple regression, the control variables were entered. This model was statistically significant ($F_{(4, 243)} = 2.519$; $p < 0.05$) and explained 4% of variance in negative attributions. After entering the cultural dimensions at model 2 the model resulted significant ($F_{(8, 239)} = 3.58$; $p < 0.001$) and explained 12% of the total variance. The introduction of the cultural dimensions adds an additional 8% variance in negative attributions, after controlling for gender, age, education and sustainability involvement. This change was statistically significant ($F_{(4, 239)} = 4.821$; $p < 0.005$). In the final model, after controlling for gender, age, education and sustainability involvement, two out of the four cultural dimensions were statistically significant, power distance ($\beta = -.171$, $p < .01$) and uncertainty avoidance ($\beta = -0.177$, $p < 0.01$), confirming hypotheses 2 and 3.

Because of unexpected results mentioned in section 4.3.2.2 regarding the calculated cultural dimensions individualism in USA, multiple regressions were conducted excluding this country. The regression indicated similar results, with power distance ($\beta = -0.159$, $p < 0.05$) and uncertainty avoidance ($\beta = -0.253$, $p < 0.01$) having a significant influence on negative attributions and a total variance explained by the model of 15%.

CONCLUSION AND GENERAL DISCUSSION

Discussion and Conclusion

The aim of this chapter was to address the extent to which national culture has an impact on the CSR attributions that mediate green advertisement with attitude and

Table 3. Sample characteristics

Variable	Colombia n=96	Netherlands n=96	USA n=56
Gender			
Male	50%	51%	53.6%
Female	50%	49%	46.4%
Age			
29 or under	82.3%	78.1%	82.1 %
30–39	8.3 %	10.4%	9 %
40–49	6.3 %	7.3 %	3.6 %
50–59	3.1%	4.2 %	7.1%
60 or over	0 %	0 %	1.8 %
Education			
13 years or less	27.1. %	18.8 %	10.7%
14–15	10.4 %	16.6%	5.4 %
16-17	20.8 %	36.5 %	62.5%
18 years or over	41.7 %	28.1%	21.4%

Note: n=248

Source: Processed by the Authors.

Table 4. Correlation matric, means, standard deviations, correlations, and reliabilities

Variables	Number of items	M	SD	1	2	3	4	5	6
1. Age	1	2.76	1.51	-					
2. Gender	1	1.51	0.501	.025	-				
3. Education	1	6.83	2.442	-.155*	.012	-			
4. Individualism	4	146.43	59.18	-.105	.085	-.062	(0.770)		
5. Power distance	4	129.69	44.32	-.072	-.087	-.070	.155*	(0.842)	
6. Masculinity	4	91.59	51.71	.023	-.018	.074	-.263**	.007	(0.760)
7. Uncertainty Avoidance	4	44.43	67.86	-.082	-.136	-.076	-.106	.086c	.093	(0.

Source: Processed by the Authors.

purchase intention. As Table 5 shows, the results indicate that there is indeed an impact; negative attributions towards green advertising are affected by national culture and more specifically, negatively affected by the dimensions power distance (p=0.007) and uncertainty avoidance (p=0.005). Contrarily to expectations, not all the dimensions of national culture affect negative attributions and as shown in Table 4, positive attributions are not significantly influenced by national culture. For the summarized results of the hypothesis testing, see Table 6.

The results suggest that national cultures with a low level of power distance and uncertainty avoidance are more likely to attribute negative motives towards green advertising. This could be related to the expectation of these cultures that people with 'higher' power, in this case the companies, are doing the right thing and not pursuing self-interest. People in cultures with a high level of uncertainty avoidance

Table 5. Multiple regression using positive attributions as the dependent variable

Variable	Coefficient value (b)	t-value	p-value
Model 1			
Intercept		17.79	0.000
Age	-0.178	-2.825	0.005
Education	0.064	1.012	0.312
Gender	-0.160	-2.577	0.011
SUS	0.009	0.140	0.889
R2 (%)		6.6%	
Adjusted R2 (%)		5%	
F statistics		4.282 and p=0.002**	
Model 2			
Intercept		16.706	0.000
Age	-0.172	-2.696	0.008
Education	0.076	1.197	0.232
Gender	-0.141	-2.249	0.025
SUS	0.016	0.256	0.798
IND	0.074	1.125	0.262
PDI	-0.076	-1.203	0.230
MAS	0.081	1.256	0.210

Source: Processed by the Authors.

and/or power distance are less likely to be skeptical about what the companies communicate. This in turn might lead to less attribution of negative motives.

That only negative attributions are significantly influenced by national culture could come because these are 'stronger' that the positive attributions and thus they differ more between stakeholders. As Vlachos et al. (2009) stated, negative attributions dominate the positive attributions leading to unfavorable attributions and behaviors.

Furthermore, that the cultural dimensions individualism and masculinity did not have a significant effect on the negative attributions could entail that only some dimensions of national culture have an influence on the cross-cultural differences of attributions. Power distance and uncertainty avoidance were also found to be the influencing cultural dimensions on marketers' perceptions of CSR (Vitell, Paolillo, & Thomas, 2003). However, research is needed to look into the other dimensions and aspects of culture.

The results extend the research of factors that influence the effectiveness of CSR communication and green advertising and the specific role of stakeholders' specific characteristics. Building on the research of Du et al. (2010), the results imply that national culture is one of the stakeholder-specific factors that companies and scholars should take into account to convey favorable attributions when creating green advertising. Furthermore, extending the research of cross-cultural differences in consumer's perceptions of CSR (Maignan, 2001; Quazi & O'brien, 2000), it implies that consumers in different cultures not only perceive CSR differently but also attribute differently towards CSR communication, specifically towards green advertising. As Leonidou & Leonidou (2011) concluded, the cross-cultural differences of green marketing could reflect this differences of expectations and demand by consumers.

Contrarily to the suggestion of Katz et al. (2001), the results indicate that not all the dimensions have an influence. Another interesting result is that both negative and positive attributions have means close to the median, implying that, in accordance to the literature, most people attribute mixed attributions (Ellen et al., 2006) or don't know why companies may be engaging in CSR communication (Du et al., 2010).

It must be acknowledged that the results show that the magnitude of the effect of cultural difference on attributions is very small, only explaining 12% of the variance. Following the literature, the results should not be underestimated even if they are of small magnitude. As stated by many researchers, the effectiveness of CSR communication is complicated and lacks literature consensus on the influencing factors, mediators and moderators. This research serves as a starting point to follow-up field research on the cross-cultural differences of perceptions and attributions towards CSR communication.

Table 6. Multiple regression using negative attributions as the dependent variable

Variable	Coefficient value (b)	t-value	p-value
Model 1			
Intercept		15.939	0.000
Age	-0.108	-1.695	0.091
Education	0.072	1.134	0.258
Gender	-0.141	-2.243	0.098
SUS	-0.003	-0.051	0.959
R2 (%)		4%	
Adjusted R2 (%)		2.4%	
F statistics		2.519 and p=0.042*	
Model 2			
Intercept		15.083	0.000
Age	-0.086	-1.379	0.169
Education	0.102	1.634	0.104
Gender	-0.098	-1.587	0.114
SUS	0.009	0.143	0.887
IND	0.100	1.555	0.121
PDI	-0.171	-2.733	0.007 **
MAS	0.104	1.626	0.105
UAI	-0.177	-2.830	0.005 **
R2 (%)		12%	
Adjusted R2 (%)		8.2%	
F statistics		3.749 and p=0.000 **	

Note: *. and **. significant at the 0.05 and o.oo1 level, respectively

Source: Processed by the Authors.

Theoretical and Practical Implications

Even tough CSR has been increasingly researched in the literature, more research is needed to understand all the mediating and moderating influences on the effectiveness of CSR communication (Du et al., 2010) and specifically the factors that influence consumers' skepticism and the attribution of negative motives (Yoon et al., 2006). According to Bögel (2015), the role of stakeholders' specific characteristics has not been thoroughly researched and might determine the CSR communication strategy.

Many of the existing research on CSR addresses the relationship with culture (e.g. Christie et al., 2003; Kim & Kim, 2010; Leonidou et al., 2010). The major contribution of this chapter to the existing academic literature concerns the integration of different theories on national culture and CSR attributions. It demonstrates the influence of national culture on the attributions towards green advertising, which has not been previously explored. The results of this research can be used as a starting point for the development of new theories and strategies to convey positive attributions in the different national cultures.

Managerially, this research puts emphasis on national culture as a stakeholder-specific factor that should be taken into account when creating green advertising. As said before, marketers do not have adequate tools for evaluating the effectiveness of green advertising (Haytko & Matulich, 2008; Do Paço & Reis, 2013; Peattie, 2001) and face the challenge of increasing awareness of CSR initiatives while minimizing skepticism and conveying positive attributions (Du et al., 2010). Understanding the influence of national culture on the motives attributed to the communication is relevant for companies that compete in international markets and accordingly, communicate their sustainability efforts in different countries.

Based on this research, the results point to power distance and uncertainty avoidance as dimensions of national culture that negatively affect negative attributions and managers should take this into account when engaging into green advertisement and consequently combine it with other strategies researched in the literature. When a company advertises its environmental efforts in countries with a low level on power distance like the Netherlands or Germany or a low level on uncertainty avoidance like Sweden or United Kingdom, people are more likely to attribute negative motives.

Therefore, companies should stress other strategies in these cultures to convey more positive attributions. As stated by Du et al., these strategies include, among others, the communication of commitment or social impact. Additionally, in relation to the study of Forehand and Grier (2003), another strategy companies could apply in these cultures is acknowledging its true motives in the communication. Emphasizing not only the social but also the business interests will increase the credibility and reduce the skepticism.

LIMITATIONS AND FUTURE RESEARCH

Next to the contributions, limitations were noticed during the process, which may result in opportunities for future research. With regard to the research sample, there are some characteristics that should be mentioned. First, the major part of the respondents was under 29 and was highly educated. It is possible that younger or higher educated people are differently informed about CSR and the environment and thus attribute differently towards green advertisement. Consequently, level of education and age are not generalizable to the entire population. Further research could use larger scales on the general population.

Secondly, due to time constraints, it was not possible to find enough responses for one of the researched countries, USA. Even though, the minimum sample size determined was met and the results excluding this culture were the same, the cultural dimensions for this country were different than assumed based on Hofstede et al., (2010). This could be because of the amount of cultures and influencing cultures in USA or the sampling method. Future research should involve more than three national cultures, higher number of respondents and preferably, a probability-sampling method.

Another limitation was the lengthiness of the survey, as 38% of respondents did not complete it. Consumers could have felt overwhelmed by the amount of information, leaving little room for the formation of attributions. Future research could shorten the survey.

Furthermore, it would be interesting for future research to examine the influence of national culture from different aspects such as the differences in social values or the use of other frameworks to compare national cultures. Additionally, it could include culture as a moderator between green advertising and attitudes and purchase behavior.

Finally, although this research provides first insights into the relation of national culture and CSR attributions, external validity should be strengthened by follow-up research. Future research should combine different characteristics with CSR attributions, such as message content, industry, company-specific factors and the advertising of other dimensions of CSR, which were not taken into account in this research. This would help identify exact profiles and strategies for the different national cultures to better understand attributions and the effectiveness of green advertising.

REFERENCES

Aguinis, H., & Glavas, A. (2012). What we know and don't know about corporate social responsibility: A review and research agenda. *Journal of Management*, 38(4), 932–968. doi:10.1177/0149206311436079

Akaah, I. P. (1990). Attitudes of marketing professionals toward ethics in marketing research: A cross-national comparison. *Journal of Business Ethics*, 9(1), 45–53. doi:10.1007/BF00382563

Bae, J., & Cameron, G. T. (2006). Conditioning effect of prior reputation on perception of corporate giving. *Public Relations Review*, *32*(2), 144–150. doi:10.1016/j. pubrev.2006.02.007

Banerjee, S., Gulas, C. S., & Iyer, E. (1995). Shades of green: A multidimensional analysis of environmental advertising. *Journal of Advertising*, *24*(2), 21–31. doi:1 0.1080/00913367.1995.10673473

Bhattacharya, C. B., & Sen, S. (2001). Does doing good always lead to doing better? Consumer reactions to corporate social responsibility. *JMR, Journal of Marketing Research*, *38*(2), 225–243. doi:10.1509/jmkr.38.2.225.18838

Birth, G., Illia, L., Lurati, F., & Zamparini, A. (2008). Communicating CSR: Practices among Switzerland's top 300 companies. *Corporate Communications*, *13*(2), 182–196. doi:10.1108/13563280810869604

Bögel, P. M. (2015). Processing of CSR communication: Insights from the ELM. *Corporate Communications*, *20*(2), 128–143. doi:10.1108/CCIJ-11-2013-0095

Burton, B. K., Farh, J. L., & Hegarty, W. H. (2000). A cross-cultural comparison of corporate social responsibility orientation: Hong Kong vs. United States students. *Teaching Business Ethics*, *4*(2), 151–167. doi:10.1023/A:1009862130160

C. L. Campbell (Ed.). (2015). Marketing in Transition: Scarcity, Globalism, & Sustainability. In *Proceedings of the 2009 World Marketing Congress*. Springer.

Carlson, L., Grove, S. J., Kangun, N., & Polonsky, M. J. (1996). An international comparison of environmental advertising: Substantive versus associative claims. *Journal of Macromarketing*, *16*(2), 57–68. doi:10.1177/027614679601600205

Choi, I., Nisbett, R. E., & Norenzayan, A. (1999). Causal attribution across cultures: Variation and universality. *Psychological Bulletin*, *125*(1), 47–63. doi:10.1037/0033-2909.125.1.47

Christie, P. M. J., Kwon, I. W. G., Stoeberl, P. A., & Baumhart, R. (2003). A cross-cultural comparison of ethical attitudes of business managers: India Korea and the United States. *Journal of Business Ethics*, *46*(3), 263–287. doi:10.1023/A:1025501426590

Cohen, J. R., Pant, L. W., & Sharp, D. J. (1996). A methodological note on cross-cultural accounting ethics research. *The International Journal of Accounting*, *31*(1), 55–66. doi:10.1016/S0020-7063(96)90013-8

Cronin, J. J. Jr, Smith, J. S., Gleim, M. R., Ramirez, E., & Martinez, J. D. (2011). Green marketing strategies: An examination of stakeholders and the opportunities they present. *Journal of the Academy of Marketing Science*, *39*(1), 158–174. doi:10.1007/s11747-010-0227-0

Cui, Y., Trent, E. S., Sullivan, P. M., & Matiru, G. N. (2003). Cause-related marketing: How generation Y responds. *International Journal of Retail & Distribution Management*, *31*(6), 310–320. doi:10.1108/09590550310476012

D'Souza, C., & Taghian, M. (2005). Green advertising effects on attitude and choice of advertising themes. *Asia Pacific Journal of Marketing and Logistics*, *17*(3), 51–66. doi:10.1108/13555850510672386

Dahlsrud, A. (2008). How corporate social responsibility is defined: An analysis of 37 definitions. *Corporate Social Responsibility and Environmental Management*, *15*(1), 1–13. doi:10.1002/csr.132

Do Paço, A. M. F., & Reis, R. (2012). Factors affecting skepticism toward green advertising. *Journal of Advertising*, *41*(4), 147–155. doi:10.1080/00913367.2012.10672463

Du, S., Bhattacharya, C. B., & Sen, S. (2010). Maximizing business returns to corporate social responsibility (CSR): The role of CSR communication. *International Journal of Management Reviews*, *12*(1), 8–19. doi:10.1111/j.1468-2370.2009.00276.x

Ellen, P. S., Webb, D. J., & Mohr, L. A. (2006). Building corporate associations: Consumer attributions for corporate socially responsible programs. *Journal of the Academy of Marketing Science*, *34*(2), 147–157. doi:10.1177/0092070305284976

Fang, T. (2003). A critique of Hofstede's fifth national culture dimension. *International Journal of Cross Cultural Management*, *3*(3), 347–368. doi:10.1177/1470595803003003006

Field, A. P. (2009). *Discovering statistics using SPSS*. Thousand Oaks, CA: SAGE Publications.

Folkes, V. S. (1988). Recent attribution research in consumer behaviour: A review and new directions. *The Journal of Consumer Research*, *14*(4), 548–565. doi:10.1086/209135

Forehand, M. R., & Grier, S. (2003). When is honesty the best policy? The effect of stated company intent on consumer skepticism. *Journal of Consumer Psychology*, *13*(3), 349–356. doi:10.1207/S15327663JCP1303_15

Fowler, A. R. III, & Close, A. G. (2012). It ain't easy being green: Macro, meso, and micro green advertising agendas. *Journal of Advertising, 41*(4), 119–132. doi:10.1080/00913367.2012.10672461

Franke, G. R., & Nadler, S. S. (2008). Culture, economic development, and national ethical attitudes. *Journal of Business Research, 61*(3), 254–264. doi:10.1016/j.jbusres.2007.06.005

Friestad, M., & Wright, P. (1994). The persuasion knowledge model: How people cope with persuasion attempts. *The Journal of Consumer Research, 21*(1), 1–31. doi:10.1086/209380

Fukuyama, F. (1995). *Trust: The social virtues and the creation of prosperity.* New York: Free Press Paperbacks.

Furlow, N. E. (2010). Greenwashing in the New Millennium. *Journal of Applied Business & Economics, 10*(6), 22–25.

Gao, Y. (2009). Corporate social performance in China: Evidence from large companies. *Journal of Business Ethics, 89*(1), 23–35. doi:10.1007/s10551-008-9982-y

Gilbert, D. T., & Malone, P. S. (1995). The correspondence bias. *Psychological Bulletin, 117*(1), 21–38. doi:10.1037/0033-2909.117.1.21 PMID:7870861

Gjølberg, M. (2009). Measuring the immeasurable?: Constructing an index of CSR practices and CSR performance in 20 countries. *Scandinavian Journal of Management, 25*(1), 10–22. doi:10.1016/j.scaman.2008.10.003

Globescan. (2012). Credibility gap persists around companies' CSR communications. *Featured Findings.* Retrieved on 13 August, 2017 from http://www.globescan.com/commentary-and-analysis/featured-findings/entry/credibility-gap-persists-around-companies-csr-communications.html

GlobeScan SustainAbility Sustainabiliy Leaders Survey. (2014). Retrieved on August 13, 2017 from http://www.globescan.com/component/edocman/?view=document&id=103&Itemid=591

Haytko, D. L., & Matulich, E. (2008). Green advertising and environmentally responsible consumer behaviors: Linkages examined. *Journal of Management and Marketing Research, 1*(1), 5–14.

Hofstede, G. (1980). Motivation, leadership, and organization: Do American theories apply abroad? *Organizational Dynamics, 9*(1), 42–63. doi:10.1016/0090-2616(80)90013-3

Hofstede, G., Hofstede, G. J., & Minkov, M. (2010). *Cultures and Organizations: Software of the Mind. Revised and Expanded* (3rd ed.). New York: McGraw-Hill.

Hofstede, G., & Minkov, M. (2010). Hofstede's fifth dimension: New evidence from the World Values Survey. *Journal of Cross-Cultural Psychology.*

Hofstede, G. H. (1984). *Culture's consequences: International differences in work-related values* (2nd ed.). Beverly Hills, CA: Sage Publications.

Hofstede, G. H., & Hofstede, G. (2001). *Culture's consequences: Comparing values, behaviors, institutions and organizations across nations* (2nd ed.). Thousand Oaks, CA: Sage Publications.

Javidan, M., House, R. J., Dorfman, P. W., Hanges, P. J., & De Luque, M. S. (2006). Conceptualizing and measuring cultures and their consequences: A comparative review of GLOBE's and Hofstede's approaches. *Journal of International Business Studies, 37*(6), 897–914. doi:10.1057/palgrave.jibs.8400234

Katz, J. P., Swanson, D. L., & Nelson, L. K. (2001). Culture-based expectations of corporate citizenship: A propositional framework and comparison of four cultures. *The International Journal of Organizational Analysis, 9*(2), 149–171. doi:10.1108/eb028931

Keegan, W. J., & Seringhaus, F. H. R. (1996). *Global Marketing Management* (5th ed.). Scarborough, Canada: Prentice-Hall Canada Inc.

Keith, D., & Blomstrom, R. L. (1975). *Business and society: Environment and responsibility.* New York: McGraw-Hill.

Kim, Y., & Kim, S.-Y. (2010). The Influence of Cultural Values on Perceptions of Corporate Social Responsibility: Application of Hofstede's Dimensions to Korean Public Relations Practitioners. *Journal of Business Ethics, 91*(4), 485–500. doi:10.1007/s10551-009-0095-z

Kirkman, B. L., Lowe, K. B., & Gibson, C. B. (2006). A quarter century of culture's consequences: A review of empirical research incorporating Hofstede's cultural values framework. *Journal of International Business Studies, 37*(3), 285–320. doi:10.1057/palgrave.jibs.8400202

Kotler, P. (2011). Reinventing marketing to manage the environmental imperative. *Journal of Marketing, 75*(4), 132–135. doi:10.1509/jmkg.75.4.132

Leonidou, C. N., & Leonidou, L. C. (2011). Research into environmental marketing/management: A bibliographic analysis. *European Journal of Marketing, 45*(1/2), 68–103. doi:10.1108/03090561111095603

Leonidou, L. C., Leonidou, C. N., & Kvasova, O. (2010). Antecedents and outcomes of consumer environmentally friendly attitudes and behaviour. *Journal of Marketing Management, 26*(13-14), 1319–1344. doi:10.1080/0267257X.2010.523710

Leung, K., Bhagat, R. S., Buchan, N. R., Erez, M., & Gibson, C. B. (2005). Culture and international business: Recent advances and their implications for future research. *Journal of International Business Studies, 36*(4), 357–378. doi:10.1057/palgrave. jibs.8400150

Maignan, I. (2001). Consumers' perceptions of corporate social responsibilities: A cross-cultural comparison. *Journal of Business Ethics, 30*(1), 57–72. doi:10.1023/A:1006433928640

Mangleberg, T. F., & Terry, B. (1998). Socialization and Adolescents' Skepticism Toward Advertising. *Journal of Advertising, 27*(Fall), 11–21. doi:10.1080/00913 367.1998.10673559

Marín, L., Cuestas, P. J., & Román, S. (2016). Determinants of consumer attributions of corporate social responsibility. *Journal of Business Ethics, 138*(2), 247–260. doi:10.1007/s10551-015-2578-4

Matten, D., & Moon, J. (2008). "Implicit" and "Explicit" CSR: A Conceptual Framework for a Comparative Understanding of Corporate Social Responsibility. *Academy of Management Review, 33*(2), 404–424. doi:10.5465/AMR.2008.31193458

Menon, S., & Kahn, B. E. (2003). Corporate sponsorships of philanthropic activities: When do they impact perception of sponsor brand? *Journal of Consumer Psychology, 13*(3), 316–327. doi:10.1207/S15327663JCP1303_12

Mohr, L. A., Webb, D. J., & Harris, K. E. (2001). Do consumers expect companies to be socially responsible? The impact of corporate social responsibility on buying behavior. *The Journal of Consumer Affairs, 35*(1), 45–72. doi:10.1111/j.1745-6606.2001. tb00102.x

Montoro, R. (2006). Improving attitudes toward brands with environmental associations: An experimental approach. *Journal of Consumer Marketing, 23*(1), 26–33. doi:10.1108/07363760610641136

Morsing, M., & Schultz, M. (2006). Corporate social responsibility communication: Stakeholder information, response and involvement strategies. *Business Ethics (Oxford, England), 15*(4), 323–338. doi:10.1111/j.1467-8608.2006.00460.x

Myers, T. A. (2011). Goodbye, listwise deletion: Presenting hot deck imputation as an easy and effective tool for handling missing data. *Communication Methods and Measures, 5*(4), 297–310. doi:10.1080/19312458.2011.624490

Nyilasy, G., Gangadharbatla, H., & Paladino, A. (2014). Perceived greenwashing: The interactive effects of green advertising and corporate environmental performance on consumer reactions. *Journal of Business Ethics, 125*(4), 693–707. doi:10.1007/s10551-013-1944-3

Parguel, B., Benoît-Moreau, F., & Larceneux, F. (2011). How sustainability ratings might deter 'greenwashing': A closer look at ethical corporate communication. *Journal of Business Ethics, 102*(1), 15–28. doi:10.1007/s10551-011-0901-2

Peattie, K. (2001). Golden goose or wild goose? The hunt for the green consumer. *Business Strategy and the Environment, 10*(4), 187–199. doi:10.1002/bse.292

Pfanner, E. (2008, July 18). Cooling off on dubious eco-friendly claims. *The New York Times,* p. C3.

Pfau, M., Haigh, M. M., Sims, J., & Wigley, S. (2008). The influence of corporate social responsibility campaigns on public opinion. *Corporate Reputation Review, 11*(2), 145–154. doi:10.1057/crr.2008.14

Pomering, A., & Dolnicar, S. (2009). Assessing the Prerequisite of Successful CSR Implementation: Are Consumers Aware of CSR Initiatives? *Journal of Business Ethics, 85*(S2), 285–301. doi:10.1007/s10551-008-9729-9

Porter, M. E., & Kramer, M. R. (2006). The link between competitive advantage and corporate social responsibility. *Harvard Business Review, 84*(12), 78–92. PMID:17183795

Quazi, A. M., & O'Brien, D. (2000). An empirical test of a cross-national model of corporate social responsibility. *Journal of Business Ethics, 25*(1), 33–51. doi:10.1023/A:1006305111122

Rallapalli, K. C., Vitell, S. J., Wiebe, F. A., & Barnes, J. H. (1994). Consumer ethical beliefs and personality traits: An exploratory analysis. *Journal of Business Ethics, 13*(7), 487–495. doi:10.1007/BF00881294

Ramasamy, B., & Yeung, M. (2009). Chinese consumers' perception of corporate social responsibility (CSR). *Journal of Business Ethics, 88*(1), 119–132. doi:10.1007/s10551-008-9825-x

Samovar, L., Porter, R., McDaniel, E., & Roy, C. (2014). *Inter-cultural communication: A reader.* Boston: Cengage Learning.

Saunders, M., Lewis, P., & Thornhill, A. (2009). *Research methods for business students* (5th ed.). Harlow, MA: Pearson Education.

Scholtens, B., & Dam, L. (2007). Cultural values and international differences in business ethics. *Journal of Business Ethics*, *75*(3), 273–284. doi:10.1007/s10551-006-9252-9

Simga-Mugan, C., Daly, B. A., Onkal, D., & Kavut, L. (2005). The influence of nationality and gender on ethical sensitivity: An application of the issue-contingent model. *Journal of Business Ethics*, *57*(2), 139–159. doi:10.1007/s10551-004-4601-z

Soares, A. M., Farhangmehr, M., & Shoham, A. (2007). Hofstede's dimensions of culture in international marketing studies. *Journal of Business Research*, *60*(3), 277–284. doi:10.1016/j.jbusres.2006.10.018

Taylor, C. R. (2005). Moving international advertising research forward: A new research agenda. *Journal of Advertising*, *34*(1), 7–16. doi:10.1080/00913367.2005.10639187

Triandis, H. C. (1989). The self and social behavior in differing cultural contexts. *Psychological Review*, *96*(3), 506–520. doi:10.1037/0033-295X.96.3.506

Triandis, H. C. (1993). Collectivism and individualism as cultural syndromes. *Cross-Cultural Research*, *27*(3), 155–180. doi:10.1177/106939719302700301

Vanhamme, J., & Grobben, B. (2009). "Too good to be true!". The effectiveness of CSR history in countering negative publicity. *Journal of Business Ethics*, *85*(2), 273–283. doi:10.1007/s10551-008-9731-2

Visser, W., & Tolhurst, N. (Eds.). (2010). *The world guide to CSR: A country-by-country analysis of corporate sustainability and responsibility*. Sheffield, UK: Greenleaf Publishing.

Vitell, S. J., & Festervand, T. A. (1987). Business ethics: Conflicts, practices and beliefs of industrial executives. *Journal of Business Ethics*, *6*(2), 111–122. doi:10.1007/BF00382024

Vitell, S. J., & Paolillo, J. G. (2004). A cross-cultural study of the antecedents of the perceived role of ethics and social responsibility. *Business Ethics (Oxford, England)*, *13*(2-3), 185–199. doi:10.1111/j.1467-8608.2004.00362.x

Vitell, S. J., Paolillo, J. G., & Thomas, J. L. (2003). The perceived role of ethics and social responsibility: A study of marketing professionals. *Business Ethics Quarterly*, *13*(01), 63–86. doi:10.5840/beq20031315

Vlachos, P. A., Tsamakos, A., Vrechopoulos, A. P., & Avramidis, P. K. (2009). Corporate social responsibility: Attributions, loyalty, and the mediating role of trust. *Journal of the Academy of Marketing Science, 37*(2), 170–180. doi:10.1007/s11747-008-0117-x

Wanderley, L. S. O., Lucian, R., Farache, F., & de Sousa Filho, J. M. (2008). CSR information disclosure on the web: A context-based approach analysing the influence of country of origin and industry sector. *Journal of Business Ethics, 82*(2), 369–378. doi:10.1007/s10551-008-9892-z

Webb, D. J., & Mohr, L. A. (1998). A typology of consumer responses to cause-related marketing: From skeptics to socially concerned. *Journal of Public Policy & Marketing,* 226–238.

Yoon, Y., Gürhan-Canli, Z., & Schwarz, N. (2006). The effect of corporate social responsibility activities on companies with bad reputations. *Journal of Consumer Psychology, 16*(4), 377–390. doi:10.1207/s15327663jcp1604_9

Zhang, Y., & Gelb, B. D. (1996). Matching advertising appeals to culture: The influence of products' use conditions. *Journal of Advertising, 25*(3), 29–46. doi:10.1080/00913367.1996.10673505

Zinkhan, G. M. (1994). International Advertising: *A Research Agenda. Journal of Advertising, 23*(1), 11–15. doi:10.1080/00913367.1994.10673427

Zinkhan, G. M., & Carlson, L. (1995). Green advertising and the reluctant consumer. *Journal of Advertising, 24*(2), 1–6. doi:10.1080/00913367.1995.10673471

ADDITIONAL READING

Banerjee, S. B. (2008). Corporate social responsibility: The good, the bad and the ugly. *Critical Sociology, 34*(1), 51–79. doi:10.1177/0896920507084623

Farache, F., & Perks, K. J. (2010). CSR advertisements: A legitimacy tool? *Corporate Communications, 15*(3), 235–248. doi:10.1108/13563281011068104

Fatma, M., Rahman, Z., & Khan, I. (2015). Building company reputation and brand equity through CSR: The mediating role of trust. *International Journal of Bank Marketing, 33*(6), 840–856. doi:10.1108/IJBM-11-2014-0166

Lee, J. W., Kim, Y. M., & Kim, Y. E. (2016). Antecedents of Adopting Corporate Environmental Responsibility and Green Practices. *Journal of Business Ethics*, 1–13.

Margolis, J. D., Elfenbein, H. A., & Walsh, J. P. (2007). Does it pay to be good? A meta-analysis and redirection of research on the relationship between corporate social and financial performance. Ann Arbor, 1001, 48109-1234.

Peterson, R. A. (1994). A meta-analysis of Cronbach's coefficient alpha. *The Journal of Consumer Research*, *21*(2), 381–391. doi:10.1086/209405

Porter, M. E., & Van der Linde, C. (1995). Toward a new conception of the environment-competitiveness relationship. *The Journal of Economic Perspectives*, *9*(4), 97–118. doi:10.1257/jep.9.4.97

Vilanova, M., Lozano, J. M., & Arenas, D. (2009). Exploring the nature of the relationship between CSR and competitiveness. *Journal of Business Ethics*, *87*(1), 57–69. doi:10.1007/s10551-008-9812-2

Weber, M. (2008). The business case for corporate social responsibility: A company-level measurement approach for CSR. *European Management Journal*, *26*(4), 247–261. doi:10.1016/j.emj.2008.01.006

KEY TERMS AND DEFINITIONS

Attribution Theory: A theory that investigates the causal explanations people give of others' behaviour. These processes of attribution are fundamental to many aspects of consumer cognitions and behaviours.

Corporate Social Responsibility (CSR): The CSR strategy of a company aims to reward the community in which it operates (both ecologically and socially). Companies implement this strategy through (1) their waste management and pollution reduction processes, (2) through the contribution of educational and social programs, and (3) by providing adequate returns to its employees.

Culture: Culture is that complex ensemble that includes knowledge, beliefs, art, morals, laws, traditions, and other abilities and habits that man acquires as a member of society. Organizational culture is a prevalent system constituted of fundamental assumptions, beliefs, values, and behavioral norms shared by the members of an organization.

Greenwashing: A practice of making a company appear more environmentally friendly than it really is.

Individualism vs. Collectivism: Individualism vs. collectivism is the extent to which people in a society are integrated into groups.

Masculinity vs. Femininity: Masculinity is the extent of preference in society for achievement, heroism, assertiveness, and material rewards for success. In masculine societies, performance is highly valued. Femininity represents a preference for cooperation, responsibility, modesty, and caring for the weak.

Uncertainty Avoidance: The extent to which individuals in a group or culture have tolerance for ambiguity and uncertainty and try to avoid these situations.

Chapter 3
Effect of Greenwashing Advertisements on Organizational Image

Tamer Baran
Pamukkale University, Turkey

Mehmet Kiziloglu
Pamukkale University, Turkey

ABSTRACT

Firms have an unfavourable effect on environmental problems that severely threatens the ecological balance. In this context, firms' responsibility must be heavy on environmental problems. In the last two decades an approach guiding firms' socially beneficial activity as well as profitably activity has emerged. Accordingly, many firms launched marketing campaigns in order to claim themselves environment friendly. But it is not possible to say all of these campaigns reflect the facts. Some firms conduct greenwashing campaigns, which means misleading activity in order to persuade external stakeholders and consumers to appear more environmentally friendly than they actually are. In this chapter, the authors explain the effect of greenwashing advertisements on organizational culture using findings of previous studies as evidence. Organizational image, greenwashing concepts, and factors that drive firms' greenwashing activities are explained and then the effect of green advertisements on organizational image is revealed through previous studies' findings.

DOI: 10.4018/978-1-5225-2965-1.ch003

INTRODUCTION

Nowadays, the fierce competition in almost every sector, have made it indispensable for firms to use new tools towards achieving competitive advantage for themselves in the market. This competition environment led firms to an approach where anything they can do to reach profit is considered acceptable. On the other hand, reaching such goals is possible only by firms persuading consumers. At this point, persuading environmentalist consumers is possible only by being or seeming environment-friendly. As firms realized the environmental sensitivities of consumers, this issue took its place in their agenda and started to be used as a tool. In a study on this subject by Polonsky et al. (1998) conducted in the United Kingdom, 78% of the CEOs of the top 50 firms in the country stated that environmentalist activities are important for their firm, while 82% stated that they will be even more important in the future. This stated finding showed itself in firms' publicity efforts in time and firms eventually started to use the emphasis on "green" more in their publicity activities. The main purpose of the emphasis on "green" by firms is undeniably the goal to establish an image that the firm is environment-friendly. However, the key here is that how these firms are "perceived by consumers", rather than "what they are" or "how they introduce themselves".

In this chapter, past evidence will be utilized to describe how consumers perceive greenwashing implementations used by firms to create an environment-friendly image. In this context, firstly, the concept of organizational image will be described, and then, detailed information will be given regarding the concept of greenwashing using examples, factors that influence firms' greenwashing activities will be discussed, and finally, how firms' organizational images are affected by their greenwashing activities will be discussed in the light of the results of previous studies.

ORGANIZATIONAL IMAGE

In general, image is a concept, a collection of meanings that we use consciously or unconsciously in our daily lives which describes persons, firms, cities, countries and objects in a positive or negative way. Image, despite being expressed in a word, is affected by social, cultural, demographic and other factors in the society we live in, and consists of many pieces that are related or unrelated to each other. Additionally, some of these pieces are more significant, while others are less significant.

The image concept, which was first defined by Sidney Levy in 1955 as 'the sum of beliefs, attitudes and impressions of persons or groups towards certain objects', have caught the attention of researchers and become subject of studies in various fields. Image may be described as a dynamic and complex concept that changes continuously (Dichter, 1985). Image was described as the impression of an object, person or organization on a person, or a collection of behaviors, ideas, attitudes, stances and beliefs related to such objects, persons or organizations (Prahalad & Hamel, 1990; Kotler & Andreasen, 1996; Lemmink et al., 2003). Van Riel and Fomburn argue that image arises from the interaction of emotions, thoughts and beliefs of individuals regarding an object, person or organization. Image is how something is known and how it is related with, described and remembered by people (Van Riel & Fomburn, 2007). Additionally, image is the interpretation and perception of an object or a person both mentally and emotionally; it is a construct that occurs via reasoning by all real and imaginary evidence at hand, and is affected by existing effects, beliefs, thoughts and emotions (Davis, 2006).

Individuals and firms unavoidably leave a certain image on people. In this sense, it may be stated that image is related to how something is known, how it is explained and remembered by people, and how it is related with. Image is described in the work of Kevin Robins named 'Image' as the similar visual or pictorial reflection of a person or an object in the mind (Robins, 1999). Therefore, image is the symbolic and visual representation of an object or an opinion. While the concept of image is an ideological construct, its effects arise from how ideas are presented and shaped, and how these are distributed via technology or interpersonal communication (Lull, 2001). Like in social life, image is important for firms also. Organization and marketing experts indicate that image establishment is the most important one among the subjects to be considered by firms in different sectors (Christensen & Askegaard, 2001).

During the twentieth century, organizational image has become one of the most significant subjects of interest for individuals of all professions deriving huge amounts of data and information as well as managers. Individuals' preferences about goods and services have changed in line with developing living conditions (Vigoda-Gadot et al., 2003). In this context, organizational image is described as the thing that comes to mind, or the picture that appears in the mind when the logo of the firm is seen (Gray & Balmer, 1998). Organizational image is established over the quality of the good or service the firm produces, tactics and strategies of distribution and marketing, events organized, achievements reached, communication among employees, sensitivities about the environment and successes or failures in fulfilling social responsibilities (Markwick & Fill, 1997). Dutton and Dukerich (1991) defined organizational image as internal and external stakeholders' perceptions on how they see and describe the firm. Additionally, organizational image shows the ideas of internal and external stakeholders of the firm regarding the firm, as well as each other.

Organizational image, in another sense, is the perception of people on how individuals know the firm based on information received from different sources by different people. While some perceptions arise by personal experience, impression and sensation, others occur by marketing and communications activities of the firm (Schultz, 2007). The establishment and alteration of people's perceptions are dependent on their culture, level of education, the social groups they belong to, their view of life, as well as the levels they are informed about the firm, and services and opportunities the firm provides to individuals (Alves & Raposo, 2010).

Organizational image is established by the sum of organizational behavior, appearance and communication. Organizational behavior is described as the collection of organizational acts that are results of organizational attitudes (Melewar, 2003). Organizational behavior consists of acts of the entire firm or its sub-structures, as well as all interactions with its surroundings (Çiftçioğlu, 2009). Organizational appearance is described as a firm's visual expression of itself (Nguyen and LeBlanc, 2001). Organizational communication is a process that turns organization identity into organization image (Gray and Balmer, 1998). Organizational communication is a societal process that facilitates the continuous exchange of information and thought between the firm and its surroundings via various departments and units that constitute the firm, which sees this process as a necessity to operate the firm and reach the firm's goals (Demirtaş, 2010). The more the organization is in contact with the target audience, the more it will be known and perceived positively (Gray & Balmer, 1998). Therefore, firms pay great importance to the communication they establish with their stakeholders and communication tools they use while establishing organizational image.

Organizational image may affect employees in a positive or a negative way. If organizational members perceive the firm's external image as negative, they may develop stress and depression, which may lead to things that are undesirable for the organization such as increased competition among members or reduced efforts for organizational goals. Members may leave their organizational roles or quit the organization eventually (Dutton et al., 1994; Meyer & Allen, 1997; Haslam et al., 2003).

When employees have perception of a positive organizational image, their trust in their firm increases, and they share their positive opinions on their firm with people around them. This situation, via individuals who hear about positive thing, may help firms survive uncertain conditions and fight hardships. That is, the organizational image established by firms acts as a strong buffer that reduces the negative effects of unexpected and sudden changes (Schukies, 1998). Additionally, organizational image plays an effective role in individuals' preferences of firms and their choice to stay in the firm (Bauer & Aiman-Smith, 1996). An individual's behavior and well-being are affected by the characteristics they see suitable for themselves and the opinions that they think other people hold about their membership of the firm. Firms may stimulate positive emotions in their members and individuals may feel pride in being members of organizations that they think have aspects liked by the society (Dutton et al., 1994).

Organizational image may be considered a resource for competitive advantage. A positive image makes it easier to attract customers (Flavian et al., 2005). A positive image is a strong tool not only for encouraging customers to choose a firm's goods and services, but only for improving their satisfaction with the firm and attitudes toward the firm (Nguyen & Leblanc, 2002). In this sense, creating a positive image is a method to increase organizational success. For example, the customer loyalty established by improving a firm's image may improve sales (Si & Hitit, 2003). Therefore, most firms spend a lot of time, resources and efforts to create a strong image. They are spending millions to spread the word about their goods and services in order to create a force (Fatt et al., 2000). The purpose of this is to increase the demand for a firm's goods and services. That is, the firm's success. A good image is a factor that provides benefits for every firm; it may achieve higher revenue than competitors in competition environment; the firm may become an organization that is preferred by qualified individuals, it may attract investors, and customers who are interested in product quality (Lemmink et al., 2003; Riordan et al., 1997). Thus, organizational image affects customers' decision making processes and behaviors (Porter & Claycomb, 1997).

The studies on organizational image show how important the image concept is for organizations. For example, Bravo et al. (2009), in their study conducted on five banks in Spain, investigated the effects of organizational image on customer behavior. The results of the study showed that a strong organizational image has a positive effect on the success of the organization in the short and long runs, and it affects customer behavior positively. In another study by Ivy (2001) where factors that differentiate universities from each other were investigated in the ever-increasing competition among universities, was found that preference of old and new universities in England and traditional and technical universities in South Africa was affected positively by their reliability in the society and perceptions of strong organizational image. In another study by Fatt et al. (2000) which aimed to improve organizational image in the light of expectations of a group consisting of the society, target audience, employees and investors, was found that ethical behaviors of the firm are the most important factors in the eyes of the public in order to achieve a strong organizational image.

Because of the increasing amount of expectations of the society from firms and firms' performances in the social dimension while consumers are making purchasing decisions, firms are observed by the society regarding issues such as attention paid to environmental issues, and fulfillment of societal responsibilities (Sabuncuoğlu & Tüz, 1998:23). Firms that operate only by commercial concerns are no longer accepted by the public, therefore, businesses pay more attention to operations that have social responsibility aspects, which in turn is aimed towards distinguishing one's firm from others and reach their target audience with a 'positive image'. In other words, the firms realized that it will not bring positive outcomes in the long run to try to profit despite the public, or without taking the public into consideration. Social responsibility activities create positive emotions in the society regarding environmentalist firms. The society appreciates these firms because it is conducting good and useful work. It likes the firms' contributions as a conscientious organization for the environment and nature. Firms that are aware of this may sometimes behave unethically in order to receive this appreciation. For example, the actual purpose of some of the firms which emphasize their environment-friendliness is to increase their sales and profits by being praise by the society. Appearance of such behaviors may affect organizational image permanently in the long run.

It is a fact that, the level of consistency of advertisements that include environment-friendly messages and have an important place in the world's agenda, is significant while assessing the social responsibility of the advertisement. Some businesses operating by a classical marketing approach use environmentalist messages in their advertisements, although there actually is not an environment-friendly product in place. This application which is called greenwashing, therefore, creates distrust towards advertisements containing environmentalist messages and lead to diminished excitement of the consumers to buy green products (Alnıaçık et al., 2010).

GREENWASHING

Regarding "greenwashing", one of the popular concepts of recent years, while it is described to be used with the purpose of helping the firm establish a positive image, there is still no consensus of a universal definition. This situation brought about the search for an answer to the question "what is greenwashing" and efforts to define the concept of greenwashing (see: Hoffman & Hoffman, 2009, Index, 2009, Wilson, 2009, Lyon & Maxwell, 2011, Delmas & Burbano, 2011, Roulet & Toulboul, 2015, Seele & Gatti, 2015).

As a result of these efforts, different definitions were developed by different writers regarding greenwashing. For example, Deen and Advocate (2002) define greenwashing as activities firms conduct to appear more environment-friendly than they actually are. Lyon and Maxwell (2011) define greenwashing as firms not disclosing negative information about their activities in terms of environmentalism and social responsibility, but selectively promote and distribute information that will emphasize their environmentalist and socially responsible activities. According to Delmas and Burbano (2011), greenwashing is any misleading activity towards creating a positive image in relevant consumers regarding the environmental uses of a good or a service, or environmentalist applications of the firms. Seele and Gatti (2015) stated that greenwashing is based on two aspects as information and distortion, and described it as unrealistic information transmitted via green messages in order to mislead stakeholders.

In addition to academic work, it is also not possible to see a universal dictionary definition of the concept of greenwashing. According to Oxford English Dictionary (2016), greenwashing is distribution of incorrect information by firms in order to establish an image as a firm that fulfills its responsibilities for the environment. Webster's New Millennium Dictionary of English (2016) claimed that greenwashing is a combination of the words "green" -which represents the environment- and "wash" -which is used as a term to hide mistakes-, and defined the concept as applications for environmentalist publicity by the firm to distract its stakeholders from activities that are not environment-friendly. Cambridge Dictionary (2016) described greenwashing as initiatives towards making people believe that firms take part in environmentalist activities more than their actual activities, and it indicated that firms may utilize concepts such as recyclable, protection, environment-friendly, repurposable, etc. in these efforts. According to MacMillan Dictionary (2016), greenwashing is described as a collection of efforts that are designed to hide especially environmentally-harmful practices and investments from third persons and make such persons believe that the firm is making investments that are environment-friendly and useful for the environment. Business Dictionary (2016) described greenwashing as a firm pursuing campaigns that support the ideas that it operates in environment-friendly ways, while producing goods and services that harm the ecosystem.

Considering the given definitions, it may be stated that greenwashing is misleading or persuading the external stakeholders, especially consumers, with the claim that firms are more environmentally responsible. Firms do this to have a positive image regarding being environment-friendly. With this purpose, the following definition was developed in this study:

Greenwashing is a collection of activities that carry the purpose of appearing more environment-friendly than the actual situation by advertisements, as well as public relations and publicity campaigns which carry incorrect information on a level of firm, product or brand in order to create a positive image in consumers and external stakeholders.

Delmas and Burbano (2011), stated that firms realize their greenwashing activities in two ways as on the level of firm and product. On the firm level greenwashing describes the emphasis on the firm rather than the product in publicity or advertisement campaigns regarding environmentalist operations. The "Ecomagination" campaign by General Electric may be an example to greenwashing on the firm level. On the level of product greenwashing, the firm emphasizes environmentalist aspects of a product. Toyota's hybrid automobile model Prius is one of the best examples of greenwashing on the level of product. It cannot be argued that environmentalist share Toyota's opinion that this car creates less damage to the environment.

Likewise, as indicated in the definition of greenwashing developed in this study, firms may also conduct greenwashing activities on the level of brands. The Turkish paper towel firm Lila, despite being active in the market with four different brands as Sofia, Maylo, Berrak and Nuo, uses environmentalist advertisements for the Sofia brand only.

Considering that greenwashing activities of firms are claims of being environment-friendly, and their efforts to persuade their external stakeholders by transmitting these claims, it will be possible to classify firms based on these factors. In this context, Delmas and Burbano (2011) used a classification based on firms having good or bad environmentalist performances, and whether they utilize publicity efforts regarding their environmentalist performance. At this point, while greenwashing firms have bad environmentalist performances, they are among firms that establish positive communication regarding their environmentalist performance. The matrix showing the classification of firms based on firms' environmentalist performance and communications regarding these performances is given in Figure 1.

Laufer (2003) stated that greenwashing consists of three parts as, confusion, fronting and posturing. These factors were shown in Figure 2.

Confusion describes the firm's transition from the centralized decision making and complex structure in applications into naturalness. Fronting may be achieved by the mediation of the firm's ethics board, adaptation specialists and legal officers.

Figure 1. A classification of firms based on environmentalist performance and communication regarding environmentalist performance
Source: Delmas and Burbano, 2011.

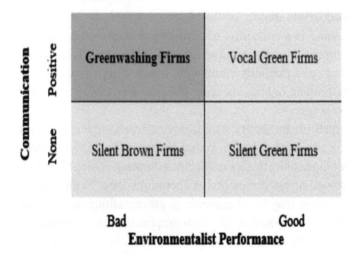

Figure 2. Factors of greenwashing
Source: Adapted from Laufer (2003)

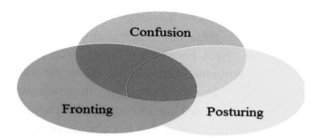

The posture of the firm towards greenwashing is related to the way it persuades its external stakeholders and internal customers regarding its total commitment to ethics.

FACTORS THAT GOVERN FIRMS' GREENWASHING ACTIVITIES

Delmas and Burbano (2011) classified the reasons that lead firms to greenwashing activities under four titles as non-external market drivers, external market drivers, organizational drivers and individual psychological drivers. Figure 3 shows the factors that lead firms to greenwashing.

Non-external market drivers consist of lax and unspecific regulatory environment, as well as activists, non-governmental organizations and media pressure. Lax and unspecific regulatory environment is related to whether regular inspections are made about greenwashing activities and whether regulations are specific or not. In other words, it is about how sufficient the laws of the country operated in for greenwashing activities and how orderly the laws work. It is possible to talk about a collection of institutions/regulations regarding greenwashing rules in various countries. For

Figure 3. Factors that lead firms to greenwashing
Source: Adapted from Delmas and Burbano (2011).

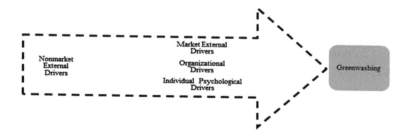

example, Trade Activities Law in Australia, the Bureau of Competition in Canada, the Federal Trade Commission in the United states of America (U.S.A.) may be examples to these (Wikipedia, 2016). However, non-external market drivers are not limited to these. In addition to these, activists, non-governmental organizations and media are also significant drivers. For example, Greenpeace, established in the year 1971 and known for its environmentalist protests, shows the organization's stance about greenwashing clearly with the website on: stopgreenwash.org. Likewise, established in 1961, the World Wide Fund for Nature, which aims to prevent damage to the environment and fix the damage that has already occurred, Foundation to Protect Life in the World (DHKD) operating in Turkey and the Turkish Foundation for Combating Soil Erosion, for Reforestation and the Protection of Natural Habitats (TEMA) may be given as examples to non-governmental organizations that influence firms' greenwashing activities (maroon.com, 2016). Social media platforms like Facebook, Twitter, etc. which are increasingly being used recently as a result of the advances in technology, and similarly ecosystems such as YouTube, video sharing platforms which are again very popular nowadays, and similar platforms constitute the media pillar of the non-external market drivers regulating firms' greenwashing activities.

Another factor that leads firms to prefer greenwashing is the market external drivers. Market drivers consist of consumer demands, investor demands and the competition conditions in the market. Firms may sometimes conduct greenwashing applications because of pressures from consumers and investors. Numerous studies found that consumers defined themselves as environmentalist and they would prefer products that are environment-friendly (ex: see, Fisher 1990, Cross 1990, Donaton & Fitzgerald 1992, cited in: Canan & Ecevit, 2005; Zinkhan & Carlson, 1995; Kalafatis et. al., 1999; Baran & Popescu, 2016). Firms prefer greenwashing in order to make themselves seem more environment-friendly against these attitudes of the consumers. Another market-related driver leading firms to greenwashing is their competitors in the sector. Firms may prefer greenwashing in order to gain competitive advantage against their competitor in the sector they operate in, or at least seem as environmentalist as their competitors (Joel, 1992; Freeman & Liedtka, 1991; Keller, 1987).

Organizational drivers are other factors that may lead to firms using greenwashing activities. At this point, the firm's characteristics, the effectiveness of the communication within the firm, the structure of the firm, its culture and organizational inertia may be influential in the firm's decision to use greenwashing or not. Whether the firm is characteristically cost-oriented or utility-oriented, the target customer base it determines, whether it is a public or private organization, and even the size of the firm may be influential in the firm's decision. For example, it is unthinkable for a firm targeting environmentalist consumers not to use greenwashing activities. In contrast, it might be argued that a firm aiming to operate in a cost-oriented manner may quit greenwashing in order to at least minimize advertising costs (Meznar & Nigh, 1995). On the other hand, while effective interdepartmental communication within the firm provides the rapid distribution of information in the firm, information might not spread rapidly in the opposite case. While rapid spread of information may contribute to the firm's innovative aspect and lead to a better understanding of greenwashing by employees and participation of employees in the process, these might take longer time or not happen at all in the opposite case (Szulanski, 1996). The firm's structure and culture are among the organizational factors that drive firms towards greenwashing. The firm's structure and culture consists of perceptions and beliefs of its members in the decision making process. This structure and this culture are classified under three parts. Selfish structure is where the firm's rules are determined based solely on the interests of the firm, benevolent structure is where the rules are determined based on the collective prosperity, and principled structure is where the rules are designed to satisfy legal obligations (Cullen et al., 2003). As it may be understood from the information above, selfish structure is the one furthest from greenwashing, and firms getting away from this structure get closer to greenwashing.

Finally, inertia may influence firms' greenwashing activities. Organizational inertia indicated resistance against organizational change, and strong maintenance of the existing structure and functions. It may be argued that organizational inertia is more common in larger and older organizations in comparison to smaller firms. In this case, larger and older organizations may naturally become late for greenwashing activities. In other words, considering organizational inertia, newer and smaller firms have an advantageous position to implement greenwashing activities in comparison to larger and older firms (Delmas & Burbano, 2011).

RELATIONSHIP BETWEEN ORGANIZATIONAL IMAGE AND GREENWASHING

The increased concerns about the environment in general and the increased awareness regarding environmental consciousness have driven firms to establish an environment-friendly organizational images or strengthen their existing images. At this point, in addition to firms that actually behave environment-friendly by risking additional costs, there are also firms that aim to establish an image of an environment-friendly firm despite not actually being environment-friendly.

Undeniably, advertising is one of the most frequently used tools in any case where firms aim to express themselves to the consumers, or in other words, establish communication with consumers (Özkaya, 2010). For example, Rosenbaum (1973) indicated that more than half of the firms in the U.S. have environment protection programs (cited in: Easterling et al., 1996). Other studies conducted in the U.S. revealed that the amount print advertisements containing greenwashing increased by more than 4 times from 1989 to 1990, while TV advertisements of the same nature increased approximately by 4 times in the same period (Ottman, 1993; (cited in: Alnıaçık et al., 2010); Joel, 1992). In the year 2011 in Hong Kong, Bank of Communications made an advertising expense of 22 million Hong Kong dollars, while HSBC Bank made an expense of 38 million Hong Kong dollars (Chan &Fan, 2015). In the year 2005, General Electric allocated a budget of $ 90 million for the "Ecomagination" advertising campaign which became a news story in the New York Times.

As indicated before, the main purpose of environment-friendly advertising applications of the firms is to create a positive organizational image in consumers. The studies conducted on the issue revealed findings about different results.

Karna et al. (2001), in their study conducted in the forestry sector in Finland that covered 167 advertisements, stated that advertising is influential in the establishment of an environmentalist image by the firm. The findings of the study revealed that firms using environmentalist elements in their advertisements are evaluated as more environment-friendly than those that are not using such elements. In the study by Alnıaçık et al. (2010) conducted in Turkey on the assessment of environmentalist claims in print advertisements by consumers, findings were presented that using environmentalist claims in advertisements for certain products helped perception of the firm as more environment-friendly. Additionally, a positive attitude towards products, firms or brands in the advertisements where environmentalist claims were used, and a higher purchasing intent were observed. Indeed, it was stated that the message in the advertisement does not even have to be presented clearly for this positive attitude to be established. Similar results were reached in the study by Chan (2000) conducted in People's Republic of China that covered 800 consumers and used a shampoo product that may be considered as a chemical-based product. As a result of the conducted study, it was stated that expressing the environmentalist claims clearly may help perception of the product, firm or brand as environment-friendly. Alnıaçık and Yılmaz (2012), in their product-based study conducted in Turkey, covering 180, indicated that environmentalist claims used in the advertisement of products that are not related to the environment (DVD players) affected the consumers' attitudes about the product's environment-friendly nature and purchasing intent in a positive way. On the other hand, it was observed that such claims did not have any effects on the attitude and purchasing intent of the consumers for products related to the environment (washing machines).

It is also possible to find studies that claim that greenwashing leads to negative perceptions and attitudes, as opposed to positive findings of the studies mentioned above. For example, the study conducted in 1973 by Fisk stated that consumers had low rates of believing in greenwashing advertisements. In the study by Newell et al. (1998) conducted in the U.S. that covered 203 consumers, presented findings suggested that consumers had negative attitudes towards advertisements containing environmentalist claims, such claims negatively affected attitudes for the brand in the advertisements, and also had negative effects on the purchasing intent of the consumers towards the products or brands in the advertisements. Additionally, consumers stated that greenwashing advertisements were exaggerated and unrealistic, and such advertisements tried to abuse their environmentalist sensitivities (Easterling et al. 1996). In Chan and Fan's study (2015) featuring 195 participants from Hong Kong and People's Republic of China, there were findings that greenwashing advertisements of firms in the banking sector led to negative perceptions and attitudes for people with lower environmental sensitivities. Likewise, Kangun et al.'s study (1991) featured statements by consumers that greenwashing advertisements were just deceptive. Iyer and Banerjee (1993), in their study named Anatomy of Green Advertising, stated that firms used advertisements towards organizational image in their greenwashing activities rather than product-based advertisements, and consumers did not find these advertisements credible and reliable despite usage of statements such as "environment-friendly", "recyclable", "reliable" and "natural".

When the previous studies on this subject mentioned above are considered, it may be safe to say that the attitude towards greenwashing advertisements may change based on the demographics of the consumer (sex, age, level of education, level of income, marital status), psychographic characteristics of the consumer (environmentalist / not environmentalist), type of the advertised product (related/unrelated to the environment), the country where the study is conducted, and various other factors. Hence, the firm's role at this point should be, to firstly determine the appropriate consumer segment, creating the content that correctly describes it, and contacting the consumer via the right channels.

CONCLUSION AND RECOMMENDATIONS

Having a positive organizational image in the eyes of the public nowadays necessitates being a firm respectful to the environment at the same time. Therefore, firms should not operate based on financial concerns only, and allocate a part of their resources to protect the environment, or at least not to harm it. If a firm, despite not being environment-friendly with its philosophy, mission, vision, managers, employees, the values reflected in its organizational culture and its activities, acts like it is environment-friendly, none of the operations of this firm related to the environment will be ethical and the firm will receive criticism about greenwashing. While such firms are trying to create an image via advertisements and other publicity activities as if they are environment-friendly when some actually are not, if the reality is exposed by the media or other authorities such as environmentalist groups, the ethical structure behind these decisions of the firms and their real purpose start to be questioned. Thus, this situation creates negative effects on the firm's organizational image, instead of positive effects.

However, activities of an organization that actually takes part in environmentalist operations are not encountered with doubt, while having persuasive power. When an actually environmentalist organization sponsors an activity related to the environment, negative interpretations such as perceiving the sole purpose as influencing an audience, being covered in media, or increasing sales will not be considered, and it will be thought that the organization acts over real environmental concerns and a sincere emotion of responsibility. This will contribute positively to the organizational image of the business.

It might not be possible to produce environmentally responsible and green products in every sector. It is an undeniable fact that many firms take part in operations that may harm the environment, and some sectors might not even operate without harming the environment by their nature. It will be more suitable for such firms to leave the notion of environment out of their corporate communication strategies instead of running environmentalist campaigns, for them to avoid having a negative organizational image in the eyes of the consumers, or at least in terms of ethics.

REFERENCES

Alnıaçık, Ü., Yılmaz, C., & Alnıaçık, E. (2010). Reklamlarda Çevreci İddalar ve Reklam Etkililiği:Başarılı Reklamlar Üzerine Deneysel Bir Araştırma. *Anadolu Üniversitesi Sosyal Bilimler Dergisi, 10*(1), 85–106.

Alves, H., & Raposo, M. (2010). The Influence of University Image on Student Behaviour. *International Journal of Educational Management, 24*(1), 73–85. doi:10.1108/09513541011013060

Baran, T., & Popescu, C. (2016). Generation Z Attitudes Toward Green Marketing: A Cross Country Study. *3th Information Society and Sustainable Development International Symposium.*

Bauer, T. N., & Aiman-Smith, L. (1996). Green Career Choices: The Influence of Ecological Stance on Recruiting. *Journal of Business and Psychology, 10*(4), 445–458. doi:10.1007/BF02251780

Bravo, R., Montaner, T., & Pina, J. M. (2009). The Role of Bank Image for Customers Versus Non-Customers. *International Journal of Bank Marketing*, *27*(4), 315–334. doi:10.1108/02652320910968377

Canan, A. Y., & Ecevit, Z. (2005). Çevre Bilinçli Tüketiciler. *Akdeniz University Faculty of Economics & Administrative Sciences Faculty Journal/Akdeniz Universitesi Iktisadi ve Idari Bilimler Fakultesi Dergisi*, *5*(10).

Chan, K., & Fan, F. (2015). How consumers perceive environmental advertising in the banking context. *Asian Journal of Business Research*, *5*(1), 69.

Chan, R. Y. (2000). The effectiveness of environmental advertising: The role of claim type and the source country green image. *International Journal of Advertising*, *19*(3), 349–375. doi:10.1080/02650487.2000.11104806

Christensen, L. T., & Askegaard, S. (2001). Corporate Identity and Corporate Image Revisited – A Semiotics Perspective. *European Journal of Marketing*, *35*(3/4), 292–315. doi:10.1108/03090560110381814

Cross, F. B. (1990). The weaning of the green: Environmentalism comes of age in the 1990s. *Business Horizons*, *33*(5), 40–46. doi:10.1016/0007-6813(90)90026-8

Cullen, J. B., Parboteeah, K. P., & Victor, B. (2003). The effects of ethical climates on organizational commitment: A two-study analysis. *Journal of Business Ethics*, *46*(2), 127–141. doi:10.1023/A:1025089819456

Çiftçioğlu, B. A. (2009). *Kurumsal İtibar Yönetimi*. Bursa: Dora.

Davis, A. (2006). *Halkla ilişkilerin ABC'si. Ümit Şendilek (çev)*. İstanbul: Kapital Medya Hizmetleri AŞ.

Delmas, M. A., & Burbano, V. C. (2011). The drivers of greenwashing. *California Management Review*, *54*(1), 64–87. doi:10.1525/cmr.2011.54.1.64

Demirtaş, M. (2010). Örgütsel Iletişimin Verimlilik ve Etkinliğinde Yararlanılan Iletişim Araçlari Ve Halkla Ilişkiler Filmleri Örneği. *Marmara Üniversitesi İİBF Dergisi*, *28*(1), 411–444.

Dichter, E. (1985). What's an Image? *Journal of Consumer Marketing*, *2*, 75–81.

Donaton, S., & Fitzgerald, K. (1992). Polls show ecological concern is strong. *Advertising Age*, *63*(3), 19–23.

Dutton, J. E., & Dukerich, J. M. (1991). Keeping an Eye on The Mirror: Image and Identity in Organizational Adaptation. *Academy of Management Journal*, *34*(3), 517–554. doi:10.2307/256405

Dutton, J. E., Dukerich, J. M., & Harquail, C. V. (1994). Organizational Images and Member Identification. *Administrative Science Quarterly*, *39*(2), 239–263. doi:10.2307/2393235

Fatt, J. P. T., Wei, M., Yuen, S., & Suan, W. (2000). Enhancing Corporate Image in Organizations. *Management Research News*, *23*(7), 28–54. doi:10.1108/01409170010782037

Fisher, A. B. (1990). What consumers want in the 1990s. *Fortune*, *121*(3), 108–112.

Fisk, G. (1973). Criteria for a theory of responsible consumption. *Journal of Marketing*, *37*(2), 24–31. doi:10.2307/1250047

Flavian, C., Guinaliu, M., & Torres, E. (2005). The Influence of Corporate Image on Consumer Trust. *Internet Research*, *15*(4), 447–470. doi:10.1108/10662240510615191

Freeman, R. E., & Liedtka, J. (1991). Corporate Social Responsibility: A Critical Approach. *Business Horizons*, *34*(4), 92–98. doi:10.1016/0007-6813(91)90012-K

Gray, E. R., & Balmer, J. M. T. (1998). Managing Corporate Image and Corporate Reputation. *Long Range Planning*, *31*(5), 695–702. doi:10.1016/S0024-6301(98)00074-0

Haslam, S. A., Eggins, R. A., & Reynolds, K. J. (2003). The ASPIRe Model: Actualizing Social and Personal Identity Resources to Enhance Organizational Outcomes. *Journal of Occupational and Organizational Psychology*, *76*(1), 83–113. doi:10.1348/096317903321208907

Hoffman, J., & Hoffman, M. (2009). What is Greenwashing? *Scientific American*, 1.

Index, G. (2009). *About greenwashing: What is greenwashing? It's whitewashing, but with a green brush*. Academic Press.

Ivy, J. (2001). Higher Education Institution Image: A Correspondence Analysis Approach. *V. International Journal of Educational Management*, *15*(6), 276–282. doi:10.1108/09513540110401484

Iyer, E., & Banerjee, B. (1993). Anatomy of green advertising. *Advances in Consumer Research. Association for Consumer Research (U. S.)*, *20*.

Joel, J. D. (1992). Ethics and Green Marketing. *Journal of Business Ethics*, *11*(2), 81–87. doi:10.1007/BF00872314

Kalafatis, S. P., Pollard, M., East, R., & Tsogas, M. H. (1999). Green marketing and Ajzen's theory of planned behaviour: A cross-market examination. *Journal of Consumer Marketing*, *16*(5), 441–460. doi:10.1108/07363769910289550

Kangun, N., Carlson, L., & Grove, S. J. (1991). Environmental advertising claims: A preliminary investigation. *Journal of Public Policy & Marketing*, 47–58.

Karna, J., Juslin, H., Ahonen, V., & Hansen, E. (2001). Green advertising: greenwash or a true reflection of marketing strategies? *Greener Management International*, 59-71.

Keller, G. M. (1987). Industry and the Environment: Toward a New Philosophy. *Vital Speeches*, *54*(5), 154–157.

Kotler, P., & Andreasen, A. R. (1996). *Positioning the Organisation: Strategic Marketig for Non-Profit Organisation*. Toronto: Prentice-Hall.

Lull, J. (2001). *Medya, İletişim, Kültür*. Ankara: Vadi Yayınları.

Lyon, T. P., & Maxwell, J. W. (2011). Greenwash: Corporate environmental disclosure under threat of audit. *Journal of Economics & Management Strategy*, *20*(1), 3–41. doi:10.1111/j.1530-9134.2010.00282.x

Markwick, N., & Fill, C. (1997). Towards A Framework for Managing Corporate Identity. *European Journal of Marketing*, *31*(5/6), 396–409. doi:10.1108/eb060639

Melewar, T. C. (2003). Determinants of Corporate Identity Construct: A Review of The Literature. *Journal of Marketing Communications*, *9*(4), 195–220. doi:10.1080/1352726032000119161

Meyer, J. P., & Allen, N. J. (1997). *Commitment in the Workplace: Theory, Research, and Application*. Thousand Oaks, CA: Sage Publications.

Meznar, M. B., & Nigh, D. (1995). Buffer or bridge? Environmental and organizational determinants of public affairs activities in American firms. *Academy of Management Journal*, *38*(4), 975–996. doi:10.2307/256617

Newell, S. J., Goldsmith, R. E., & Banzhaf, E. J. (1998). The effect of misleading environmental claims on consumer perceptions of advertisements. *Journal of Marketing Theory and Practice*, *6*(2), 48–60. doi:10.1080/10696679.1998.11501795

Nguyen, N., & LeBlanc, G. (2001). Image and Reputation of Higher Education Institutions in Students' Retention Decisions. *International Journal of Educational Management*, *15*(6), 303–311. doi:10.1108/EUM0000000005909

Nguyen, N., & Leblanc, G. (2002). Contact Personnel, Physical Environment and The Perceived Corporate Image of Intangible Services by New Clients. *International Journal of Service Industry Management*, *13*(3), 242–262. doi:10.1108/09564230210431965

Özkaya, B. (2010). İşletmelerin Sosyal Sorumluluk Anlayışının Uzantısı Olarak Yeşil Pazarlama Bağlamında Yeşil Reklamlar. *Öneri, 9*(34), 247-258.

Polonsky, M. J., Rosenberger, P. J. III, & Ottman, J. (1998). Developing green products: Learning from stakeholders. *Asia Pacific Journal of Marketing and Logistics, 10*(1), 22–43. doi:10.1108/13555859810764454

Porter, S. S., & Claycomb, C. (1997). The Influence of Brand Recognition on Retail Store Image. *Journal of Product and Brand Management, 16*(6), 373–387. doi:10.1108/10610429710190414

Prahalad, C. K., & Hamel, G. (1990). The Core Competence of The Corporation. *Harvard Business Review, 68*(3), 79–81.

Riordan, C., Gatewood, R. D., & Bill, J. B. (1997). Corporate Image: Employee Reactions and Implications for Managing Corporate Social Performance. *Journal of Business Ethics, 16*(4), 401–412. doi:10.1023/A:1017989205184

Robins, K. (1999). *İmaj Görmenin Kültür ve Politikası*. İstanbul: Ayrıntı Yayınları.

Roulet, T. J., & Touboul, S. (2015). The intentions with which the road is paved: Attitudes to liberalism as determinants of greenwashing. *Journal of Business Ethics, 128*(2), 305–320. doi:10.1007/s10551-014-2097-8

Sabuncuoğlu, Z., & Tuz, M. (1998). Örgütsel Psikoloji. Alfa Yayınevi, 3.

Schukies, G. (1998). *Halkla İlişkilerde Müşteri Memnuniyetine Dönük Kalite*. İstanbul: Rota Yayınları.

Schultz, M. (2007). *Organizational Image. International Encyclopedia of Organization Studies*. Sage Publications.

Seele, P., & Gatti, L. (2015). Greenwashing Revisited: In Search of a Typology and Accusation-Based Definition Incorporating Legitimacy Strategies. Business Strategy and the Environment.

Si, S. X., & Hitit, M. A. (2003). A Study of Organizational Image Resulting from International Joint Ventures in Transitional Economies. *Journal of Business Research*, 1–8.

Szulanski, G. (1996). Exploring internal stickiness: Impediments to the transfer of best practice within the firm. *Strategic Management Journal, 17*(S2), 27–43. doi:10.1002/smj.4250171105

Van Riel, C. B., & Fomburn, C. J. (2007). *Essentials of Corporate Communications: Implementing Practices for Effective Reputation Management.* New York: Routledge Publishing. doi:10.4324/9780203390931

Vigoda-Gadot, E., Vinarski-Peretz, H., & Ben-Zion, E. (2003). Politics and Image in The Organizational Landscape: An Empirical Examination Amongst Public Sector Employees. *Journal of Managerial Psychology*, *18*(8), 764–787. doi:10.1108/02683940310511872

Wilson, N. J. (2009). *What is Greenwashing? Don't let the truth-stretchers pull the wool over your eyes.* Academic Press.

Zinkhan, G. M., & Carlson, L. (1995). Green advertising and the reluctant consumer. *Journal of Advertising*, *24*(2), 1–6. doi:10.1080/00913367.1995.10673471

ADDITIONAL READING

Banerjee, S., Gulas, S. C., & Iyer, E. (1995). Shades of Green: A Multidimensional Analysis of Environmental Advertising. *Journal of Advertising*, *24*(2), 21–31. doi:10.1080/00913367.1995.10673473

Lemmimk, J., Schuijf, A., & Streukens, S. (2003). The Role Of Corporate Image and Company Employment Image in Explaining Application Intentions. *Journal of Economic Psychology*, *24*(1), 1–15. doi:10.1016/S0167-4870(02)00151-4

KEY TERMS AND DEFINITIONS

Green Advertisement: Green advertisement addressees the relationship between a product and environment, promotes a green, and presents a corporate image of environmental responsibility.

Greenwashing: A sum of practices used with the purpose of helping the firm establish a positive image regarding the environment.

Organizational Image: A concept including the sum of organizational behavior, appearance, and communication.

Chapter 4
Advertising and Organization's Green Behavior

Augustin Constantin Mitu
Petroleum-Gas University of Ploiesti, Romania

Daniela Steluta Uta
Petroleum-Gas University of Ploiesti, Romania

ABSTRACT

Following the development of marketing theory concerning the policies in general, promotional policy has known an impressive development. Today, the practice fields professionals operating with relatively sophisticated notions and concepts, which are fine-tuned and pragmatic in terms of results. For example, it is significant that concepts such as rating and market share have already entered into ordinary language, including being properly understood by consumers covered. Annually large amounts of money for advertising are spent; almost all large companies allocate non-negligible amounts for such purposes. The launch of new brands is accompanied by consistent advertising and promotional campaigns conducted on multiple levels to cater to potential consumers with tangible and intangible components associated with the various products, services, or brands.

INTRODUCTION

The aim of this chapter is to bring to the attention of specialists an integrative approach to promotion policy, insisting on the advantages anchoring promotional policy in the context of all green marketing activities, an aspect often ignored the practice field.

DOI: 10.4018/978-1-5225-2965-1.ch004

Actual research conducted revealed that promotional activity is still in a phase crystallization growth and diversification, the advertising market is marked by some examples of less professionalism or attempts less successful by reference to the final results recorded among consumers.

On another plan, the proposed chapter highlights the fact that promotional policy, namely advertising, need to be improved by including legal regulations and requirements related to natural resource management and technologies developed on the specific market - specific, the need to use resources in a sustainable manner and to use those technologies that protect the environment.

Another aspect refers to the role that promotional activities plays in informing consumers and their role in the process of modeling the consumer behavior. Consumers are generally receptive to different promotional messages, which must, however, be actually helpful to people whom they are addressed. Some campaigns, for example, does not provide consumers with the information they really need and is likely to cause ambiguity that does not serve the goals and objectives of various promotional programs.

This chapter will highlight the fact that, at present, on the Romanian market advertising put too much emphasis on grounding more rigorous approaches in terms of quantity of messages that are conveyed through various media, to the detriment of measuring the effects of these efforts in the consumer or end user of goods and services.

GREEN MARKETING AND ECO-FRIENDLY ADVERTISING

Unfortunately, a majority of people believe that green marketing refers solely to the promotion or advertising of products with environmental characteristics (Polonsky, 1994). According to the same author, Green or Environmental Marketing consists of all activities designed to generate and facilitate any exchanges intended to satisfy human needs or wants, such that the satisfaction of these needs and wants occurs, with minimal detrimental impact on the natural environment. Green marketing intends to minimize the impact of marketing activities on the environment and such protect it while building a sustainable business.

The importance of green marketing activities is also revealed by the consumer's concerns regarding environment protection and waste disposal. Consumer awareness is influenced by a number of factors including increased media coverage, greater awareness of environmental problems, the rise of pressure group activities, stringent legislation (both national and international) and the impact of major industrial disasters on public opinion (Kallafatis et al., 1999).

Kotler (2008) states that the main purpose of marketing is to transform consumer needs into profitable business ideas and the consumers concerns regarding environment protection makes no exception from this rule. Still, green marketing needs a coherent strategy implementation in order to have notable results.

Marketing strategy is the main component of organization's marketing policy (through which it establishes the concrete paths of achieving the objectives which it has set), which may take various embodiments: market strategy, product strategy, price strategy, distribution strategy, promotional strategy etc. In this chapter, further, the concept of marketing strategy title will be used generically to refer to operationalize the vision of modern marketing across the organization.

Management teams start to substantiate a market strategy adapted to resources (material, financial and manpower) available in the market to achieve certain objectives, namely customer satisfaction in order to obtain profit. Building on the foundations of the market economy, the modern organization aims not only economic goals but also social and environmental goals, to harmonize its interests with those of the community in which it operates. Social objectives can be embodied in the phrase "corporate social responsibility" (for example, a company that produces alcoholic beverages or cigarettes - harmful products in principle - can be considered to have social responsibility?).

Development of marketing strategies evolved greatly, as the transition from classical to modern marketing. Thus, specialists address currently market strategy in the context of strategic marketing, marketing that represents the current approach, which differs from the previous stage of marketing, called for differentiation, marketing management. Strategic marketing essentially involves developing well-founded long-term decisions (the most important being the very market strategy) to ensure and strengthen the existence on the market of a company operating in a competitive environment.

Green marketing strategy uses the same instruments as modern marketing strategies but considering how company's consumer will react to a green communication approach. For this, it is needed an accurate segmentation of consumers not considering it is classical approach (age, gender, incomes) but rather consumers intention to adopt a green behavior and their lifestyle defined as activities, interests, and opinions (Shrum, McCarthy, Lowray, 1995).

Throughout the years companies started to understand that corporate social responsibility must include not only internal green procedures (in order to reduce environmental impact of its activities) which can prove to be profitable for the company, but also to integrate environmental concerns into their product and service development and so respond to consumers environmental consciousness (Ginsberg & Bloom, 2004).

Marketing strategy elaboration is concretizing in the marketing mix, respectively the appropriate dosage of the four marketing policies: product, price, distribution and promotion. All experts agree that the elements of the marketing mix are:

- The product, which requires specific decisions on wide assortment attributes (bodily constituents and disembodied), communications on the product and its image
- Price, respectively decisions regarding its level and structure, discounts policy, amenities and payment terms, credit rating etc.
- Distribution, solving specific problems related to distribution channels, distribution system, locating, establishing sales techniques, transport, storage and warehousing, logistics and other aspects of product and information flows accompanying physical distribution
- The promotion, which requires determination of the means and techniques to facilitate the sales process.

Due to the complexity of market activities, mostly related to services marketing, some authors propose to extend the marketing mix components to reflect the contribution from the sale of items such as personnel, customers, physical support of providing the service, ambiance etc.

Though conceptual issues related to the marketing mix are already at a stage that enables the operationalization of this important tool of modern marketing, in practice there are many difficulties of application, generated by several causes, among which the most important lies in the high degree of specialization to achieve the vital functions of the modern organization. Such difficulties are common especially among companies in countries like Romania, that have appropriated marketing after 1990, here businesses deal rather sequentially marketing mix components at the expense of systemic approach. In fact, it is harmful interference to the level of what specialists (Pop et al., 2000) call strategic marketing and operational marketing. The dimensions of the operative customize strategic marketing are:

- Decisions' bearer;
- Decisions' object;
- The decision-making process.

Clearly, the marketing mix falls within the implementation of strategic marketing because the strategic direction of the modern organization is the bearer decisions on the policy mix of product, price, distribution and promotion (Wilson&Gilligan, 2012). Tactical decisions taken at the operational marketing level, by departments' responsible for product, price, distribution and promotion should be integrated into the global vision of strategic marketing, only then marketing mix becomes an effective operationalization tool for the market strategy of the modern organization.

In this context, the role of promotional programs in the marketing mix can be outlined with clarity:

- The promotional program is a component of the marketing mix, which should be consistent with all other components, in terms of multiple interdependencies.
- The promotional program involves the development and substantiation of the promotional strategy of the modern organization, a strategy that forms an integral part of marketing strategy, together and interdependent with the product, price and distribution strategies.
- Components and the structure of promotional programs are proper to the strategic marketing since at this level the marketing mix is elaborated.
- Operationalization of the promotional strategy is a matter of operative marketing, located at the level of the department responsible for the promotional activities of the modern organization.

PROMOTIONAL PROGRAMS: A THEORETICAL APPROACH

Develop and substantiate promotional strategy is achieved through consideration of criteria or levels of differentiation, which make up what experts call typology promotional strategies. The criteria of differentiation and related strategic options are: theoretical

- The overall objectives of the promotional activity (strategy to promote overall company image, promote the exclusive product strategy, the company's strategy to expand image);
- Conduct duration (permanent strategy promotional activity, intermittent promotional activity strategy);
- The role of promotional activity (offensive strategy, defensive strategy);
- Position to market structures (focused strategy, differentiated strategy, undifferentiated strategy);
- Headquarters of promotional activity (by their own forces, through specialized institutions).

The role of the promotional program in the marketing mix is strongly connected of the appropriate is also linked to the proper disposal of two other important aspects associated promotional strategy, namely:

- Determining promotional budget and
- Control and evaluation of the promotional activity result.

Across promotional activities for determining the budget, it can be proposed several ways, which are found in almost all the literature: setting a percentage of turnover; how much the companies afford to spend; budget comparison with competitors; analysis of objectives; use of marketing experiments. Content analysis of such means denotes that there is no single method for determining the promotional budget, practitioners resorting to such means in various proportions and combinations, which are combined in the mix promotional based on the marketing strategy of the modern organization.

The problem of determining the promotional budget is closely related to controlling and evaluating promotional activities. In this respect, there are also somewhat different approaches in the literature, approaches generated from the impossibility of assessing the various activities and promotional techniques. Clearly, the problem of results evaluation is associated with the advertising. This approach is justified by the overwhelming weight of the advertising budget in the promotional budget. In other words, for all practical aims, it is traced, especially, how the money is spent or what amounts allocated to advertising produce concrete results.

This problematic area still raises many questions, evaluating the results of promotional activities is a constant concern of all specialists dealing with promotional policy in general and advertising in particular. Starting from the practical importance of assessing the effects of promotional activities, especially those related to green advertising, this paper submits to specialists an approach operationalized by the authors in order to draw conclusions with a high range of generalization.

Promotional programs' role in the green marketing mix can be addressed in a more thorough manner by a more detailed reporting of the marketing mix components in order to highlight more clearly the capability of this marketing instrument for the specialty practice.

For successful marketing, marketing theory and practice revealed, clear, a need to uniform approach marketing policies (product, price, distribution and promotion). It's about the systemic approach to the marketing strategy of the modern organization, as the only way of amplifying the synergy implied by operation of open systems. The organization must communicate continually and systematically with its market's environment in order to fulfill its economic and social objectives.

To secure the place of promotional programs in the green marketing mix, systemic approach provides the most appropriate theoretical model because it leverages two fundamental properties of general systems theory: social stability and equifinality (Demetrescu, 1971; Bertalanffy, 1972). The enterprise and its market environment constitute a social system that enjoys equifinality and so it can get the desired result from different initial conditions and in a variety of ways. However, this system also enjoys stability as a necessary condition for its ability to work, since it did not lose its identity, with all the changes and transformations that occur in the elements.

In this vision, the promotional program is circumscribed to the green marketing mix in terms of needed knowledge of qualitative and quantitative aspects, expressed as objectives attached to the four marketing policies.

- Regarding the objectives attached to the product policy, qualitative aspects of interest include a wide variety of features, variables, reasons etc. which are objectives of studying the market and consumers. In this context, for example, it is aimed to identify patterns of consumption or use, consumer reaction to various stimuli related to the product itself, the reasons for accepting or rejecting products, the consumers' perception of satisfaction offered different products, determining product attributes used by consumers for their purchase decision making etc. In this context, studies are conducted to determine, for example, the type of packaging desired by consumers for a given product (going as far to addressing details label, watermark etc.), the preferred grammage for understanding consumer opinion about the quality of the product, finding the differences, if any, in perceptions of different brands or types etc. Such studies are very useful for manufacturers because it allows them adapting products to the real requirements of a specific market. Adaptation is a condition sine qua non for both market penetration and, especially, to achieve a share of sales according to market strategy that has been adopted.

The issues addressed in quantitative marketing research with respect to product policy are also very complex. Thus, designed and performed behavioral studies aimed dimensions such as knowledge of consumer brands products / services available in the market, buying different brands, quantities purchased, frequency of purchase, frequency of consumption / use, reasons for acceptance / rejection products / brands, buying intentions, the criteria for choosing brands, evaluation of product attributes etc.

- Regarding price policy, qualitatively, the first aim is to understand how important the variable "price" is for the consumer in the purchase decision process. The qualitative approach to price is inserted in behavior studies, usually in two forms:
  - Through the consumers' hierarchy of variables considered in the purchase decision process, variables that include the price.
  - Through the consumers' direct evaluation of the price importance, but in a more complex way, namely by introducing the concept of

"price / quality" ('value for money', a term already established among researchers in this field). This approach is more relevant because it allows knowledge of the link between price and product quality in the minds of consumers. This explains, for example, what are the reasons that lead some consumers to accept a higher price or to not consider necessarily high a price as they consider the utility to a certain quality of product / service.

Quantitative studies on price policy address also useful elements necessary to support price mix. Using representative samples of consumers it is tested the acceptability of different price levels, taking into account the change in other components attached to the product (tangible or disembodied). There are also very efficient quantitative studies that apply the technical knowledge of consumer expectations regarding product price ("price sensitivity"). This applies particularly to the market launch of new products and / or services or of new ranges of products already on the market. In such studies, consumers are placed on a possible prices scale, removing answers aberrant and computing averages thus enabling knowledge of the potential price consumers to expect and that are actually real market prices which may be considered for financial arrangements to business plans.

- At the level of distribution policy, in terms of quality, conducted behavioral studies are focused towards actual purchasing habits, aiming to understand the significance granted by consumers to distribution.

Applying relevant techniques (mainly in-depth interviews and group discussions), to test the reactions and perceptions of consumers for different distribution variants/ strategies, in the idea of exploring the motivational field, components and determinants, preferences and other relevant elements of the operational plan. Such studies reveal, in particular, consumers' attitudes about the different distribution channels or outlets.

Also, on this path, it is possible to underline mutations occurring among consumers as a result of adopting certain ways of distribution and sales, as well as the effects of changes made in market variables. Such studies present a great attraction for market decisions makers in the field as they are able to adapt adequately to its dynamism. Incidentally, in this context, it is significant that, in the present, the distribution is an area of fierce competition, which is added to the now classic competition, of the product and price policy. The so-called "full competition" has flexible limits.

Qualitative studies highlight consumer's interest in various other aspects of distribution and sale itself: the practice of price reductions depending on the location or time of sale, the acceptance of the grouped sale for products or services, the perception of specific forms of distribution / sale during certain periods (Christmas, New Year, Easter), knowing the criteria considered in choosing different forms of distribution or sale etc. Qualitative studies also pay a great attention to the knowledge of information sources to which consumers appeal when deciding to purchase products from certain outlets. Whether for personal sources, whether they resort to marketing sources, their knowledge is very useful, directly for use in various promotional techniques.

Finally, specific objectives are targeted when the conducted qualitative studies are among its distributors (producers, for those with their own distribution network, or wholesalers) or retailers. This kind of qualitative studies specifically address the problems related to the perception of facilitations packages granted to the actual point of sale (transport, settlement, encompassing assortment, supply frequency etc.).

Regarding the quantitative aspects of behavioral studies concerning distribution, the objectives differ, depending on observation units considered: consumers themselves, wholesalers and retailers.

- Among consumers is aimed the knowledge of some aspects from the sphere of distribution, such as: frequency of purchase, quantities bought, place a purchase, temporal aspects (time of year, day / days of the week, time / times of day, etc.); calling a specific service (transport, testing, commissioning, etc.).
- Among wholesalers / retailers address in particular the following relevant issues related to the distribution policy: a criteria for choosing suppliers; quantity supplied in assortment structure, brands and suppliers etc. in terms of value, weights, odds; supply frequency; services; running a flow of goods, information, financial; policy of stocks; system of warranties / service; competitive system.

Quantitative studies conducted among wholesalers and retailers produce, among other things, a very interesting result for policy makers: the characteristics of the so-called „ideal distributor" (of course, hypothetical) and then assessing the "relative distance" between real and ideal distributors. Polarity profile obtained is a significant measure for understanding the strengths and weaknesses of distributors, namely a scientific way of approaching competition.

- Finally, in the sphere of promotion policy, in terms of quality, the necessary studies have goals particularly important because their results are used primarily for designing promotional campaigns. In essence, the studies are orientated in order to know:

○   Consumer attitudes toward various sources of information, in terms of credibility and significance in their buying decision making. It can also be studying consumer perception not only of advertising (it is true that studies of this kind are focused, however, on various ways of designing advertising, the publicity in general) but also on other promotional aspects. In this context, an emphasis is put on shaping the image of businesses / brand among consumers, and the elements considered in the formation and evolution of that image. For example, studying the impact of social responsibility on the image of companies, or public relations undertaken by different companies in order to obtain a favorable picture for its market activity.

○   Consumer perceptions of various advertising media, including the activities of creating them. Besides, qualitative studies are the only tool that can be applied for such purposes as quantitative approaches are either not appropriate or would be very costly. In this sense, there are numerous studies of consumer attitude on the television or radio commercial spots, advertisements through billboards, advertising inserts in newspapers and magazines, advertisements placed on transport etc. Consumers are presented with many variants already created, or possibly to create (presentation is usually in the context of group discussions, but not excluded in some cases in in-depth interviews, or other techniques in the arsenal of qualitative research) and so, the version perceived closest to the purpose of "issuer" is used in the respective promotional campaign. Great emphasis is placed in such studies, on knowing the consumer's coordinated perception in receiving the same advertising message, transmitted through multiple media.

In terms of quantitative studies conducted for promotional policy, the followed objectives are numerous, whether in research are included only final consumers, or are involved, as well, distributors and retailers. Essentially, regardless of the studies' sphere, objectives envisaged can be grouped into two broad categories:

•   Objectives targeting the knowledge, in quantitative terms, the number of persons reached by various promotional activities, among which: sources of information considered appealing by consumers; sources' credibility; assessment of the importance of various sources in the process of their purchasing decisions.

•   Objectives related to evaluating the effectiveness of various promotional activities: evoking a spontaneous or suggested content of promotional messages; comparing the effectiveness of a promotional messages, among some defined consumer segments; an overall assessment of the promotional campaigns conducted through several activities, the idea of knowing the most appropriate media; comparative assessment of the effectiveness of promotional campaigns conducted for competing products or services on the market.

It says that these two categories of objectives must be pursued systemically. Knowing your goals in the first category nominated above is insufficient to substantiate adequate promotional mix decisions, because, for example, audience research cannot reach any conclusion about how the messages sent were actually received by consumers. They must be completed with efficacy studies or research outlining clearly what consumers have perceived a certain promotional message. It stresses this point because many studies on the effectiveness of promotional activities highlighted the confusion and distorted perception, which cannot be attributed to consumers but to the defective design and / or transmission of messages.

In the context of the above, promotional programs must take into account and integrate the results of behavioral studies carried out in all four marketing policies course within the context of established market for enterprise or organization. Moreover, specialists in charge of marketing management include the development program of a promotional campaign in the overall planning of marketing activities, which ends with a general plan of action, involving research to be synchronized with concrete activities of such a program.

Specialty's theory and practice devoted numerous types and designs of promotional programs, which were considered and implemented by specialists in many countries. The multitude of theoretical and practical examples of promotional programs makes them difficult to present exhaustive, even in summary form. For this reason, it is considered appropriate and pragmatic revealing, conceptually, some types of promotional programs, in terms of their instrumental approach. This approach brings into question the essential objective of a promotional program, which in practical marketing, presents the biggest attraction for management teams. They are interested primarily in specific aspects of promotional strategies contribution to building and strengthening market image associated with products, services, brands, and companies, as appropriate.

In this perspective, it is considered useful to reveal the characteristics of the main types or models of the promotional programs, which, according to their fundamental objective, may take the following forms:

- **Promotional Programs for Creating/Strengthening the Overall Image of Products or Services:** This kind of programs is considering products or services of interest to a certain company, which are promoted without having regard to specific elements (production or trademark, functional and technical features etc.). Such promotional programs are characteristic of specific markets, with relatively few competitors, which bring to market the products or services very similar and relatively less differentiated.

- **Promotional Programs for the Creation/Strengthening Specific Brand Image:** This program focuses solely on image or trademarks and may be characteristic for companies that bring more to market various products or services. In these promotional programs, brands are promoted individually without any explicit link between them. For example, promote different brands on the toothpaste or shampoo market, in an individual name, brands which are made by the same manufacturer. The great advantage of such an approach lies in preserving the image of the manufacturer, meaning that an eventual failure on the market to a certain brand name, the manufacturer will not compromise (or will have a minor effect on it). This type of promotional programs is characteristic for relatively large companies that cannot always meet high-quality level for all products or services brought to the market. Generally, such programs are considered tactical promotional tools, which support sales.

- **Promotional Programs for the Creation/Strengthening Production Brand Image:** In the event of such promotional programs, the main focus is on promoting the image of different brands of products, brought to market by the same manufacturer, including any range within them. In creating individual brand image is an explicit link with the manufacturer's name. Manufacturer's brand is the "umbrella" and refers most often to different products (eg: Samsung brings to market smartphones, refrigerators, televisions, etc., each with an individual name, but "linked" to the manufacturer's name). This category includes the general promotion of corporations, which includes all its products and services, such as, for example, the companies Ericsson, Philips, Nokia, and Gillette. Such programs are considered strategic and promotional tools are meant to promote the corporation itself.

- **Promotional Programs for the Creation/Strengthening of Trademark Image:** This category of promotional programs is specific especially for large distribution companies, or chains of outlets, which sell a variety of products or services under a single trade brand. Such companies assure themselves a high quality of products. Typically, these companies have their own laboratories for testing, verification and certification of quality real manufacturers being "absolved" of any liabilities in the eyes of final consumers. Companies that sign up as a promoter for this category of promotional programs are usually of high prestige, which exceed many times the national market frame in which they operate. For example, one can mention the famous store Harrods's in

London (where they shop, among others, famous Hollywood stars, heads of state, etc.), or prestigious Mark & Spencer chain of grocery stores. Promotional programs in this category are considered, as well, strategic, promotional tools meant to promote the corporation itself.

In designing and implementing promotional program there are several steps that must be followed regardless of the type of program approached. To highlight them clear, Kotler proposes in the Principles of Marketing (2008) a synthesized representation as in Figure 1.

Measuring performance of promotional programs is a concern of greatest significance to specialists in companies that initiate and finance such programs. As is known, promotional budgets are more than consistent, at least for multinational companies, thus justifies the interest in measuring the performance of each promotional program and overall promotional strategy.

In order to obtain better results for the promotional activity, modern science supplies new measuring instruments for their evaluation, instruments that somehow differ from classic approach (Demetrescu, 1982, p.117). It is about the concepts of efficiency and effectiveness.

Figure 1. Planning promotional programs
Source: Proposed by Authors.

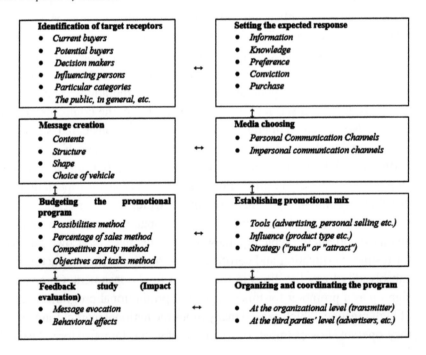

1.   The concept of efficiency, always used for evaluating the actions of an economic nature, refers to resources spent. The best-known indicator of efficiency is profit. In promotional messages case, efficiency is connected with the given resources or costs of production and distribution. In this context, lower costs of production and broadcasting of promotional messages are the expression of its effectiveness.

2.   Instead, the concept of efficacy, more often applied at present by decision makers, introduces a measure of the degree in which the objective of marketing is achieved - for example, a promotional program without taking into account the resources (human, material, money). The number of consumers who retained the right promotional message is a convenient measure of the effectiveness or performances of the operating promotional activities' system.

Two examples (adapted from Cătoiu & Teodorescu, 2004, p.130) are instructive to deduce how a promotion policy can be formulated by applying concepts of efficiency and effectiveness:

•   Producing and broadcasting promotional message costs 500,000 monetary units and allows a "touch" of 500,000 customers, of which 250,000 retain the right message. A consumer who retained the right message "costs" two units of money.

•   Producing and broadcasting promotional message costs 1,500,000 monetary units and allows a "touch" of 1,500,000 customers, of which 500,000 retain the right message. A consumer who retained the right message "costs" three monetary units.

The combined analysis of these two examples, through the concepts of efficiency and effectiveness, leads to conclusions relevant to how this promotional politic problem can be phrased:

•   In the first example, the efficiency is 2 monetary units / consumer, and in the second example, the efficiency is 3 monetary units / consumer.

•   Instead, the effectiveness of the message - in other words the number of "target" achieved - is 250,000 customers in the first case and 500,000 customers in the second case.

The question is: Should be given priority to efficiency or effectiveness? The answer to this dilemma is nuanced. In the short term, and taking into account the resources, it is better to give priority to efficiency, but long-term efficacy is preferable because it ensures a safer market. One is that a firm has a total of 250,000 customers, and quite another to have a market of 500,000 consumers. The problem itself is addressed to decision makers and the right answer is, essentially, embedded in the modern company's market strategy.

In practice, promotional programs performance measurement is done at two levels:

- First, at the level of promotional messages' "sender", based on monitoring publicized messages, an activity that takes place in specialized departments of producers / distributors, agencies, media / advertising, television channels, radio stations etc. At this level are calculated or determined several indicators or specific variables, such as, for example:
  - Overall daily duration of advertising message broadcast on a specific TV channel, for example, divided per different periods of the day;
  - The number of consumers who were exposed to the advertising message (for example, viewers, readers, radio listeners, etc.);
  - The cost of the advertising message based on the estimated number of "targets" achieved, according to the estimated annual number of consumers exposed to the message;
  - The structuring of advertising messages on product ranges and brands, taking into account all the brands for which advertising was made by the whole competition. This structure is particularly useful for understanding competition's promotional strategy.
- Second, at the level of promotional messages' "receiver", in this case, the "final consumer" which is, in fact, the "recipient" of any promotional communications. Also at this level the goal is to identify specific issues, such as:
  - The importance attributed by consumers to different sources of information when gathering information necessary to support the purchase decision process;
  - Evaluation of the usefulness of various media supports used for broadcasting promotional messages, in other words, of different modalities to advertise products and services;
  - Measurement of the penetration level among final consumers of certain advertising;
  - Knowing the degree to which different promotional messages were correctly perceived by the relevant consumers, through the evocation source, content (characters, situations, the message that was intended to transmit etc.) and slogan.

Measuring promotional messages performance at the "transmitter" level in green marketing case is relatively difficult to approach in real terms due to the fact that the participants in this activity (producers / distributors, advertising agencies, television channels, etc.) it considers such data as strictly confidential. Such behavior is understandable, to a point, though, in authors' opinion, it is more than exaggerations related to the so-called "secrecy" regarding this activity.

In the same context, on the market, there are no data or information available related to measuring promotional messages performance at the "final consumer" level. A large variety of studies were made in order to determine the impact of green advertising on consumer buying behavior (Pau & Ong, 2007) attitude towards green advertising (Ahmad et al., 2009) and green advertising perception (Hartman & Apaolaza-Ibanez, 2009). None of these studies offer a real measurement scale for the green advertising impact on final consumer's perception or retention of messages. This is why the authors of this chapter realized its own research at country level.

RESEARCH ON ROMANIAN ADVERTISING MARKET

In order to determine the impact of promotional programs at final consumer level the authors conducted its own research on Romanian advertising market. The research was conducted based on the methodological aspects illustrated in Table 1.

Research Results

Information sources to which consumers appeal when gathering information for substantiating the decisional buying process have, according to the expressed opinions, different degrees of importance. In Table 2 is presented a synthesized situation of the main information sources used by consumers.

Analysis of this information provided by the interviewees, by considering variants answered "very important" and "important", highlights the following hierarchical perception by consumers of information sources mentioned:

- Visit stores (outlets) = 74%;
- Commercials generally = 60.9%;
- Friends, colleagues, acquaintances = 56.4%;
- The advice provided by sellers = 33.5%.

This hierarchical order highlights the great importance that consumers attach to marketing sources, in the process of gathering information necessary to support purchasing decisions. An important role also has personal sources of information (friends, acquaintances, colleagues), confirming that they enjoy high credibility

Table 1. Research methodology

Collectivity	Romania's population aged 15 and over
Observation Unit	Person (aged 15 and over)
Survey Unit	Household (as in official statistics)
Sample Size	1.000 respondents, representative sample at national level
Definition of Sample	The general public, male and female gender, aged 15 years and over
Sample Location	Urban and rural (14 cities and 20 villages)
Sampling Methodology	Random model; General community stratification according to demographic concentration; Multistage sample; Lists of respondents / Kish grid
Number of Sampling Points	90
Interviewing Method	Interviews "face to face" (one person / household)
Research Reliability	± 3,2%
Chestionar	Prepared in accordance with research purposes
Features of Grouping Collected Information	• The sex of the interviewee • Age group of the person interviewed • Geographical residence area • Employment status of the interviewed person • The education of the interviewee
Final Results	Tables presenting the information gathered and analyzed - presented below. Note: Data in the tables are automatically retrieved from the computer, so that may have deviations (± 0.2%) generated by canonical statistical rounding.

Source: Authors' Conception.

Table 2. Importance given to information sources

Scale	Commercials Generally	Stores Visit	Friends, Colleagues, Acquaintances	The advice Offered by Sellers
	% of the Total Column, for the Entire Sample			
Very important	20.2	30.2	17.4	6.6
Important	40.7	43.8	39.0	26.9
Neither important nor unimportant	22.6	18.1	27.6	33.9
Unimportant	8.4	3.2	9.8	17.8
Not important	5.4	2.6	3.6	12.3
Do not know	2.6	2.0	2.5	2.6

Source: Authors' Conception.

among consumers, although not quite as precise, as emphasized specialists (Cătoiu & Teodorescu, 2000, p.59).

In addition to this hierarchical order of importance of information sources aggregated data above highlights the precarious credibility that support sales staff enjoys among consumers. The advice offered by sellers is perceived as important by a relatively small number of consumers, compared to other sources of information. This reveals, in context, a low level of training of sales staff. Negative perceptions of sellers' competence are able to argue redirecting promotional actions involving customer contact staff towards its preparation in offering professional assistance to the needs and demands of consumers.

A more detailed analysis of gathered data highlights differences in expressed opinions of respondents based on socio-demographic features. In Table 3 are presented the main differences based on these features.

Note: the above analysis did not include variants "uneducated" and "refusing to declare" from the feature "education level" because of the low number of cases, irrelevant to any statistical treatments. The inclusion of these data in the tables was performed only to ensure accurate information on the entire sample.

In order to evaluate the utility of various media used to broadcast promotional messages respondents were asked to say how useful they consider certain media supports. Their answers are gathered in Table 4.

The above information reveals the existence of three main "classes" of media for disseminating promotional messages, through the usefulness attributed by interviewees. Thus, taking into account, cumulative, responses variants "very useful" and "useful" results a hierarchical order with the following configuration:

Table 3. Differences in expressed opinions based on socio-demographic features

Visit Stores **(74% of Total Sample Size)**	• Female gender (79.6% of their total) • People in the age group 36-54 years (75.7%) • Persons residing in Bucharest (88.1%)
Commercials Generally **(60,9% of Total Sample Size)**	• Female gender (64.5% of their total) • People in the age group 15-35 years (68.5%) • Persons residing in Bucharest (68.2%) • Educated people with "high school / post-secondary school" (67.6%)
Friends, Colleagues, Acquaintances **(56,4% of Total Sample Size)**	• Female gender (58.5% of their total) • Persons residing in Bucharest (67.6%) • People work status of "permanent employee" (59.8%) • Educated people with "higher education" (64%)
The Advice Provided by Sellers **(33,5% of Total Sample Size)**	• People in the age group 55 years and above (41.7% of their total) • People work status of "retired" (42.1%) • Persons educated in "professional school" (41%)

Source: Authors' Conception.

Table 4. Perceived usefulness of media support

Scale	Television	Radio	Posters/ Outdoor Posters	Means of Transportation	Daily Press	Illustrated Magazines	Internet	Tram Stations etc.	Sports Sponsorships	Culture Sponsorships
	% of the Total Column, for the Entire Sample									
Totally useless	4.0	3.8	5.1	7.7	5.5	7.6	18.8	14.3	11.0	10.6
Useless	5.6	9.5	14.0	24.3	10.4	12.9	16.7	26.0	16.8	15.8
Neither useful nor useless	13.2	25.1	32.4	33.8	27.7	26.4	17.8	25.7	23.5	23.9
Useful	44.9	42.4	32.8	23.1	41.6	37.5	16.9	21.6	26.9	26.7
Very useful	30.6	16.9	11.9	5.9	11.4	11.5	11.7	4.5	12.5	13.3
Do not know	1.7	2.3	3.8	5.2	3.3	4.0	18.0	7.8	9.4	9.6

Source: Authors' Conception.

- Promotional messages broadcast media assessed as having a high degree of utility:
  o **Television:** 75.5%.
  o **Radio:** 59.3%.
  o **Daily Press:** 53.0%.
- Promotional messages broadcast media assessed as having a medium degree of utility:
  o **Illustrated Magazines:** 49.0%.
  o **Posters/Outdoor Posters:** 44.7%.
  o **Sponsorship of Cultural Events:** 40.0%.
  o **Sponsorship of Sporting Events:** 39.4%.
- Promotional messages broadcast media assessed as having a low degree of utility:
  o **Means of Transportation:** 29.0%.
  o **Internet:** 28.6%.
  o **Tram, Bus Stations, etc.:** 26.1%.

A more detailed analysis of this information underlines significant differences in consumer evaluation of advertising supports. For example, certain categories of respondents consider certain advertising supports as being "useful" or "very useful" as it is shown in Tables 5, 6 and 7.

In conclusion, one can view that Romanians in the age group 15-35 years, living in urban areas with a high or medium level of education consider television, radio and daily press as the main sources of information as well as the most credible ones. This is very important in designing the media plan for any Romanian company.

Table 5. Interviewees segments that assessed messages broadcast media as having high degree of utility

Television **(75,5% of Total Sample Size)**	• People in the age group 15-35 years (79.5% of their total) • Persons residing in Bucharest (90.1%) • Students (86.3%) • People with education level "middle" and "high school" (over 79% per segment)
Radio **(59,3% of Total Sample Size)**	• People in the age group 55 years and above (62.6% of their total) • Persons residing in Bucharest (63.9%) • People with low education "gymnasium" (66.2%)
Daily Press **(53% of Total Sample Size)**	• People in the age group 15-35 years (55.9% of their total) • Persons residing in Bucharest (73.1%) • Students (65.5%) • People with education level "high school" (59.4%)

Source: Authors' Conception.

Table 6. Interviewees segments that assessed messages broadcast media as having medium degree of utility

Illustrated Magazines (49% of Total Sample Size)	• Female gender (52% of their total) • People in the age group 15-35 years (52.9%) • Persons residing in Bucharest (56.5%) • Students (57.4%) • People with low education "high school" (56.2%)
Posters/ outdoor posters (44,7% of Total Sample Size)	• People in the age group 15-35 years (49.9% of their total) • Persons residing in Bucharest (64.6%) • People with low education "gymnasium" (52%)
Sponsorship of Cultural Events (40% of Total Sample Size)	• People in the age group 15-35 years (42.9% of their total) • Persons residing in Bucharest (67.1%) • Students (47.7%) • People with education level "higher education" (48.2%)
Sponsorship of Sporting Events (39,4% of Total Sample Size)	• People in the age group 15-35 years (42.5% of their total) • Persons residing in Bucharest (66.5%) • People with education level "higher education" (47%)

Source: Authors' Conception.

Table 7. Interviewees segments that assessed messages broadcast media as having low degree of utility

Means of Transportation (29% of Total Sample Size)	• Persons residing in Bucharest (50.3% of their total) • People with education level "gymnasium" (34.6%)
Internet (28,6% of Total Sample Size)	• Male gender (30% of their total) • People in the age group 15-35 years (39.4%) • Persons residing in Bucharest (48.8%) • Students (66.6%) • People with education level "higher education" (43.7%)
Tram, Bus Stations etc. (26,1% of Total Sample Size)	• Persons residing in Bucharest (50.6% of their total) • Students (28.4%) • People with education level "gymnasium" (29.5%)

Source: Authors' Conception.

Note: the above analysis did not include variants "uneducated" and "refusing to declare" from the characteristic "level of education", due to reduced number of cases irrelevant to any statistical treatments. The inclusion of these data in the tables was performed only to ensure accurate information on the entire sample.

LIMITS ON THE DESIGN AND IMPLEMENTATION OF PROMOTIONAL PROGRAMS

There are two types of limits in design and implementation of promotional programs at Romanian market level:

• Conceptual and methodological limits;

- Limits arising from the experimental applicative framework. Among conceptual and methodological limits in design and implementation of promotional programs the fallowing can be listed:

  ○ In designing promotional programs are being used many notions and concepts from multiple scientific disciplines, many of which are used in the form of the English language which causes some difficulties of translation. In addition, many notions and concepts are not adapted to the Romanian market.

  ○ Designing promotional programs is difficult because of the confusion between definitions and meanings, advertising agencies and their clients confront with the need to agree on a common language, so as to be clear what objectives are established and which are the best means to achieve them.

  ○ If in other marketing activities, there are many models approached - as, for instance, purchase and consumption behavior - in terms of promotional programs does not exist yet validated instruments in theory and proven to be effective on the practical activity. It is true that it seems very difficult to develop universal "recipes" for problems to which promotional programs are called to respond, and lack of theoretical support in this regard is very difficult to overcome. In other words, almost every promotional program is more an ad hoc approach, rather than one that is already checked based on a model.

  ○ Failure anchorage of designing and implementing promotional programs, within the coordinates of marketing science or rather a sequential approach to this issue, to the detriment of a systemic approach. This limit of conceptual and methodological nature has its origins in the training of both the user's advertising staff and experts working within media agencies. In the advertising user case, usually the problematic of promotion policy is not properly approached or is not based on a market strategy and aggregating with other components of the marketing mix, ie product policy, price policy and distribution policy. In the media companies' case, this inter-correlation is less present, specialists of advertising agencies dealing exclusively with proposing promotional programs to customers. These promotional programs are practically almost totally broken from components of the marketing mix of the user's company. Also, on the advertising companies, the promotional policy is not treated in fact as a coherent and unified system. In this context, resolutions and sequential solutions prove, most often to be a palliative approach, which does not generate desired effects at advertising user level.

The practical-experimental framework of designing and implementing promotional programs bring to the attention of specialists boundaries that cannot be ignored. Among the most important of these limits can be listed as follows:

- Assimilation and application of the marketing concept and tools require, ab initio, guidance and practical foundation of all activities based on the study and knowledge of the real needs of final users. This practice in Romania is more a goal than a current activity, both at users of advertising and media agencies level. Clearly, any promotional activity must be based on relevant marketing research studies. It is true that the question is whether such studies must be undertaken by users of advertising or media agencies. Theoretically, this is irrelevant, because it only matters the ultimate effect, the promotional program's performance. If users do not have well-prepared specialists, ignore research and media agencies are strictly limited to their work, without making, or ask users to conduct appropriate studies and research. As a result, promotional programs appear to be of most often very far from what the consumers need.
- In practice, there are relatively few specialized promotional activities that have a scientific, explicit and detailed enough foundation. This limit of the practical activity can be explained largely by the lack of, insufficient substantiation or relatively superficial treatment of theoretical foundation of promotional activities and this can't be made exclusively at the expense of users of advertising and media agencies. What can be criticized, for both, users and media agencies, is that they treat relatively superficial such issues?
- Research conducted by the authors of this paper revealed the fact that, often, media agencies and logistics solutions use inappropriate materials or poor implementation promotional programs. These shows a lack of professionalism in the advertising, which does not monitor the conduct of the promotional programs designed, or do this lightly. In addition, media agencies do not assess any effect of such deficiencies on the promotional program overall performance.

CONCLUSION

Even though the authors' research was not explicitly meant for green advertising, it has a wide range of applicability. Leonidu and Leonidu (2011) show that 93.4% of green advertising is sponsored by manufacturing companies due to the fact that they are more likely to damage the environment by consuming resources. According to the same authors, most of the firms involved in green advertising were big conglomerate organizations, consisting of multiple strategic business units and producing a wide range of products, not necessarily green products.

In this context, green advertising is not necessarily meant for green products but rather for products and services that have a negative impact on the environment. Green promotional products need to focus on specific organizational activities designated to the real protection of the natural and social environment.

Green promotion needs to communicate substantive environmental information to consumers that have meaningful links to corporate activities. According to Polonsky and Rosenberg (2001), environmental communication can be used to communicate tactical activities, such as relevant environmental sponsorships or minor product modifications. Promotional programs' design and implementation need to be clearly formulated in accordance with company's green activities so consumers may not perceive it as greenwash.

A promotional program can be considered green when respecting the rules of effectiveness and efficiency mention in the body of this chapter and when it allows impact measurement as accurate as possible.

Another important request of a greener promotional program is using the media for messages broadcast with the greater impact on consumers' perception. In this research case, the media considered by Romanian consumers with the greatest utility for messages broadcast is television, followed by radio and daily press.

In the present days, promotional programs have a relatively diverse set of instruments ready to be used due to the accumulation of scientific development on the conceptual, methodological and practical-experimental field, even though, as mentioned above, there are several limits to overcome.

Elaboration and implementation of promotional programs are facilitated by modern marketing knowledge gained in the study of markets and consumers. There is also a proper marketing set of instruments, such as, for example, marketing strategies and programs that incorporate promotional programs.

Following the development of marketing theory regarding marketing policies in general, promotional strategy benefits of an important boost of the framework. Today professionals are operating with relatively sophisticated notions and concepts, fine-tuned and pragmatic in terms of results. For example, it is significant that concepts such as audience, market-share, and rating have already entered into ordinary language, including being properly understood by consumers covered.

Consumers are generally receptive to different promotional messages, which must, however, be actually helpful to people whom they are addressed. The fact that green campaigns, for example, does not provide consumers with the information they really need is likely to cause ambiguity that does not serve the goals and objectives when designing and implementing green promotional programs.

REFERENCES

Ahmad, H., Shah, I. A., & Ahmad, K. (2009). Factors in environmental advertising influencing consumer's purchase intention. *Cell, 333*, 5339752.

Al Pop, N. (2000). *Marketing Strategic*. Editura Economică.

Cătoiu, I., & Teodorescu, N. (2001). Comportamentul consumatorului. Abordare instrumentală. *Editura Uranus, Bucureşti, 2001*, 130.

Cătoiu, I., & Teodorescu, N. (2004). *Comportamentul consumatorului. Teorie şi practică*. Bucureşti: Editura Economică.

Demetrescu, M. C. (1971). *Metode cantitative în marketing*. Bucureşti: Editura Ştiinţifică.

Ginsberg, J. M., & Bloom, P. N. (2004). Choosing the right green-marketing strategy. *MIT Sloan Management Review, 46*(1), 79.

Kotler, Ph., & Keller, K. (2008). *Managementul Marketingului*. Bucureşti: Editura Teora.

Kotler, Ph., Saunders, J., Armstrong, G., & Wong, V. (2008). *Principiile Marketingului*. Bucureşti: Editura Teora.

Leonidou, L. C., Leonidou, C. N., Palihawadana, D., & Hultman, M. (2011). Evaluating the green advertising practices of international firms: A trend analysis. *International Marketing Review, 28*(1), 6–33. doi:10.1108/02651331111107080

Polonsky, M. J. (1994). An introduction to green marketing. *Electronic Green Journal, 1*(2).

Polonsky, M. J., & Rosenberger, P. J. III. (2001). Reevaluating green marketing: A strategic approach. *Business Horizons, 44*(5), 21–30. doi:10.1016/S0007-6813(01)80057-4

Shrum, L. J., McCarty, J. A., & Lowrey, T. M. (1995). Buyer characteristics of the green consumer and their implications for advertising strategy. *Journal of Advertising, 24*(2), 71–82. doi:10.1080/00913367.1995.10673477

Von Bertalanffy, L. (1972). The history and status of general systems theory. *Academy of Management Journal, 15*(4), 407–426. doi:10.2307/255139

Wilson, R. M., & Gilligan, C. (2012). *Strategic marketing management*. Routledge.

ADDITIONAL READING

Hartmann, P., & Apaolaza-Ibáñez, V. (2009). Green advertising revisited: Conditioning virtual nature experiences. *International Journal of Advertising*, 28(4), 715–739. doi:10.2501/S0265048709200837

Kalafatis, S. P., Pollard, M., East, R., & Tsogas, M. H. (1999). Green marketing and Ajzen's theory of planned behaviour: A cross-market examination. *Journal of Consumer Marketing*, 16(5), 441–460. doi:10.1108/07363769910289550

Phau, I., & Ong, D. (2007). An investigation of the effects of environmental claims in promotional messages for clothing brands. *Marketing Intelligence & Planning*, 25(7), 772–788. doi:10.1108/02634500710834214

KEY TERMS AND DEFINITIONS

Advertising Research: A systematic process of marketing research conducted to assess and improve the efficiency of advertising.

Eco-Friendly Advertising: A innovative and creative form of advertising part of the green movement.

Impact Measurement of the Promotional Campaign: An assessment of the effectiveness of the promotional campaign.

Marketing Strategy: A way to reach the marketing objectives established after the situation analysis of the internal and external media in the context of the business mission.

Promotional Plan: An important marketing tool, part of the marketing strategies aiming to ensure meeting of its objectives.

Tactical Promotional Tools: The tools used in advertising, public relations, and sales strategies to communicate about an organization' products and services and get people to buy them.

Chapter 5
Organisational Culture:
An Essential Factor for Increasing the Competitiveness of Companies

Mihaela N. Otelea
Petroleum-Gas University of Ploiesti, Romania

ABSTRACT

Organizational culture is one of the determinants of a company's competitiveness, and consequently, realistic analysis of the link between these two elements can provide relevant information to optimize it and, on this basis, to increase the company performance. The direct implications of organizational culture are important in business efficiency. Increasing the quality of human resources, efficient exploitation of material resources, and financial mean the achievement of provisioned levels of turnover, market share, or value added. Organizational culture, through its forms and manifestations (symbols, rules of behavior, customs, ceremonies, history, prestige, and authority of managers and employees), influences and leads to a series of behaviors and attitudes so that employees can tap the full potential for achieving goals. Eliminating fear in an organization is an essential requirement, as it encourages people to take more risks, responsibilities, and initiatives. Remarkable results can be achieved if performance will be measured properly and if a direct reward is chosen.

DOI: 10.4018/978-1-5225-2965-1.ch005

INTRODUCTION

Performance has always been the focus of companies' management. Therefore, rapid changes taking place, at the present, in the business environment, make appropriate the managers' orientation to practicing, in business, strategic management, rigorous foundation of business strategies and implementing them correctly, being essential for achieving higher performances.

Low performances or failures of many companies, are because of their inability to adapt to the requirements of the market and its rules of operation. In this context, the organizational culture plays an important role. Basically, the managers unawareness to the importance of organizational culture has made it impossible to support high performance. On such a dynamic market, companies can reach and can exist only if they have products and/or innovative services related to attractive prices. A company is competitive on the market only if it has a strong and positive organizational culture, able to mobilize people, energies for achieving the desired objective.

Improvement of organizational culture is required by the registration of decreasing performance of products/services that have not been adapted to the market, in the event of a merger acquisition, so that the so-called cultural shock to be easily overcome. The meeting of two types of organizational cultures, rules, values and beliefs of different rites, it involves a cultural adaptation, both for expatriate managers, as well as domestic workers. The complex and time-consuming process, the cultural adaptation must be supported by the application of effective methods and measures.

Organizational culture is one of the determinants of a company's competitiveness and, consequently, realistic analysis of the link between these two elements can provide relevant information to optimize it and, on this basis, to increase the company performance.

The direct implications of organizational culture are important in business efficiency. Increasing the quality of human resources, efficient exploitation of material resources and financial mean the achievement of provisioned levels of turnover, market share or value added.

Organizational culture, through its forms and manifestations (symbols, rules of behaviour, customs, ceremonies, history, prestige and authority of managers and employees), influences and leads to a series of behaviours and attitudes so that employees can tap the full potential for achieving goals.

Eliminating fear in an organization is an essential requirement, as it encourages people to take more risks, responsibilities and initiatives. Remarkable results can be achieved if performance will be measured properly and if a direct reward is chosen. Modern management systems try to better intertwine with the interests of the company's employees, trying to reward team work, thus promoting the values and rules. Teams made up of motivated employees for business increase productivity.

Establishing such a team and creating strong relationships with a particular company could pose real challenges for managers.

The author was motivated to start this research by the interest in organizational culture and the correlation between different types of organizational cultures and performances of a company.

Throughout the paper, the author followed the development of a methodology to assess the competitiveness at company level, shaping organizational culture, competitive relationship and outlining possible ways to improve it.

Organizational culture, by its nature, has many facets. Some are better explored and assessed by qualitative methods and quantitative methods others. The application of both methods provides a better understanding of the research object.

As a rule, successful companies have "something of their own" to distinguish them from others and to characterize the mode of action of their employees. Studies show that the cultural values present in high-performance businesses are as follows:

- **Orientation Towards Teamwork:** People are willing to put the objectives of the team above their own.
- **Sincerity:** Communication is sincere and open, ensuring the share of information and minimizing secrets.
- **Empowering Employees:** Authority and responsibility are decentralized and broadly delegated.
- **Respect for the Individual:** Companies are tolerant to cultural differences between people, professionally or socially.
- **Customer - Orientated:** It considers that the activity should be determined by market conditions and the obligation to satisfy customers.
- **Competitive Spirit and Desire to Win:** All employees are mobilized by the desire for success, achievement.
- **Entrepreneurial Attitude:** There is openness to innovation and risk-taking.
- **Assuming Personal Responsibility:** It is assumed that the interest for results is critical for business success.
- **Continuous Learning:** Continuous renewal for skills and attitudes.
- **Trust:** Employees are convinced that each of them fight as hard as they can for the interests of the company.

To sustain a high level of performance over the long term, the organizational culture must meet three basic conditions simultaneously:

- To be strong through a coherent and rigorous value system, communicated to all employees of the company by the leaders and shared widely.
- To be strategically adequate.

- To be adaptive.

THE CONCEPT OF CORPORATE CULTURE

Corporate culture is a relatively recent concern of the management theorists.

Numerous researchers have defined the term of organizational (corporate) culture, in an attempt to grasp it in its essence. Further are some relevant definitions. Griffin (1990, p. 20), considers culture as a set of values, belonging to an organization that helps its members to understand the purpose, the way of action and what they deem important. Davis (1984, p. 38), considers organizational culture as a set of values and beliefs shared by the staff of an organization with some meanings and which provide rules for an accepted behavior. Jones (1979), who believes that, formally, the corporate culture refers to shared beliefs, values and assumptions that characterize members of an organization. Schein (1985), relying on the advice given to several economic organizations, has developed a complex definition of corporate culture, according to which its components are defined as follows:

- Conduct rules observed when people meet, such as: language, ways of expressing respect s.o;
- Rules that develop in the working teams.
- Dominant values adopted by the Organization.
- The philosophy of the policy towards members of the Organization.
- Rules implemented in the Organization for an efficient operation.
- Spirit and climate in the Organization, in terms of comfort and the way its members interact with outsiders.

Hofstede (1996), defines culture as collective mental programming that makes the difference between members of different organizations. Hofstede considers that there are three levels of mental programming: universal, collective and individual level. Mental programming relies on collective level. A clearer definition was given by Robbins and Coutter (1996), according to which corporate culture is a system of shared meanings, models of the values, symbols, rituals, myths and practices that have evolved over time. "Shared Meanings" in the definition means the organization specific philosophy, values, beliefs and attitudes adhered to by the organization members and that govern their behavior and actions. All of the above interpretations can be translated into the following definition: corporate culture comprises the set of artificial products, basic values and concepts, ways of thinking and generally accepted behavior in an organization based on common actions (Zorleţan, Burduş & Căprărescu, 1995, p. 193).

Forms of Corporate Culture Manifestation

Each company identifies a specific type of organizational culture, corresponding to its specific values. Corporate culture influences and change attitudes, beliefs and behaviors, and if they correspond to the company's strategy, one can speak about effectiveness and performance.

Organizational cultures are grouped into several categories according to certain criteria, such as: culture configuration, contribution to the company's performance, level of risk assumption and reaction speed to changes, vision of time.

Based on culture configuration and values that underlie corporate structure, four types of organizational culture can be identified (Harrison, 1987).

Role or Temple Type Culture

This kind of culture characterizes large corporations with formal, classic, bureaucratic and well ranked structures - State-owned enterprises, local administrations etc.

Beehive Type Culture

Unlike other types of corporate cultures, in which the employee is subordinate to the Organization and contributes to the attainment of its objectives, in the beehive type culture professionals and their individual goals represents the essence of the company.

Power Type Culture

The Organization of this type responds quickly to society changes. Power company culture type provides company a high competitive spirit, its competitiveness depending on the personality of both managers and experts' competence.

Network Type Culture

In such a culture, the company management is viewed in terms of a chain of challenges that involve finding solutions. The central element is the execution of the task and provision of resources specific to each company level. Companies governed by this kind of culture are competence and dynamism oriented.

Table 1 synthesizes the peculiarities of the main types of corporate cultures, creating thus the possibility to make a comparison between them.

Depending on their nature and contribution to the company performance, there are positive cultures focusing on participation, trust, environmental adaptation,

Table 1. Corporate culture defining elements

Defining Elements	Types of Cultures			
	"Temple"	"Beehive"	"Power"	"Spider Network"
Key element	Professional Specialization	Power	Personality	Network nodes
Open to outwards	High	Low	Low	High
Dynamism	Low	Low	Emphasized	Emphasized
Predominating authority	Formal	Formal	Informal	Formal
Motivation	Balanced positive-negative	Predominating negative	Predominating positive	Predominating positive
Corporate climate	Calm	Tense	Tense	Tense
Contribution to the company's performance	Low	High	High	High
Area of manifesting competition	Professional specializations	Task achievement	Competent authority	Hierarchical vs. competent authority functional

Source: The Author's conception.

communication and flexibility, and negative culture characterized by traits such as lack of confidence in the individual, separating the leader from workers, lack of dialogue, rigidity, and concentration of decision at higher levels. A negative culture gradually leads to company bankruptcy.

A strong culture, but with negative aspects, results in a decrease in the performance recorded. Thus, not culture intensity, especially its ability to adapt to the environment makes it a tool for success.

Time plays a decisive role in the culture of a community and thus in the business practice. According to the time factor, i.e. depending on how companies organize their time, at least two types of cultures are identified (Huţu, 1999): (1) Monochronic culture, where time is perceived in a linear manner (absolute time), stretches from past through the present to the future and is segmented (in stages) and tangible (by calendar). (2) Polychronic Culture - where there is a different perspective on time (relative time), with reference to its flow in relation to the events and facts of life. Increased productivity and competitiveness are ensured.

Hofstede (1996) makes another classification of cultures, according to the orientation of Corporate Management. It defines six models of corporate culture: (1) Process/ results. In process-oriented companies, employees tend to prefer standard, routine activities, avoiding changes and risks. In those centered on results, employees focus their work on achieving certain goals, making special efforts in this regard based on the initiation and implementation of changes to the risk-taking involved. Thus, they have an increased potential to achieve outstanding performance. (2) Employees/Jobs. In companies focused on employees' decisions are adopted within the group, which leads to involvement of all employees in achieving the general goals of the company. In work oriented corporate cultures, the focus is on the professional activity, decisions being taken at a higher level. This creates an obstacle to intra-organizational communication, with negative effects on the growth and maintaining company competitiveness. (3) *"Limited" / "Professional"*. Employees in 'limited' type culture organizations, identify themselves with the company rather than with the professional branch of which they belong. On the contrary, employees in the "professional" type culture consider that the main criterion is their professional competence, which motives development and lifelong learning. (4) Open/closed system. Members of "open system" organizations believe that the new employee must adapt quickly, while those in the "closed system" manifest much reluctance towards newcomers. To achieve increased productivity, open system type cultures are preferred and justified. (5) Low / intense control. In companies where little control is exercised, there is a relaxed atmosphere, a calm organizational climate, which favors innovation and productivity. When intense control is applied, it appears some "respect" towards the organization, but with inhibitory effect on skills development. (6) Prescriptive/pragmatic. The prescriptive organizational culture is oriented to strict adherence to behavioral rules and organizational procedures, while the pragmatic ones focus on customer satisfaction and are market oriented.

So far, the literature has not created a well outlined Romanian cultural model. Based on specialized studies, we have highlighted a number of elements that characterize most of the Romanian companies. Thus, we mainly identify two types of corporate cultures, the one characterized by bureaucracy and entrepreneurial elements.

Culture with bureaucracy elements is typical for state owned companies, autonomous companies, state owned educational and health institutions and can be characterized as inertial, focused on the system interior and extremely involved in the political life of the country. Within these organizations there is a significant difference between proclaimed values and real actions. This leads to confusion, distrust, lack of respect within the company and creates a communicative abyss between company management and operating levels.

Cultural rigidity specific to these companies resulted in lowering their performance, with repercussions for the entire economy - high rate of inflation and unemployment, high level of taxes and fees, high ratio between prices / wages, with extensive implications on the living standard.

Currently, the entrepreneurial culture crystallizes, especially in private capital companies established after the creation of free market mechanisms in Romania. Most new entrepreneurs do not have the knowledge and the skills needed to create a coherent strategic perspective or a dynamic adaptation to the external environment, but intuition on company development and communication with the company staff determines a sense of belonging, involvement and engagement in solving problems. Utmost importance is given to the effort of constructing new meanings, through the promotion of values such as respect for customers, employees and the community, concern for products and services quality, creativity, openness and personal development within the company.

According to State (2004, p. 173), Romanian two types of culture are present in Romanian companies:

1. **"Modern" Type:** Positive attitude towards foreign investment; dominant preference for private property; preference for certain streamlining strategies, rather radical constructivism; the dominant option for meritocracy based on professional competence and work performance; intense and constant concern for increasing competitiveness;
2. **"Remnant" Type:** Able to hold back a quick change: most employees' preference for direct involvement in electing company leadership regardless of its type's property; dominant preference for a strong hand in leading companies, resulting into a high degree of instability and not an option for an authoritarian style, based on respect; faith in that company management relationships with various media and political groups can be important for its proper functioning.

We can affirm that the basis for the development of strong culture, suitable in terms of strategy and tailored, was created.

CORPORATE CULTURE: COMPETITIVENESS - WAYS FOR IMPROVEMENT

An assumption increasingly common with managers of various companies is that there is a direct and positive relationship between a strong corporate culture and the company performance seen in terms of profit, productivity and creativity. This has led many businesses to initiate programs on "corporate culture remodeling", "corporate culture development", "cultural revolution", etc.

Models Quantifying the Relationship Between Organizational Culture and Business Competitiveness

Performance measurement and evaluation is achieved by using objective and/or subjective criteria and instruments. We turn to a wide range of quantitative indicators (volume) and qualitative indicators (efficiency).

The large number of variables analyzed in terms of competitiveness of companies is a strength point, and the lack of aggregation in a coherent methodology represents a weak point.

Intense interest on the competitiveness takes into account: indissoluble relationship between competitiveness, living standard, productivity, economic growth and poverty eradication; and shaping competitiveness as a standalone field of economic science, begins to crystallize and individualize through a specific set of concepts and instruments.

In our opinion, the organizational culture variables with major impact on company competitiveness are:

- **Number of Training Hours/Employee:** Direct proportional correlation with labor productivity, turnover and product quality.
- **Absenteeism Rate:** Reverse proportional correlation between turnover, labor productivity and company image.
- **Degree of Stability of the Staff:** Direct proportional correlation between productivity and company image.
- **Specialization Degree:** Direct proportional correlation to the quality of products and market share.
- **Accepted Risk Level:** Direct proportional correlation between productivity and company image.

Study on Quantifying the Relationship Corporate Culture: Company Competitiveness

In our research we aimed that, on the basis of data from the real economy, to examine through statistical methods to what extent corporate culture-specific variables influence on the degree of competitiveness of a company.

The method of data processing, for central, median tendency, we employed frequencies and percentages of answers to each question, and out of the non-parametric tests, to test variables significance, we used test F and for the degree of association of two variables – we used the Pearson correlation coefficient. We have also conducted regression analysis for the purpose of measuring the influence of each of the selected variables of corporate culture on the company's performance.

In using these methods, we made reference to a series of questions formulated so as to capture aspects such as: general value fund of corporate culture; socio-professional climate; training and professional development; social relationships within companies; and relations between managers −and subordinates on communication and cooperation.

The answers have been processed using SPSS for Windows 14 - Statistical Package for the Social Sciences, with a focus on relative frequencies and modal value of the participants' answers and on the Pearson test for the degree of association of two variables.

The method of selection of the companies included in the sample was non-random sampling, thus the choice of items was made taking into account the proportion of various parts of the community quotas.

The questionnaire was conducted in four sections: (A) Identification of the company; (B) Organizational (corporate) culture; (C) Company performance; and (D) Organizational Culture-Competitiveness Relationship.

In terms of business profile, the sample was structured as follows - over half come from services performance, about one-fifth of the number of companies acting as "*production*" and a quarter have profile right "*production and services*" as shown in Figure 1.

Decisions but, in particular, way of making decisions is defining the company's activity. Thus, in the case of 43% of the companies the decision adopted is transmitted to the employees, but it interferes with changes in 40% - requesting the opinion of those involved in the implementation of decisions, which leads to decrease in the

Figure 1. Structure of the company sample according to the activity profile
Source: Processed by author.

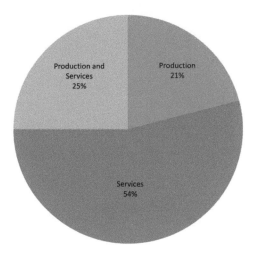

staff resistance implementing the decisions and a good substantiation thereof, in other words, we practice participatory-advisory management, and in 17% cases - the decision is transmitted without consultation.

In close connection with adopting the decision are company communication and the regulations underlying the decisions making process. Thus, in the majority of companies there are clear regulations, in one-third of their number participatory management is practiced, and in the case of less than tenth - informal communication is predominant, as it appears in Figure 2.

Meeting customer requirements is essential given the current economy. For the sample examined, a quarter of companies treat their customers equally, while most companies adapt to their requirements anticipating and customizing the clients. In recent years, customer loyalty programs (CRM - Customer Relationship Management) have been created and developed, allowing tilting the balance in favor of the second way of treating clients as shown in Figure 3.

Integrating new employees in the company is an important component of the corporate culture of a company. Thus, most companies provide support to their new colleagues and in fewer companies, new colleagues are treated with reserve and restraint, according to data in the Figure 4. One of the cases can see the special attention given the group, confirmed by the index size for individualism/collectivism.

Figure 2. The distribution of sample, based on the answers regarding direction of employees' decisions
Source: Processed by author.

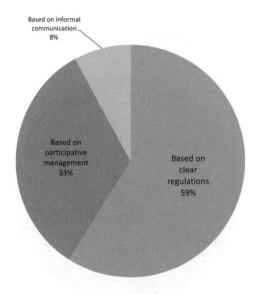

Figure 3. Structure of the sample, according to the answers on how clients are being treated
Source: Processed by author.

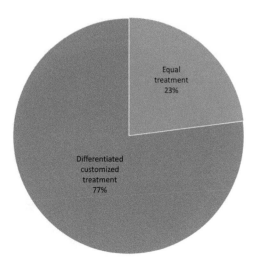

Figure 4. The structure of the sample, based on the answers regarding how new employees are integrated
Source: Processed by author.

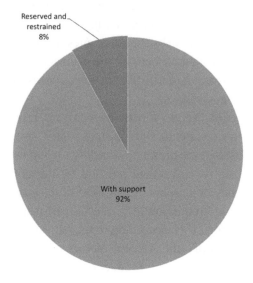

In terms of reasons of the new hires, most companies have as main reasons, business development and opening new branches, seasonal business increase, insufficient staff training and resignations occurred, each with weights specified in the Figure 5.

115

Figure 5. The structure of the sample, based on the answers regarding the main reasons of employment
Source: Processed by author.

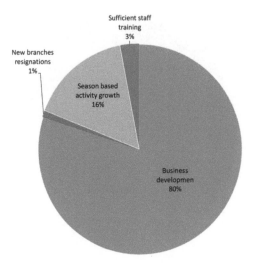

Vocational training is considered useful in achieving duties in most companies, in much less companies, it is considered a way of loyalty to employees and only in very little companies it is seen as a source of spending growth as specified in Figure 6.

In one of the cases can be observed the high degree of awareness for the the importance of vocational training by the companies' management. Also, vocational training is a major and constant concern for the management of about three quarters of the companies, and in case of fourth of them, it is an occasional concern, according to the data in the Figure 7.

In terms of existence of disputes with their employees, in over three quarters of the companies they were not registered, showing thus a quiet, stimulating organizational climate, unlike the rest that are present, according to data in the Figure 8.

In terms of competitive advantage pursued by the companies, in the order determined by frequency of answers, it consisted of the quality and promptness of the service provided, differentiation of products, performance of employees and decrease in the production costs, according to the data submitted in the Table 2.

When seeking to identify the success factors of the company directed, the frequency of answers placed on top: product quality; organizational culture; staff training (Table 3), which was an encouraging support for our approach to quantify the relationship between organizational culture of a company and its competitiveness.

In terms of corporate culture - competitiveness relationship, we achieved ordering in relation to importance (*from 1 - important to 7 - less important*) corporate culture variables in insurance company performance. Consequently, the average of staff

Figure 6. The structure of the sample, based on the answers regarding characterization of vocational training
Source: Processed by author.

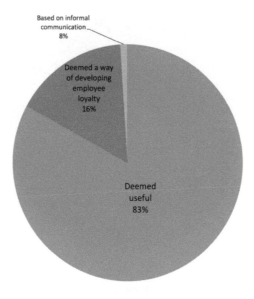

Figure 7. The structure of the sample, based on the management vision of vocational training
Source: Processed by author.

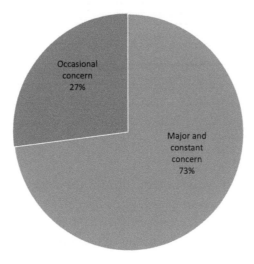

Figure 8. The structure of the companies' sample, based on existence of labor disputes in the company
Source: Processed by author.

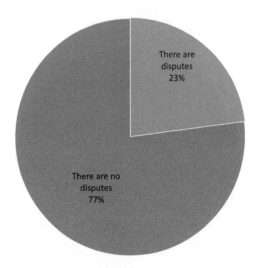

Table 2. Distribution of answers on the types of competitive advantages tracked by companies analyzed

Competitive Advantage	Answers	
	Number	Weights
Product differentiation	43	29.5%
Performance of employees	34	23.3%
Decrease in production costs	21	14.4%
Quality and efficiency of servicing provided	46	31.5%
Others	2	1.4%
Total	146	100.0%

Source: The author's conception.

qualification obtained the average score of 2.62, the degree of risk accepted - 3.52, expenditure on social responsibility - 4.63, number of hours of training - 2.97, degree of staff stability - 2.64, rate of absenteeism - 5.34 and labor disputes 6.19. Based on the recorded average scores, corporate culture variables are scaled as follows:

1. Average level of qualified staff.
2. Degree of staff stability.
3. Number of hours of training.

Table 3. Distribution of answers regarding the factors ensuring the success of the companies analyzed

Success Factors	Answers	
	Number	Weights
Quality of products	71	24.0%
Staff training	59	19.9%
Corporate culture	66	22.3%
Innovation	28	9.5%
Risk taking	23	7.8%
Collaborative ties	47	15.9%
Others	2	0.7%
Total	296	100.0%

Source: The author's conception.

4. Level of risk accepted by company management.
5. Expenditure on social responsibility.
6. Rate of absenteeism.
7. Working conditions.

In order to achieve the proposed model of linear regression type between corporate culture and competitiveness, it was necessary to standardize values entered for the seven variables of corporate culture, namely six of competitiveness, since variables have different units of measure (percentage, absolute, currency values). With these standardized values we proceeded through aggregation, to obtain synthetic values for organizational culture, i.e. competitiveness.

We mention that where intensity of appreciation was done on regular intervals, the interval center has been taken into account.

Analysis of correlation between the selected variables that define the corporate culture of the company and those chosen on performance thereof was carried out on three levels:

1. Synthetic influence of corporate culture of the company on company synthetic performance;
2. Influence of each variable of corporate culture on company synthetic performance;
3. Influence of each variable on the variables of each company's performance (emphasizing bilateral correlation).

The details of this research conducted at each level are shown below.

In view of considering the significance, especially the intensity of the bond between variables, in the primary level of our study we used Pearson correlation coefficient. This registered a value of 0.533 for company competitiveness-corporate culture relationship, which shows:

1. A direct relationship between variables considered (the sign of the coefficient being positive);
2. A significant link in the statistical sense.

The Table 5 is important because it gives information on the effectiveness of the regression model applied. Table 5 shows the correlation coefficient Pearson marked with R (also known as multiple R or multiple correlation coefficient, if the model contains more than one independent variable). Since R = 0.533, shows that between the two variables, there is a strong correlation. This appreciation and the following considerations regarding *R2* have in mind that the data being transformed by standardization into a dimensioned value, we eliminate some of the false correlation elements existing in the unprocessed empirical values.

The third column of the table contains the coefficient of determination R2 = 0.284, meaning that 28.4% of the dependent variable version - business competitiveness -

Table 4. Company competitiveness: corporate culture correlation

		Company Competitiveness	Corporate Culture
Company competitiveness	Pearson coefficient	1	0.533**
	Level of significance		0.000
	N	100	100
Corporate culture	Pearson coefficient	0.533**	1
	Level of significance	0.000	
	N	100	100

Source: The author's computation.
Note: ** - statistically significant value.

Table 5. The effectiveness of the regression model

Model	R	R2	R2 Adjusted	Standard Error of the Estimation
1	0.533	0.284	0.277	178.10118

Source: The author's computation.

can be explained by the independent variable version - company corporate culture. The fourth column shows the R2 adjusted coefficient. R2 coefficient is generally higher (compared to R2 adjusted), being influenced by the number of independent variables subjected to analysis and the sample volume. Since we are interested in generalizing the results to population level, R2 adjusted is a better estimator. In our case, R2 adjusted is 0.277, the difference being minimal as compared to R2. We say that, in general, company corporate culture influences in 27.7% its competitiveness.

In the Table 6, ANOVA, the F test checks if the prediction we make is better than the one based on chance, hazard, in other words, the model is validated. Since Fcalc = 38.924 and Ftab= 3.84, it appears that it is very unlikely that the connection is the result of hazard.

The next step shows the regression non-standardized coefficients (B) and the standardized coefficients (beta). The non-standardized coefficient for the organizational culture is b = 1.837 and represents the slope of regression.

Based on the results shown in Table 7 regarding regression coefficients a = − 38.938, b = 1.837, we can write the regression equation:

$$Y = a + bX = -38.938 + 1.837\,X,$$

Table 6. Results of model's testing

Model	Variants	Degrees of Freedom (df)	Variants/df	Test F	Level of Significance
1 Regression	1234656.086	1	1234656.086	38.924	0.000
Residual values	3108563.137	98	31720.032		
Total	4343219.223	99			

Source: The author's computation.

Table 7. Regression coefficients

Model		Non-Standardized Coefficients		Non-Standardized Coefficients	T Test	Level of Significance
		B	Standard Error	Beta		
1	(Constant)	− 38.938	23.243		− 1.675	0.097
	Corporate culture	1.837	0.294	0.533	6.239	0.000

Source: The author's computation.

where:

Y = company competitiveness;
X = corporate culture.

Below is the results interpretation: for an increase by one unit of the corporate culture, its competitiveness shows a 1.837 units growth. Units for each variable are dimensionless, due to the said standardization process.

Our study approached the structural form of the model, analyzing the influence of corporate culture on competitiveness.

Thus, the relationship between competitiveness and the rate of absenteeism is inversely proportional, recording a Pearson coefficient of - 0.313, with an acceptable level of significance of 0.002, which confirm that at a high rate of staff absenteeism, company competitiveness decreases.

Vocational training- competitiveness relationship is directly proportional. The Pearson coefficient value is 0.248 with acceptable significance level of 0.013. This confirms that if vocational training of employees is a priority of the company's management, its performance continues to grow.

For average staff qualification - company competitiveness relationship, the Pearson coefficient value is 0.198, the level of significance at limit of acceptance of 0.049, which confirms the obvious reality as in the case of a company having highly qualified personnel, its competitiveness is superior.

Level of stability of the staff slightly influences company competitiveness, since the Pearson coefficient was 0.091. The level of significance, well above the allowed limit of 0.05, indicates a rather insignificant link.

Also, the answers received show that the degree of risk assumed by the company's management while adopting decisions does not considerably influence its competitiveness (the Pearson coefficient is 0.035. The high significance level indicates that the connection between the variables is statistically insignificant.

Disputes between labor and company competitiveness relationship is inversely proportional, but its intensity is reduced (Pearson coefficient of -0.094). The high significance level indicates that the connection between the variables is statistically insignificant.

Expenditure on social responsibility actions has a direct connection with obtaining superior performance. Pearson coefficient has a value of 0.522 and the significance level is 0.000, which shows directly the proportional relationship, statistically significant between the two variables.

For the second level of the study, i.e. determination of the influence of each organizational culture variable on the company competitiveness, social responsibility expenses, training and absenteeism rate stand out as significant factors.

ISSUES OF CORPORATE CULTURE: COMPANY COMPETITIVENESS RELATIONSHIP, SHOWN BY OUR RESEARCH

The research conducted on a sample of 100 firms aimed to quantify the influence of corporate culture on company competitiveness. Thus, a Pearson coefficient of 0.533, an adjusted R^2 of 0.277, with a level of significance of 0.000 have been calculated. This certifies that there is a direct strong connection between the variables considered and, at the same time, that nearly a third of company's achievements, and recorded performances, are due to a viable corporate culture. After implementation of the linear regression model type, $Y = a + bX$, where Y is company competitiveness, and X is the corporate culture, the value of the coefficient b was 1.837, which shows that at an absolute unit growth of the company corporate culture, competitiveness records an increase by 1.837 units.

The study goal was the determination of the individual influence of relevant variables of corporate culture on the company competitiveness and also a third level has taken into account the correlation between company competitiveness and corporate culture variables.

Thus, following calculation of the Pearson correlation coefficients, it was found that the variables: amount of costs with social responsibility actions; the number of training hours/employee, the average qualification of employees and the absenteeism rate influence company competitiveness (Table 8). This certifies, once again, the paramount importance of human resources in business and its unique creative potential.

In terms of variables: the degree of staff stability; the number of labor disputes and the level of risk accepted in adopting decisions have not identified any statistically significant connections to company performance. This can also be explained by the researched sample, namely the majority weight of companies in the field of provision of services.

In terms of correlations between company competitiveness and corporate culture variables, the following have been found:

Turnover varies in direct proportion to the number of training hours/employee and inversely with the rate of staff absenteeism;

Average labor productivity varies in direct proportion to the number of hours of training and staff qualification and inversely with the rate of staff absenteeism;

The market share held by the company is strongly correlated with the following variables: quality of products/services and average staff qualification. A poor connection has been confirmed in terms of the level of risk accepted by the company management in the decision-making process;

Table 8. Company and corporate culture variables correlations

Correlations	Pearson Coefficient (r) Level of Significance (p)
Company competitiveness - Expenditure on social responsibility	0.522** 0.000
Company competitiveness - Staff absenteeism rate	-0, 313** 0.002
Company competitiveness - Number of hours of training / employee	0.248* 0.013
Company competitiveness - Average qualification of the staff	0.198* 0.049
Company competitiveness - Number of labor disputes	-0.094 0.354
Company competitiveness - Degree of stability of the staff	0.091 0.366
Company competitiveness - Level of risk accepted	0.035 0.728

Source: The author's computation.
Note: **, *- statistically significant value

The relationship directly proportional to the level of staff qualification and the degree of staff stability became apparent in terms of quality of products/services provided;

The company image is influenced directly proportional by the amount of expenditure with social responsibility, the average qualification of staff and its degree of stability. Also, the inverse relationship with staff absenteeism rate and the number of labor disputes has been confirmed.

CONCLUSION

The study on the impact of organizational culture on the competitiveness of firms has highlighted the need to raise awareness of the importance of organizational culture in order to obtain components for superior performance.

Such factors are "responsible" for the success of firms analysed are: quality of products/services - which received 24.0% of the responses, organizational culture, chosen by 22.3% of respondents and training / qualification of personnel with weight 19.9%. These factors are interdependent and need special attention to supporting and developing each recorded performance by firms.

From the above analysis, organizational culture is a factor that determines whether the organization can effectively achieve a particular performance or not, which leads to the organization's response and attitude on any particular incident or on an external environmental change.

Three types of capital resources can be identified as sources of a competitive advantage: organizational resources, human resources and physical resources. The organizational planning and control and the organizational structure of the company are examples of organizational resources of a company.

Involvement and ownership are key measures in an organizational culture. These aspects of organizational culture include two competitive advantage sources: human resources and organizational resources.

The phenomenon of a business culture and social complexity plays an important role in defining the competitive advantage and survival of many companies (King & Zeithaml, 2001).

Therefore, the direct implications of organizational culture are important in business efficiency. Increasing the quality of human resources, efficient exploitation of material resources and financial mean the achievement of provisioned levels of turnover, market share or value added.

Organizational culture, through its forms and manifestations (symbols, rules of behavior, customs, ceremonies, history, prestige and authority of managers and employees), influences and leads to a series of behaviors and attitudes so that employees can tap the full potential for achieving goals.

Teams made up of motivated employees for business increase productivity. Establishing such a team and creating strong relationships with a particular company could pose real challenges for managers.

The vitality of a team is an art (Bourdais, 2005). When within a company, decisions and actions revolve around the same objective, the result means competitiveness on all levels, thus ensuring development on the short, medium and long term.

A research in the relationship between the organization and its environmental opportunities and threats, as well as its strengths and weaknesses on the internal perspective, was made until what is today known as the SWOT analysis (Barney, 1993). Other measures of corporate performance measurement and therefore a competitive advantage have also been developed (Brown & Laverick, 1994).

Conventional measures developed include financial measures such as capitalization of assets, depreciation and undervalued assets, goodwill, brands and value added (Brown & Laverick, 1994).

A strong culture, of positive type, which meets internal and external environment requirements, is a contributing factor to increasing business performance through the beneficial influence that it has on the management system. Culture influences the conception of the centralization-decentralization report, on delegation, risk tolerance, staff involvement in decision-oriented strategic decisions.

Companies in Romania in certain failures occur, the elimination of which requires, above all, an effort to change attitudes entire research and innovation chain-implementation-production. For many Romanian companies was preserved traditional pyramid organizational structure with many hierarchical levels, which perpetuates barriers to communication, maintaining structural rigidity and reduces the ability to adapt to change. To avoid these drawbacks is also necessary rethinking ways to boost employee. Rewards should be based on the achievements of all functional departments and not only on the successes of individuals or departments separately.

In terms of topic, the author concluded that Romanian companies are dominated by crop type "role", which makes management practices often have strong bureaucratic accents with clear procedures, but rigid.

Culture of type "task" is better tailored to the complex and fluctuating environment, similar to the current one. However, the adoption of strong leadership change is needed, hence the need for elements of culture type "power".

Performing companies are defined by a high degree of adaptation of information systems on organizational structure, the existence of systems to motivate employees, reduced conflicts and adopt a proactive behaviour.

In author's opinion, the priorities of Romanian companies in the coming years would be to:

- Increase capacity to provide products at competitive prices subject to modernization and upgrading of productive and thorough understanding by employees of "industrial culture", characterized by professionalism, technological and administrative discipline, rigor, strict adherence to deadlines, care for our heritage;
- Development of innovation ability.
- Developing the capacity of marketing (promotion) in international markets.
- Attracting foreign direct investment, including the "green field".

Strategic orientations of the primordial gyrations during the same period will be:

- Increase of the existing market share.
- Entering new markets.
- Outsourcing of activities.
- Horizontal integration (mergers, acquisitions, joint-venture).
- Vertical integration upstream-downstream.

A strong culture, of positive type, which meets internal and external environment requirements, is a contributing factor to increasing business performance through the beneficial influence that it has on the management system. Culture influences the conception of the centralization-decentralization report, on delegation, risk tolerance, staff involvement in decision-oriented strategic decisions

In conclusion, the reasons for the success or failure of companies are multiple, but they are closely linked with the resources, skills and characteristics of the environment in which it operates.

In the context of the current economic and financial crisis is of vital importance to know the factors generating success for activity of companies and how they can be measured. The conclusions drawn as a result of the theoretical studies and, most importantly, practice undertaken may constitute useful suggestions for improving the activity of companies.

REFERENCES

Barney, J. (1993). Firm resources and sustained competitive advantage. *Journal of Management, 17*(1), 99–120. doi:10.1177/014920639101700108

Brown, D. M., & Laverick, S. (1994). Measuring Corporate Performance. *Long Range Planning, 27*(4), 89–98. doi:10.1016/0024-6301(94)90059-0

Davis, S. (1984). *Managing Corporate Culture*. Harper & Row Publishers.

Griffin, R. W. (1990). *Management* (7th ed.). Mifflin Co.

Harrison, R. (1987). *Organization Culture and Quality of Service*. London: The Association for Management Education and Development.

Hofstede, G., & Ochiană, G. (1996). *Managementul structurilor multiculturale: Software-ul gândirii*. Bucureşti: Editura Economică.

Huţu, C. A. (1999). *Cultură organizaţională şi transfer de tehnologie*. Bucureşti: Editura Economică.

Jones, A. P., & James, L. R. (1979). Psychological climate: Dimensions and relationships of individual and aggregated work environment perceptions. *Organizational Behavior and Human Performance, 23*(2), 201–250. doi:10.1016/0030-5073(79)90056-4

King, A. W., & Zeithaml, C. P. (2001). Competencies and Firm Performance: Examining the Causal Ambiguity Paradox. *Strategic Management Journal, 22*(1), 75–99. doi:10.1002/1097-0266(200101)22:1<75::AID-SMJ145>3.0.CO;2-I

Orlowski, D. (1982). *Die internationale Wetthewerbsf.* Göttingen: Vanderhoeck und Ruprecht.

Robbins, S. P., & Coulter, M. (1996). *Management* (5th ed.). Englewood Cliffs, NJ: Prentice-Hall, Inc.

Schein, E. H. (1985). *Organizational Culture and Leadership.* San Francisco: Jossey Bass.

State, O. (2004). *Cultura organizaţiei şi managementul.* Bucureşti: Editura ASE.

Zorleţan, T., Burduş, E., & Căprărescu, G. (1995). *Managementul tranziţiei.* Bucureşti: Editura Holding Reporter.

ADDITIONAL READING

Băcanu, B. (2006). *Practici de management strategic: metode şi studii de caz.* Iaşi: Editura Polirom.

Burdus, E., Caprarescu, G., Androniceanu, A., & Miles, M. (2003). *Managementul schimbării organizaţionale.* Bucureşti: Editura Economică.

Burnete, S. (1999). *Comert international: teorii, modele, politici.* Bucureşti: Editura Economică.

Câmpeanu-Sonea, E., & Osoian, C. L. (2004). *Managementul resursei umane: recrutarea, selecţia şi dezvoltarea profesională.* Cluj-Napoca: Editura Presa Universitară Clujeană.

Câmpeanu-Sonea, E., & Sonea, A. (2005). *Comunicare, conflict şi dialog în procesul managerial.* Cluj-Napoca: Editura Presa Universitară Clujeană.

Cătăniciu, N. et. al. (2009). *Productivitatate, salarii, ocupare şi conexiunea dintre ele din perspectiva integrării în Uniunea Europeană,* Călăraşi: Editura Agora.

Ciobanu, I., & Ciulu, R. (2005). *Strategiile competitive ale firmei.* Iaşi: Editura Polirom.

Deal, T., & Kennedy, A. (1998). *The Rites and Rituals of Corporate Life // The Manager's Bookshelf - A Mosaic of Contemporary Views.* Duluth: Harper & Row Publishers.

Deal, T. E., & Kennedy, A. A. (1990). *Corporate cultures: The rites and rituals of corporate life* (2nd ed.). Addison-Wesley.

Denison, D. R. (1990). *Corporate culture and organizational effectiveness.* New York: John Wiley & Sons.

Dygert, C. B., Jacobs, R. A., & Popa, C. (2006). *Managementul culturii organizaţionale: Paşi spre succes.* Iaşi: Editura Polirom.

Ghiţă, R. (2006). *Globalizarea firmei.* Bucureşti: Editura Economică.

Hoffman, V. (1999). *Management - fundamente socioumane.* Bucureşti: Editura Victor.

Huţu, C. A. (2007). *Cultură organizaţională şi leadership: fundamentarea capacităţii competitive a firmei.* Bucureşti: Editura Economică.

Ionescu, Gh. Gh. & Toma, A. (2001). Cultura organizaţională şi managementul tranziţiei, Bucureşti: Editura Economică.

Isaic - Maniu. Al., Mitruţ, C., Voineagu, V. (1999). Statistică pentru managementul afacerilor, Bucureşti: Editura Economică.

Isaic-Maniu, Al., Pecican, E., Ştefănescu, D., Vodă, V., & Wagner, P. (2003). *Dicţionar de statistică generală.* Bucureşti: Editura Economică.

Krugman, P. (1994a, March–April). Competitiveness: A dangerous obsession. *Foreign Affairs, 73*(2), 28–44. doi:10.2307/20045917

Labăr, A. V. (2008). *SPSS pentru ştiinţele educaţiei.* Iaşi: Editura Polirom.

Makin, P., & Cox, Ch. (2006). *Schimbarea în organizaţii.* Iaşi: Editura Polirom.

Manfred, F. R. Kets de Vries (2001). *The leadership mystique: a use's for the human enterprise*, Financial Times Prentice Hall.

Moldoveanu, G., & Dobrin, C. (2007). *Turbulenţă şi flexibilitate organizaţională.* Bucureşti: Editura Economică.

Moran, R. T., & Stripp, W. G. (1991). *Dynamics of successful international business negotiations.* Gulf Professional Publishing.

Navarro, P. (2009). *Sincronizarea strategiei de afaceri cu ciclurile economice.* Bucureşti: Editura All.

Nicolescu, O. (2000). *Sisteme metode şi tehnici manageriale ale organizaţiei.* Bucureşti: Editura Economică.

Nicolescu, O., & Mereuţă, C. (2007). *Avantaje competitive ale industriei prelucrătoare din România în Uniunea Europeană, Asociaţia pentru prognoze şi studii economico-sociale*. Bucureşti: Editura Bren.

Nicolescu, O., & Nicolescu, L. (2005). *Economia, firma şi managementul bazate pe cunoştinţe*. Bucureşti: Editura Economică.

Nicolescu, O., & Verboncu, I. (2008). *Metodologii manageriale*. Bucureşti: Editura Universitară.

Ogrean, C. (2007). *Coordonate manageriale ale competitivităţii firmei - o perspectivă globală*. Sibiu: Editura Universităţii Lucian Blaga.

Oţelea, M. (2013). *Cultura organizaţională şi competitivitatea firmei*. Ploieşti: Editura Universităţii Petrol - Gaze.

Pecican, Ş. E. (2005). Econometria pentru... economişti (2nd. ed.), Bucureşti: Editura Economică.

Petrescu, I. (1996). *Gândirea şi aptitudinile managerului*. Braşov: Editura Lux Libris.

Pfeffer, J. (2010). *Resursele umane în ecuaţia profitului*. Bucureşti: Editura All.

Pîrvu, F., Stănescu, A., & Lungu, A. (2011). *Management*. Bucureşti: Editura ASE.

Popa, I., & Radu, F. (1999). *Management internaţional*. Bucureşti: Editura Economică.

Popescu, D. (2010). *Comportament organizational*. Bucureşti: Editura ASE.

Porter, M. (1980). *Competitive Strategy. Techniques for Analyzing Industries and Competitors*. New York: The Free Press.

Porter, M. (1990). *The Competitive Advantage of Nations*. New York: The Free Press. doi:10.1007/978-1-349-11336-1

Reinert, E. S. (1995). Competitiveness and its predecessors—a 500-year cross-national perspective. *Structural Change and Economic Dynamics*, *6*(1), 23–42. doi:10.1016/0954-349X(94)00002-Q

Render, B., Stair, R. M. Jr, & Hanna, M. E. (2003). *Quantitative analysis for management* (8th ed.). New Jersey: Pearson Education Inc.

Robey, D. (1986). *Designing Organizations* (2nd ed.). Illinois: Irwin, Homewood.

Russu, C. (2003). *Economie industrială*. Bucureşti: Editura Economică.

Russu, C., & Hornianschi, N. (2005). Competitivitatea - criteriu determinant al procesului de integrare europeană and Experienţa Uniunii Europene privind măsurarea competitivităţii în Cursul de schimb şi competitivitatea in perspectiva aderării la Uniunea Europeană (pp.41-62, 63-126). Pelinescu, E. (Ed.), Bucureşti: Editura Expert.

Scott, B., & Lodge, G. (1985). *US Competitivenes and the World Economy*. Boston: Harvard Business School Press.

Sima, V., Gheorghe, I. G., Orzan, M. C., & Orzan, Gh. (2008). The Romanian Entrepreneurial Profile from the Perspective of Cultural Dimensions: A Case Study for Prahova County-Romania. *Communications of the IBIMA*, 4(8), 65–75.

Stoetzel, J. (1983). *Les valeurs du temp présént: une enquête européene*. Paris.

Uri, P. (1971). *Bericht uber die Wettbewerbsfahigkeit der Europaschen Gemeinschaft*. Luxembourg.

Vlăsceanu, M. (2003). *Organizaţii şi comportament organizaţional*. Iaşi: Editura Polirom.

World Economic Forum. (2008). *The global competitiveness report 2008–2009*. World Economic Forum Geneva. Retrieved from http://www.weforum.org/en/index.htm [Google Scholar].

KEY TERMS AND DEFINITIONS

Business Performance Measurement Systems: The formal, information-based routines and procedures managers use to maintain or alter patterns in organizational activities.

Competitive Advantage: A superiority that makes an organization better than the competition in the customers' minds.

Metrics of Organizational Culture: Those qualities that are shared by high-performance companies as the ingredients of a strong culture. Using these qualities as metrics to track, business leaders can finally understand whether their company is on the path to culture success.

Organizational Culture: Organizational culture, through its forms and manifestations (symbols, rules of behaviour, customs, ceremonies, history, prestige, and authority of managers and employees), influences and leads to a series of behaviours and attitudes so that employees can tap the full potential for achieving goals.

APPENDIX

Questionnaire on the Quantification of the Relationship Between Organizational Culture and Competitiveness of the Company

A. Company's Identification Data

1. Company's name
2. Company's year of establishment
3. Which is the form of organization of your company?
   a. SRL
   b. SA
   c. SNC
   d. Other, specify..............
4. Specify the ownership of the company:
   a. Private capital
   b. Public capital
   c. Mixed capital
5. Specify the type of activity that you carry out:
   a. Production
   b. Services
   c. Production and services
6. Number of employees in the last year
   a. Average rate of absenteeism
7. Turnover in the last year
   a. Profit rate
8. Market share held in the last year
   a. The percentage of returns/products/services refusals recorded in the last year

B. Organizational Culture

9. What is the modality chosen by the company management to communicate your decisions?
   a. It communicates you the decision, without consulting you
   b. It communicates you the decision, but it makes changes without discussing it with you
   c. First it consults you and then it adopts the decision

10. What is guiding the behavior of the employees within your company?
    a. The regulations that establish clearly what should be done in various situations
    b. Regulations are useful, but they are not sufficient in all cases
    c. The unwritten rules, because regulations are rather formal
11. What do you think is the best way to treat your customers?
    a. Equally
    b. You have to adapt to the customer and to his requirements
    c. Regular customers should be treated differently
12. How do you react when a new colleague is employed in your department?
    a. You provide support for a rapid integration
    b. You are reserved towards him/her as you do not know that person
    c. You treat him/her with indifference
13. Number of employments in last year within your company was:
    a. 0 – 3
    b. 4 – 7
    c. Over 7
14. What are the main reasons of employment?
    a. Business development
    b. High rate of resignations
    c. Seasonal growth of business
    d. Insufficient skills of the current employees
15. What was the number of withdrawals from activity in for last year?
    a. 0- 3
    b. 4- 7
    c. Over 7
16. Do you consider the vocational training:
    a. Useful for carrying out the tasks
    b. A way of enhancing the employees' loyalty
    c. A factor for increasing the expenditures
    d. A disturbing element of the production process
17. Vocational training of the employees:
    a. Represents a major concern of your company management
    b. It is done occasionally, sporadically
    c. It is of no interest to the company
18. If at the previous question you answered with 17.1, estimate the annual average number of training hours for each employee
    a. 8 - 16 hours
    b. 17 - 40 hours
    c. Over 40 hours

19. The percentage of employees with specialist studies for the position held is:
    a.   Less than 60%
    b.   Between 61% and 80%
    c.   Over 80%
20. During the last year were there any labor disputes within your company?
    a.   Yes
    b.   No
21. If you answered "Yes" at the previous question, how many were there?
    a.   1 – 3
    b.   4 – 7
    c.   Over 7
22. Do you think that the decisions having a major impact on your company's activity are adopted in case of?
    a.   High risk
    b.   Average risk
    c.   Low risk
23. The risk estimated at the previous question is determined by one of the following options. Choose the appropriate option for your company.
    a.   The company's image on the market
    b.   Direct competition
    c.   Labor productivity
    d.   Legislative-regulatory framework
    e.   The evolution of the national currency rate
    f.   Fluctuations in the company's environment (market, customers, suppliers, etc.)
24. Specify the modalities used by your company to ensure an efficient communication with society.
    a.   Social responsibility
    b.   Public relations
    c.   The activity of selling agents
    d.   Other, specify
25. If you answered a at the previous question, what was the amount of the costs for this activity for the last year:
    a.   1.000- 5.000 RON
    b.   5.001- 10.000 RON
    c.   10.001 – 50.000 RON
    d.   Over 50.000 RON
26. Specify which of the following features represent the strengths, respectively the weaknesses for the organizational culture of your company.
    a.   Average level of qualification

    b.   Accepted risk

    c.   Amount of the costs with social responsibility

    d.   Vocational training

    e.   Degree of stability of the staff

    f.   Number of labor disputes

    g.   Absenteeism rate

27.   Evaluate with a mark from 1 to 5 (1 – slightly important, 5 – very important) the way in which the following values are found in your company

    a.   Considerate treatment of the employees

    b.   The existence of transparent and open leadership

    c.   Ensuring the incentive organizational climate for increasing the skills and the productivity

    d.   Facilitating access to vocational training

    e.   Rewarding the professional performance

C. The Company's Performance

28.   Which of the following types of competitive advantages are tracked by your company?

    a.   Differentiation (quality of products)

    b.   The employees' performance

    c.   Reduced production costs

    d.   Quality and promptness of the service offered

    e.   Other, specify

29.   What do you think are the three (3) most important factors of success of your company?

    a.   Quality of the products

    b.   Staff training

    c.   Organizational culture

    d.   Innovation

    e.   Risk taking

    f.   Collaboration-cooperation relationships with other companies

    g.   Other, specify

D. Organizational Culture: Competitiveness Relationship of the Company

30. Order from 1 to 7 (1 – the most important, 7 – the least important) the following variables of the organizational culture with impact on the competitiveness of your company.

    a. Average level of qualification of the staff
    b. Accepted level of risk
    c. Amount of the costs with social responsibility actions
    d. Number of hours of vocational training
    e. Degree of stability of the staff
    f. Absenteeism rate
    g. Number of labor disputes

E. Respondent's Identification Data

Department
Indicate the period during which you worked within this company
Age
Gender

Chapter 6
Organic Markets, Participatory Guarantee Systems, and Community–Supported Agriculture for Sustainable Food Communities

Ozge Yalciner Ercoskun
Gazi University, Turkey

ABSTRACT

Local and organic food is of global importance and benefits our health, community, and environment. Today, people come together and build a food community to access local and organic food directly from the farmers under a chain of trust. It is an amazing opportunity to support small farmers and reach fresh produce. Organic markets, participatory guarantee systems, farm shares or community supported agriculture, work exchange, and other co-operatives allow us to connect with one another and perpetuate social and ecological sustainability. This chapter analyzes these direct organic marketing mechanisms and community building ways towards green economy. It demonstrates these cultures and gives some best practices in the creation of sustainable food community networks around the world. The chapter concludes with emphasizing the significance on the sociality and locality, thus contributing to the long-term goal of sustainable development and resilience.

DOI: 10.4018/978-1-5225-2965-1.ch006

INTRODUCTION

The production of organic food by environmentally friendly cultivation techniques (e.g. drip irrigation, natural farming, companion planting, crop rotation, composting) is a worldwide growing trend. The multinational seed companies push hard the governments all around the world to use their infertile and genetically modified seeds (GMO) by free trade agreements. That is a great threat against the food security of the world. The use of local seeds is forbidden by governments under the pressure of big international companies and western countries. The biodiversity of ecosystems are under pressure due to GMO's, pesticides and chemicals used in agriculture. As all the food is grown locally, the reduction of food transportation radically reduces the environmental impact of food chain. People living in a town can access high-quality organic food directly from producers. Organic markets promote an urban healthy lifestyle by enabling city inhabitants to be better informed and buy organic and safe food directly from farmers (Meroni, 2007). They also contribute to the survival of local producers, promote a conviviality not found in the city supermarkets and reconnect city and countryside.

The organic markets, which get only minimum support from municipalities and NGOs, provide new and alternative retail channels for small organic producers. Farmers can earn more and consumers can find organic food easier. Alternatively, in community supported agriculture (CSA) and participatory guarantee systems (PGS), fresh, organically grown and reasonably priced box of vegetables are directly delivered to the doors of the supporters. These services foster awareness of tradition, taste and the natural seasonal availability and healthy food. Being in touch with the surrounding region, getting the best from it and the luxury of receiving organic food to home bring the feeling of confidence to its provenance.

From global dependency to local sustainability, the shift towards more localized and productive living strategies is not a choice, but an inevitable direction for humanity. This chapter focuses on the organic markets and food communities towards green economy, enabling both community prosperity and economic sustainability. Organic markets abound with the vibrant colours, smells and sights that define the multicultural city, meaning organic markets are one of the best ways to soak up the local culture. In many examples, these markets are a meeting point and provide space for social relationships and interaction. This study examines the main features of an organic market for a vibrant space for the community. It also searches the users of the markets and their preferences. The organic market culture is defined and different types of activities held in the market are explained in this chapter.

On the other hand, there are some other direct marketing mechanisms for the organic or locally grown products such as participatory guarantee systems and community supported agriculture. Participatory Guarantee Systems (PGS) are local quality certification systems. The community certified producers who are based on a mutual trust, social network and knowledge exchange. Community Supported Agriculture (CSA) is another mechanism for communities to purchase local and fresh products directly from a producer nearby. It is built on a farm share. A farmer offers shares to the local people. Local people buy a share into the farm, they support seasonal products with money, and in exchange, they will receive a box of local, organic produce directly from the farm every week.

The objectives of this chapter are to demonstrate organic market culture, to analyze an understanding what PGS and CSA are and how they work and to provide operation information on how to set-up and manage them for being a sustainable food community. The chapter also gives case study insights on how different communities around the world have managed to develop flourishing local economies with PGS and CSA. Firstly, the importance of developing direct models for being a sustainable food community is defined following by the shift of consumer behavior in the context of green economy. Then the role of organic markets is emphasized, best practices in the creation of sustainable food community networks are given from around the world such as Brazil, France, USA, Japan and India etc. The next section specifically focuses on Turkish case and Turkish consumers, the rapid growth of Turkish ecological markets and best practices of PGS and CSA social networks in metropolitan cities in Turkey. The chapter concludes by an evaluation which is made on the significance on these social networks of sustainable food communities, thus contributing to the long-term goal of sustainable development.

ORGANIC MARKET CULTURE

Considerable confusion surrounding the term 'organic' still exists (Chryssochoidis 2000). While many consumers have heard of the term and are aware of its central features – namely, that it is chemical-free – most are unfamiliar with organic farming standards and practices (Davies et al., 1995; Harper and Makatouni, 2002; Hill and Lynchehaun, 2002). Furthermore, variables such as the level of market development, the use of other positively associated food terms (e.g., 'cage-free' and 'natural') and the product category (e.g., farmed salmon) can serve to heighten consumer confusion.

The term organic farming is referred to "an agricultural production management system which improves soil health, biological diversity of flora-fauna and animal husbandry through the use of organic inputs like composts, vermicompost, farmyard manure, bio-fertilizers, green manure, poultry manure, crop residues, botanical agents for control pest and diseases, natural energy conservation practices and low cost agronomic practices". The organic agriculture improves soil production capacity, soil biological cycles and biological activity which contributes for sustainable agricultural production (Murthy et al. 2014, p.249). The term 'organic' causes significant confusion. While many consumers are aware of the term and know that it is chemical free, they are not familiar with its standards and practices. Furthermore, the other positive terms such as natural, cage-free, chemical-free and without additives raise consumer confusion.

Organic food presents an alternative lifestyle to the interested people who are close to environmentalism, vegetarianism, and alternative medicine. Interest in organic food has grown rapidly and awareness about health and environmental effects of pesticides, genetically-modified organisms, and food safety is created by media. Organic food has a multi-billion dollar global industry with quick growth (Hughner et al. 2007). The popularity of organic foods and organic markets raises important questions of interest to governments, growers, distributors, retailers, planners, and marketers. Culture is one of the main factors that has an impact on consumer behavior, ideas and wishes. Behaviour is a learnt process and culture has power on the behavior in a certain group of society. Culture is the circulation of values, norms and traditions among society between generations. Health awareness culture boomed organic foods in the developed countries as change of eating behaviors. This caused emergence of the organic market culture as well.

Organic markets where organic food is sold are important sites of public space for many people, and serve opportunities for local economic development and employment. They create social interaction and connection, social inclusion, the meeting of different cultures and the improvement of a sense of community. There is a growing interest in the use of organic markets as meeting points for local communities, but research is needed to explore the economic and social success of some organic markets.

Today, organic markets play crucial role in local green economy, food procurement and place making. 'Third place' is a concept put by Oldenburg (1989) to find the diverse spaces where community is in spontaneous interaction. Markets are defined as spaces of informal contact, which bring different groups together and revitalizing community spirit (Morales, 2011). They provide social interaction, social ties, social mixing across groups and social inclusion. Social inclusion brings gender, age, ethnicity and immigrant issues. Social interaction can be defined such as a greeting between customer and stallholder or an extended dialogue between customers and stallholders. The organic marketplace can be a public space where marginalized people spend time and sell cheap goods. The location of the organic market plays an important role. If a market is in a poor location, badly designed, inaccessible by public transport, and not protected from bad weather, market success fails. A market strategy also needs that the market site is accessible, particularly to older people, people with disabilities and those with children, as well as providing a site that has good protection from the weather, seating, wide enough aisles and other attributes that attract customers to the market. For an organic market to function well as a social space include essential attributes were as follows (Watson&Studdert, 2006):

- **Attractive Features of the Site:** Variety of organic products that fits the need and taste of the community,
- **Places to Linger:** Cafes, food caravan, seating areas near to the site,
- **Access to the Site:** Access to public transport and relevant parking by automobile,
- **An Active Stallholder Community:** Connected stallholders,
- **Well Designed Physical Environment:** Layout of the stalls, wide enough aisles, protection from bad weather, enough seating, grocery cart, weighing scale etc.
- **Effective Management:** Well operated by city councils or associations.

Watson (2009) studied marketplaces in the UK and found that the market sites play an inportant role as social space across four dimensions: rubbing along, social inclusion; theatricality/performance and mediating differences. The physical layout of the market can make rubbing along easier where there are spaces for eat and drink, food van or buffets near the market. Social inclusion means active participation of marginalized groups such as unemployed, minority, young or old, disadvantaged or strangers to improve their living environment. Market places as a democratic public realm, serve a space for interaction, concerning the care of them. Performance and theatricality are the other social ties for the sales of the product in the market where the salesmen come together for a festive and enjoyable space. Many people from different origins, class, gender and sexuality meet and mix up in the marketplaces in day and night or different days of the week and they improve locality in that city.

SOLIDARITY ECONOMY

Solidarity economy is based on social economy which has many levels involving neighborhood economic organizations to the district, national up to global ones. This type of economy can be named as community or self-help economy that gives an opportunity to new social innovations, self-managed or voluntary trading and alternative exchanges. Pearce (2003) divides economy into three categories, first system is private and profit-oriented, and the second system is equal, public service-oriented. Third system refers to the social economy which involves social firms and community enterprises in local level, social businesses and voluntary organizations in national level, and fairtrade companies in global level. Workers cooperatives play important role at all levels.

Solidarity economy is a kind of social economy which is an alternative to conventional market-based competitive systems. It is created by a collaborative action of local people which try to re-define new economic practices of labour, knowledge and innovation, rather than profit-based competitive vision (Miller, 2010). Solidarity economy is alive with networks with cooperative spirit. The vision of these networks are built on trust, equity, diversity and ecological responsibility. Communities in the solidarity economy build cooperation culture. Rather than isolating, they foster mutual support and solidarity towards shared responsibility and directly decision-making. Instead of prioritizing profit, they encourage commitment for social, economic, and environmental justice. The main idea is summarized as: "alternatives are everywhere and our task is to identify them and connect them in ways that build a coherent and powerful social movement for another economy. In this way, solidarity economy is not so much a model of economic organization as it is a process of economic organizing; it is not a vision, but an active process of collective visioning" (Miller, 2010, p.3). "Cooperation and mutuality" are emphasized. "Economic and social justice" are accepted as priorities. The "responsibility to work towards ecological health" is a core focus. Robust "democracy" at all levels, placing people and communities as the active agents of their own lives towards weaving other values together. And finally, these values give a strong emphasis on "diversity and pluralism" which bring people, working together, towards sustainable economy.

In summary, solidarity economy is a way of thinking about the environment that serves spaces of hope and possibility for building a more democratic and sustainable economy. It is a network to imagine, discuss and create visions for another economy based on shared values (Miller, 2010). The economic principle that defines the networks within the solidarity economy is reciprocity. Reciprocity in organizations can be defined in three ways (Restakis, 2006):

1. In co-operatives, reciprocity is based on mutuality, where the enterprise is collectively owned by members for their mutual benefit, and in the social co-ops, for the benefit of the larger community,
2. In non-profits, the reciprocity is based on the distribution of surplus, to use for the social objectives of the enterprise.
3. In charitable and voluntary organizations, reciprocity takes the form of gift economy which offers resources or services for distribution to recipients, with no expectation of come back (Ercoskun, 2015).

Johnston (2001, p.47) calls "a conduit to a broader notion of citizenship, where an obsessive focus on individual choice is replaced, or at least supplemented with a broader notion of community, sustainability, justice, and democracy". Seyfang (2005) promotes direct marketing mechanisms as alternative models of sustainable consumption, including cooperative local distribution food systems, and non-monetary community barter networks etc. They will transform the meaning of sustainable consumption and intensity of everyday practices, and they will shift the consumer to prosumer by creating co-production platform.

Co-production is based on five main principles. First is that people from all ages can give a real work to the organic production in the farms. Second, volunteering should be honored as work. Third is reciprocity, that we give and receive help. This raises awareness that we need each other and improves a 'giving back' attitude. Fourth is social capital, we must invest to bring people together and support them to make a group in order to have positive results. And fifth is respect, that everyone's voice is equal and that there must be ways to understand when something does not work.

Alternative food networks or other direct marketing mechanisms of natural and organic products try to build relationships among producers and consumers. The community capitals framework put by Flora &Bregendahl (2012) shows the holistic idea of these networks. Built, financial, political, natural, human, cultural and social capital are the seven capitals which have impact on each other and build an useful outcome towards sustainability providing ecosystem health, social inclusion and solidarity economy.

The other direct marketing mechanisms of natural or organic products such as Participatory Guarantee Systems (PGS) and Community Supported Agriculture (CSA) are in the category of solidarity economy. They work as a cooperative and they exchange organic products. The exchange is between producer and consumer or prosumer is built on a direct and mutual trust-based mechanism (Birhala & Mollers, 2014). The main framework of these two parties fits the permaculture ethics which are: 1) care of the world, 2) care of the people and 3) re-distribute surplus with fair share (Mollison et al., 1991).

PGS and CSA are the alternatives to socio-technical regime and embeds organic agriculture in the local. Ther attempt to build viable, vibrant, ecological and equal relationships in the food chain networks. The vision is to encourage local food production and consumption, promotes land ownership, reduces food mileage and increase biodiversity which supports natural capital, build food communities towards social capital, trains consumers about healthy food which enhances cultural capital, shares risk between urban and rural people (financial capital), develops relationships with local government (political capital) and adds value to more knowledge, labor and produce (human capital). These fit to Flora&Bregendahl community capitals framework explained above. These systems such as PGS and CSA improve transition initiated by innovative stakeholders through change in the locality.

OTHER DIRECT MARKETING MECHANISMS 1: PARTICIPATORY GUARANTEE SYSTEMS (PGS)

Participatory Guarantee Systems (PGS) are known as local quality certification systems. The community certify producers which are based on a mutual trust, social network and knowledge exchange (IFOAM website). PGS initiatives are mostly small organic farmers and their customers are the local communities nearby. International Foundation for Organic Agriculture (IFOAM) supports PGS as one of the other direct marketing mechanisms and a complementary tool to third-party certification in the organic sector and promotes PGS to the governments. PGS started forty years ago. This organic quality assurance guarantee first evolved by the organic farming community in Brazil, South America. So-called low-cost system was successful and it has led to the registration under many national councils by NGOs, platforms or communities making sustainable agriculture (Shetty et al., 2014). Third party certification provide the development of local economy and build transparent relationships between farmer and customer. PGS initiatives verified many organic farmers around the world and details of the process vary by the country.

The key elements of PGS can be defined as (IFOAM website, Cerci, 2015):

- **Shared Vision:** A shared vision is needed between farmers and customers which is based on common principles and values on well-being, food security, farmers' rights and gender equality.
- **Participation:** The reliability of the production quality depends on the farmers, customers and third parties.
- **Transparency:** All management and procedures are documented and all stakeholders know the information flow, process and decision mechanisms.
- **Trust:** PGS advocates provide trust and reliability chain.
- **Horizontality:** No-one is on the top, there is no hierarcy but heterarchy.
- **Learning Process:** Mechanisms exist to support farmers, seals or labels define the organic status.

Social control works when a community feels responsible and a member of the network, there are pre-agreed decisions written by the moderators of the network and accepted by the members. The producer accepts improvement on organic production techniques to minimize the mistakes to be repeated. Knowledge exchange and capacity building for producers are ingredients of PGS. Some PGS initiatives have obligatory attendance to training at season. PGS supports the organic movement which will raise the demand for third-party certification. Organic movement involves low-income producers and prosumers. So, people in this community become aware of each other's need and purchasing power other members. In this process, the community can identify who is unemployed or incapable of working, then PGS can help people in need. Members of the system can pay a small amount extra for the low income families, all the share is carried by the community (Lamb, 1994). Also, the community can organize the leftover food go directly to families in need, food bank or societies for the protected children. The aim is that nothing goes to waste.

Moreover, PGS attract new or transitioning organic producers. The learning process and exchange of knowledge between producers and prosumers develops new techniques and improve organic farming. PGS producers have a certificate and a logo to present their PGS organic status. In some countries, PGS producers are on the internet and can be accessed through messaging systems.

The main focus of PGS is to support local and direct relationships between farmers and stakeholders. International organizations including IFOAM, MAELA, UN-FAO, encourage PGS as alternative means for small organic farmers to participate to a system of committed organic production and to provide more stakeholders with quality assured organic products. PGS have gained attention especially in 2012, UN Conference on Sustainable Development (Rio +20) (IFOAM website).

OTHER DIRECT MARKETING MECHANISMS 2: COMMUNITY SUPPORTED AGRICULTURE (CSA)

IFOAM defines CSA as a partnership and mutual commitment between a farm and a food community on producing and buying local and/or organic food. Community purchases a share of farmer's harvest in that season and they help the farm work, in return, the farm supplies healthy fresh produce to the community of supporters (IFOAM website).

URGENCI, the International Network of Community Supported Agriculture, describes CSA as follows: a local solidarity-based partnership between producers and communities, a framework to assist communities to collaborate with their producers to re-connect to the field where their food is grown. There are four components of CSA which can be drawn as (URGENCI website):

- **Partnership:** This commitment is between farmers and consumers during each season,
- **Local:** It is a local exchange to support a local green economy,
- **Solidarity:** It is a solidarity between stakeholders sharing advantages of healthy produce regarding the environment, health and culture. It also involves paying a fair price to the farmers to live sufficiently. It is a mutual deal to take the risks of the produce in that season.

- **The Farmer/Consumer Tandem:** It is a direct contact and an including trust without a hierarchy.

There are many models of CSA which are shaped according to the commmunity's requirements. For instance, in England, there are several initiatives such as whole farm CSAs, consumer supported box schemes, intentional communities community gardens and charitable programs. Therefore, CSA improves by developing novel local food systems. However, we can categorize such as (Soil Association, 2011):

- **Farmer-Driven:** Farmer organizes a subscription system. This is common in the U.S., In England, this is similar to the consumer supported box scheme, a vegtable box is sent to the addresses by the farmer but consumers are attracted to the farm by various activities.
- **Prosumer-Driven:** Prosumer is the combination of producer and consumer. Consumer becomes prosumer when she/he contributes to the local producing process regarding the environment and health (Ozesmi, 2016). Prosumers join or organize the scheme in contact with the farmer and select the product according to their demand.
- **Farmer Cooperatives:** Two or more farmers cooperate for giving a variety of products for their prosumers. This allows speacialization on the crops or livestock. There are examples of them in Germany and Japan.
- **Farmer-Prosumer Cooperatives:** Farmers build cooperative networks to supply different demands but prosumers can also co-own the land with the farmers to work together to produce and send food. Stroudco Food Hub in England is a model owned by farmers and prosumers, delivering local artian food and drink to the doors (Stroudco Food Hub website).

CSA system has many advantages such as (Soil Association website): a) farmers can get a safe income, b) farmers and prosumers have an equal responsibility and share the loss when crop fails c) it is an engagement and farmers can get feedback from prosumers about the quality of the food d) activities in the farm enhance solidarity and sociality of the community.

What drives households to join a community supported farm? The most important reasons in the studies are quality of produce, support for local farming, environmental and food safety concerns. Bougherara et al. (2009) rank some important motivations such as: 'getting fresh or organic vegetables', 'support local farms', 'respect environment', 'reduce packaging', 'knowing the origin of the food', 'making something healthy'. Some other reasons can be defined as 'sharing the risk between prosumers and farmers' and increasing the 'sense of community'. CSA supporters are active for the environment, they are against the pesticides and have strong interaction when buying produce. In summary, ecological thinking play a vital role in joining CSA.

A member in a CSA helps reduce food miles, she/he supports agriculture without chemicals. This type of agriculture improves water quality, creates healthy soil, increases biodiversity, and improves wildlife habitat and landscape. Financially, this support helps local economy, creates or saves local jobs, local and small farmers. Culturally, local agriculture and farming tradition in that area survives. Member's philosophical, spiritual and ethical values keep alive. She/he develops a personal connection to the local food and place. She/he accesses special produce, heritage species etc. Member can join tours, events or farm festivals. This is a connection to the land and participation to the social movement. Embracing human capital brings access to healthy nutritious and safe food. This is also a gate to organic, natural, fresh, and tasty food that is not genetically modified. Member can share her/his food preparation knowledge with others, she/he learns more about farmer, land, grow process and other realities of agriculture. Food storage or preparation techniques can be learnt from other CSA members and farmers. Ecological farming or animal production methods can be learnt more. Socially, this is the connection to the land with others. Member joins others to support alternative agriculture by making connection with local farmer and help build food community feeling part of it. Politically, member supports alternative forms of agriculture. She/he reacts industrialized agriculture and improves relationships with local food system advocates. She/he makes coalitions with the supporters of healthy food communities and develops dialogues with government and decision makers (Flora &Bregendahl, 2012).

CSA system has disadvantages such as (Soil Association website): a) if prosumers intervene the farmers so much, farmers can lose control on the organization, b) planning and program are needed for box schemes and activities c) prosumers can work in the field intensely and can cause inconvenience for the farmers. d) there is lack of training in farmers, both in terms of production and communicating with the prosumer groups e) there is a lack information and long-term commitment on the prosumers side f) there is a challenge of raising awareness in means of agro-ecology. g) the cost of local organic produce can be challenging, external costs, travel costs and health costs should be considered h) hard access to healthy food, large-scale corporate actors dominate the market.

BEST PRACTICES IN THE WORLD

In this section, best practices of PGS and CSA in the world will be summarized according to IFOAM and URGENCI database. IFOAM tries to update its database by global surveys. It is estimated that 109,317 farmers are currently participated in

PGS globally, 49,945 of them are certified through PGS. PGS are found over 72 countries, of these 20 countries have developed or developing PGS, 33 countries show cases and 19 countries have just operated PGS in 2015 (Figure 1).

IFOAM applied a survey to PGS initiatives in 2012. When creating statistics, it is not easy to distinguish PGS intiatives between producers involved and producers certified. So, the number of certified producers can be higher. In 2012, more than 31,000 small farmers involved in PGS. The Philippines was a pioneer country with 850 certified and 10,500 involved producers. The second country was India, with 2,512 certified and 5,370 involved producers. The third country was Brazil, with over 2,754 certified and 3,692 involved producers. Asia contains the highest number of producers involved in PGS, more than 3,860 certified and 16,000 involved producers. Latin America is the second continent with more than 5,600 certified and over 9,600 involved producers. More than 3,400 producers are involved in PGS in Africa. More than 2,000 producers involved in PGS in Europe and North America. These initiatives exist mostly in France, Italy, Spain and the U.S., and Canada. There are more than 170 certified and 250 involved producers in PGS in Oceania according to 2012 IFOAM survey (Castro, 2013). IFOAM online global PGS database is updated regularly (Figure 1).

Some PGS initiatives such as Sapphire Coast PGS in Australia and Sistema ABIO in Brazil promote learning and sharing cooperatively. Nature & Progrès in France, which is the oldest PGS, established in 1964, emphasizes the significance of

Figure 1. IFOAM PGS Database in 2015
Source: IFOAM website.

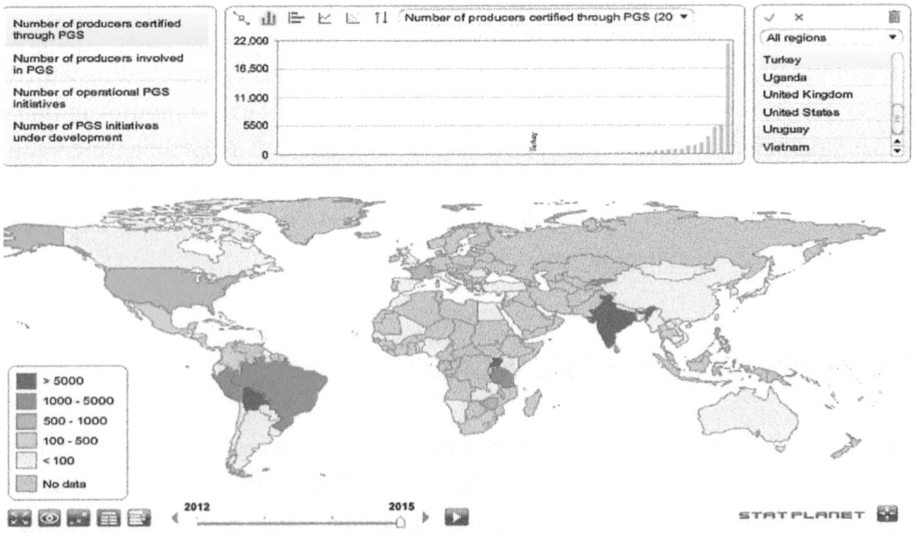

participation to knowledge exchange process which is a motivation for the producers. Organic farming techniques, traditional knowledge, and innovative practices are shared in a forum to share in this network. Moreover, local experiences, specific features of soil, traditional seeds, the climatic conditions and the market characteristics are practical for the producers. Some PGS initiatives such as Keystone in India, and MASIPAG in the Philippines use traditional seeds, practices and restore forgotten ones. PGS in Tanzania and India built farmer field schools. Some PGS use online platforms for sharing their knowledge and online manuals, publish online bulletins and forums such Certified Naturally Grown in the US or Sapphire Coast PGS in Australia. This facilitates the meetings and distance learning for sharing experiences and reaching PGS guides about efficient practices (Kirchner, 2014).

CSA started in the 1960s in Germany, Switzerland, and Japan. Some consumers and farmers built cooperatives to fund farming and pay the full costs of equitable and ecological agriculture. In Europe, many of the CSA-style farms were inspired by the economic ideas of Rudolf Steiner, and experimental farms were built. In 1965, the first CSA projects, called Teikei in Japanese, started against the loss of arable land. Jan Vander Tuin brought the idea to the United States in 1984 from Europe. He co-founded a CSA named Topinambur, located near Zurich, Switzerland. In the 1980s, its popularity spread over the U.S. and Europe. North America has at least 1,300 CSA farms, with estimates ranging as high as 3,000 (Zsolnai&Podmaniczky,2010). It gained importance in the 2000s. In 2008, URGENCI – The International Network of Community Supported Agriculture was established. URGENCI is the pioneer network for promoting CSA globally. CSA models have many different names in many countries. The food communities using CSA are listed in Table 1 (Henderson, 2010, Cerci, 2015 and related website adresses).

URGENCI made a study on the Mediterranean basin in 2016. Most of the countries in this basin transform into urban and industrial model rather than rural and agricultural character. However, the countries in the south and east shores like Morocco, Egypt, Algeria and Lebanon are still characterized by high level of employment in agriculture. The frequent model is small farming in these countries. The people living in the city are close linked to the farms through mutual trust-based networks. Lack of formal CSA partnerships cause irregular demand of food from these farms. In the north shores of the the Mediterranean basin, the demand of organic food is high in the industrial countries. URGENCI (2016) mapped the situation of CSA movement in the the Mediterranean countries. It divides the CSA movement into four types: 1. Mass movement 2. Consolidated movement 3. Experimental movement and 4: Embryonic movement, these ones also include ecological, solidarity-based food networks (Figure 2).

Table 1. The food communities using CSA around the world

Country	Year	Name	Numbers	Website
Japan	1975	Teikei, the Movement of the Japan Organic Agriculture Association	3,000 members (80% prosumers, 20% producers)	http://www.joaa.net/english/teikei.htm
France	2001	AMAP (Associations pour le maintien d'une agriculture paysanne)	226 registered AMAP groups around 570 farms and 40,000 prosumers	http://www.reseau-amap.org/
France	2011	La Ruche Qui dit Oui!	360 Assemblies with the support of 60,000 locals and 2,000 producers	https://laruchequiditoui.fr
UK	2011	The Food Assembly	10,000 members	https://thefoodassembly.com/
UK	1976	Box Schemes (under Soil Association)	20 producers	https://www.soilassociation.org/organic-living/buy-organic/find-a-veg-box-scheme/
Italy	1994	GAS (Gruppi di Acquisto Solidale)	600 GAS groups linking 10-80 families each	http://www.retegas.org/
Portugal	2002	RECIPROCO		http://www.comunidadesparticipativas.org/
Belgium	2006	GASAP	75 GASAP around 25 producers	http://www.gasap.be/
Germany	1988	Buschberghof	300 prosumers	http://buschberghof.de/
Spain	2007	Ehne Bizkaia	80 producers, 800 prosumers	http://ehnebizkaia.eus/index.php/es
Croatia	2002	GSR (Grupa solidarne razmjene)	15 GSR, 80 families	http://zmag.hr
Romania	2008	ASAT (Asociația pentru susținerea Agriculturii Țărănești)	33 producers, 180 prosumers	http://asatromania.ro/
Switzerland	2008	FRACP (Fédération romande d'agriculture contractuelle de proximité)	80-150 members	http://www.acpch.ch/la-federation/
Canada		Ontario CSA Farm Directory	More than 200 farms	http://csafarms.ca/
USA			4,000 producers, 150,000 prosumers	http://www.justfood.org, http://localharvest.org http://www.csaware.com http://www.agriculture.ny.gov/AP/organic/CommunitySupported.html
USA	1976	Farm Fresh To You	4,000 families	http://www.farmfreshtoyou.com/
China	2008	Little Donkey Farm	700 members	http://www.littledonkeyfarm.com/
SriLanka	2013	Good Market	160 vendors	http://www.goodmarket.lk

Source: Author's compilation.

Figure 2. Map of the situation of CSA movement in the the Mediterranean countries
Source: URGENCI, 2016.

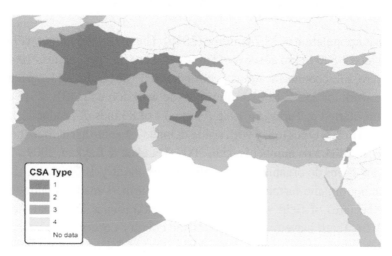

In Type 1, mass movements can be considered in France and Italy (Figure 2). These countries involve many partnerships such as GAS, La Ruche Qui dit Oui and AMAP (Table 1). AMAP movement has significant numbers such as 226 registered AMAP groups that account for around 570 farms and 40,000 prosumers. In some regions, 20% of the population is in the CSA network (AMAP website).

In Type 2, we can find well-established and developing movements such as Spain and Croatia (Figure 2). In Spain, CSA is one of the popular direct organic food mechanism, a farmers' network named Ehne Bizkaia in the Basque country is pioneer which involves 80 producers, 800 prosumers (Table 1). CSA in Croatia develops rapidly since 2012, reaching to 4,000 prosumers.

Type 3 is shaped by experimental initiatives in Turkey, Morocco, Palestine, Lebanon, Greece and Algeria (Figure 2). These countries accommodate some 1-10 CSA networks. Sharaka group in Palestine functions since 2000. 5 CSA intiatives plus 20 ecological solidarity-based groups exist in Morocco since 2008. There are many farms delivering box schemes in Turkey. However, three main PGS network are given in the next sections. The model in these countries are still developing, these experimental iniatives are trust-based, some are based on written contract, others are not and consfering fair share for all members.

Type 4 symbolizes embryonic movements in Egypt, Tunisia and the Former Yugoslav Republic of Macedonia (FYROM) (Figure 2). In these countries, some local and organic food movements, festivals function well. Nawaya, an NGO in Egypt, organizes farm visits and markets. The concept of CSA is known but there still needs some actors to activate and implement dynamically.

TURKISH ORGANIC MARKETS AND BEST PRACTICES OF PGS AND CSA IN TURKEY

Turkey has a population of 78.74 million (2016). The area of the country is 780,580 sq km, of which 9,820 sq km are covered in water. The GDP per capita is 10,444 USD. Agriculture still accounts for almost 35% of the GDP (2011). In 2011, agriculture still provided work for 25.5% (24.1 million) of the work force (TOBB, 2013). Organic agriculture started in Turkey in 1985 for export of 8 kinds of products, and then it is increased to 300 types today with rising demand. Organic agriculture began in 49 provinces in 2004, this number is 65 in 2009 (Karakoc & Baykan, 2009). Small and fragmented farms do organic farming all over the country. In 2002, 12,428 farmers were making organic farming. In 2011, 42,000 farmers made organic farming in 614,000 hectares of field with a yield of 659,000 tonnes (National Action Plan 2013-2016). Tenth Development Plan of the country covering the years of 2014-2018, aims to increase organic agriculture areas to 5% of total agriculture area. As seen in Figure 3, Aegean coastal provinces and southeastern Anatolia plains produce highest organic yield in the country. Major organic crops in Turkey are; cotton, wheat, apple, grape, corn, tomato and olive. Apple was at top of the list in 2004 and cotton was in 2008 (Karakoc & Baykan, 2009).

Figure 3. Distribution of organic production in the provinces of Turkey in 2010
Source: Proposed by the Author.

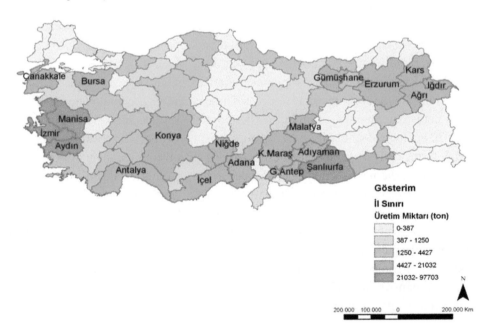

Industrial investments, mining projects, hydroelectric power stations, deforestation and depopulation of villages are the main factors hindering the development of clean, ecological food production. Governments have constantly tried to reduce the rural population. The Metropolitan Law of 2012 cancelled the village status of thousands of settlements and turned them into districts of the central, metropolitan municipalities, with potentially serious results for small farmers.

Turkey's first 100% ecological farmers' market was set up in Sisli, Istanbul in the leadership and coordination of the Bugday Association in 2006. Whilst there were 48 stalls at the beginning, in ten years, the number of stalls has gone up to 300. Since 2010, approximately 600 tons of fresh fruits and vegetables are sold every year on the Sisli farmers' market. The market is visited by about 500 visitors every Saturday. Today, the number of markets increased to 5 in Istanbul. The Bugday Association and Kartal Municipality opened a 100% Ecological Market in Kartal in 2009 (Sehirlioglu, 2015). The Anatolian side's first ecological market was designed as an attractive center. Fresh fruit and vegetables, cotton, pasta, bread, shampoos, cleaning products and textile products are sold on 200 stalls. 271 tonnes of products were sold in 2015 in this market. There is an ecological strawbale cafe, which serves as a meeting point for sustainable living workshops, discussions on ecology, art activities, and concerts. The market is controlled with Bugday's standards for 100% Ecological Markets in order to meet producers and consumers in a cozy space. It is open every Sunday and organic and healthy food can be easily accessed (Kartal Municipality website). Diverse ecological markets have been set up in Izmir, Eskisehir, Bursa, and Ankara.

The farmers' market retains its place mainly as a "producers' market" as opposed to a traders' market. The consumers buy directly from the producers themselves. Today, the farmers' markets that are founded by Bugday host a variety of organic certified products, ranging from fresh produce to packaged foods, textiles, cosmetics, cleaning supplies etc. They are closely inspected and supervised by Buğday's team of agricultural engineers. The farmers' markets host concerts, workshops, and seminars (Nance, 2012). The Bugday Association 100% Ecological Market Coordinator Batur Sehirlioglu said the association opened Turkey's first 100% Ecological Market in 2006: "We have been working since then to make these ecological markets a place where ecological life habits are popularized and people join in workshops and discussions. The markets was home to the first Ecology Book Days in 2012."

Why 100% Ecological Markets are popular in Turkey (Sehirlioglu, 2015)? The reasons can be listed such as:

- Ecological products are recognized and become prevalent in a fair, sustainable, reliable shopping model in inner market.
- It is a social responsibility project of the municipality and an NGO.
- Municipal services are beneficial to society and environment.

- Being role model to other municipalities.
- Innovative certificated food market raises the quality of public services.
- Well-known by the power of media.
- Variety of fresh products is sold directly from producer to consumer.
- Marketplaces are accessed easily; different income groups can be seen.
- Municipality can use this marketplace for sociality, education, communication, and cultural activity space.

In recent years, cloth bag studio, real cleaning studio, children play studio, drama studio, SlowFood children activities, book marketing activities, toy and child dress exchange activities, genetically modified corn activities, talks, films, and celebrations were held in 100% Ecological Markets (Figure 4).

Celik (2013) made a survey in the Istanbul 100% Ecological Markets. He found that consumers prefer organic products for health, nutrition and respect to environment. 200 respondents to his survey were average 35-40 years old, married with two children, graduated from university, public employees with a salary of 2,500 TL, who have their own residences and buy organic food at least once a week and the top organic food is tomato. So, organic consumers in Turkey belong to younger age groups, they pay attention to their children's health, they have high education levels and belong to middle and upper middle income groups. Azak and Miran (2015) made a survey on the Izmir-Bostanli eco-market. They found that respondents are aware of organic production and certification. They heard these concepts from newpapers and magazines. They preferred organic egg mostly. They found the prices high, the diversity is low. Organic consumers have problems with the durability and expiration dates. If there is more durability they will purchase more. Trust is another barrier, they would like to know if the product exactly comes from an organic origin (Mutlu, 2007). New meat and milk products, also baby products can be introduced to the organic market. The researchers suggest the municipality

Figure 4. Activities in 100% ecological markets
Source: Sehirlioglu, 2015.

for price arrangements, improve shopping volume, finding governmental subsidies for food mileage. The media can support organic markets with programs and advertisements (Yildirim, 2015).

Moreover, the Bugday Association gave impetus to CSA practices in 2006 with the Bahce (Garden) Project. Members received vegetable boxes to their door and paid to the association regularly. Guneskoy, an eco-village initiative in Ankara, started organic agriculture in 2005. A box of organic vegetables is delivered weekly to 100 families in Ankara in 2006. A variable amount of 8-10 kg of vegetables is put in a box and 28 different kinds of vegetables are served to the door of the supporters of project in Ankara throughout the season. In 2008, total production was about 15 tons in 0.7 ha (Ercoskun et al., 2010). Similar practices were developed in Izmir (Imeceevi) and Cengelkoy, Istanbul. There are around 10 CSAs and/or Ecological Solidarity-based Partnerships in Turkey including those led by the Yeryuzu Association in Istanbul, and many small groups around Izmir. There are around 1,000 people who get a share from one of these 10 initiatives (Temurcu, 2016). These prosumers mostly know the producer in person or have direct relation with him-her. CSA communities build solidarity in growing and consuming fresh, natural or organic produce. The prosumers support producers with pre-payment, they try to reduce food mileage and reduce transportation costs by making collective orders and logistics. CSA communities try to protect traditional seeds, these CSAs can be sometimes producer and sometimes prosumer-initiated. Turkish people, in a transition from rural to industrial society, have generally contacts with their parents, relatives or friends in their villages. These relatives send fresh local food to them to the cities. When urban-dwellers visit their villages on holidays, they turn back with large amount of food to home. This seems an agriculture-supported community. Sometimes workers at companies or institutions make collective order of local food like honey, hazelnut, olive oil or cereal from their villages regularly. When producers are in the network of email list or in the social media, they can access to more prosumers. When they present their product lists, serve easiest ways of orders and delivery, they can benefit more. CSA models of Guneskoy, which were producer initiated, worked well in recent years. This initiative had organic production and simple contract including CSA principles for the season. Other initiatives are built on a mutual trust, close relationship and prosumers make pre-payment or contribute to other costs.

All CSA initiatives in Turkey emphasize the value of ecological production without chemicals, artificial fertilizers and care of soil and environment. Some of the producers make natural production which means traditional small-scale no-chemical farming and free-range naturally-grown husbandry. Producers apply agro-ecological techniques, permaculture principles and Fukuoka style natural agriculture. Turkey is still a fertile place with clean resources for CSA initiatives who come together, learn from each other and make plan collectively. Urban dwellers protect their contacts with the villages which are valuable. Young people work in the cities but sometimes they turn to the villages and start to make small scale farming. This learning process needs time and energy (Temurcu, 2016). Although some grants or credits proposed for organic production and national policies are drawn for large-scale mono-cultural production. These can be overcome with sufficient legislation and regulations for small scale producers. The credits can be proposed to the farmers who can offer education and practice programs for the starters. More CSAs are necessary for supporting people to create more solutions.

PGS is a new model for Turkey. In 2009, two initiatives emerged, the BU-KOOP in Istanbul (a cooperative) and the DBB group in Ankara. Then the CAYEK in Canakkale was established in 2013. The DBB and the CAYEK are counted as PGS. The BU-KOOP is similar to an eco-coop that provides logistics with a small sales center. The DBB promotes the formation of small CSA groups, and there are a number of food communities under it. Relatively recent producer driven groups include the Tahtaciorencik Village Ecological Living Collective (TADYA) in Ankara, and the Bayramic Yenikoy in Canakkale (Temurcu, 2016).

The Ecological Life Initiative-CAYEK has been organizing activities gathering environment-friendly producers together since 2012 (CAYEK website). Group members meet in every two weeks, they communicate via social media and organize organic agriculture activities. Their Facebook profile contains over 1,700 members. They have mailing list and internet shopping possibility. They have amoderator committee of 8 people. Their product categories can be listed as fresh vegetable and fruit, cereal, jam, tomate paste, animal products, cleaning products and olive products. The CAYEK members aim to respect to food, restore air, water and soil. Their producers are sustainability-sensitive and climate- friendly. Their producers try to improve soil with organic production and reduce erosion. They use efficient amount of water, collect rainwater. They use natural and tradition solutions and regard biodiversity with the support of bio-cycles. They aim to use renewables and make recycling. The controllers of then CAYEK visit their member farms regularly and fill some forms including categories of land management, soil efficiency, water use, weed, insects, diseases, seeds, buffer zones and biodiversity. A summary report is presented to the all CAYEK members emphasizing the importance of soil and water efficiency, biodiversity protection, natural production without pesticides-herbicides, use of traditional seeds in the member farms (Gidatopluluklari website).

The DBB (Natural Food, Conscious Nutrition Group) is a PGS group in Ankara, Turkey which aims to create mutual trust, enhace communication between producers and prosumers. The communication and coordination of orders are made with the mailing lists. This list has more than 1,200 members living in Ankara who are sometimes active (Temurcu, 2015) since 2011. Almost 30 producers are registered in the DBB from Central Anatolia, Aegean, and West Mediterranean Regions. Prosumers can be the member of the maling list and obey the participation rules. There is a committee of 8 moderators who approve the participation, coordinate the orders and facilitate the communication. Producers serve a presentation file stating the natural or organic production and opening their farms to the members. Prosumers take the responsibility for all the operation processes, they are encouraged to take part in the production, bulk orders, transportation and visits, the feedback is important for the producers and products. Annual meetings are held and working groups present their observations and studies. Regular surveys are made in the mailing lists for the satisfaction of the members. Prosumers sometimes have complaints on shipping costs, delivery of the production and damaged product. They have dreams or plans to be a producer. The DBB made collaborative activities with the SlowFood Ankara, the Doga Association, and the Bugday Association. The moderators published their news in popular magazines and newspapers. They organize tours to the villages near Ankara, some of the producers have stalls in Ayranci organic market in Ankara (DBB website). This large and flexible network works well in Ankara which has a heterarchical structure, no formal platform and sincere intraction between rural and city people.

The BUKOOP (Bogazici Members of Consumer Cooperative) was established in 2009 by a group of academics and campus employees of Bogazici University, Istanbul. They found many producers making natural or organic agriculture and organized pre-orders from them. There is a small sales center about 40 sqm in the north campus who can buy natural or organic vegetables, fruit, animal products, cereal, jam, tomato paste, olive oil, honey etc. (Figure 5). All these products can be ordered through their website as well. The BUKOOP is different from the CAYEK and the DBB explained above. It has a formal cooperative status, which has cooperative members. It is a product based on internet shopping system. The attractive side is the voluntary system operating the sales center. It is a non-profit organization formed by students, academic, and administrative staff who open the sales center, coordinate the products, place them to the shelves, operate the financial records and make payments, announcements to the members. 20 core teams of 50 volunteers make nearly 500 people in cooperative groups (BUKOOP website). The work-sharing is made by the members in charge of products, shift is organized for the sales center and packaging activities are held in this center. The BUKOOP cooperates with women associations such as the Yasamevi Women Solidarity Association in Sanliurfa, the Karapurcek Women Association in Balikesir, and other village cooperatives such as the Vakifli Village Agricultural Development Cooperative in

Hatay and the Sindi Village Agricultural Development Cooperative in Datca. They have collaborative work with the Tohumizi Association and the Ciftci-Sen, make talks and field visits, and provide a participatory guarantee system for developing self-control mechanisms (Dalli, 2015). The BUKOOP publishes a bulletin, and has an active Facebook and a Twitter account and small videoclips in Youtube for explaining their voluntary system (Figure 5).

CONCLUSION

Many developing societies in the agrarian relations face important problems in terms of their conditions of survival within the developing tendencies of capitalistic changes that are undergoing. The commercialization of the inputs that are needed for production and consumption and the integration of the villagers/producers to the extending markets through producing agricultural products and consuming industrial products force villagers to sustain their life more and more through the means of commercial relations, big seed firms, and extending cash economy. The conventional agriculture made by globalized firms, wholesale market legislations, and seed act impede organic food producers in the developing countries. It is not possible to reach ecological sustainability and social interaction by globalized firms, which aim to increase their profits, international competitiveness and economic growth. It can be succeeded by small local communities to meet their requirements from local resources. This will happen if communities develop economic cultures to improve their quality of life within the limits of their own locales, while building the integrity and stability of the ecological world. So, organic markets, PGS, CSA or any kind of other alternative techniques of distributing and selling healthy food gain more importance.

Figure 5. BUKOOP website (bukoop.org) and sales center in the campus
Source: Captured by Author.

Organic marketplaces provide space for civic and economic synergies between local authorities, NGOs, producers and the community. These places serve the variety of food from nature directly to city environment. This contributes to community health, producer welfare, food system protection. It also enhances locality, sociality, creative, and recreative environment. A vibrant organic market can be perceived as a catalyser for the community empowerment with positive feedbacks in civic, economic and social life. It also raises ecological awareness. New habits emerge such as bringing cloth bags to the marketplace, composting, recycling, prefering reusables, and reacting to GMOs etc. After creating synergy between city inhabitants and villagers in the organic markets, some other gains are listed below:

- Contribute to personal growth, community building and service to the Earth.
- Find a group of committed people for a network who will leave behind their egos.
- Involve everybody, both villagers and city inhabitants in the transition.
- Trust the process, be consistent, celebrate the successes.
- Build a bridge to local government.
- Disseminate ideas, build social networks between old and young, rural, and city people.
- Everyone is equal (horizontal and heterarchical approach, no hierarchical and no top to bottom).

These direct mechanisms to access organic food aim to raise awareness of adults and children for consuming organic food in the cities, learning the process of organic cultivation and to create shortest communication link between producers and consumers. If people take part in the production, the added value for them is that they know what they get, where it comes from etc and this induces the social cohesion and the sense of responsibility towards the environment. They become prosumers.

Increasing prosumer involvement depends on the number of consumers taking part and social responsibility for the food they consume. Producers should raise awareness on this demand and leave profit based vision and see the demands of local market and produce in a more efficient way. Cooperation between PGS or CSA members can be increased when the production risks are shared and return to conventional market is prevented. The problem of low volume of products can be solved by involving more producers to the network. However, the differentiatin of natural, organic or conventional products should be made carefully by the controllers. Also the prices of these products can be regulated by a share fund. Purchase of food and packaging, food mileage and cold chain facilities are the other important issues for the prosumers.

Prosumers can get food from different farms, share their ideas, improve community activities and create a share fund. PGS or CSA communities can participate to the courses about social community, responsibiliy, solving complex problems, and networking. Experience sharing programs, mentoring and training activities in permaculture or agroecology assist building learning from other networks. Producer empowerment is one of the key issues in PGS or CSA. This means increase in skills and knowledge, personal growth and strengthening self-confidence. Women in organic markets, PGS or CSA are empowered when they have equal access to the training and technical support. Knowledge exchange directly contributes to this producer empowerment. This exchange can be made as producer to producer on natural or organic practices, or producer to prosumer or vice versa which contribute to traditional knowledge, dissemination and empower producers to use local inputs and breeds regarding natural resource management in these communities. Use of traditional seeds, breeding local species, organic input production, agroforestry, biodiversity enhacement with variety of cultivated species, vermicompsting, mulching, rainwater swales, and other permaculture techniques used in PGS or CSA network contribute to the long-term goal of sustainable development and resilience. One important issue is the producer access of PGS or CSA should not be limited and all producers benefit these networks equally. Well-established networks provide support and inspition to other iniatives which are under development. The tools of flexible iniatives can be adaptable to other contexts. In this way, sharing these experiences contribute to organic agricultural practices.

Farms of the producers attract the communities as meeting points and encourage organic farming, community gardening etc. International organizations such as FAO, IFOAM and URGENCI play important role to raise awareness of local and national governments and support them to build food communities or giving space for these partnerships. Local governments can promote PGS or CSA and local food platform sor food policy councils to become prevalent in schools, hospitals, and homes for the elderly and other social service facilities.

Today's global economic model succeeds in creating competition by dividing people from one another. To build cooperative, and harmonious societies we need an approach that creates more opportunities for people from different places and ages to interact- work together, and have fun together. A healthy society is one that encourages close ties and mutual interdependence, granting each individual a net of unconditional emotional support.

REFERENCES

AMAP website, Associations pour le maintien d'une agriculture paysanne. (n.d.). Retrieved July 23, 2016, from http://www.reseau-amap.org/

Azak, S., & Miran, B. (2015). *Turk Tuketicilerin Organik Pazara ve Organik Urunlere Yonelik Davranislarinin Analizi: Izmir Ornegi.* Retrieved July 23, 2016 from http://www.eto.org.tr/?p=1341

Birhala, B., & Mollers, J. (2014, August). *Community Supported Agriculture in Romania: Solidarity partnerships as viable innovations for small farms?* Paper presented at the EAAE 2014 Congress 'Agri-Food and Rural Innovations for Healthier Societies'. Ljubljana.

Bougherara, D., Grolleau, G., & Mzoughi, N. (2009). Buy local, pollute less: What drives households to join a community supported farm? *Ecological Economics*, *68*(5), 1488–1495. doi:10.1016/j.ecolecon.2008.10.009

BUKOOP website. (n.d.). Retrieved July 26, 2016, from http://www.bukoop.org

Castro, F. (2013). *Overview of Participatory Guarantee Systems in 2012.* The World of Organic Agriculture and Emerging Trends 2013. Retrieved July 28, 2016, from https://shop.fibl.org/fileadmin/documents/shop/1606-organic-world-2013.pdf

CAYEK website. (n.d.). Retrieved July 26, 2016, from http://www.cayek.org, https://www.facebook.com/groups/cayekcanakkale/

Celik, S. (2013). Kimler, neden organik gida satin aliyor? Bir alan arastirmasi. *Selcuk University Journal of Institute of Social Sciences*, *30*, 93–108.

Cerci, A. (2015, June). *Gida Hakkı ve Gida Topluluklari.* Paper presented at 3rd Ankara Ecological Society and Living Days, Ankara.

Dalli, C. M. (2015, June). *Kentte Alternatif bir Örgütlenme Modeli: BuKoop.* Paper presented at 3rd Ankara Ecological Society and Living Days, Ankara.

DBB website, Dogal Besin, Bilincli Beslenme. (n.d.). Retrieved July 26, 2016, from https://ankaradbb.wordpress.com/

Ercoskun, O. Y. (2015). Creating Resilient Communities: Local Currencies and Time. In A. J. Vasile, I. R. Andrea, & T. R. Adrian (Eds.), *Green Economic Structures in Modern Business and Society* (pp. 1–19). Hershey, PA: Information Science Publishing. doi:10.4018/978-1-4666-8219-1.ch001

Ercoskun, O. Y., Gokmen, A., & Gokmen, I. (2010). Can We Create Networks For Sustainable Living In Our Cities and Villages? In *Proceedings of International Conference on Organic Farming In Scope of Environmental Problems* (pp.181-190). Gazi Magosa, the Turkish Republic of Northern Cyprus: EMCC Press.

Flora, C. B., & Bregendahl, C. (2012). Collaborative community-supported agriculture: Balancing community capitals for producers and consumers. *Int. Jrnl. of Soc. of Agr. & Food*, *19*(3), 329–346.

Gidatopluluklari website. (n.d.). Retrieved July 28, 2016, from http://gidatopluluklari. org/

Henderson, E. (2010, February). *The World of Community Supported Agriculture*. Paper presented at Urgenci Kobe Conference. Retrieved July 28, 2016, from http:// www.chelseagreen.com/blogs/elizabeth-henderson-the-world-of-community-supported-agriculture/

Hughner, R. S., McDonagh, P., Prothero, A., Shultz, C. J., & Stanton, J. (2007). Who are organic food consumers? A compilation and review of why people purchase organic food. *Journal of Consumer Behaviour*, *6*(2-3), 94–110. doi:10.1002/cb.210

IFOAM website. (n.d.). Retrieved May 29, 2016, from http://www.ifoam.bio/en/organic-policy-guarantee/participatory-guarantee-systems-pgs

Johnston, J. (2001). Consuming social justice: Shopping for fair-trade chic. *Arena Magazine*, *51*, 42–47.

Karakoc, U., & Baykan, B. G. (2009). *Turkiye'de Organik Tarım Gelisiyor*. BETAM Research Note, 35, Bahcesehir Uni., Istanbul.

Kartal Municipality website. (n.d.). Retrieved July 26, 2016, from http://en.kartal. bel.tr/content/projects-ecological-market.aspx

Kirchner, C. (2014, October) *Participatory Guarantee Systems (PGS) Practitioners*. Paper presented at IFOAM Organic World Congress, Istanbul.

Lamb, G. (1994). Community supported agriculture. *Threefold Review*, *11*, 39–43.

Meroni, A. (2007). *Creative Communities: People inventing sustainable ways of living*. Milan: Edizioni Poli.Design.

Miller, E. (2010). Solidarity Economy: Key Concepts and Issues. In E. Kawano, T. Masterson, & J. Teller-Ellsberg (Eds.), *Solidarity Economy I: Building Alternatives for People and Planet* (pp. 1–12). Amherst, MA: Center for Popular Economics.

Mollison, B., Slay, R. M., Girard, J. L., Bourgignon, C., & Bourguignon, L. (1991). *Introduction to permaculture*. Tyalgum, Australia: Tagari Publications.

Morales, A. (2011). Marketplaces: Prospects for social, economic, and political development. *Journal of Planning Literature*, *26*(1), 3–17. doi:10.1177/0885412210388040

Murthy, R. S., Mazumdar, P., Rani, M., Tabassum, S., & Chandra, K. (2014). Rapid Growth of Eco-friendly Low Cost Sustainable Organic Agriculture Production Systems in the World. In P. K. Shetty, C. Alvares, & A. K. Yadav (Eds.), *Organic Farming and Sustainability* (pp. 249–258). Bangalore: NIAS Books and Special Publications.

Mutlu, N. (2007). *Consumer attitude and behavior towards organic food: Cross-cultural study of Turkey and Germany* (Unpublished master thesis). Institute for Agricultural Policy and Markets, Universitat Hohenheim, Germany.

Nance, G. A. (2012). Organic Farming in Turkey and the Contribution of Bugday to the Sector's Development. *The World of Organic Agriculture 2012, Europe Country Report: Turkey* (pp. 221-225). Retrieved July 26, 2016, from http://www.organic-world.net/fileadmin/documents/yearbook/2012/altin-2012-turkey-221-225.pdf

National Action Plan on Organic Agriculture 2013-2016, Turkey. (n.d.). Retrieved July 26, 2016, from http://www.tarim.gov.tr/BUGEM/Belgeler/Bitkisel%20%C3%9Cretim/Organik%20Tar%C4%B1m/UlusalEylemPlan-2013-2016.pdf

Oldenburg, R. (1989). *The Great Good Place: Cafes, Coffee Shops, Community Centers, Beauty Parlors, General Stores, Bars, Hangouts and How They Get Through The Day*. New York: Paragon House.

Ozesmi, U. (2016). *TEDxReset Talks Prosumer Economy for a Future*. Retrieved June 13, 2016, from, https://www.youtube.com/watch?v=8ceCiWie0lM&feature=share

Pearce, J. (2003). *Social Enterprise in Any Town*. Calouste Gulbenkian Foundation.

Restakis, J. (2006). *Defining the Social Economy-the BC context*. Prepared for BC Social Economy Roundtable. Retrieved November 23, 2016, from, http://bcca.coop/sites/bcca.coop/files/u2/Defining_Social_Economy.pdf

Sehirlioglu, B. (2015). *%100 Ekolojik Pazar*. Retrieved March 24, 2016, from http://ekolojikpazar.org/author/batur/page/2/

Seyfang, G. (2005). Shopping for sustainability: Can sustainable consumption promote ecological citizenship? *Environmental Politics*, *14*(2), 290–306. doi:10.1080/09644010500055209

Shetty, P. K., Alvares, C., & Yadav, A. K. (Eds.). (2014). Organic Farming and Sustainability. National Institute of Advanced Studies, Bangalore, India.

Soil Association. (2011). *The impact of community supported agriculture.* Retrieved July 26, 2016, from http://www.communitysupportedagriculture.org.uk/wp-content/uploads/2015/03/The-impact-of-community-supported-agriculture.pdf

Soil Association website. (n.d.). Retrieved July 26, 2016, from https://www.soilassociation.org/

Stroudco Food Hub website. (n.d.). Retrieved July 20, 2016, from http://www.stroudco.org.uk/how-it-works/

Temurcu, C. (2015, June). *DBB- Ankara'da bir aracisiz dogal urun orgutlenmesi/ katilimci onay sistemi modeli.* Paper presented at 3rd Ankara Ecological Society and Living Days, Ankara.

Temurcu, C. (2016). *Turkey. Mapping Local and Solidarity-Based Partnerships Between Producers and Consumers In The Mediterranean Basin.* Retrieved July 26, 2016, from http://urgenci.net/wp-content/uploads/2016/03/UR_Med-MAPPING_RESULTS-0416.pdf

TOBB. (2013). *Turkey Agriculture Sector Report.* Retrieved July 25 2016, from http://www.tobb.org.tr/Documents/yayinlar/2014/turkiye_tarim_meclisi_sektor_raporu_2013_int.pdf

URGENCI. (2016). *Mapping Local and Solidarity-Based Partnerships Between Producers and Consumers In The Mediterranean Basin.* Retrieved July 26, 2016, from http://urgenci.net/wp-content/uploads/2016/03/UR_Med-MAPPING_RESULTS-0416.pdf

URGENCI website. (n.d.). Retrieved July 26, 2016, from http://urgenci.net/the-network/

Watson, S. (2009). The Magic of the Marketplace: Sociality in a Neglected Public Space. *Urban Studies (Edinburgh, Scotland)*, *46*(8), 1577–1591. doi:10.1177/0042098009105506

Watson, S., & Studdert, D. (2006). *Markets as sites for social interaction*. Bristol: The Policy Press.

Yildirim, A. E. (2015). *Organik Pazar Arastirmasi*. Retrieved July 22, 2016, from http://www.tarimdunyasi.net/2015/07/22/organik-pazar-arastirmasi/

Zsolnai, L., & Podmaniczky, L. (2010). Community-supported agriculture. In The Collaborative Enterprise: Creating Values for a Sustainable World (pp. 137-150). Oxford, UK: Peter Land Academic.

ADDITIONAL READING

Allard, J., & Davidson, C. (Eds.). (2008). *Solidarity economy: Building alternatives for people and planet*. Lulu.com.

Brown, C., & Miller, S. (2008). The impacts of local markets: A review of research on farmers markets and community supported agriculture (CSA). *American Journal of Agricultural Economics, 90*(5), 1298–1302. doi:10.1111/j.1467-8276.2008.01220.x

Henderson, E., & Van En, R. (2007). *Sharing the harvest: a citizen's guide to Community Supported Agriculture*. Chelsea Green Publishing.

Lockeretz, W. (Ed.). (2007). *Organic farming: an international history*. CABI. doi:10.1079/9780851998336.0000

Lyson, T. A. (2012). *Civic agriculture: Reconnecting farm, food, and community*. UPNE.

Ritzer, G. (2010). Focusing on the Prosumer. In *Prosumer revisited* (pp. 61–79). VS Verlag für Sozialwissenschaften. doi:10.1007/978-3-531-91998-0_3

Schneider, K. R., & Schneider, R. G. (2009). Genetically modified food. Retrieved September, 26, 2010 from http://www.academia.edu/download/32482742/FS08400.pdf

Willer, H., & Lernoud, J. (2016). The world of organic agriculture. Statistics and emerging trends 2016 (pp. 1-336). Research Institute of Organic Agriculture FiBL and IFOAM Organics International.

KEY TERMS AND DEFINITIONS

Community-Supported Agriculture: A farm share for local consumers to buy local, seasonal produce directly from a farmer in their community.

Food Community: People come together and build a food community to access local and organic food directly from the farmers under a chain of trust.

GMO: Any organism whose genetic material has been altered using genetic engineering techniques.

Participatory Guarantee Systems: Locally focused quality assurance systems. Local community certify producers, built on a foundation of trust, social networks, and knowledge exchange.

Prosumer: The combination of producer and consumer. Consumer becomes prosumer when she/he contributes to the local producing process regarding the environment and health.

Solidarity Economy: Community or self-help economy that gives an opportunity to new social innovations, self-managed, or voluntary trading and alternative exchanges.

Third Place: The variety of places where community is practiced in spontaneous interaction.

Chapter 7
Approaches on Trends, Constraints, and Transformations of Romanian Organic Agrifood Market

Georgiana-Raluca Ladaru
Bucharest University of Economic Studies, Romania

ABSTRACT

In current economies, the organic agrifood markets have started to gain more proactive dimensions by volume, revenue, and demand. Analysing the trends, constraints, and transformations of Romanian organic agrifood market represents an actual research subject, which should be understood as a growing part of agricultural economics and marketing research. Starting from the general assumption that organic agrifood market represents a share of one percent and growing, the main aim of this chapter is to reveal the primary transformation and constraints from a multiperspective approach.

INTRODUCTION

In recent years, the organic market has followed an upward trend although many national markets worldwide have registered negative growth rates. Therefore, both supply and demand of organic products continued to grow (Burcă-Voicu, 2012). On most markets, the organic sector is part of the total trade, as the organic goods are sold to the consumers via the main market and store networks and specialised stores, like organic or natural stores, weekly markets or farm shops (Orboi, 2013).

DOI: 10.4018/978-1-5225-2965-1.ch007

But despite this global growth in consumer demand and sales, the organic food market is still relatively small (Hughner et al., 2007).

A pertinent and complex analysis of the organic agrifood market trends requires a third-factor analysis: the supply, the demand and the prices.

Regarding the supply, in recent times organic food supply chains have shifted from local and fragmented chains to geographically much longer ones, which has often involved multinationalization (The International Fund for Agricultural Development, Rural Development Report 2016). However, organic food supply is limited as compared to demand, which is why the prices of organic agri food products are sensitively higher than conventional ones. (FAO)

Regarding the demand, several studies confirmed that the consumer behavior regarding the purchase of food products is increasingly channeled and more focused on acquiring "healthy" products and having an "eco-friendly" way of life, while investing more in information and in maintaining their health through food and a "healthy" lifestyle (Burcă-Voicu, M, 2012). Regarding the socio-demographic profile of the organic product buyers, most studies agree that it is mainly women, who buy larger quantities and more frequently than men. Slight differences between gender groups are observed as regards their willingness to pay. The age factor does not seem to play an important role either, with the younger seeming slightly more willing to buy (more and expensive) due to their greater environmental consciousness (Arvanitoyannis & Krystallis, 2004).

Knowing the market factors of the agrifood organic products its a good start, but a solid evolution of the organic products market can only be achieved through the creation of trade policies that are tailored to the specifics of each region, taking into account several factors, including the degree of urbanization, the existing professional categories, the degree of influence of the environment and the sensitivity of inhabitants of an area facing this problem. Other studies show that organic food's share of total food consumption depends heavily on political regulation, including legal definitions and standards, financial support to farmers, and a national labeling system. Other important structural factors are soil conditions, an effective and efficient distribution system, and the size of the premium price demanded for organic food products. Macro factors such as the food culture and the culture's level of postmaterialism and environmental concern play an additional role (Thøgersen, 2010).

Following the premise shown above, the present study aims at carrying out an analysis of the organic agro-food products market in Romania, taking into account the increasing tendencies of the producers and consumers orientation towards organic agro-food products. Thus, the study is structured in four parts: the first part presents the analysis of the supply of organic agrifood products, the second part presents an analysis of the prices of organic agrifood products, the third part presents an analysis of the demand for agrifood products and the last part presents an analysis of the exports and imports with organic agrifood products. The study ends with a set of conclusions resulting from the analysis.

THE ANALYSIS OF SUPPLY OF ORGANIC AGRIFOOD PRODUCTS

The supply of organic products is mainly given by organic farming. The volume of supply also depends on a number of other factors, such as: climatic factors, technical factors, technical and technological development factors of production, production capacity, economic factors linked to price, cost-related economic factors.

At present, there are approximately 12,000 certified organic farmers in Romania, of which a high percentage is represented by individual producers, as well as commercial companies (agricultural farmers). Organic agriculture is present both in the vegetable sector (vegetables, fruits, cereals, soybeans) and zootechnics (sheep, cattle, poultry, goats, pigs, equines, apiculture).

As far as the number of processors is concerned, they are fewer than the manufacturers. The main weakness of the organic food industry is currently the processing, packaging and marketing of products. This gap of the industry is mainly determined by the high costs of industrial and packaging facilities that meet the standards of organic farming. Romania has a lack of processors in this field. The growing demand and the lack of processors in the country determine the agricultural organic products to follow external routes, and only a small part of this type of food is found on the domestic market.

The organic agrifood products that are processed are:

- **Vegetable Products:** Wheat, sunflower, corn, peas, soybeans, fruits (cherries, cherries, raspberries, blueberries, sea buckthorns, nuts, etc.);
- **Animal Products:** Eggs, milk, meat;
- **Bee Products:** Honey, wax, propolis, pollen.
- The main networks of stores that have introduced organic products into their range and have set up special spaces for such products are: Carrefour, Cora, Gima, La Fourmi, Mega Image. The best-selling BIO products through the organized trading network are eggs and dairy products.

Organic products in Romania are marketed in several ways:

- Farm gate
- Seasonal markets
- **Traditional Retail:** Specialized stores
- **Modern Retail:** Hypermarkets, supermarkets, cash & carry stores
- **Online Stores:** www.rangali.ro; www.organikshop.ro; www.biomania.ro - network marketing (Life Care); www.elemental.ro, www.farmacianaturii. ro, www.naturalia.ro, www.casamatei.ro, www.superbio.ro, www.pcfarm. ro, www.naturafarm.ro, www.bioatura.ro, www.naturalmall.ro, www. naturashop.ro şi www.naturaland.ro.
- Online Stocks for organic products (www.agricultura-ecologica.ro)

The offer in the organic food market refers on two categories of products:

- Biological and ecological food products resulting from strict adherence to certain technologies required to obtain these products;
- Biologically-imagined products that are intermediable between biologically-ecological food products and current food products (within these products can also be included the farm products or the products of the farmer).
- The annual growth rate of the European agri-food market is 20-40%. This increase is the natural consequence of the growing concern of consumers for their health and safety, with an increasing emphasis on the relationship between sustainable development and organic farming, emphasizing that the practice of this type of agriculture facilitates the realization of three categories of objectives, namely: economic, social and environmental objectives.

The evolution of the number of operators registered in organic farming and the evolution of the surface cultivated in ecological system in Romania is presented in Figure 1.

According to the Ministry of Agriculture, nearly 3200 organic operators were registered in 2010, with 1,000 operators less than in 2008. If in 2008 there was an increasing trend of the number of organic operators in Romania, the effects of the economic crisis in the near future caused a decrease in the support from the Romanian state and the need to produce a lot and inexpensively food, which led to almost 1 000 eco-producers in Romania in 2 years to withdraw or change their business orientation, as can be seen in the above figure. Looking in the next period analysed, in 2015 the number of registered operators tripled compared to the beginning of the analysis, respectively 2006, thus in 2015 there were registered over 12000 operators.

Regarding the processed organic agrifood sector, in 2012 there was a significant increase in the number of registered operators in organic farming, their number increasing five times compared to 2006 when there were 3409 operators. It is also

Figure 1. Number of operators registered in organic faming
Source: http://www.madr.ro/ro/agricultura-ecologica/dinamica-operatorilor-si-a-suprafetelor-in-agricultura-ecologica.html.

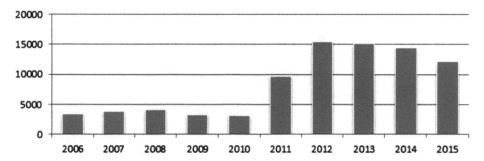

noticed that with the increase of the number of registered organic farmers there is also the diversification of the range of organic products including: products processed from cow and sheep milk, processed products from soy, sunflower oil, various assortments of bakery products, processed rice products, cereal flakes, herbal teas as well as organic wine. One of the reasons for the increase in the number of operators is represented by the existing of support measures for the conversion period granted on the basis of Art. 68 of Regulation (EC) No 73/2009, establishing common rules for direct support schemes for farmers under the common agricultural policy and establishing certain support schemes for farmers.

If in 2012 we could speak of a high level of operators registered in organic farming, we can not say the same thing in 2015 when their number decreased by 21%.

The above figure shows the distribution of organic operators in counties. Based on the analysis of the data presented, Suceava County has a leading position in this ranking, with favorable results in animal production, pasture and meadow. On the next place we find Mureş County, which records about 500 operators practicing organic farming. On the other side of the ranking there are Ilfov, Giurgiu, Olt, Vâlcea, Dâmbovița counties with a number of operators under 20.

Regarding the area cultivated in the ecological system in Romania, the evolution between 2006 and 2015 is presented in Figure 3.

In 2015, Romania is on the twentieth place at European level, with an area of 175571 ha, while at the opposite pole, with the smallest area cultivated in an ecological system, Malta is only 27 ha. Speaking of countries with a record area cultivated in the ecological system, we see Spain recording 1,410,531 ha, and then Italy with 1,093,646 ha.

Regarding the evolution of Romania during the period 2006-2015, it registered an ascending rhythm with considerable values from one year to another. The increase was achieved gradually excepting 2008 when was registered a decrease of 16%

Figure 2. Distribution of operators by county in 2014
Source: http://www.bio-romania.org.

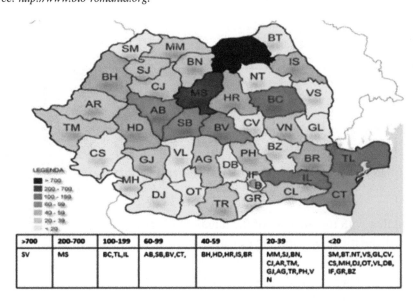

>700	200-700	100-199	60-99	40-59	20-39	<20
SV	MS	BC,TL,IL	AB,SB,BV,CT,	BH,HD,HR,IS,BR	MM,SJ,BN, CJ,AR,TM, GJ,AG,TR,PH,V N	SM,BT,NT,VS,GL,CV, CS,MH,DJ,OT,VL,DB, IF,GR,BZ

Figure 3. Area cultivated in ecological system Romania (ha)
Source: http://epp.eurostat.ec.europa.eu/tgm/refreshTableAction.do?tab=table&plugin=1&pcode=tag00098&language=en.

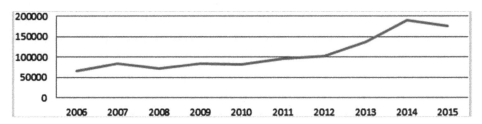

compared to the value registered in the previous year. The year 2012 represents the year when the area cultivated in the ecological system grows significantly, keeping the growth rate until 2014, and in 2015 it will register a 7% decrease regarding the previous year.

As for the year-to-year variation of the area, and analyzing in percentages, there is an increase of 29% in 2007 compared to 2006, when Romania has a total ecological area of about 65000ha. Subsequently, ecological agriculture is gaining, rising in 2012 by 30% respectively with 31496 ha, compared to 2008 when it registered 71597 ha.

Figure 4 shows the evolution of the share of ecological system surface from the total agricultural area used.

Figure 4. Share of ecological system surface from the total agricultural area used (%)
Source:http://epp.eurostat.ec.europa.eu/tgm/table.do?tab=table&init=1&language=en&pcode=ts
dpc440&plugin=1.

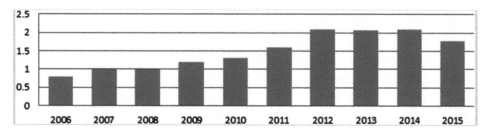

Analyzing the structure of organic products, we see that the highest percentage is held by cereal cultivation where wheat occupies a leading position in the ranking. The data in Figure 5 show that in 2007 the wheat-covered area occupies 8145 ha, and in 2011 the cultivated area grows significantly, being 21302 ha in Romania. The progress made by Romanian farmers is clearly observed - if in 2006 there are 7,175 ha of land on which wheat is cultivated, the situation is changing radically in 2012, this area trebled and registered an ascending rhythm until 2015, thus arriving at an area of 31800 ha of wheat.

Regarding the cultivation of other cereals, such as corn, barley, oats or rice, Romania does not have an unfavorable situation in this chapter, as the offer is constantly increasing especially in maize. From the table above, it appears that the area cultivated with maize in the organic system occupies the second place after the cultivation of the wheat.

Figure 5. The area cultivated in organic farming with cereals (ha)
Source: http://appsso.eurostat.ec.europa.eu/nui/submitViewTableAction.do.

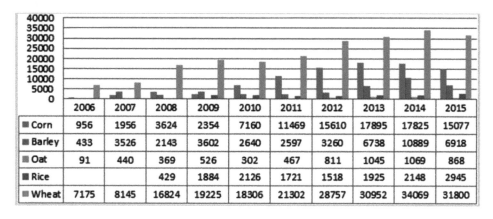

	2006	2007	2008	2009	2010	2011	2012	2013	2014	2015
Corn	956	1956	3624	2354	7160	11469	15610	17895	17825	15077
Barley	433	3526	2143	3602	2640	2597	3260	6738	10889	6918
Oat	91	440	369	526	302	467	811	1045	1069	868
Rice			429	1884	2126	1721	1518	1925	2148	2945
Wheat	7175	8145	16824	19225	18306	21302	28757	30952	34069	31800

Regarding the share of certified crops in the organic system, in 2015 the grain crops for grain production and permanent meadows (pastures and meadows) are placed first, followed by industrial crops. At the opposite side there are both dried protein crops for the production of grains and root crops, and especially fresh vegetables, melons, strawberries, mushrooms with a very low percentage.

Analyzing zootehnics sector in the Romanian ecological system, we see its growing trend. From the chart below we can see the high percentage of sheep breeding in 2009, namely 51470 heads, but the situation is not very favorable because in 2010 the percentage decreases by more than half. Later, in 2011 it will reach half of the value registered in 2009.

Regarding organic cattle breeding we notice a significant decrease in the level of 2010 when it registered 5,358 heads compared to 2006 when it registered with 6007 more heads. If we analyze the situation as a whole we observe a significant decrease of 40% in 2012 compared to 2006. Organic birds breeding represent another strength of Romania, in 2009 the number of birds being 9400 heads and in the following year its number doubled. In 2011 the number of breeding birds growed for five times regarding the value registered in 2009.

ORGANIC AGRIFOOD PRODUCTS PRICES

The price is an important factor on the market of any agri-food product and according to the National Federation of Ecological Agriculture in Romania presents the following prices on the organic agri-food market:

The prices of organic agro-food products start from 5 ROL and reach up to 30 ROL, depending very much on the specifics of the product. It can be said that the price of these products is at a very high level compared to the price of an agri-food product. For example, in the case of bakery products the price of a homemade bread produced in the organic system is 5 ROL / 1200 gr, and the one produced in the

Figure 6. The evolution of organic farming in zootechnics sector (heads)
Source: http://appsso.eurostat.ec.europa.eu/nui/submitViewTableAction.do.

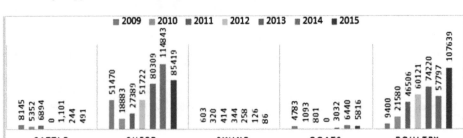

Table 1. Organic agrifood products prices (ROL)

Category	Product	Price of the Ecological Product (per Kilo)	Price of the Conventional Product (per Kilo)
Bakery and pastry preparations	White bread from home	20	14
	Bread with rye	23.6	9.2
	Cake with nuts	10	8
Fruits and vegetables	Apples	5	4
	Natural apple juice*	10	8
	Bananas	19.50	4.5
	Tomatoes	15	4
Bee products	Honey	25	20

Source: http://www.fnae.ro/ecoaliment3.pdf, cât şi date preluate din magazinul Carrefour.

normal system is 3,5 ROL. On the other hand, the price of bananas or tomatoes for example is much higher compared to the price of the same conventional product.

Demand for Organic Agrifood Products

Demand for organic goods and services is steadily increasing over the current period. In recent years, consumers have become increasingly interested in quality agricultural and food products. Quality products include products from organic farming.

One factor of influence of the organic agri-food market is green purchasing by promoting public authorities by positively influencing the industry for the development of these technologies. Organic farming is an essential contributor to economic growth and local and regional diversification and to the development of local identity and markets, thus contributing to the revitalization of rural and urban communities.

The intensive use of chemicals in the agricultural sector, both for fertilization and for crop cultivation, has led to a growing market demand for clean products from a growing number of consumers. This type of application is part of a more comprehensive and lasting movement, towards preserving and protecting the environment.

The consumer's benefits are the following: purchasing seasonal and fresh produce, knowledge of products and area of origin. For the producer, the main advantages are: profit growth, direct relationship with consumers, a new role of the farmer, promotion of local products / varieties.

Direct sale in all its forms is the most important selling channel for organic products for both the consumer and the farmer. There are different methods of direct sale: farmers in the city: local markets, buyer groups, promotional events etc; Farmers on the farm: the farm gate, agro-ecological farms, etc.

Direct marketing and farmers' markets are very important in rural areas, especially in combination with local agroeco tourism and restaurants. Retail markets can harness more products than healthy and environmentally friendly food stores and are an important point of contact for many consumers with organic products. Some supermarkets also have support initiatives for increasing the consumption of organic products.

Consumer demand for organic products is mainly focused on developed economies, and this can be explained mainly by two factors: high prices used to market organic food, in close connection with the purchasing power of consumers in these regions; the level of education and information on the benefits of organic products (food safety, environmental protection, health, etc.).

The growing demand for organic agro-food products was also due to the confrontation of the population with undesirable metabolic effects, which are becoming more and more frequent, the main cause being food imbalances. So, when the population faced nutritional problems, a large number of consumers chose the reorientation of behavior for cleaner and purer biological products.

The negative influence of the consumption of organic products is due to the high prices, so that in Romania a significant percentage of organic farming production is not sold on its own market.

The Romanian market for organic food products in 2012 had a value of aproximately 80 million Euros, half of this value coming from Romanian products, namely from honey, wine and bakery, and the other half of imports made by big retailers. The most demanding organic food is the fresh one, especially fruit, dairy, and cereal products.

Manufacturers and distributors are looking for solutions to succeed in expanding this market, from which it can be remarked: (Stanciu, 2008)

- The presence of products in major retail distribution networks;
- Constancy of supply;
- Competitive prices;
- Informing consumers of the benefits of using these products;
- Effective product promotion that will not create confusion among consumers but rather help them to better choose the products.

The largest export share isfor technical crops such as soy, sunflower, flax, followed by wheat, honey and other products. Annually, ecological products worth 130-140 million euros are sold, about half of which is obtained from exported goods, representing in 2007 about 8% of the value of agricultural products and food products exported by Romania.

Export and Import of Organic Food Products

The organic product market has grown significantly over the past three years, with more Romanian producers being certified to practice organic farming. Nevertheless, the tripling of the number of certified producers in the last year is not reflected in the growth of organic products sold on the Romanian market. The owners of the specialized shops say that over 70% of the products on the shelf are imported, because the Romanian farmers do not have the possibility to sell merchendise but only the raw material, which is 90%destined for the export. The balance will return to Romanian products when the strategy for promoting organic products is changed. Farmers need to be helped to produce organic food, not just to set up organic farms to produce raw materials for export.

In the Table 2, we can see the situation of exports and imports in Romania and in Europe.

Table 2. Number of exporters and importers in Romania and Europe

Year	Indicator	Romania	Europe
2015	Exporters	2	-
	Importers	3	3472
2014	Exporters	1	-
	Importers	3	-
2013	Exporters	1	-
	Importers	1	-
2012	Exporters	3	-
	Importers	3	-
2011	Exporters	-	3320
	Importers	2	2030
2010	Exporters	-	878
	Importers	13	1845
2009	Exporters	-	4157
	Importers	16	264
2008	Exporters	37	515
	Importers	11	3295
2007	Exporters	37	190
	Importers	14	2650
2006	Exporters	-	27
	Importers	3	1168

Source: http://www.organic-world.net/statistics-data-tables.html?&L=0.

Regarding the export of organic food products, it can be noticed that Romania has 37 exporters in 2007 and 2008 with a decreasing trend, reaching in 2015 only 2 exporters nationwide. The situation differs from the point of view of the number of exporters in Europe. If in 2007 Europe had 190 exporters, in 2008 the situation and number of exporters increases by 325. As for the number of importers, there is an obvious increase in Romania up to the level of 2009. After 2009 the evolution registered a decrease, reaching in 2015 at the level of only 3 importers.

CONCLUSION

The organic agro-food market is in the full process of forming, by analyzing the demand and supply of such productsit can be seen an increasing trend of orientation towards these types of products.

The supply of organic agrifood products registered upward trends in the period 2006 - 2015, both in terms of primary production (positive developments were recorded both in terms of the area cultivated with organic agri-food products and as number of producers), as well as at the level of processors and retailers.

On the other hand, the demand for organic agro-food products recorded oscillating evolutions during the analyzed period (2006 - 2015), being influenced directly by the applied prices. Thus, the still low level of consumption of organic agro-food products at national level is due to high prices, so that in Romania a significant percentage of organic farming production is not sold on its own market. This negative impact is also amplified by the negative trade balance with organic agri-food products. Over 70% of the organic agro-food products come from the import, because the Romanian farmers do not have the possibility to market agrifood products but only the raw material, which is 90% destined for the export. Thus, in order to turn the balance in favor of Romanian organic products and to increase their consumption at national level, an effective strategy for the promotion of organic products is necessary. Farmers need to be supported in the production of finished products, not just in the creation of organic farms to produce raw material for export, and thus the purchaising costs for the final consumers will be more accessible and attractive for them.

REFERENCES

Al Stanciu, O. (2008). *Dimensiuni ale comportamentului consumatorului produselor ecologice pe piata romaneasca in viziunea marketingului modern* (Unpublished doctoral dissertation). The Bucharest University of Economic Studies.

Arvanitoyannis, I. S., & Krystallis, A. (2004). *Current state of the art of legislation and marketing trends of organic foods worldwide*. World Scientific.

Burcă-Voicu, M. (2012). The Evolution of the Organic Food Market in Romania-Trends, Opportunities and Threats in the Current International Economic Context. Romanian Review of International Studies, 4(2).

FAO. (n.d.). *Why is organic food more expensive than conventional food?* Available at http://www.fao.org/organicag/oa-faq/oa-faq5/en/?ncid=txtlnkusaolp00000618

Hughner, R. S., McDonagh, P., Prothero, A., Shultz, C. J., & Stanton, J. (2007). Who are organic food consumers? A compilation and review of why people purchase organic food. *Journal of Consumer Behaviour, 6*(2-3), 94–110. doi:10.1002/cb.210

Orboi, M. D. (2013). Aspects regarding the evolution the organic food market in the world. *Research Journal of Agricultural Science, 45*(2), 201–209.

The International Fund for Agricultural Development. (n.d.). *Rural Development Report 2016*. Available at https://www.ifad.org/documents/30600024/8f07f4f9-6a91-496a-89c1-d1b120f8de8b

Thøgersen, J. (2010). Country differences in sustainable consumption: The case of organic food. *Journal of Macromarketing, 30*(2), 171–185. doi:10.1177/0276146710361926

ADITIONAL READING

Ho Milne, J. A. (2005). Societal expectations of livestock farming in relation to environmental effects in Europe. *Livestock Production Science, 96*(1), 3–9. doi:10.1016/j.livprodsci.2005.05.014

Hoffmann, I. (2011). Livestock biodiversity and sustainability. *Livestock Science, 139*(1), 69–79. doi:10.1016/j.livsci.2011.03.016

Istudor, N., & Petrescu, I. E. (2015). Influence of accesing European founds for rural development over the credits for agricultural sector in Romania. *Calitatea, 16*(S1), 4.

Popescu, A. (2012). Research regarding oil seeds crops development in Romania in the EU context. *Economics of Agriculture, 59*(1), 129–137.

Roşca, V. (2009). *Tehnologii moderne de producere a răsadurilor de legume* (p. 176). Chişinău: Editura Print-Caro.

Sima, V., & Gheorghe, I. G. (2016). The Potential of Young People from Rural Communities in Romania. In N. Istudor, I. de los Rios, & J. V. Andrei (Eds.), *Rural Communities in the Global Economy: Beyond The Classical Rural Economy Paradigms* (pp. 232–252). New York: Nova Science Publishers, Inc.

KEY TERMS AND DEFINITIONS

Agricultural Economics: A branch of applied economics concerned with the application of economic theory in optimizing the production and distribution of food and fibre.

Consumption of Organic Products: The consumers' attitudes toward organic products and their behavior rearding organic products.

Demand for Organic Products: Demand for organic products is likely to grow because consumers are more likely to see organically grown food as a healthy and nutritious option to conventionally grown products, studies show.

Organic Farming: An agricultural production system that involves much more than choosing not to use pesticides, fertilizers, genetically modified organisms, antibiotics, and growth hormones. It requests certifications.

Organic Food Industry: A branch of industries based on principles and criteria for organic food processing.

Organic Products: Products made from materials produced by organic agriculture.

Chapter 8

The Evolution of the Feed Industry Towards Its "Sustainabilization"

Alfredo J. Escribano
Independent Researcher, Spain

ABSTRACT

Livestock production requires important amounts of resources, which are limited. Therefore, the feed industry is under pressure to combine food security and sustainability. Hence, it is going through an important process of remodeling (both in focus and in practice). The feed industry should make good use of this context as a way to evolve towards a more sustainable future, and constitute itself as a player in global sustainability efforts. The present chapter reviews the concept of quality (using meat products as model) and gives examples of how to modulate animal products healthiness/safety and reduce the environmental impact of the sector through animal feeding practices. Finally, it provides an overview of the main research areas and ongoing projects that the main global organizations involved in the feed sector are currently running in order to successfully overcome sustainability challenges.

INTRODUCTION

Consumers' Behavior Toward a More Sustainable Food System

Different facts and episodes surrounding the food industry (food waste, groundwater pollution, etc.) have lead that consumers' attitudes and preferences have been turning greener during the last two decades. However, this shift is not being fast enough

DOI: 10.4018/978-1-5225-2965-1.ch008

(sustainability is an issue needing urgent solutions) and is not always converted in to changes in the purchasing behavior.

Due to this, consumers' behavior must be modulated through marketing strategies and product modifications (labeling, production system, composition, etc.). This is particularly important in the livestock sector, due to the environmental impacts of some production systems. An important part of the such impacts come from the great nutritional needs of the animals, which requires rethinking the feeding system and the feed industry. This is why this sector is presented as a case for the present chapter.

BACKGROUND

The Sustainability Crisis, Livestock Sector Externalities, and Global Population Trends

From a historical perspective, pro-growth economic policies have encouraged rapid accumulation of natural, financial and human capital. As a result, an excessive depletion and degradation of natural resources has been experienced in conjunction with a strong impact on social, environmental and economic equilibria (Orecchini, Valitutti, & Vitali, 2012).

Sustainability challenges call for urgent action. They are multitudinous, urgent, and complex. They are beyond the capacities of our current institutions to address, caused by path-dependent behaviours, and require substantial change from systems with crippling inertia (Van der Leeuw, Wiek, Harlow, & Buizer, 2012).

Global population and food demand for animal products is predicted to increase globally (FAO, 2006). However, livestock production requires important amounts of resources (feed, land, water) which, in turn, are limited. Due to this, it is necessary to increase the sustainability and efficiency of the livestock sector, where the feed industry has great a potential and role to play. Beef is one of the productions on the spotlight, as it makes a substantial contribution to environmental pollution. Globally, beef supply chains are estimated to emit about 2.9 gigatonnes of CO2-eq, about 40% of all livestock emissions using a life-cycle approach (Gerber, Henderson, Opio, Mottet, & Steinfeld, 2013). However, it also has great positive environmental externalities (Escribano, 2016a).

Moreover, it is necessary to take into account ruminants' great contribution to food security (providing protein, energy and also essential micronutrients). Also, they can be fed reducing the human-animal competition for food-feed, as well as the effect of grazing in the revaluation of pastures and lands. Finally, their positive contribution as carbon sinks should not be forgotten, despite it not being accounted for in certain environmental impact studies (Gerber et al., 2015; Escribano, 2016b).

According to A. J. Escribano, Gaspar, Mesías, M. Escribano, and Pulido (2015), in order to be sustainable, livestock production must be economically viable, socially acceptable (fair, equitable, and human health protective), and environmentally respectful. Moreover, it should also be low-input, regenerative, make good use of a farm's internal resources, and be based on locally sustainable agricultural practices.

Consumers' Perceptions and Behavior Towards Animal Products

In order to provide with solutions for the industry and global society, it is first needed to understand consumers' perceptions towards meat. First of all, a definition of perception is provided. Perception has been defined as the act of apprehending by means of the senses and/or the mind. Hence, perception not only relates to basic senses such as visual, flavour and taste attributes, but also to formed learning or experiences. Some of our non-cognitive learning mechanisms such as conditioning and imitation are predominant in the early formation of food habits. Therefore, perception incorporates complex aspects of consumer behaviour such as learning, motivational and contextual factors (Troy & Kerry, 2010; Koster & Mojet, 2007). This concept along is dynamic and evolves according to consumers' context does it. This is why the concept of quality must be understood and constantly defined in order to be oriented to the market. Thus, meat quality has evolved from security and safety to ethics, sustainability and convenience.

Slowly but increasingly, consumers seem to be becoming aware of the need to increase the sustainability of the livestock sector, mainly looking for: quality, safety (avoiding illnesses caused agrochemical's residues –pesticides and veterinary drugs-, but also health promotion –functional foods-), and environmental sustainability (which in turn affects human health). Due to this, many companies are adding sustainability in their CSR (Corporate Social Responsibility) politics.

However, it seems that consumers are still not clearly willing to pay more for animal origin products carrying sustainability attributes. This means that producers find difficulties to sell these products at profitable prices, which reduces the development of marketing channels, feeding a loop characterized by reduced per capita consumption and low presence of these products in the market (Escribano et al., 2016a, b). For instance, consumers' demand and willingness to pay for organic products is reduced in many countries (Mesías, Martínez-Carrasco, Martínez-Paz, & Gaspar, 2011; Olivas, Díaz, & Bernabeu, 2013; Schleenbecker & Hamm, 2013; Costanigro, Kroll, Thilmany, & Bunning, 2014), especially with regard to beef (Mesías, Escribano, Gaspar, & Pulido, 2008). According to Krystallis, Arvanitoyannis, and Chryssohoidis (2006), this poor demand is partly due to a low perception of the differences between these and conventional products (i.e. between organic and pasture-based conventional meat). This fact could be even more marked in the case of consumers used to the presence of extensive livestock systems in their countries. As a strategy to increase awareness and willingness to pay for sustainable animal products, there is agreement of the fact that consumers' knowledge and perceptions about these products should be improved. In the case of organic meat, the level of knowledge and awareness is even lower (Escribano, 2016a). In comparison with extensive production systems, efforts should be made on their environmental and social contribution of sustainable livestock systems (A. J. Escribano, Gaspar, Mesías, Pulido, & M. Escribano, 2014).

White and Brady (2014), based on a literature review of 46 studies estimating WTP for pure and impure (organic, grass-fed, natural) environmental meat attributes, estimated the consumer willingness to pay (WTP) for environmental meat attributes and explored the extent to which WTP could offset on-farm costs of reducing water use. They found that a 10% premium is the ideal WTP, resulting in water use reductions between 24.4 L and 41.4 L.

Other attributes such as 'local' and 'fresh' are also experiencing greater acceptance. However, there are no clear definitions of these concepts, which lead to confusion among consumers with regard to the differences between different claims ('local', 'organic', 'fresh', 'sustainable', etc.) (Adams & Salois, 2010; Campbell, Mhlanga, & Lesschaeve, 2013; Pugliese, Zanasi, Atallah, & Cosimo, 2013; Rikkonen, Kotro, Koistinen, Penttilä, & Kauriinoja, 2013; Gracia, Barreiro-Hurlé, & López-Galán, 2014) and probably lower market share than expected. Therefore, consumers' level of knowledge of these products must be improved. In this regard, nutritionists' efforts could be made on formulating diets that include local resources (by-products, farm crops, etc.) and allow achieving adequate production levels at affordable economic and environmental cost.

The Concept of Quality and Its Dynamic Nature: Consumer Perception of Meat Products and Quality Attributes

Perceptions of meat qualities vary between contexts due to differences in needs, availabilities to meet their needs and psychological influences. The consumer therefore forms the decision to purchase meat on the basis of a large number of cues (Troy & Kerry, 2010). In this sense, Korzen and Lassen (2010) described two contexts, the "everyday context" (relating to buying, preparing and eating) and the "production context" (relating to primary production, slaughtering and meat processing).

Consumers have difficulty in evaluating meat quality, resulting in uncertainty and dissatisfaction. Additionally, the understanding of what quality means for the different consumers has been achieved through the use of different models. With regard to quality, models can be mainly classified into those that approach the product as:

- **A Food:** Safety, nutrition, sensory, and ethical (Peri, 2006).
- **An Object of Trade:** Certification, traceability, convenience, and price (Peri, 2006).
- **A Product Before Purchase:** Costs, extrinsic quality cues, and intrinsic quality cues (Grunert, Larsen, Madsen, & Baadsgaard, 1996).
- **A Product After Purchase:** Meat preparation, experienced quality, and sensory characteristics (Grunert et al., 1996).

Many authors have identified the major quality attributes of meat products. The Total Food Quality Model developed by Grunert, Bredahl, and Brunsø (2004) is worthy to mention. It describes meat's intrinsic and extrinsic quality cues perceived by consumers on the basis on which quality expectations are formed. Grunert et al. (2004) also analysed the quality perception attributes before and after purchase:

- **Before Purchase:**
  - Shopping situation.
  - Cost.
  - Extrinsic quality.
  - Intrinsic quality.
  - **Expected Quality:**
    - Taste.
    - Health.
    - Convenience.
    - Process.
- **After Purchase:**
  - **Meal Preparation:**
    - Taste.
    - Health.
    - Convenience.
    - *Process.*

The main attributes affecting purchases are described below:

Intrinsic or Background Cues

- **Nutritional Value**
- **Meat Colour and Freshness:** Colour is the first quality attribute for consumers in red meat. They use it as an indication of freshness Water-holding capacity (Renerre & Labas, 1987). Moreover, it is also related to long shelf life and good eating quality (Hood & Mead, 1993). Colour is highly related

to freshness, which has been also pointed out as a major cue in assessing the safety of meat (Cowan, 1998; Henson & Northern, 2000).

- **Marbling:** The presence and extent of marbling (intramuscular fat) are really important as it is assumed that they directly influence eating experience (flavour, juiciness, tenderness and palatability). However, fat scores are not always a good indicator of eating quality, as Bonny et al. stated in 2016 after studying European conformation and fat scores in cattle. Besides, fat levels exceeding 7.3% have been identified as too high by health-conscious consumers, consequently, meat with a fat content between 3 and 7.3% is generally considered acceptable (Miller, 2002). However, these values are market specific (Troy & Kerry, 2010). In this sense, animal nutritionists and the farming industry must assess the desired marbling degree in order to produce meats that match consumers' needs through the tools available (genetics, feeding strategy, production systems, slaughter weight).

- **Fat Colour:** The yellow colour does not affect the palatability of the cooked product, but is considered objectionable by most consumers because fat is usually white or off-white, a yellow appearance often suggesting (incorrectly) that the tissue necessarily originated from an old, malnourished or unhealthy animal (Kauffman & Marsh, 1987).

- **Visible Drip/Water-Holding Capacity:** Exudates from muscle and condensation of moisture on the surface of the meat are also important cues for consumers (Den Hertog-Meischke, van Laack, & Smulders, 1997).

- **Packaging Materials:** Plastic-based films are the materials of choice for the majority of meat products presented at retail level (Troy & Kerry, 2010). Mesías, Gaspar, Á. F. Pulido, Escribano, and F. Pulido (2009) analysed consumers' preferences for Iberian dry-cured ham, one of the most typical and highly prized meat products in Spain. These authors found that the most important attributes in shaping the preferences of the consumers for Iberian dry-cured ham were the Type of ham (43.5%) and the Price (38.5%) and the attribute that least affected the choice of the different types of ham was the Purchasing Format (5.6%).

- **Tenderness and Flavour:** Experienced quality cues such as tenderness and flavour are well known as being of immense importance to consumers at point of consumption.

Extrinsic Quality Cues

- **Price**
- **Origin**

- **Animal Production System:** Animals bred and fed with due consideration to animal welfare and without artificial hormones and additives
  ○ Organic
  ○ Free-range
  ○ GMO
  ○ Store type and size
  ○ Merchandising
  ○ Etc.

Holbrook (1999) identifies eight universal types of consumer value, namely: efficiency, play, excellence, aesthetics, status, ethics, esteem, and spirituality.

- **Efficiency, Excellence:** Nutrition, absence of chemical residues
- **Hedonic Consumption Value:** Enjoyment of its sensory characteristics
- **Cultural, Social Expectations, and Norms:** Such as status, esteem.
- **Edible Foods:**
  ○ Aesthetics
  ○ Ethics
- **Moral Values:** Moral values broadly relate to an individual's beliefs and may be understood as culturally defined standards by which people assess desirability, goodness, beauty, and guidelines for social living (Macionis and Plummer, 1997). Significantly, as values are internalized by the individual, emotions as well as reasoning are involved.

In line with Holbrook's classification, it has been widely reported that the increasing importance given to credence quality attributes, that is those qualities, is a consequence of increasing concerns among consumers on safety, health, convenience, locality, ethical factors, etc. These credence attributes mainly focus on the quality of the production process (extrinsic characteristics of meat) and if credence quality attributes are confirmed by trusted extrinsic cues (e.g. label information) they become the search quality attributes available at the time of shopping (Bernués et al., 2003b). Then, trends in consumer lifestyles with regard to meat when purchasing, are related to increasing use of extrinsic cues in quality perception, especially associated with increased awareness of the link between food and health (Grunert, 2006).

Grunert, Skytte, Esbjerg, and Hviid (2002) studied the influence of different attributes of pork on purchases: stunning of animals before slaughter, course of chilling, farmers' own feed, animal-friendly conditions at the farm and transportation, lean meat (not fatty), non-GMO feed, no pesticide residues on meat, date and weight of slaughter, maturation of meat, breed, low use of energy and water in production, uniformity of meat cut, low ph-value of meat, electricity stimulation of meat.

Taking into account all the attributes discussed above, it is timely to cite the study carried out by McEachern and Schröeder (2002), which shows (Table 1) an interesting rating of selection criteria for fresh meat.

Information Asymmetry

Consumers still have difficulty in accurately predicting experienced quality by perception at the point of purchase (Grunert et al., 2004), which poses a real challenge for the meat industry in order to understand consumers' attitudes and then adapt to them. Moreover, consumers lack understanding of the science behind the meat products, and many times they show contradictory attitudes (such as wishing more naturally reared animals while preferring white fat and more tender meats). From the industry point of view, the know-how in modulating meat products intrinsic quality (tenderness, nutritional profile, etc.) is high, so that the challenge remains on the side of communication. Thus, the industry must train consumers and learn how to better communicate the quality attributes present in the meat products it sells.

THE FEED INDUSTRY: SCOPE AND SIZE

Animal feeds play a leading role in the global food industry and feed is the largest and most important component to ensuring safe, abundant and affordable animal proteins. The global feed industry continues to expand in volume and value in response to increases in world population and demand for animal protein worldwide, including for livestock, dairy and fish. Generally, IFIF has observed a growth of production

Table 1. Selection criteria for fresh meat

	Number of Rural Respondents	Number of Urban Respondents	All Respondents
Price	6	10	16
Country of origin	7	7	14
Taste	8	6	14
Visible attributes (fat level, colour, etc.)	7	7	14
Quality label mark	2	2	4
Animal welfare	2	2	4
Organic	1	2	3
Freshness/sell-by date	1	2	3

Source: (McEachern and Schröeder, 2002).

particularly in the developing world, with the developed world remaining more or less stable. Global commercial feed manufacturing generates an estimated annual turnover of over US $370 billion. In 2015, compound feed production was close to 1 billion tonnes worldwide. This numerical milestone is a marker, not only for the achievements of this industry, but also for the opportunities as well as for the challenges that will be faced in the future (de Athayde, 2015). Commercial production or sale of manufactured feed products takes place in more than 130 countries and directly employs more than a quarter of a million skilled workers (IFIF, 2013).

Due to this, the feed industry is probably more scientifically active than ever in the search for feed materials and feed additives that allow increasing sustainability (economically viable, environmental protection and socially fair – including of course human health). In this sense, the increase in efficiency is essential as Earth resources are limited and global population is predicted to growth by 50% in 2050, as predicted by FAO (2006). This will require that agricultural production increase by 60% (compared to 2005/2007 production), including an increase in animal production and animal products with limited resources. Particularly, demand for livestock products will continue to intensify over the decades to come. Meat consumption is projected to rise nearly 73% by 2050; dairy consumption will grow 58% over current levels. Estimates show that between 2010 and 2050 animal protein production is expected to grow by around 1.7% per year, with meat production projected to rise by nearly 58%, aquaculture by 90% and dairy by 55%. This should be good news for the feed industry and our partners along the agri-food chain. However, such growth comes with significant challenges and it is vital that our sector, as well as the wider agricultural chain, meet these demands in a sustainable, safe and affordable manner, while maintaining consumer trust and confidence in the food supply chain (de Athayde, 2015). In meeting these future demands, sustainability and animal welfare are not optional, and this reflects many consumers' concerns and wishes (Cutait, 2013).

In this scenario, those who are at the greatest economic disadvantage must also be cared of, as they bear the heaviest burden of increase in price rise of food, including livestock products being one of the essentials, as they are components of a balanced diet (Agnihotri, Rajkumar, & Dutta, 2006; Agnihotri, Verma, & Rajkumar, 2012). In developing countries, increasing animal productivity to reduce animal numbers is not only limited by technological and socio-economic constraints, but also interferes with the multiple objectives of smallholders to keep livestock. In these economies, the role on self-reliance as well as the diversification of income sources with the farms are almost a pre-requisite for their economic sustainability (A. J. Escribano, Gaspar, Mesías, & M. Escribano, 2016). Livestock in developing countries not only provide food, they also provide, for example, manure and draught power to support crop cultivation and financial security (Udo et al., 2011). Due to this, there is a need also to produce food at affordable prices, and continued innovation as well as regulatory convergence and free and fair trade are key elements to meet future challenges. In order to search for these less social goals, international organizations have a great responsibility, such as IFIF (the International Feed Industry Federation), which represents the global feed industry and constitutes an essential pillar of the food chain that provides sustainable, safe and nutritious food. Along with IFIF, FAO plays an essential role, as it is committed to facilitating dialogue between regulators and private sector, and continues to provide extensive information and capacity development on different issues regarding animal nutrition and animal feeding.

MAIN FOCUS OF THE CHAPTER: THE FEED INDUSTRY AS A KEY PROVIDER OF SOLUTIONS WITHIN THE AGRO-FOOD CHAIN

Environmental Sustainability

Sustainability must be considered as a business issue. For businesses, sustainability is becoming a commanding and essential principle. A sustainable corporation should create profits for its shareholders while protecting the environment and improving the lives of those with whom it interacts; it should operate so that its business interests and the interests of the environment and society intersect. Then, the transition of society towards its 'sustainabilization' depends on the industry, both in terms of causes of the crisis and potential contribution to its solution (Orecchini et al., 2012). With respect to the food/feed industry, challenges and opportunities have never been greater. It has become apparent that anything less than a very proactive approach to addressing current challenges may not be sufficient.

Production of feed ingredients has a major contribution to total GHG emissions from livestock production (de Vries & De Boer, 2010). However, emissions of CO_2 and N_2O from production of feed ingredients can be reduced by selection of crops with a higher yield (or lower N demand per unit output) (De Boer et al., 2011).

Potential to Increase the Environmental Sustainability of the Feed Industry: A Summary of the Available Feeding Strategies and Nutritional Tools

As a consequence, lots of research has been published the last two decades in order to reduce the environmental impact of livestock production system (and particularly the influence of different diets and active compounds) in terms on GHGs (Greenhouse Gasses) emissions. Over the past 30 years, the feed conversion rates have on average been reduced by 30% reaching approximately a level of 1.2: 1 for farmed fish feed,

1.8: 1 for poultry feed and 2.5: 1 for pig feed. The expertise the EU feed industry holds in resource efficiency, which is also expressed through the optimal use of co- and by-products from food and non-food processing industries, is one of the very reasons of its success (FEFAC, 2014).

In this sense, Wanapat, Cherdthong, Phesatcha, and Kang (2015) reviewed dietary sources (feed management, plant secondary compounds, organic acids, defaunation, immunisation and biological control, and lipids) and their effects on animal production and environmental sustainability. This author summarized the methane abatement strategies, mechanism of abatement, considerations for use and reducing efficiency of CH4. De Boer et al. (2011) also provided with useful strategies to mitigate greenhouse gas emissions from livestock. Other authors have evaluated other strategies, such as the optimization of diets, pasture management and feeding system in order to improve farms sustainability (i.e. Tamminga, Bannink, Dijkstra, & Zom, 2007; Capper, 2012; White & Capper, 2013; O'Brien, Capper, Garnsworthy, Grainger, & Shalloo, 2014; White, Brady, Capper, & Johnson, 2014; and White & Capper, 2014, in cattle production). Nutritional management is a powerful tool to increase the sustainability of production systems. With regard to the beef sector, White, Brady, Capper, McNamara, and Johnson (2015) identified the relative role of nutritional management in minimizing beef production systems' environmental impact in an economically viable, socially acceptable manner. For this purpose, they used an economic and environmental diet optimizer. Diets to minimize land use, water use, and/or greenhouse gas (GHG) emissions were optimized under different scenarios (with regard to different genetics and reproductive management). The authors found that, despite reducing farms environmental impact can lead to increase in feed cost, such cost is less than stakeholder willingness to pay for improved efficiency.

Regarding sources of feed, also agricultural by-products are useful in this sense, as they help reducing the food-feed waste constitutes a body of research and efforts for researchers, companies and organizations. Each year, the EU feed industry utilises up to approximately 90 million tonnes of several hundreds of different types of co-products in animal feed. The feed industry thus creates a sustainable outlet for processing. In line with this, new feed materials are being evaluated as sources of nutrients and beneficial active compound for livestock, such as seaweeds (Makkar et al., 2015) or insects, which are key to ambitious climate targets (Walsh et al., 2015).

In ruminants, the balance between energy and protein is really important and worthy of mention. In this sense. Oltjen, Kebreab, and Lapierre (2013) published a book on nutrition and metabolism of these two key parameters with a focus on sustainable animal production.

The understanding of ruminal microbiology as well as its relationship with rumen development is essential (Puniya, Singh, & Kamra, 2015). In this sense, the research carried out by Yáñez-Ruiz, Abecia, and Newbold (i.e. 2015) is providing new and important knowledge for future farm strategies that will allow to increase farms' sustainability. As the understanding of rumen microbiology is being improved, researchers are becoming more aware of the potential to improve feed utilization by the manipulation of microbial compositions and diets. It is thus possible to talk about the concept of 'sustainable animal diets' reflected in FAO (2014). By deepening into the feeding strategies to modulate rumen microbiology, Choudhury et al. (2015) studied the role of bacteriophages in controlling different rumen microbes. Also, the doctoral thesis published by Dschaak in 2012 is worthy to mention as a review of rumen modifiers to manipulate ruminal fermentation, and in this case also to improve nutrient utilization and lactational performance in dairy cows. Below, Table 2 summarizes the main strategies that focus on modulating rumen microbiota as a path to reduce CH4 (methane) and N (nitrogen) losses from ruminants.

However, the implementation of these strategies may have implications (trade-offs) in the emissions of the rest of gasses as well as on the technical management of the farms, and on its economic performance. As a result, site specie and dynamic (temporal scale) evaluations must be carried out in order to avoid negative consequences.

As a summary, it can be concluded that the main aims and potential contribution of animal nutrition science are to optimize animal nutrition in relation to productivity,

Table 2. Main available strategies to modulate rumen microbiota

Feed Management	Plant Compounds
Roughage to concentrate ratio	Condensed tannins
replacing grass silage by maize silage	Saponins
Increase hemicelluloses/starch	Essential oils
improving forage digestibility	Organosulfur compounds
Reducing cell wall	
Organic Acids	**Defaunation**
Malate	Chemical
Fumarate	Feed additives
Nitroethane	**Lipids**
Nitrate	Fatty acids
Thiamine	Oil, seed oils, tallow
Rumen Development and Programming: Dietary interventions, metagenomics, etc.	
Microbial Feed Additives (Probiotics)	
Bacteriophages	

Source: Authors' Conception.

the environment, product composition and nutrient content, and health. For this purpose, below the main areas of research are summarized (Aarhus University, 2016):

- **Characterization of Feedstuff Composition and Quality:** With regard to nutritional and environmentally damaging components
- **Determination of Nutrient Requirements in Relation to the Animals:** Different physiological needs and the overall nutrient utilization and balance
- **Initiatives Concerning Feedstuffs:** In order to reduce the emission of greenhouse gas and ammonia from the farm animals and the environmental impacts of the livestock production (N, P, heavy metals)
- **Optimization of Animal Nutrition:** With focus on the environment, production/productivity and efficient resource utilization while taking welfare and product quality into consideration.

Food Safety and Human Health Improvement

Food safety is a major concern in the livestock sector, and overall confidence in food safety was down in the early 1990s, tended to rise and peaked in the mid-1990s, and has declined since (Food Marketing Institute, 1991-2000). As a consequence, feed companies are, out of necessity, now becoming major players within the food safety issue. The commitment by the feed company to provide customers with products of the highest quality has been deemed vital to the success of the business. Therefore, feed companies must become early leaders in assuring that all products are Hazard Analysis and Critical Control Point (HACCP) certified (Maxwell, 2006). Only by working together with all stakeholders is it possible to ensure feed and food safety.

FEFAC's (The European Feed Manufacturers' Federation) principles state that safe feed is non-negotiable and belongs in the precompetitive part of the feed chain. The EU feed industry has had to learn hard lessons from past feed safety incidents and measures have been put in place to safeguard compliance with the stringent rules posed by the EU, which are in fact among the most demanding at global level. In many aspects, the requirements imposed on feed business operators are stricter than in the food chain (FEFAC, 2014).

Toxic substances such as dioxins, mycotoxins, heavy metals, pesticides, veterinary drugs and polycyclic aromatic hydrocarbons are almost ubiquitous in the environment. Thus, they can also be present in ingredients for animal feed (Kan & Meijer, 2007). The recent ban in the use of antibiotic for growth promotion should be used as a marketing strategy since consumers' preferences seem to be changing in US in this respect; as it already occurred in other countries, such as the European ones. Reducing the use of antibiotics in livestock husbandry is one of the greatest challenges the livestock sector faces at global level. Antimicrobial resistance has become a serious threat to the effectiveness of currently used antibiotics, both in human medicines and animal production (FEFAC, 2014). Withdrawing GET (growth-enhancing technologies: steroid implants, in-feed ionophores, in-feed hormones and beta-adrenergic agonists) from U.S. beef production would reduce both the economic and environmental sustainability of the industry (Capper & Hayes, 2012).

Hence, the feed industry's role in food safety and human health improvement is key, such that this sector must make use of consumers' behaviour and take care of public health as an opportunity to improve its perception and guide its sustainabilization. In this sense, the feed industry must take benefit of the opportunity brought by consumers' preferences changes towards sustainable food (those healthy included, for being increasingly socially acceptable). Thus, this sector would position itself as a green and responsible one, provider of 'natural' feed additives, as an alternative to: (i) the traditional health management based on the use of preventive antibiotics; (ii) antibiotic used for growth promoting (still allowed in some countries).

However, it is not an easy task, as consumers are day by day more requiring, as are regulations. Moreover, the global market put together all these requirements so that companies have narrow paths to go through in order to fulfil global requirements. These regulatory hurdles that must be overcome include differences in the use of antibiotics, animal proteins, genetically modified materials, etc.

Moreover, there are still some gaps that require special attention with regard to food/feed safety. One of the challenges is that on top of the almost 1 billion tonnes of feed produced by the feed industry, around 300 million tonnes of feed is produced directly by on-farm mixing. This poses challenges, as food safety authorities do not regularly audit mixing by farmers and regulatory authorities only inspect when there is a problem. IFIF believes it is vital for the feed industry and for the sustainability of the whole feed and food chain that clear standards apply throughout the whole feed chain, and both industrial and on-farm mixers should be controlled and inspected on a regular basis (IFIF, 2013).

However, the nutritional tools that can be used nowadays must be safer than ever (i.e. no use of antibiotic growth promoters), which is requiring dramatic changes in the way that feed companies operate.

Potential to Increase Food Safety and Improve Human Health: A Summary of the Available Feeding Strategies and Nutritional Tools

In this sense, Tiwari and Rana (2015) reviewed the content and applications of plant secondary metabolites. Placing particular emphasis on animal nutrition, Jouany and Morgavi (2007) reviewed the great diversity of already available non-antibiotic feed additives (called 'natural products' and 'alternative feed additives' in the cited paper) that could potentially improve animal health and productivity in ruminant production. Functionality and potential effects of probiotics, dicarboxylic acids and its salts, as well as enzymes and plant-derived products (saponins, tannins and essential oils) were presented. Later, Hart, Yáñez-Ruiz, Duval, McEwan, and Newbold (2008) reviewed this field of plant extract and modulation of rumen fermentation, while Benchaar et al. (2008) reviewed essential oils use in ruminant nutrition and production.

However, these 'natural products' have important limitations. One of which being the stabilization of active compounds concentrations. Moreover, the synergetic and antagonist effects must be assessed. Also, the minimum effective doses are still not well-known for many of the products in animal diets. With regard to these products, policymakers must take action, since it is needed to legislate more precisely, especially with regard to labelling. In the search for transparency, the author's opinion is that it is important that their ingredients (active compounds and their quantity) be declared. However, this would be in contrast with private companies' interests. This will force companies to protect their products (patents, registers), with the required time and investments this leads to.

In relation with the active compounds in plants, and the reduction of association between livestock and land stated by many authors (Escribano et al., 2015; Escribano, 2016a, b), Provenza, Meuret, and Gregorini (2015) carried out an interesting study which concluded that phytochemically impoverished pastures and feedlot diets can adversely affect the health of livestock and the flavour and nutritive value of meat and milk products for humans. Regarding animal products quality, the authors claimed that flavours of produce, meat, and dairy have become blander, and processed foods have become more desirable as people have learned to link synthetic flavours with feedback from energy-rich compounds that obscure nutritional sameness and diminish health. According to this study, the roles plants and animals once played in nutrition have been usurped by processed foods that are altered, fortified, and enriched in ways that can adversely affect appetitive states and food preferences. These researchers convey the current need to amend foods, and to take nutrient supplements, then showing that this could be reduced by creating phytochemically rich plants and herbivores and by creating cultures that know how to combine foods into meals that nourish and satiate.

Products With Heathier Fatty Acid Profiles

Red meat and dairy products have been associated with a number of unfavourable health conditions, linked to the contribution to the intake of fat, saturated fatty acids, cholesterol, salt, and other substances that may have negative health implications (Olmedilla-Alonso, Jiménez-Colmenero, & Sánchez-Muniz, 2013; Realini et al.,

2014). Composition of meat and dairy products varies with respect to numerous factors and animal diet is the factor which can most easily be manipulated and which has one of the most profound effects on its composition (Troy & Kerry, 2010). Here, animal nutritionists must be aware of consumers' needs by keeping in touch with the industry, and design diets that allow to obtain meats (and meat products) that match consumers' demands, thus playing a role in social sustainability (human health-food safety).

Unsaturated fatty acids, such as Omega-3, have positive effects of these fatty acids in relation to cardiovascular diseases, different types of cancers and neurological health (Abuajah, Ogbonna, & Osuji, 2014). Consequently, the presence of these fatty acids in food is of great interest in terms of human health. Similarly, potential positive effects of CLA (Conjugated Linoleic Acids) on human health have been found. Omega-3 and CLA are ingredients that in general are considered healthy, and it has been reported that the enrichment of beef with one of these compounds increases consumer scores compared with conventional meat, while enrichment with both compounds seems to not affect consumers' overall liking (Realini et al., 2013).

A lot of effort has been made to increase the content of certain polyunsaturated fatty acids in milk and meat products. Specifically, Conjugated Linoleic Acid (CLA) and Omega-3. However, ruminants physiology provoke that the achievement of the desired products is not always easy through feed materials, and that the use of feed additives developed to facilitate such goal, are sometimes too much expenses to be included in ruminants diets. From the milk industry side, farmers are required to produce milk with a high % of fat, while high content on Omega-3 and/or a higher proportion of unsaturated/saturated fatty acids, which is not easy to achieve. From the consumer perspective, their higher prices render them affordable for a specific market niche. Due to this, dairy industry is currently rewarding farmers focused on producing these products.

Consumers' Behaviour Towards These Functional Products

These trends towards healthy products is also especially important clear in the case of the consumption of eggs because of their strong negative association with cholesterol levels and their extremely intensive systems of production. Thus, the introduction of variants that are more in harmony with current consumer demands represents an interesting market alternative (Mesías et al., 2011). The authors found that hens' feed was the second attribute in importance. In this sense, both feed industry and organic regulations must take steps forward to both meet consumers' demands and produce sustainably.

Realini et al. (2014) estimated the relative importance of animal diet (conventional, enriched with n-3, with CLA, or with n-3 plus CLA) of beef loin in three Spanish cities, finding that consumer liking scores of beef enriched with n-3 or CLA fatty acids improved, while the combination of both did not. Kallas, Realini, and Gil (2014) investigated consumers' preferences towards beef meat enriched with polyunsaturated fatty acids (omega-3 and conjugated linoleic acid), and found that consumers informed about the health effects of these fatty acids were willing to accept meat with a higher amount of visible fat if it is enriched with beneficial fatty acids.

Thus, consumers' perception of the healthiness of beef has become an important determinant of beef consumption. Van Wezemael, Verbeke, de Barcellos, Scholderer, and Perez-Cueto (2010) found that although beef was generally perceived as healthful, negative effects of beef consumption on health were also expressed by surveyed participants. Labelled and lean beef were perceived as signalling healthful beef, which can guide the feed sector in how to do business (and technical work).

EXAMPLES OF SUSTAINABILITY STRATEGIES IMPLEMENTATION IN THE FEED INDUSTRY: PROJECTS AND CSR

In order to encourage feed producers to quantify, report, better understand and reduce the environmental impact, FEFAC has developed, jointly with the American Feed Industry Association (AFIA), feed specific LCA guidelines in 2013.

These guidelines were built on existing general guidance from the ENVIFOOD protocol from the EU Food Sustainable Round Table and served as input to the FAO LEAP (Livestock Environmental Assessment and Performance) Feed guidelines, which were published for public review in March 2014. In May 2014, DG ENVI selected FEFAC's submission as regards feed for food producing animals as one of the pilots of the PEF (Product Environmental Footprint), which aims to be an EU harmonised methodology for

measuring the environmental impact and performance of a product. FEFAC also underlines responsible production of the raw material supply according to internationally agreed principles as a very important aspect of sustainability (FEFAC, 2014).

Another key part of IFIF's mission is to support worldwide trade and ensure that future demands for feed and food can be met efficiently. IFIF works to promote a balanced regulatory framework to support a fair global playing field to facilitate market access and support the competitiveness of the feed and livestock industries. Engagement with international institutions is vital for this and IFIF collaborates with the FAO, the World Organisation for Animal Health (OIE), the Codex Alimentarius Commission and other international bodies to help set international regulatory standards for the whole feed chain, and to support fair trade. IFIF has a strong collaborative relationship with the FAO dating back many years, and IFIF and the FAO Animal Production and Health Division organise the annual International Feed Regulators Meeting (IFRM) (de Athayde, 2015).

Measuring the environmental performance and impact of this industry is another major aim for IFIF. Meeting the sustainability challenge means producing more and using less, at an affordable cost. In order to achieve these goals, IFIF started three key projects:

- **SFIS (the Specialty Feed Ingredients Sustainability Project):** This project is intended to establish the positive role of the use of Specialty Feed Ingredients (SFIs) on the environmental impact of livestock production, which will have a direct positive impact on the future environmental footprint of the feed and food chain. The possibilities for reducing the environmental impact of the industry go through the concept of feed efficiency, which basically means produce more with less. Improving production traits, such as growth rate, annual milk production, fertility and efficiency of feed conversion, by breeding or precision management, will reduce net GHG emissions, because fewer animals, and hence less feed, are needed to produce the same amount of product (Thomassen, Dolman, Van Calker, & De Boer, 2009; Gill, Smith, & Wilkinson, 2010). This will allow to feed more people with fewer resources. In this field of action, the efficiency of utilization of protein is quite popular, as nitrogen losses poses great environmental impacts. To give some figures, by reducing the crude protein level in compound feed by only 1% when supplementing amino acids, the nitrogen excretion by the animal will be lowered by 10% in the manure as a result. Besides, the use of local and/or unusual feed resources (such as agricultural by-products) is one of the areas of study. In this sense, Arriaga (2010) published a doctoral thesis addressing the cattle nutrition strategies to mitigate gaseous nitrogen losses from fairy farming. According to De Boer et al. (2011), Precisely meeting the N requirements of the animal, during the various stages of its productive life, reduces N excretion per unit of product produced, and, therefore, related N_2O and NH_3 emissions (i.e. precision N feeding).
- **LEAP (UN FAO-LED Partnership on Livestock Environmental Assessment and Performance):** IFIF, together with the American Feed Industry Association (AFIA) and the European Compound Feed Manufacturers' Federation (FEFAC), have joined the LEAP. The overarching goal of this initiative is to contribute to improved environmental performance of the livestock sector while considering social and economic viability. The partnership will contribute towards the achievement of this goal through support to decision-making by providing guidance on environmental

assessments and their subsequent application. Research benefits of this partnership could lead to changed diet patterns and composition for farm animals and fish, further reducing GHG emissions attributed to livestock production. Activities planned for the initial three-year phase of the project included:

- ○ Establishing science-based methods and guidelines on how to quantify livestock carbon footprint.
- ○ Creating a database of greenhouse gas emission factors generated for the production of different kinds of animal feed.
- ○ Developing a methodology for measuring other important environmental pressures, such as water consumption and nutrient losses.

- **FAO Global Agenda of Action in Support of Sustainable Livestock Development:** Together the partners develop and implement an ambitious agenda to ensure that sector growth contributes to socially desirable objectives. Areas of work:
  - ○ Closing the Efficiency Gap: to transfer and adapt resource use efficient technologies.
  - ○ Restoring Value to Grassland.
  - ○ Waste to Worth: this aims at recovering and recycling nutrients and energy contained in animal manure.

SUMMARY AND CONCLUSION

The feed industry is a central element with a great potential that must not be despised in order to achieve global sustainability goals. The strategies used must also be in line with complex and changing consumers' demands towards food products of animal origin. Many aspects, such as environmental impact and food safety/quality can be modulated through animal nutrition, and this is the path to follow (avoiding the use of nocive substances, such as antibiotic growth promoters). Technologies such as nutrigenomics (the impact of foods on genes), personalised food for health, and the exploitation of animal derived bioactive components are not science fiction already. Veterinarians, nutritionists and other stakeholders must work hand in hand with a common approach: maintain animal performance through nutritional strategies.

This has pushed private companies and academic researchers to increase their knowledge on animal nutrition, and particularly, on what have been called 'natural' feed additives, feed materials. Smart feeding or precision livestock feeding has thus become an obsession for every nutritionist, as diet formulation is key to achieve such need for increased animal performance and for the reduction of prevalence of nutritional disorders, such as ruminal acidosis.

Fortunately, these efforts have been useful, and nowadays there is great and increasing scientific knowledge available to help on this task.

SOLUTIONS AND RECOMMENDATIONS

However, their externalities and trade-offs are numerous, which requires site specific and dynamic evaluations of their suitability. In this sense, the collaboration between the feed industry and academia within the context of sustainability science is key.

Not only must feeding strategies and feed additives be evaluated and used, but also the huge amount of agricultural/industrial by-products, as well as new feed materials that are sources of nutrients and beneficial active compound for livestock, such as seaweeds (Makkar et al., 2015) or insects.

From the above, one can infer the pivotal role of animal nutrition to meet consumers' demands and to achieve global goals and concerns. Therefore, in order to provide with specific products (functional, sustainable, etc.) and/or at affordable prices in sufficient amounts, a great development of the feed industry will be observed in the coming years, with a focus on sustainability and by means of technical efficiency (produce more with less), for which nutritionists and food engineers' technical knowledge will be essential. Hence, the feed industry, the meat industry needs to invest in and embrace an innovation agenda in order to be sustainable.

FUTURE RESEARCH DIRECTIONS

Communication and bi-directional (professionals of the sector – consumers) understanding remains a challenge. In this sense, the industry must really work hard and tune consumer groups such as millennials, using the adequate language and media. In this sense, two recommendations for the agricultural industry and its sub-industries (Howard, 2015): 1. Industry communicators should consider current industry representation on social media and identify ways to proactively supply information to consumers. 2. Industry communicators should identify social media platforms and other media outlets that can be used to reach consumers and provide information proactively and reactively. Social media tools must be used to change the negative information that consumers have received regarding beef through such media. It is especially important because consumers often search for information on food safety on the Internet (Charanza, 2011).

REFERENCES

Aarhus University. (2016). Animal Nutrition and Environment, Department of Animal Science. *Project partners*. Retrieved from http://anis.au.dk/forskning/projekter/nometmet/project-partners

Abuajah, C. I., Ogbonna, A. C., & Osuji, C. M. (2015). Functional components and medicinal properties of food: A review. *Journal of Food Science and Technology, 52*(5), 2522–2529. doi:10.1007/s13197-014-1396-5 PMID:25892752

Adams, D. C., & Salois, M. J. (2010). Local versus organic: A turn in consumer preferences and willingness-to-pay. *Renewable Agriculture and Food Systems, 25*(4), 331–341. doi:10.1017/S1742170510000219

Agnihotri, M. K., Rajkumar, V., & Dutta, T. K. (2006). Effect of feeding complete rations with variable protein and energy levels prepared using by-products of pulses and oilseeds on carcass characteristics, meat and meat ball quality of goats. *Asian-Australasian Journal of Animal Sciences, 19*(10), 1437–1449. doi:10.5713/ajas.2006.1437

Agnihotri, M. K., Verma, A. K., & Rajkumar, V. (2012). *Sustainable animal products production for food security*. Paper presented at the National Seminar on Vet for Health; Vet for Food; Vet for the planet, New Delhi, India.

Arriaga, H. (2010). *Cattle nutrition as a strategy to mitigate gaseous nitrogen losses from dairy farming* (Doctoral Thesis). University of Barcelona, Spain.

Benchaar, C., Calsamiglia, S., Chaves, A. V., Fraser, G. R., Colombatto, D., McAllister, T. A., & Beauchemin, K. A. (2008). A review of plant-derived essential oils in ruminant nutrition and production. *Animal Feed Science and Technology, 145*(1-4), 209–228. doi:10.1016/j.anifeedsci.2007.04.014

Bonny, S. P. F., Pethick, D. W., Legrand, I., Wierzbicki, J., Allen, P., Farmer, L. J., ... Gardner, G. E. (2016). European conformation and fat scores have no relationship with eating quality. *Animal, 10*(6), 1–11. doi:10.1017/S1751731115002839 PMID:26755183

Campbell, B. L., Mhlanga, S., & Lesschaeve, I. (2013). Perception versus reality: Canadian consumer views of local and organic. *Canadian Journal of Agricultural Economics, 61*(4), 531–558. doi:10.1111/j.1744-7976.2012.01267.x

Capper, J. L. (2012). Is the Grass Always Greener? Comparing the Environmental Impact of Conventional, Natural and Grass-Fed Beef Production Systems. *Animals (Basel), 2*(2), 127–143. doi:10.3390/ani2020127 PMID:26486913

Capper, J. L., & Hayes, D. J. (2012). The environmental and economic impact of removing growth-enhancing technologies from U.S. beef production. *Journal of Animal Science*, *90*(10), 3527–3537. doi:10.2527/jas.2011-4870 PMID:22665660

Charanza, A. D. (2011). *Consumers' dependency on media for information about food safety incidents related to the beef industry* (Master's thesis). Texas A&M University.

Choudhury, P. K., Salem, A. Z. M., Jena, R., Kumar, S., Singh, R., & Puniya, A. K. (2015). Rumen Microbiology: An Overview. In A. K. Puniya, R. Singh, & D. N. Kamra (Eds.), *Rumen Microbiology: From Evolution to Revolution* (pp. 3–16). New Delhi: Springer India; doi:10.1007/978-81-322-2401-3_1

Costanigro, M., Kroll, S., Thilmany, D., & Bunning, M. (2014). Is it love for local/ organic or hate for conventional? Asymmetric effects of information and taste on label preferences in an experimental auction. *Food Quality and Preference*, *31*, 94–105. doi:10.1016/j.foodqual.2013.08.008

Cowan, C. (1998). Irish and European consumer views on food safety. *Journal of Food Safety*, *18*(4), 275–295. doi:10.1111/j.1745-4565.1998.tb00221.x

Cutait, M. S. (2013). Letter from the Chairman. In International Feed Industry Federation Annual Report 2012/13 (p. 5). International Feed Industry Federation.

De Athayde, A. (2015). Towards Sustainable Feed & Food – Working Together at International Level. *International Animal Health Journal*, *2*(2), 28–30.

De Boer, I. J. M., Cederberg, C., Eady, S., Gollnow, S., Kristensen, T., Macleod, M., ... Zonderland-Thomassen, M. A. (2011). Greenhouse gas mitigation in animal production: Towards an integrated life cycle sustainability assessment. *Current Opinion in Environmental Sustainability*, *3*(5), 423–431. doi:10.1016/j. cosust.2011.08.007

De Vries, M., & De Boer, I. J. M. (2010). Comparing environmental impacts for livestock products: A review of life cycle assessments. *Livestock Science*, *128*(1-3), 1–11. doi:10.1016/j.livsci.2009.11.007

Den Hertog-Meischke, M. J. A., van Laack, R. J. L. M., & Smulders, F. J. M. (1997). The water-holding capacity of fresh meat. *The Veterinary Quarterly*, *19*(4), 175–181. doi:10.1080/01652176.1997.9694767 PMID:9413116

Dschaak, C. M. (2012). *Rumen modifiers to manipulate ruminal fermentation and improve nutrient utilization and lactational performance of dairy cows* (Doctoral Thesis). Utah State University, Logan, UT.

Escribano, A. J. (2016a). Organic Livestock Farming: Challenges, Perspectives, And Strategies to Increase its Contribution to the Agrifood System's Sustainability – A Review. In P. Konvalina (Ed.), *Organic Farming - A Promising Way of Food Production* (pp. 229–260). InTech. doi:10.5772/61272

Escribano, A. J. (2016b). Beef Cattle Farms' Conversion to the Organic System. Recommendations for Success in the Face of Future Changes in a Global Context. *Sustainability*, *8*(6), 572. doi:10.3390/su8060572

Escribano, A. J., Gaspar, P., Mesías, F. J., & Escribano, M. (2016). The role of the level of intensification, productive orientation and self-reliance in extensive beef cattle farms. *Livestock Science*, *193*, 8–19. doi:10.1016/j.livsci.2016.09.006

Escribano, A. J., Gaspar, P., Mesías, F. J., Escribano, M., & Pulido, F. (2015). Comparative Sustainability Assessment of Extensive Beef Cattle Farms in a High Nature Value Agroforestry System. In V. R. Squires (Ed.), *Rangeland Ecology, Management and Conservation Benefits* (pp. 65–85). New York, NY: Nova Science Publishers, Inc.

Escribano, A. J., Gaspar, P., Mesías, F. J., Pulido, A. F., & Escribano, M. (2014). A sustainability assessment of organic and conventional beef cattle farms in agroforestry systems: The case of the 'dehesa' rangelands. *ITEA. Información Técnica Económica Agraria*, *110*(4), 343–367. doi:10.12706/itea.2014.022

European Feed Manufacturers' Federation (FEFAC). (2014). *The Feed Chain in Action Animal Nutrition – the key to animal performance, health & welfare.* Bruxelles, Belgium: Fefac.

FAO. (2006). Global Perspective Studies Unit: Food and Agriculture Organization of the United Nations. World agriculture: towards 2030/2050. Interim Report. Prospects for food, nutrition, agriculture and major commodity groups. Rome, Italy: FAO.

FAO. (2014). Towards a concept of sustainable animal diets. FAO Animal Production and Health Report. No. 7. Rome, Italy: FAO.

FAO (Food and Agriculture Organization of the United Nations). (1983). World Food Security: a Reappraisal of the Concepts and Approaches. Director General's Report. Rome, Italy: FAO.

Food Marketing Institute (FMI). (1998). Trends in the United States: Consumer attitudes and the supermarket. Washington, DC: Research Department, Food Marketing Institute.

Gerber, P. J., Steinfeld, H., Henderson, B., Mottet, A., Opio, C., Dijkman, J., & Tempio, G. (2013). *Tackling climate change through livestock: A global assessment of emissions and mitigation opportunities*. Rome: FAO.

Gill, M., Smith, P., & Wilkinson, J. M. (2010). Mitigating climate change: The role of domestic livestock. *Animal*, *4*(03), 323–333. doi:10.1017/S1751731109004662 PMID:22443938

Gracia, A., Barreiro-Hurlé, J., & López-Galán, B. (2014). Are Local and Organic Claims Complements or Substitutes? A Consumer Preferences Study for Eggs. *Journal of Agricultural Economics*, *65*(1), 49–67. doi:10.1111/1477-9552.12036

Grunert, K. G. (2006). Future trends and consumer lifestyles with regard to meat consumption. *Meat Science*, *74*(1), 149–160. doi:10.1016/j.meatsci.2006.04.016 PMID:22062724

Grunert, K. G., Larsen, H. H., Madsen, T. K., & Baadsgaard, A. (1996). *Market orientation in food and agriculture*. Norwell, MA: Springer US. doi:10.1007/978-1-4613-1301-4

Grunert, K. G., Skytte, H., Esbjerg, L., & Hviid, M. (2002). *Dokumenteret kødkvalitet. MAPP project paper*. Aarhus: The Aarhus School of Business.

Hart, K. J., Yáñez-Ruiz, D. R., Duval, S. M., McEwan, N. R., & Newbold, C. J. (2008). Plant extracts to manipulate rumen fermentation. *Animal Feed Science and Technology*, *147*(1-3), 8–35. doi:10.1016/j.anifeedsci.2007.09.007

Henson, S., & Northern, J. (2000). Consumer Assessment of the Safety of Beef at the Point of Purchase: A Pan-European Study. *Journal of Agricultural Economics*, *51*(1), 90–105. doi:10.1111/j.1477-9552.2000.tb01211.x

Holbrook, M. B. (1999). *Consumer Value: A Framework for Analysis and Research*. London: Routledge. doi:10.4324/9780203010679

Hood, D. E., & Mead, G. C. (1993). Modified atmosphere storage of fresh meat and poultry. In R. T. Parry (Ed.), *Principles and applications of modified atmosphere packaging of food* (pp. 269–298). London: Blackie Academic and Professional. doi:10.1007/978-1-4615-2137-2_11

Howard, M. L. (2015). *The Effect of Social Media on Consumer Perceptions of the Beef Industry* (Master's Thesis). University of Tennessee. Retrieved from http://trace.tennessee.edu/utk_gradthes/3373

IFIF (International Feed Industry Federation). (2013). *The International Feed Industry Federation Annual Report 2012/13*. Retrieved from http://ifif.org/uploadImage/2013/10/1/c838a3d3dbb286acb4685f331c1b70241380656385.pdf

Jouany, J. P., & Morgavi, D. P. (2007). Use of 'natural' products as alternatives to antibiotic feed additives in ruminant production. *Animal, 1*(10), 1443–1466. doi:10.1017/S1751731107000742 PMID:22444918

Kallas, Z., Realini, C., & Gil, J. M. (2014). Health information impact on the relative importance of beef attributes including its enrichment with polyunsaturated fatty acids (omega-3 and conjugated linoleic acid). *Meat Science, 97*(4), 497–503. doi:10.1016/j.meatsci.2014.03.015 PMID:24769150

Kan, C. A., & Meijer, G. A. L. (2007). The risk of contamination of food with toxic substances present in animal feed. *Animal Feed Science and Technology, 133*(1-2), 84–108. doi:10.1016/j.anifeedsci.2006.08.005

Kauffman, R. G., & Marsh, B. B. (1987). Quality characteristics of muscle as food. In J. F. Price & B. S. Schweigert (Eds.), *The science of meat and meat products* (3rd ed.; pp. 349–369). Westport, CT: Food and Nutrition Press, Inc.

Korzen, S., & Lassen, J. (2010). Meat in context. On the relation between perceptions and contexts. *Appetite, 54*(2), 274–281. doi:10.1016/j.appet.2009.11.011 PMID:19944122

Koster, E. P., & Mojet, J. (2007). Theories of food choice development. In L. Frewer & H. van Trijp (Eds.), *Understanding consumers of food products* (pp. 93–124). Cambridge: Woodhead. doi:10.1533/9781845692506.1.93

Krystallis, A., Arvanitoyannis, I., & Chryssohoidis, G. (2006). Is there a real difference between conventional and organic meat? Investigating consumers' attitudes towards both meat types as an indicator of organic meat's market potential. *Journal of Food Products Marketing, 12*(2), 47–78. doi:10.1300/J038v12n02_04

Makkar, H. P. S., Tran, G., Heuzé, V., Giger-Reverdin, S., Lessire, M., Lebas, F., & Ankers, P. (2015). Seaweeds for livestock diets: A review. *Animal Feed Science and Technology, 212*, 1–17. doi:10.1016/j.anifeedsci.2015.09.018

Mesías, F. J., Escribano, M., Gaspar, P., & Pulido, F. (2008). Consumers' attitudes towards organic, PGI and conventional meats in Extremadura (Spain). *Archivos de Zootecnia, 57*, 139–146.

Mesías, F. J., Martínez-Carrasco Pleite, F., Martínez-Paz, J. M., & Gaspar, P. (2011). Functional and Organic Eggs as an Alternative to Conventional Production: A Conjoint Analysis of Consumers' preferences. *Journal of the Science of Food and Agriculture*, *91*(3), 532–538. doi:10.1002/jsfa.4217 PMID:21218489

Miller, R. K. (2002). Factors affecting the quality of raw meat. In J. P. Kerry, J. F. Kerry, & D. Ledward (Eds.), *Meat processing—Improving quality* (pp. 27–63). Cambridge, UK: Woodhead Publishing Co. doi:10.1533/9781855736665.1.27

O'Brien, D., Capper, J. L., Garnsworthy, P. C., Grainger, C., & Shalloo, L. (2014). A case study of the carbon footprint of milk from high-performing confinement and grass-based dairy farms. *Journal of Dairy Science*, *97*(3), 1835–1851. doi:10.3168/jds.2013-7174 PMID:24440256

Olivas, R., Díaz, M., & Bernabeu, R. (2013). Structural Equation Modeling of lifestyles and consumer attitudes towards organic food by income: A Spanish case study. *Ciencia e Investigación Agraria*, *40*(2), 265–277. doi:10.4067/S0718-16202013000200003

Olmedilla-Alonso, B., Jiménez-Colmenero, F., & Sánchez-Muniz, F. J. (2013). Development and assessment of healthy properties of meat and meat products designed as functional foods. *Meat Science*, *95*(4), 919–930. doi:10.1016/j.meatsci.2013.03.030 PMID:23623320

Oltjen, J. W., Kebreab, E., & Lapierre, H. (Eds.). (2013). *Energy and protein metabolism and nutrition in sustainable animal production* (Vol. 134). Wageningen Academic Publishers. doi:10.3920/978-90-8686-781-3

Orecchini, F., Valitutti, V., & Vitali, G. (2012). Industry and academia for a transition towards sustainability: Advancing sustainability science through university–business collaborations. *Sustainability Science*, *7*(S1), 57–73. doi:10.1007/s11625-011-0151-3

Peri, C. (2006). The universe of food quality. *Food Quality and Preference*, *17*(1-2), 3–8. doi:10.1016/j.foodqual.2005.03.002

Provenza, F. D., Meuret, M., & Gregorini, P. (2015). Our landscapes, our livestock, ourselves: Restoring broken linkages among plants, herbivores, and humans with diets that nourish and satiate. *Appetite*, *95*, 500–519. doi:10.1016/j.appet.2015.08.004 PMID:26247703

Pugliese, P., Zanasi, C., Atallah, O., & Cosimo, R. (2013). Investigating the interaction between organic and local foods in the Mediterranean: The Lebanese organic consumer's perspective. *Food Policy*, *39*, 1–12. doi:10.1016/j.foodpol.2012.12.009

Puniya, A. K., Singh, R., & Kamra, D. N. (Eds.). (2015). *Rumen Microbiology: From Evolution to Revolution.* New Delhi, India: Springer India. doi:10.1007/978-81-322-2401-3

Realini, C., Font, I., Furnols, M., Sañudo, C., Montossi, F., Oliver, M. A., & Guerrero, L. (2013). Spanish, French and British consumers' acceptability of Uruguayan beef, and consumers' beef choice associated with country of origin, finishing diet and meat price. *Meat Science, 95*(1), 14–21. doi:10.1016/j.meatsci.2013.04.004 PMID:23644048

Realini, C. E., Kallas, Z., Perez-Juan, M., Gomez, I., Olleta, J. L., Beriain, M. J., ... Sañudo, C. (2014). Relative importance of cues underlying Spanish consumers' beef choice and segmentation, and consumer liking of beef enriched with n-3 and CLA fatty acids. *Food Quality and Preference, 33*, 74–85. doi:10.1016/j.foodqual.2013.11.007

Rikkonen, P., Kotro, J., Koistinen, L., Penttilä, K., & Kauriinoja, H. (2013). Opportunities for local food suppliers to use locality as a competitive advantage – a mixed survey methods approach. *Acta Agriculturae Scandinavica, Section B — Soil & Plant Science, 63*, 29–37. doi:10.1080/09064710.783620

Schleenbecker, R., & Hamm, U. (2013). Consumers' perception of organic product characteristics. A review. *Appetite, 71*, 420–429. doi:10.1016/j.appet.2013.08.020 PMID:24012637

Tamminga, S. A., Bannink, A., Dijkstra, J., & Zom, R. (2007). *Feeding strategies to reduce methane loss in cattle.* Report 34. Animal Sciences Group, Wageningen UR Livestock Research: Lelystad.

Thomassen, M. A., Dolman, M. A., Van Calker, K. J., & De Boer, I. J. M. (2009). Relating life cycle assessment indicators to gross value added for Dutch dairy farms. *Ecological Economics, 68*(8-9), 2278–2284. doi:10.1016/j.ecolecon.2009.02.011

Tiwari, R., & Rana, C. S. (2015). Plant secondary metabolites: A review. *International Journal of Engineering Research and General Science, 3*(5), 661–670.

Troy, D. J., & Kerry, J. P. (2010). Consumer perception and the role of science in the meat industry. *Meat Science, 86*(1), 214–226. doi:10.1016/j.meatsci.2010.05.009 PMID:20579814

Udo, H. M. J., Aklilu, H. A., Phong, L. T., Bosma, R. H., Budisatria, I. G. S., Patil, B. R., ... Bebe, B. O. (2011). Impact of intensification of different types of livestock production in smallholder crop-livestock systems. *Livestock Science, 139*(1-2), 22–29. doi:10.1016/j.livsci.2011.03.020

Van der Leeuw, S., Wiek, A., Harlow, J., & Buizer, J. (2012). How much time do we have? Urgency and rhetoric in sustainability science. *Sustainability Science, 7*(S1), 115–120. doi:10.1007/s11625-011-0153-1

Van Wezemael, L., Verbeke, W., de Barcellos, M. D., Scholderer, J., & Perez-Cueto, F. (2010). Consumer perceptions of beef healthiness: Results from a qualitative study in four European countries. *BMC Public Health, 10*(1), 342. doi:10.1186/1471-2458-10-342 PMID:20550647

Walsh, B. J., Rydzak, F., Palazzo, A., Kraxner, F., Herrero, M., Schenk, P. M., ... Obersteiner, M. (2015). New feed sources key to ambitious climate targets. *Carbon Balance and Management, 10*(26), 1–8. doi:10.1186/s13021-015-0040-7 PMID:26661066

Wanapat, M., Cherdthong, A., Phesatcha, K., & Kang, S. (2015). Dietary sources and their effects on animal production and environmental sustainability. *Animal Nutrition, 1*(3), 96–103. doi:10.1016/j.aninu.2015.07.004

White, R. R., & Brady, M. (2014). Can consumers' willingness to pay incentivize adoption of environmental impact reducing technologies in meat animal production? *Food Policy, 49*(Part 1), 41–49. doi:10.1016/j.foodpol.2014.06.007

White, R. R., Brady, M., Capper, J. L., & Johnson, K. A. (2014). Optimizing diet and pasture management to improve sustainability of U.S. beef production. *Agricultural Systems, 130*, 1–12. doi:10.1016/j.agsy.2014.06.004

White, R. R., Brady, M., Capper, J. L., McNamara, J. P., & Johnson, K. A. (2015). Cow–calf reproductive, genetic, and nutritional management to improve the sustainability of whole beef production systems. *Journal of Animal Science, 93*(6), 3197–3211. doi:10.2527/jas.2014-8800 PMID:26115306

White, R. R., & Capper, J. L. (2013). An environmental, economic, and social assessment of improving cattle finishing weight or average daily gain within U.S. beef production. *Journal of Animal Science, 91*(12), 5801–5812. doi:10.2527/jas.2013-6632 PMID:24146151

White, R. R., & Capper, J. L. (2014). Precision diet formulation to improve performance and profitability across various climates: Modeling the implications of increasing the formulation frequency of dairy cattle diets. *Journal of Dairy Science, 97*(3), 1563–1577. doi:10.3168/jds.2013-6859 PMID:24393175

Yáñez-Ruiz, D. R., Abecia, L., & Newbold, C. (2015). Manipulating rumen microbiome and fermentation through interventions during early life: A review. *Frontiers in Microbiology, 6*, 1133. doi:10.3389/fmicb.2015.01133 PMID:26528276

ADDITIONAL READING

AAFCO (Association of American Feed Control Officials). (2000). *Official Publication, Association of American Feed Control Officials Inc*. West Lafayette in AAFCO Press.

Maxwell, C. V. (2006). Future of the feed/food industry: re-inventing animal feed. In T. P. Lyons & K. A. Jacques (Eds.), *Nutritional Biotechnology in the Feed and Food Industries* (pp. 11–27). Nottingham: Nottingham University Press; Retrieved from http://en.engormix.com/MA-feed-machinery/formulation/articles/future-feed-food-industry-t229/p0.htm

Mennecke, B. E., Townsend, A. M., Hayes, D. J., & Lonergan, S. M. (2007). A study of the factors that influence consumer attitudes toward beef products using the conjoint market analysis tool. *Journal of Animal Science*, *85*(10), 2639–2659. doi:10.2527/jas.2006-495 PMID:17526667

Mesías, F. J., Escribano, M., Rodríguez de Ledesma, A., & Pulido, F. (2005). Consumers' preferences for beef in the Spanish region of Extremadura: A study using conjoint analysis. *Journal of the Science of Food and Agriculture*, *85*(14), 2487–2494. doi:10.1002/jsfa.2283

Mesías, F. J., Gaspar, P., Pulido, Á. F., Escribano, M., & Pulido, F. (2009). Consumers' preferences for Iberian dry-cured ham and the influence of mast feeding: An application of conjoint analysis in Spain. *Meat Science*, *83*(4), 684–690. doi:10.1016/j.meatsci.2009.08.004 PMID:20416637

KEY TERMS AND DEFINITIONS

Food System/Agro-Food System: All processes and infrastructure involved in feeding a population: growing, harvesting, packing, processing, transforming, marketing, consuming, and disposing of food. The most common food system is the agro-industrial food system that is global.

Chapter 9
Partnership of Rural Tourism and Organic Farming to Achieve Goals of Green Economy:
Rural Tourism and Organic Farming

Predrag Vuković
Institute of Agricultural Economics, Serbia

Svetlana Milorad Roljević-Nikolić
Institute of Agricultural Economics, Serbia

ABSTRACT

Practice has shown that the best results in solving problems that burden rural areas give mechanisms which coordinate development of agriculture with other economic activities on the principles of sustainable development. Partnership in the development of rural tourism and organic agriculture represent a logical sequence of things. People today are aware of the complex problem of burdening the global food chain and natural resources with the remains of persistent pesticides, nitrates, and the worsening of organoleptic properties and nutrient-like food. The concept of organic farming insists on the natural balance of interests. For this reason, tourists who come to the rural areas expect that they will be able to consume organically produced healthy food. The chapter analyzes the concept of rural tourism and organic farming, their dynamic development in the world and in Serbia. It points out the importance of its connectivity to eliminate existing negative trends which burden life in rural areas and possibilities to implement the goals of the green economy.

DOI: 10.4018/978-1-5225-2965-1.ch009

INTRODUCTION

Tourism is one of the fastest growing activities in the last ten years. The UN Environment Program and UNWTO (World Tourist Organization) 2005 report that tourism is an activity that has grown by around 25 per cent in the past 10 years. It now accounts for around 10% of the world's economic activity and is one of the main generators of employment. However, it also has major impacts on the natural and built environments and on the wellbeing and culture of host populations. In roughly that same period, the concept of sustainable development has become widely accepted as the way to a better future.

Many authors highlight that in last few decades the concept of sustainable tourism development has become almost universally accepted as desirable and politically appropriate approach to, and goal of, tourism development (Godfrey, 1996; Hall, Roberts & Morag, 2003; etc.). UNWTO (2007) gave important role to sustainable tourst development of tourst destination. This organization insist on sustainability as key factor for successful destination management. Ritchie and Croach (2003) highlight conection between competivnes of torust destination and sustainability development.

Also in last few decades rise interest for organic food. Areas with protect nature is in better position for organic farming. Toursts who shows interst for rural tourism, ecpecially for ecotourism have great interest for consupmtion organic food during their staying in rural torust destination.

The Republic of Serbia has great potenital for development rural toruism. More than 80% of territory cover rural areas and on this area lives approximatly 45% of total population. Also this areas are very good preserved. The same resources gives also potentials for development organic farming.

CONCEPT OF RURAL TOURISM

Rural areas today are burdened with numerous problems (aging population, migration to urban city centers, unemployment, reduction in macroeconomic indicators, etc.). These kinds of problems are present in most countries. The tendency is to stop these negative trends and initiate in the opposite direction. A synergetic character of tourism allows connection of a large number of economic and non-economic activities and with its positive multiplicative effects gives possibility to achieve economic development of rural areas.

Until this moment, many authors and international organizations who research development of rural tourism have tried to give uniform and universally accepted definition of rural tourism, but reason that this definition doesn`t exist until now, unfortunately lies in complexity of the issue. Namely, rural tourism touches two important branches of national economy – agriculture and tourism. Second important issue is that rural areas have different definition in many countries. Table 1 shows some criteria for rural settlements that use different countries.

The OECD Rural Development Programme uses a pragmatically based series of indicators:

- At the local level, a population density of 150 persons per square kilometer is the preferred criterion.
- At the regional level, geographic units are grouped by the share of their population which is rural, into the following three types:
  - Predominantly rural (> 50 per cent).
  - Significantly rural (15-50 per cent).
  - Predominantly urbanized regions (< 15 per cent).

These two issues are reason that until now there no universal and uniform definition of rural tourism. One of the best definitions gave OECD (1994, p.14) in report *Tourism Strategies and Rural Development*. Author of this report, Lane B. understood complexity of the definition rural tourism and suggested work definition. He suggested characteristic of rural tourism on the way that it can be recognized as typical.

- Located in rural areas.

Table 1. Selected national criteria for "rural" settlements

Country	Criteria
Australia	Population clusters of fewer than 1 000 people, excluding certain areas, e.g. holiday resorts
Austria	Towns of fewer than 5 000 people
Canada	Places of fewer than 1 000 people, with a population density of fewer than 400 per square kilometer.
Denmark and Norway	Agglomerations of fewer than 200 inhabitants
England and Wales	No definition - but the Rural Development Commission excludes towns with more than 10 000 inhabitants.
France	Towns containing an agglomeration of fewer than 2 000 people living in contiguous houses, or with not more than 200 metres between the houses.
Portugal and Switzerland	Towns of fewer than 10 000 people.

Source: OECD (1994): Tourism Strategies and Rural Development, General Distribution, OECD/GD (94) 49, p.9-10. Web site: http://www.oecd.org/dataoecd/31/27/2755218.pdf (accessed on 06/29/2017).

- Functionally rural; built upon the rural world`s special features;
- Rural in scale.
- Traditional in character, growing slowly and organically, and connected with local families.
- Sustainable. In the sense that its development should help sustain the special rural character of an area, and in the sense that its development should be sustainable in its use of resources. Rural tourism should be seen as a potential tool for conservation and sustainability, rather than as an urbanizing and development tool.
- Of many different kinds, representing the complex pattern of rural environment, economy and history.

The same document emphasizes the factors one must consider when determining rural tourism (type of vacation, intensity of vacation use, location, management, style, degree of integration with the community) (OECD, 1994).

El-Hage Scialabba and Williamson (2004) clarified distinguishes of the following types of tourism that can be taking place in rural areas:

- **Ecotourism:** Under the right circumstances, ecotourism has proven to be one of the most effective means to finance biodiversity conservation. In most rich biodiversity areas, actual revenue flows for ecotourism are better than non-timber forest products and biopharmacy, and comparable only to agroforestry. Because the dominating land use in protected areas and buffer zones is agriculture and forestry, ecotourism is an opportunity for the creation of additional income to farmers/foresters and to generate financial means for the management of protected areas, especially where governmental park management agencies have little resources.
- **Agro-Tourism:** The symbiotic relationship between tourism and agriculture that can be found in agrotourism (i.e. holidays on farmland) is a key element of an environmentally and socially responsible tourism in rural areas. Rural hospitality offers new employment and income generating opportunities for rural populations, including agrotourism as expression and cultural exchange of agricultural practices, artistic heritage and craftsmanship and culinary traditions. Agrotourism may take several forms: holiday farms, farmhouse bed-and-breakfast, farm camping, mountain resorts, equestrian centres and other forms of rural accommodations. Such facilities are an innovative payment system for environmental services generated on and around agricultural lands.
- **Agro-Ecotourism:** While ecotourism is nature-based and agro-tourism is farm-based, agro-ecotourism is a combination of both. The rural landscape, usually a combination of wild and agro-ecosystems, is the most important

resource for tourism development. It is obvious that a diversified agricultural landscape, with semi-natural habitats, has a greater aesthetic and recreational potential over uniform, degraded and/or polluted agricultural areas. In Europe, agri-environmental policies often promoted organic agricultural activities as a most effective means for landscape conservation. Agro-ecotourism in certain locations provides a strong economic incentive to small farmers to commit to biodiversity-friendly agriculture management.

- **Eco-Organic Tourism:** When agro-ecotourism involves around an organic farm, it is referred to as eco-organic tourism. The valorisation of specific elements of the agro-ecosystem landscape offers an additional economic resource for environmental protection. Conversion to organic management in agricultural areas and the development of connected activities such as tourism are increasing. When farms are organically-managed, they increase the motivation for tourists' visits. New tourist expectations have enhanced the quality of the supply such as diversified farm landscape, environmentally-sound farm-house architecture and local/typical gastronomy.

European Federation of Rural Tourism ("EuroGites") at the general conference held on 29th September 2005 held at Yalta in Ukraine adopted a "general standards of rural tourism" (Table 2)

DYNAMIC DEVELOPMENT OF RURAL TOURISM IN THE REPUBLIC OF SERBIA

Accepting views on the phase development of rural tourism with the corresponding characteristics that Zodorov (2009), it can be concluded that in the Republic of Serbia, as well as in most other countries, rural tourism has developed in an identical way with the same features, even the duration of the phases can be precisely determined.

The first phase could be named independent establishment. Rural tourism in Serbia started to develop since the seventies of the twentieth century. The villages that were so called the "pioneers" of the development were Sirogojno, Seča Reka and Devići. At that time, the leading tourist agencies "Yugoturs" and "Putnik" were involved in the business of bringing foreign tourists to rural areas. Thus, according to the 1992 Serbian Tourist Association, there were about 35,000 foreign tourists from 21 countries in Knić municipality. The largest number of tourists was recorded from Great Britain, Germany, Russia and Italy (Todorivić. & Bjelac, 2009; Milojević, 2004; UN WTO, 2003; Štetić & Todorović, 2009).

Table 2. The criteria for defining the framework of rural tourism by the European Federation of Rural Tourism ("EUROGITES") from 2005

No.	Criterion	Explanation
1.	Position of the household in the natural environment, a village or small town	Less than 5,000 residents in the village / town or in typical / traditional neighbourhoods.
2.	Rural area with emphasize characteristics of traditional agriculture and the outstanding natural values	Outstanding natural values (natural park, etc.). Traditional agriculture excluded industry.
3.	Tourism is not the main or predominant activity or source of income in the surrounding area.	The ratio of the number of tourist beds and residents in rural areas should not exceed 1:1 ratio.
4.	Good environment, quiet and peaceful location, no noise and pollution	Acceptable noise and odors that is characteristic of traditional agricultural production.
5.	Authentic accommodation and environment	-
6.	Hospitality	Personal care host about the guest (tourists).
7.	Small capacity units	The upper limit capacity is 40 beds, if not legally designated or prescribed by internal standardization by members.
8.	Respect the legal criteria for evaluation	Respect for standards adapted to evaluate quality
9.	Social sustainability in the context of multi-functional activities in rural areas	The application of the criteria of "Agenda 21" for tourism. [1]
10.	Connection with the local community and traditional culture.	Minimum integration activities within the communities in the region, guests have the opportunity to make contact with local realities if they want to.
11.	Local products and gastronomy	Available in the environment.
12.	Culture (folklore, handicrafts, customs, heritage, etc.)	Available in the environment.
13.	Excluding criteria: • Urban and industrial locality and their surroundings. • Areas of extreme mass and developed tourism. • Noise, pollution etc.	

Source: Ružić, P., (2009): Rural tourism, Institute for agriculture and tourism, Poreč, p.16.

Note: 1) Considering that tourism has simplified impact on economic and social development, it is reasonable to highlight the „social costs of tourism", as well as determining the consequences of its development. Many tourist places, adapting to the needs of tourism development are losing their originality and uniqueness. For this reason, it has developed a concept called „Sustainable tourism". Sustainable tourism is defined as the positive approach that seeks to reduce tensions and frictions that arise from complex interactions between the tourism industry, visitors, the environment and society as a host. Such a tourism including work for lasting quality of natural and human resources, which is particularly emphasized in the document *Agenda 21*.

Table 3. Indicators in the development of rural tourism in Serbia in the period from 1990 to 2000 according to the data of the Tourist Organization of Serbia

Year	1990	2000
Number of villages	50	41
Number of farms	800	170
Number of beds	3 000	800

Source: Milojević, Lj., (2004). Rural Tourism in Serbia, p.30, UNWTO. Rural Tourism in Europe: Experiences, Development and Perspectives, p. 27 -31, Proceeding from Seminars, Belgrade (Serbia and Montenegro, 24-25 June 2002), Kielce (Poland, 06-07 June 2003), Yaremcha (Ukraine, 25-26 Sept. 2003) published by UNWTO 2004. Web link: http://www.idestur.org.br/download/20120219145557.pdf (accesses: 01/24/201.)

The reasons for the emergence of negative trends in the development of rural tourism in the observed decade should be seen primarily in the deep political, social and economic crisis that reflected on all segments of the society, and hence on tourism.

The second phase, dedicated development started in 2006. In the period from 2006 to 2008, the Ministry of Agriculture, Forestry and Water Management of the Republic of Serbia allocated a total of 91,580,215 dinars for development of rural tourism and diversification of economic activities in the countryside. In 2008, there were 173 users of these funds (141 registered agricultural producers, 23 associations of citizens, 7 legal entities and 2 agricultural cooperatives). The largest amount of funds was distributed to the region of Western Serbia and AP Vojvodina, while most districts were distributed in Zlatibor region, and the least in the North Backa region. The analysis of the types of investments indicates that as much as 91% of the funds allocated were directed to the restoration of traditional rural farms (adaptation, upgrading and renovation of facilities, procurement of equipment, etc.), while 9% were allocated for promotional and educational activities. (Analysis of budget support to the development of rural tourism in Serbia and the diversification of economic activities in the countryside, 2009)

Vuković et al. (2015) state that until the year 2011, there were no reliable indicators of rural tourism development in Serbia. That is when *The Master Plan of Sustainable Development of Rural Tourism* (2011) was made, which presented the results that 106 local tourist organizations made in cooperation. According to this source, rural tourism encompassed 2.7 million overnight stays, which is the sum of individual overnight stays in rural tourism (145,354). This data comes from the municipalities and LTOs. As pointed out in this document, no central institution is in charge of gathering this data, except the Council of each municipality or the LTO, (p.15). The number of common tourist overnight stays usable for rural tourism (2,556,128). The Master Plan states: the common tourist overnight stays usable for rural tourism mean accommodation in rural areas that can be used by tourists who visit the rural areas, but cannot be called "rural households". Rural tourism provides more than 32,000 beds (registered and unregistered), where more than 10,000 beds are in the countryside. The total number of beds is estimated to bring more than 5 billion RSD annually in income and 5 bn. RSD in direct income to the tourism sector. The income of 10 bn. RSD does not include visitors who stay for a night or stay with their friends or family (although they also spend money on tourism and other services during their stay) and it does not include the indirect contribution to the local economy in the sense of income and employment. The income of 10 bn. RSD is 16% of direct GDP from travel and tourism, as calculated by the *World Council for Travel and Tourism in Serbia* for the year 2010, which is 64.2 bn. RSD (pp.74-75). Based on this, we can conclude that rural tourism today has an up-going trend in development.

DEVELOPMENT ORGANIC FRAMING TRENDS IN EURPOE AND SERBIA

For the reason that food is nowadays polluted with presistent pesticides, nitrates and all the worse organoloeptic and nutritonal elements, peopele shows rise interest for organic food.

Roljević (2014) stated that organic farming represents a comprehensive system of farm management and food production that protects environment, preserves biodiversity and natural resources. The sustainability of organic production is reflected in the rational use of natural resources, without exhausting, but rather through maintaining and increasing their diversity, leaving no negative impacts on the environment. This system is controlled and subject to inspection, which is why it has the trust of consumers in terms of quality and food safety.

FiBL-IFOAM, 2016 represent data that organic agriculture nowadays is practice in 172 countries and covered 40.3 million ha (1% of global agricultural land), on which there are registered 1.8 million farms.

In the EU, organic farming is practiced by 10.3 million ha, which represents 23.5% of global land area under organic production. The number of registered organic producers in 2014 at the EU amounted to 257,525, which is 2.4% compared to the total number of farms (Eurostat, 2016).

Eurostat gives data that most of the area coverd by organic farming is located in Spain (1,968,570 ha), Italy (1,492,579 ha), France (1,322,911 ha) and Germany (1,060,291 ha), which disposes of 50% of the total organic surface of the European Union etc. (Figure 1).

Figure 1. Area under organic production in EU member states
Source: Eurostat (09/14/2017).

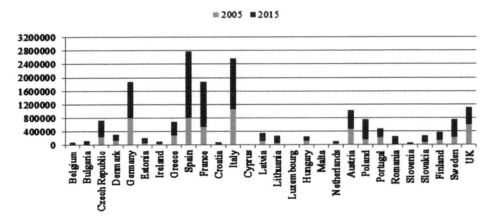

In EU dynamic of rise organic farmers shows almost linear trend (Figure 2.). Most registered organic producers are located in Italy (52,609), Spain (34,673), France (28,884) and Germany (25,078) and account for 52% of the total number of organic producers in the EU.

EU has support policy for organic agricultrue. It is regulated by the Council Regulation (EC) No 834/2007. This Councile definine the official EU aims, objectives and principles of organic farming and production. Council Regulation follow two Commission regulations, Commission Regulation (EC) No. 889/2008 with the detailed rules for production, labeling and control, including the first amendment to the rules on production of organic yeast and Commission Regulation (EC) No. 1235/2008 detailed rules regarding the import of organic products from third countries.

Figure 2. The number of organic producers in the EU during the period 2005-2015
Source: Eurostat, accessed on 05/25/2017.

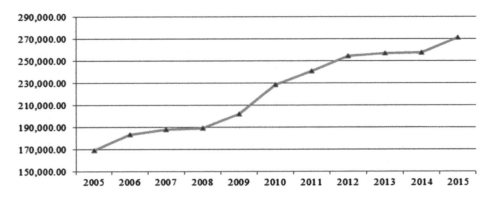

In the Republic of Serbia exist great potential for organic farming. This attitude is based on well preserved ecological agricultural resources, economic and social capacities, fact that rural population shows interest for organic agriculture, etc. If all these potentials would be put in function of organic agriculture, competitiveness of agriculture production and rural development while giving a positive contribution to the overall socio-economic development of the country (Roljević et al., 2012).

FiBL/IFOAM givs data that in 2006 in the Republic of Serbia under organic production were only 740 ha, but nowadays it is 15,298 ha (certified and areas in conversion), accounting for 0.4% of agricultural land in Serbia (MAEP, 2015). FiBL/IFOAM givs precise data that arable crops covered almost 55%, orchards and vineyards 19% represent dominated structure of crop production, while vegetable gardening practices covered only 1% of soil in organic production system (Table 4).

CONNECTION BETWEEN RURAL TOURISM AND ORGANIC AGRICULTURE

The modern trends in the tourism market move further from the concept of mass tourism offered by vacations in destinations located on the seashore and/or mountain ski resorts. There is striving towards activating all segments of tourist demand in order to achieve the best results in tourism development. In this way the countries, i.e. destinations that do not possess the resource bases for developing the so-called

Table 4. Areas under organic production in Serbia in 2015

Category	In the Period of Conversion (ha)	Certified Areas (ha)	Total (ha)
Cereals	2,069.05	2,182.89	4,251.94
Industrial plants	1,216.25	1,458.14	2,674.38
Vegetable	45.61	124.89	170.50
Fodder crops	397.58	104.81	1,440.39
Fruit	1,291.13	1,603.98	2,895.10
Medicinal and Aromatic Plants	2.67	68.27	70.94
Rest	1,844.55	50.39	1,894.93
Total arable land	6,866.84	6,531.36	13,398.19
Meadows and pastures	802.63	1,097.19	1,899.83
Total	7,669.47	7,628.55	15,298.02

Source: Direction for National referent laboratories, MAEP, 2015.

„mass tourism" seek their chance on the tourism market by offering alternative tourism products. (Vuković et al., 2015.)

This is precisely where Serbia's key to success on the tourism market lies. Great resource bases significant for the development of organic agriculture on one hand, as well as rural tourism on the other, create the possibility of their interaction and forming a specific tourism product that could be made into a brand, and as such, be positioned on the tourism market. In this way, Serbia could create a completely new tourism image, and reposition itself on the market as a tourist destination.

The focus of long-term research of the Poon, A., is to understand the changes that have taken place in the tourism market and their impact on the competitiveness of destinations and tourism enterprises. (Poon A., 1993; 1994; 2003; 2007 etc).

She makes a distinction between the two concepts of tourism, the so-called "old" and "new" one. The concept of "old tourism" has been implemented during the fifties, sixties and the seventies of the twentieth century. It can be recognized by the mass attitude, standardized quality of services, rigidly packaged tourist products, strict roles management, implementation new services technology, production and production frameworks etc. Also, next factors made influence for this form of tourism development:

- The entry of large multinational corporations into tourism.
- Franchising.
- Economic growth is inspired by teaching of *Keynes. J. M.*
- The availability of cars and cheap gasoline.
- The appearance of jet planes, etc.

This kind of tourism approach has destroyed the sense of visitors regarding the values of local communities, and has heightened the neglect of the environment of the destination, both by tourists and residents. Also, this kind of tourism minimizes the personal contacts of tourists with representatives of the local community.

Poon, state that in recent years has been emerged the concept of "new tourism". Its main features are: flexibility, segmentation, integrity, focuses on the environment and tourists as a consumer (person). She insisted that concept of "new tourism" has been changing rules of the "market game". It is based on new strategy approach. Reason is success on the market. Travel and tourism industry have experience radical and rapid transformation, which is why the competitiveness strategy is more important than ever. In order to survive the competitiveness of industrial players within the concept of mass tourism, it was necessary to apply the marketing and standardization that this concept required, while the so-called "Tourism transition" focused on a limited choice and flexible, short breaks to attract tourists interested in sustainable tourism, rural tourism, etc., or more for individual and flexible holiday

/ stay programs in the appropriate tourist destinations. „New tourism" with changes sets the rules of the game in the economy and requires new strategies to ensure competitive success (Poon, 2003).

From the 1970s to the present, the service sector has experienced great expansion and has become the dominant sector in many economies. Over time, interest in service quality has increased, as studies have shown that this is a prediction for the success and survival of enterprises in a competitive environment, in other words, providing quality services to clients creates an opportunity for companies to gain a competitive advantage (Poon, 2003).

Today's tourist is determined by his own personal needs. Tourist destinations that are able to meet the personal needs of tourists are more competitive on the market. This particularly applies to rural tourism destinations that are by definition addressed to meet the personal needs of visitors. This is in line with the definition of rural tourism, which suggests that it is small in scale and small intensity.

Modern tourists who go to rural destinations want to completely consume so-called "rural tourism experience". In that sense, they want to escape from the modern way of life which one of the most recognized characteristic is "fast food". Modern tourists who spend their vocation in rural tourist destination want to eat "slow food", or beter word food made by organically produced agricultural products. Rural tourist destinations that can offer such more organic products are more competitive.

As numerous studies have shown, it is precisely the segment of foods in the tourist supply, one of the important components of the overall tourist experience of a destination and, consequently, of its competitiveness. Hence, great opportunities for organic production are opened up as a food tourism destination in rural areas.

Each rural area has some natural specificity that affects the agricultural production and the food consumed therein. For this reason, there are a large number of different culinary specialties that can be found in different tourist destinations. The Republic of Serbia has a great geographical diversity from the Pannonian flat lend located in the north part of the county, to the hilly and mountainous area characterized by the south, which allows for a number of different culinary specialties in the tourist supply.

In the Republic of Serbia has done pretty small on linking rural tourism with organic farming so far. It can be said that these are sporadic attempts. Considering the potentials that exist for the development of rural tourism, as well as organic agriculture, it is justified to expect some strategic approach at the state level. It provides opportunities for developing specific tourist brands for destinations that are located in characteristic natural sites. Especially if we understand the geographical diversity that the country has and which provides opportunities for the development of various types of organic farming production. It is also a possibility for development of tourist competitiveness of Serbia, which offers various rural tourism products. The range of tourist offer spreads both on-board and extra-board a tourist offers.

RURAL TOURISM AND POSSIBILITIES TO ACHIEVE AIMS OF GREEN ECONOMY

The development of rural tourism is just launched by the whole mechanism of various activities that are included in the tourist supply (construction, rent, trade, etc.). An important place in this offer is organically produced food. This also enables the development of the local economy.

Implicit characteristic of sustainable tourism development is localization. Sustainable tourism development should ideally, focus on satisfying the development needs of local communities trough, for example, promoting local product supply chains, encouraging local crafts and industries optimizing the retention of tourism earnings within the destination ensuring that development is within local environmental and social capacities. The achievement of such localization is, in turn, depended upon local control of tourism development. Indeed, a fundamental objective of sustainable development is the satisfaction of basic needs and encouragement of self-reliance based upon grassroots, endogenous development process (Sharpley, 2003; Galtung, 1986; Streeten, 1977).

If all the principles of sustainable development of rural tourism and organic agriculture are consistently respected, also can be expected development of a green economy with all its characteristics. There is interaction between development of rural tourism and organic agriculture.

One of the key problems of successful management of rural tourism is possibility to define frame of rural tourist destination on which it could be implemented (principles, plans, strategies, etc.). Rural tourist destination can be understood as farm, village, local countryside, or rural area in whole (for example, some rural region). Problem is who is responsible for its successful development of tourist destination. UNWTO (2007) suggest Destination Management Organization. But in rural tourism it must be defined what kind of area this organization will be covering. This is important question because successfulness of implementing strategies depends on it. Maybe better word is that if tourism is recognized as perspective and potential business for local economy who and how it will be leading this system. Solving this problem has direct implication on development of green economy.

UNWTO (2007) define that the VICE model presents destination management as the interaction between the visitors, the industry that servers them, the community that hosts them and the environment where this interaction takes place. The last of these, the environment, can be understood in its broadest sense to include built and natural resources on which many tourism products are based. (Figure 3) To ensure a balance of interests, it is essential that rural tourist destinations must be observed at micro and macro levels. At the micro, as well as farms in rural tourism and at the macro level as well as rural areas in which it can be implement the concept in

Figure 3. "VICE" model
Source: UNWTO (2007): "A Practical Guide to Tourist Destination Management", Madrid, p. 13.

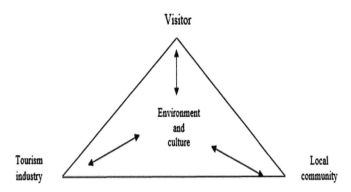

order to ensure long-term economic growth and competitiveness of whole area as a tourist destination. Expectations are that the positive effects of developing rural tourism will reflect in all sectors of the economy that are directly or indirectly linked to tourism, such as, for example, agriculture, trade, transport, civil engineering, etc. If will be respected principles developing rural tourism consistently, in that case it can be achieving growth of so-called "green economy".

According to this model, it is the role of destination managers to work through partnership and joint destination management plan in order to UNWTO (2007, p.13):

- Welcome, involve and satisfy Visitors.
- Achieve a profitable and prosperous tourist industry.
- Engage and benefit host Communities.
- Protect and enhance the local Environment and culture.

One of the questions that arise is whether the development of tourism in itself carries negative implications for the preservation of rural areas, its natural and human (anthropogenic) value? In order to solve this dilemma in the management of rural tourist destinations got on importance concept of sustainable development. The concept has evolved over time. The original idea, which was in the beginning put emphasis on first plan only on the preservation of the environment, today it has grown into a system of complex relationships. In the case of tourism, it should be noted that the World Tourism Organization (UN WTO), through the concept of sustainable development suggests a balance of interests of all stakeholders. In this sense, it suggests use of "VICE" model (Visitor, Industry, Community, Environment and Culture).

Tourism is in special position in the contribution it can make to sustainable development and the challenges it presents. Firstly, this is because of the dynamism and growth of the sector and the major contribution that it makes to the economies of many countries and local destinations. Secondly, it is because tourism is an activity which involves a special relationship between consumer/visitors the industry, the environment and local communities. (UN WTO, 2005; 2007).

On the basis of guidelines, which in 2004 gave the IUCN (International Union for Nature Conversation) in order to achieve the guidelines of the "green economy", important role must have the management of rural tourist destinations. Management allows the formulation of the vision of sustainable development, which should be based on consultations larger number of stakeholders, sets goals for achieving the vision and tourist standards, provides strategic direction and development activities, assess the potential impacts of tourism on the environment, applies adaptive resource management in line with tourism and biodiversity.

It is a complementary process.

Organic farming and rural tourism have multiple complementarities in development, which is reflected in the following:

- Sustainability of organic agriculture and rural tourism is based on the rational use of natural resources. The intention is to preserve and increase their diversity with minimum negative impacts on the environment.
- Organically produced agricultural products are subject to inspection and control, hence the trust of tourists who come to rural destinations that they will exactly be able to consume these organic products, which increase revenues of producers, as well as farmers who offer tourist services.
- Rural tourism is, by definition, small-scale and low intensity. As such it is found to comply with the organic products which, according to numerous studies have shown give lower yield of crops in comparison with conventional agriculture. However, these yields can be compensated with numerous benefits that organic farming offer, such as, for example, increased soil fertility, reduced pollution, conservation of agro-eco system, income security, strengthening communities, improving the health of the population, etc.

UNWTO (2012) gave key messages to achieve goals of green economy:

- Tourism as an economic sector can significantly contribute to the growth of the world economy. This attitude is based on the fact that the tourism economy accounts for 5% of the world's GDP and accounts for 8% of the total employment. International tourism is in the fourth place (after fuels, chemicals and automotive products) in the value of global exports. There are around four billion estimated domestic arrivals every year and in 2010, some 940 million international tourists were recorded. Tourism represent one of the five top export earners in over 150 countries. Also tourism represent one of the main source of foreign exchange for 1/3 of developing countries and „least developed countries" (LDC).

- Tourism is facing with significant challenges in its development. Some of the challenges are: business improvement in the IT sector, rapid development of traffic, environmental pollution, international terrorism, etc.

- The development of green tourism enables the creation of new *"Green jobs."* Tourism is a labor intensive economic activity. It is estimated that directly and indirectly employs about 8% of the global workforce. It is also estimated that one job in the core tourism industry creates about one and a half additional or indirect jobs in tourism related economy. If the concept of greening tourism will take important place in future of tourism business, it is assumption that percentage would be rise. This attitude is based on the fact of the synergistic character of tourism that includes a large number of economic activities (trade, agriculture, construction, etc.).

- The role of tourism is, among other things, to support local economy and reducing local poverty. This attitude is based primarily in the fact that the tourists during staing in some destination through their consumption contribute to the local economy . Tourism contributes to the development of an entire sector of services that is directly and indirectly linked to tourism.

- Investing in the development of "Green tourism" contributes to reducing energy costs, water and waste water consumption, developing ecosystems, preserving cultural heritage, and contributing to energy efficiency.

- Modern tourists require green tourism. This is caused primarily by the fact the growth of environmental awareness of population. A certain part of the tourists is ready to pay from 2 to 40% more for this type of service. Modern tourists are sophisticated in their requirements. Hence, today's modern tourist offer is oriented towards the individual demands of tourists as consumers.

- In order to develop green tourism, private sector must be developmed, especially small and medium-sized firms. Practice has shown that awareness of advantages of green tourism has been present so far mainly in large-scale companies. An important role in this process should be put on process of education owners and employees of small and medium firms which are involved in distribution of tourist services.

- In order to make tourism more "green", it is necessary to use the mechanisms of marketing and management of tourist destinations. In this respect, all stakeholders must have a coordinated management both horizontally and vertically. In this way, all economic activities that are included in the chain of tourist supply will generate revenues. Some of the necessary steps in this porcess are zoning, protected areas, environmental regulations, labor standards, health standards, environmental standards and health requirements, especially energy, emissions, water, waste and sanitation.

- It is very important investment of Government and the other of administrative organs in the development of "green tourism" and private sector. In this sense, important role take the policy towards protected areas, preservation of cultural heritage, preservation of water and soil, sanitation system, public transport, renewable energy sources. Governments often use concessions and subsidies to promote development of green tourism.

CONCLUSION

Tourism has been developing rapidly in the last few decades. The particular expansion has been recorded since the seventies of the twentieth century. This is also the case in the Republic of Serbia. The only period when development made stagnation was recorded during the 1990s, due to well-known events in the territory of the former Yugoslavia (wars, sanctions, deep political, economic and social crisis, etc.).

Since 2008, the Ministry of Agriculture and Forestry of the Republic of Serbia has started to allocate dedicated funds for the development of rural tourism, which contributed to its accelerated development. Today, there is almost no region in Serbia without the development of some of the forms of rural tourism (eco, agro, agro-eco, eco-organic tourism - UNFAO definition).

In Serbia, more than 85% of the territory consists of rural areas, which are largely well preserved. They provide a great opportunity for the development of organic agriculture. However, the development of organic agriculture in Serbia is still not at the level that it could be in terms of potential.

In Republic of Serbia rural tourism has started to develop in the seventies of the twentieth century and its dynamics in the development has different intensity over the time. A similar dynamic has had organic agriculture. Having in mind very good preservation of natural areas in Serbia today is reasonably asks the question using comparative advantages for rural tourism and organic agriculture, the ability to connect them and shifts them into a competitive advantage.

Rural tourism and organic agriculture are complementary activities. Both are low intensity and small volume. This is because they put the environment in the forefront. As one of the possibilities that would contribute to the development of both organic agriculture and rural tourism, it is possible to connect them in a tourist offer. In this way, the Pension supply will be enriched and made possible by the creation of a large number of different specialties from organically produced agricultural products.

The expectations are that in this way specific tourism products based on food tourism could be formed, which in a number of ways could enrich the overall tourist offer - from the classical boarding house to tourism events that would attract a certain number of tourists to rural areas. By doing so, rural tourism destinations that would connect these two complementary activities would also become more attractive to the market, i.e. more competitive in relation to those destinations that do not have this kind of tourist supply.

An important role is played by the management of rural tourism destinations. In rural tourism this is one of the essential issues, because rural tourism destinations themselves, as well as rural tourism, are difficult to define. They can be farms, villages or entire rural areas. UNWTO in 2007 suggests the destination management organization as a form of public and private partnership that would allow easier management of these destinations. In so far as the regulation of legal regulation is one of the priority tasks in order to solve such problems.

Having in mind all the foregoing, it is reasonable to expect appropriate activities to make link between organic agriculture and rural tourism. The results that could be achieved would be in favor of development and rural tourism and organic agriculture. This is in line with general market trends that show growth in demand for both types of business.

ACKNOWLEDGMENT

This article is part of the research project *"Sustainable agriculture and rural development in the function of accomplishing strategic objectives of the Republic of Serbia within the Danube region"*, No. III - 46006, financed by the Ministry of Education, Science and Technological Development of the Republic of Serbia.

REFERENCES

Analysis of budget support to the development of rural tourism in Serbia and the diversification of economic activities in the countryside. (2009). Retrieved from Ministry of Agriculture, Forestry and Water Management of the Republic of Serbia - Sector for Rural Development, Direction for National referent laboratories, MAEP, 2015: http://www.dnrl.minpolj.gov.rs/o_nama/organska.html

EUROSTAT. (n.d.). Retrieved from http://ec.europa.eu/eurostat/statistics-explained/index.php/Organic_farming_statistics

Galtung, J. (1986). *Towards a new economics: On the theory and practice of self-reliance. In The Living Economy: A New Economics in the Making.* London: Routledge.

Godfrey, K. B. (1996). Towards sustainability? Tourism in the Republic of Cyprus. *Practicing responsible tourism: International case studies in tourism planning, policy and development*, 58-79.

Hall, D., Roberts, L., & Mitchell, M. (2003). *New directions in rural tourism.* Ashgate Publishing Ltd.

Lane, B. (1994). What is rural tourism? *Journal of Sustainable Tourism*, 2(1-2), 7–21. doi:10.1080/09669589409510680

OECD. (1994), *Tourism Strategies and Rural Development.* General Distribution, OECD/GD (94)49, 9-10. Retrieved from http://www.oecd.org/dataoecd/31/27/2755218.pdf

Poon, A. (1990). Flexible specialization and small size: The case of Caribbean tourism. *World Development*, 18(1), 109–123. doi:10.1016/0305-750X(90)90106-8

Poon, A. (1993). *Tourism, technology and competitive strategies.* CAB international.

Poon, A. (1994). The 'new tourism' revolution. *Tourism Management*, 15(2), 91–92. doi:10.1016/0261-5177(94)90001-9

Poon, A. (2003). Competitive strategies for a 'new tourism'. *Classic reviews in tourism*, 130-142.

Poon, A. (2007). Local Involvment in Tourism. In *Proceedings of Meeting on the Trade and Development Implications of Tourism Services for Developing Countries.* UNCTAD XII pre-event.

Roljević, S. (2014). *Productivity of alternative small grains in the organic farming system* (Doctoral dissertation). Faculty of Agriculture, University of Belgrade, UDC 631.147: 633.11 (043.3)).

Roljević, S., Grujić, B., & Sarić, R. (2012). *Organic agriculture in terms of sustainable development and rural areas development.* Academic Press.

Ružić, P. (2009). *Rural Tourism.* Pula: Institute for Agriculture and Tourism Porec.

Sciabalabba, N. E. H., & Williamson, D. (2004). *The scope of organic agriculture, sustainable forest management and ecoforestry in protected area management.* Food and Agriculture Organization of the United Nations. Retrieved from ftp://ftp.fao.org/docrep/fao/007/y5558e/y5558e00.pdf

Sharpley, R. (2003). Rural Tourism and Sustainability - A Critique. In New Directions in Rural Tourism. Academic Press.

The Master Plan for Sustainable Rural Tourism Development in Serbia. (2011). Ministry of finance and economy of the Republic of Serbia.

Todorović, M., & Bjeljac, Ž. (2009). Rural tourism in Serbia as a way of development in undeveloped regions. *Acta Geographica Slovenica*, *49*(2), 453–473. doi:10.3986/AGS49208

Todorović, M., & Stetic, S. (2009). *Rural tourism.* Belgrade: University of Belgrade, Faculty of Geography.

UN WTO. (2003). Rural Tourism in Europe: Experiences, Development and Perspectives. In *Proceeding of Seminars* (pp. 115-121). UNWTO.

UNEP. (2012). Tourism in the green economy–background report. UNWTO.

UNWTO. (2004). Rural Tourism in Europe: Experiences, Development and Perspectives. In *Proceeding from Seminars* (pp. 27-31). UNWTO. Retrieved from http://www.idestur.org.br/download/20120219145557.pdf

UNWTO. (2007). *A Practical Guide to Tourism Destination Management.* Retrieved from http://pub.unwto.org/WebRoot/Store/Shops/Infoshop/4745/8BCE/AD9A/ECA8/048B/C0A8/0164/0B7A/071115_practical_guide_destination_management_excerpt.pdf

Vuković, P., Čavlin, G., & Čavlin, M. (2015). Komplementarnost u razvoju ruralnog sa banjskim, spa i wellness turizmom. *Ekonomika Poljoprivrede*, *62*(1), 259–270. doi:10.5937/ekoPolj1501259V

Zdorov, A. B. (2009). Comprehensive development of tourism in the countryside. *Studies on Russian Economic Development*, *20*(4), 453–455. doi:10.1134/S107570070904011X

ADDITIONAL READING

Barlybaev, A. A., Akhmetov, V. Y., & Nasyrov, G. M. (2009). Tourism as a factor of rural economy diversification. *Studies on Russian Economic Development, 20*(6), 639–643. doi:10.1134/S1075700709060094

Björk, P. E. T. E. R. (2001). Sustainable tourism development, fact or fiction in small tourism companies. *LTA, 3*(01), 328–345.

Bogdanov, N. L., Robertson, B., Đorđević-Milošević, S., & Klark, L. (2007). *Small rural households in Serbia and rural non-farm economy*. UNDP.

Bramwell, B. (1994). Rural tourism and sustainable rural tourism. *Journal of Sustainable Tourism, 2*(1-2), 1–6. doi:10.1080/09669589409510679

Dwyer, L., & Kim, C. (2003). Destination competitiveness: Determinants and indicators. *Current Issues in Tourism, 6*(5), 369–414. doi:10.1080/13683500308667962

Getz, D., & Page, S. (Eds.). (1997). *The business of rural tourism: International perspectives*. Cengage Learning EMEA.

Ghobadian, A., Speller, S., & Jones, M. (1994). Service quality: Concepts and models. *International Journal of Quality & Reliability Management, 11*(9), 43–66. doi:10.1108/02656719410074297

Gross, M. J., Brien, C., & Brown, G. (2008). Examining the dimensions of a lifestyle tourism destination. *International Journal of Culture, Tourism and Hospitality Research, 2*(1), 44–66. doi:10.1108/17506180810856130

Lane, B. (1994). What is rural tourism? *Journal of Sustainable Tourism, 2*(1-2), 7–21. doi:10.1080/09669589409510680

Lane, B. (2005). Sustainable rural tourism strategies: A tool for development and conservation. *Revista Interamericana de Ambiente y Turismo-RIAT, 1*(1), 12–18.

Padel, S., Lampkin, N., & Lockeretz, W. (2007). The development of governmental support for organic farming in Europe. *Organic farming: An international history*, 93-122.

Parasuraman, A., Zeithaml, V. A., & Berry, L. L. (1988). Servqual: A multiple-item scale for measuring consumer perc. *Journal of Retailing, 64*(1), 12.

Ritchie, J. B., & Crouch, G. I. (2003). *The competitive destination: A sustainable tourism perspective.* Cabi. doi:10.1079/9780851996646.0000

Sima, V., & Gheorghe, I. G. (2015). Changing Consumption Patterns in Green Economy. In *Agricultural Management Strategies in a Changing Economy* (pp. 186–212). IGI Global. doi:10.4018/978-1-4666-7521-6.ch009

Wang, Y., Lo, H. P., & Hui, Y. V. (2003). The antecedents of service quality and product quality and their influences on bank reputation: Evidence from the banking industry in China. *Managing Service Quality: An International Journal, 13*(1), 72–83. doi:10.1108/09604520310456726

Westhoek, H., Van Zeijts, H., Witmer, M., Van den Berg, M., Overmars, K., Van der Esch, S., & Van der Bilt, W. (2014). Greening the CAP. *An analysis of the effects of the European Commission's proposals for the Common Agricultural Policy, 2020.*

Willer, H., & Lernoud, J. (2016). *The world of organic agriculture. Statistics and emerging trends 2016* (pp. 1-336). Research Institute of Organic Agriculture FiBL and IFOAM Organics International. https://shop.fibl.org/fileadmin/documents/shop/1698-organic-world-2016.pdf

KEY TERMS AND DEFINITIONS

Natural Potential of Serbia: Represents the agricultural area with which Serbia has (i.e., there is about 5,111,000 hectares of agricultural land in Serbia, in other words 239,000 hectares of orchards, 3,333,000 hectares of plowed fields and gardens, about 67,000 hectares of vineyards, 625,000 hectares of meadows, and 834,000 hectares of pastures).

Organic Farming: A viable, natural alternative to the intensification of production methods and presents a production management system that promotes the recovery of ecosystems.

Rural Tourism Product: Represents a mix of services and local products that are characteristic for rural areas. An attempt to provide tourists with a personal contact with the rural environment, or to provide them with a sense of physical and social environment (ambience) characteristic of the rural location in which they reside. This means that tourists, to the extent possible or to the extent that tourists want, will be able to participate in agricultural activities, as well as to familiarize themselves with the tradition, history, culture, customs, gastronomy, the way and style of life of the local (rural) population, as well as all the natural attractions of the respective rural area.

Sustainable Development: Sustainable development is a new, generally accepted concept of human society that is based on the controlled development without growth that exceeded the capacity of the environment and nature in general. Sustainability means living in conditions of reasonable comfort within natural limits, means to live with nature without leaving behind a large footprint.

Chapter 10
The Role of the Educational System in Promoting Local Culture Within Rural Areas in Romania

Cristina Iridon
Petroleum-Gas University of Ploiesti, Romania

Cristina Gafu
Petroleum-Gas University of Ploiesti, Romania

ABSTRACT

The present chapter presents the results of a research developed within a series of rural schools in Romania (Prahova and Buzău County) regarding the role of the educational system in preserving the individuals' cultural identity and in promoting the local culture within the rural areas. Schools, be they urban or rural, are meant to contribute to capitalizing, reevaluating, and valuing the local cultural identity. The present analysis takes into account both the formal activities (included in the study programs or in the units of study planning: topics of discussion, study themes, optional courses, etc.) and non-formal events (traditional local festivals, school feasts, religious/folk celebrations, etc.) organized with the support of the local community projects, workshops conceived by the teachers in order to preserve the local culture and to make the young generation aware of their identity values.

DOI: 10.4018/978-1-5225-2965-1.ch010

INTRODUCTION

The III millennium overwhelms the entire world with its speed in geographical remodeling, historical confrontations, political changes, social adjustments, economic growth or cultural shocks (movements) which bring about not only benefits, but also lots of drawbacks for the mankind.

For almost a decade Romania has become part of the European Union experiencing globalization, which drew on a free circulation of material and spiritual values, having a great impact on regions, countries, but, more important, on individuals. This worldwide phenomenon can be considered a double edge sword because, "transnational flows of people, financial resources, goods, information and culture" (Hassi & Storti, 2012, p.3), even if they offer people the chance to enrich horizons or to have better jobs and better living conditions, they also alter the feeling of belonging to a group by wiping out national, ethnical, religious, social or cultural borders. The process of global homogenization generated a counteract movement all over the world – perceived not only at macro-levels (nationally), but also within micro-entities such as small communities (locally): it amplified the natural reflex of resistance, a phenomenon expressed in different forms of exhibiting and exploiting peculiarity, contrast and diversity. The counterbalancing trend resides in rediscovering, revaluing, redefining, valorizing national and local cultural values, in conceiving and applying strategies meant to preserve and promote national, ethnic and local identities.

BACKGROUND

The concept of globalization has been over popularized in its raw, narrow interpretation, the intense contact between different societies, civilizations and cultures being understood from a perspective which sharpened the tendencies to borrow, to import, to reproduce all kind of patterns which mold the individual and collective mentalities in the contemporary world. The homogenization (convergence) theory for example reverberates in different syntagmas such as "standardized and unique world culture", "universal culture" (Hassi & Storti, 2012, p.8), "replication of uniformity" (Hannerz, 2009, p.1). Seen as the new *doctrine* of the XXth century civilization, globalization has been considered the result of "a multiplicity of linkages and interconnections that transcend the nation states (and by implication the societies) which make up the modern world system", defining a "process through which events, decisions and activities in one part of the world can come to have a significant consequence for individuals and communities in quite distant parts of the globe." (McGrew, 1990, p.470) From this point of view, the impact of the phenomenon has been assessed as pertinent to all the world's five billion people, their environment, their roles as citizens, consumers or producers with an interest in collective action designed to solve common problems (Rosenau, 1996, pp. 3.4). More than that, there are opinions which envisage globalization as a functional variant to deal with the challenges of the modern/postmodern world, the process ensuring "an increasing homogenization of all human societies, regardless of their historical origins or cultural inheritances." (Fukuyama, 1992, pp.XIV, XV).

The overestimation of the effects generated by the increased circulation of economic, social, cultural values, of ideologies, of mentalities during the last decades is reflected in theories which release restrictive concepts such as global culture/world culture, Americanization or McDonaldization. The availability of contemporary communities and individuals to become attached to similar life experiences, to social and economic practices, to material and spiritual goods (in the sense that there is an worldwide open access to the same products and services, cultural brands, commodities, or consumerism assets) has been comprehended as a facilitator of a new cultural paradigm – the global culture/the world culture.

The American patterns defined by economic strength, political power, tolerance, freedom of expression, creativity, a good sense of pragmatism and opportunism (both financial and cultural) has been the subject of mimetic tendencies all over the world. In this respect, the term *Americanization* is used to refer to a replication of the American and/or Western cultural tradition. (Hassi & Sorti, 2012, p.9) Initially circumscribed by economic parameters, the thesis of McDonaldization has been expanded to a more general meaning:

McDonaldization is the idea of a worldwide homogenization of cultures through the effects of multinational corporations. [...] The McDonaldization model refers to the principles that the McDonald's franchise system has been able to successfully spread across borders and into the global market place. [...] It impacts social structures and institutions in its country of origin, as well as, in other developed and developing countries around the world. The McDonaldization thesis' relevance to issues of globalization asserts that social systems in today's society are becoming increasingly McDonaldized, and more significantly that the fundamental tenets of its principles have been successfully exported from the United stated to the rest of the world. (Hassi & Sorti, 2012, p.10)

Nevertheless, the process of globalization, mostly popularized by exploiting its broad meaning of homogenization and uniformity, is more complex and has generated various series of phenomena in terms of impact and consequences on all economic, social, cultural and even politic dimensions within modern contemporary life: Globalization is a multidimensional phenomenon that encompasses not only economic components but also cultural, ideological, political and similar other facets. (Hassi & Sorti, 2012, p.3)

However, strong homogenization tendencies, besides their direct effects (energetic transfers, standardization, development of a unique world culture, convergence, cohesion etc.), has determined a certain predisposition to search for proper and effective mechanisms to protect national cultures and identity specific patterns. From this point of view, the problem of the national cultures faced with the assault of the foreign cultures has been increasingly emphasized. Within this competition, reinforcing and reaffirming local cultures and traditions seemed to play an important part in various strategies embraced by many communities all over the world in their fight to maintain their identity and even legitimate their existence as identifiable cultural entities:

... local cultures exposed to compete with foreign as a united culture that embraces the community in order to maintain its existence. The durability of the local culture is being tested in the face of global penetration of foreign culture. The problem is that the durability of the local culture is relatively weak in the face of foreign cultural invasion [...] the most appropriate strategy to strengthen the resilience of local culture is by absorbing both sides and be a head of foreign culture to them be combined with the local culture so there is still a mix of local culture in it. (Kustyadji, 2014, p.46)

The merger theory seen as an emergency survival solution reflects only a restrictive approach of the defiance reaction, as the role of the local cultures has become more and more significant and relevant in the context of the opposition against globalization. The mixture between foreign and local cultures within the resistance scenario has been referred to by different concepts – glocalization, hybridization - which, in fact, encapsulate the same essence: the influential positive effect of the local culture. Glocalization can be defined as the interpenetration of the global and the local, resulting in unique outcomes in different geographic areas. (Ritzer, 2011, p.159); glocalization to be meaningful must include at least one component that addresses the local culture (Khondker, 2004, p.17). By means of glocalization a heterogenization process is identified, in which global and local culture shape a new paradigm in which globalization is refracted through the local as Roudometof formulated in his work *Glocalization: A Critical Introduction* (2016). Hence, the concept of glocalization cannot elude the role of the communities as mediators and agents enabled with the power and legitimacy to adapt, innovate and maneuver processes emerging from a new economic, social and cultural reality. From this point of view, glocalization is also understood as the mechanism by which people in a local place mediate and alter national, regional, and global processes. (https://quizlet.com/3113884/chapter-4-local-culture-popular-culture-and-cultural-landscapes-vocab-flash-cards/)

The new theories regarding the processes of *t*ranslocal fusion and cultural mixing/ cultural blending surpass the idea of homogenization as they are focused on the fact that national or local cultures are not blurred and they do not disappear overwhelmed by the power of the external exchanges. More than that, in Ritzer's opinion, the new model deriving from the interaction between external and internal cultural values, hybridization, is a very positive, even romantic, view of globalization as a profoundly creative process out of which emerges new cultural realities, and continuing, if not increasing, heterogeneity in many different locales. (2011, p.159). The new construct refers to the integration of both the global and the local cultural values resulting in distinctive and hybrid cultures (which are neither global, nor local) and cannot be reduced to either the local or the global culture. (Ritzer, 2011) There are opinions arguing that hybridization may be seen as an equivalent for glocalization or that glocalization is the heart of hybridization. The term hybridization would describe a process which implies an amalgam of cultural patterns or a melting similar with a cultural "alloy", the intersection of internal and external flows represents rather an interconnection of distinctive features: hybridization is not a synonym for fusion without contradiction but rather can be helpful in accounting for particular forms of conflict generated in recent cross cultural contact. […] hybridization is equivalent to sociocultural processes in which discrete structures or practices, previously existing in separate form, are combined to generate new structures, objects, and practices (Canclini, 2001, pp.XIV, XV).

The fact that awareness of the globalization impact leads to the awareness of cultural differences can be perceived as a paradox. The specialists who adhere to the heterogenization scenario (also labeled differentiation) have outlined precisely the resistance movement of the local communities who struggle to raise barriers meant to prevent the assault of the external influences which would make cultures look alike. In fact, local cultures experience a certain type of dynamics which implies continuous transformation and reinvention due to the influence of global factors and forces […] cultures do not remain unaffected by global flows and globalization, in general, but the actual crux of the culture remains intact and unaffected (Haasi & Sorti, 2012, p.7) and, more important, these flows do not eradicate local cultures, they only change some of their traits and reinforce others. (Haasi & Sorti, 2012, p.8) The heterogeneity theory also draws attention to the fact that cultures in contact remain distinct one from another, the focus being shifted on diversity, variety and plurality. As a consequence, the new created paradigm acquires a multidimensional layout.

No matter the approach – sociolinguistic, anthropological, ethnological, philosophical – culture (be it national or local) is considered a peculiar mark of the identity profile, the collective programming of the mind which distinguishes the members of one group or category of people from another. (Hofstede, 1994, p.5)

The concept of culture refers to a dynamic process influenced not only by the diachronic dimension (historical variables), but also by synchronic changes (social, economic, cultural variables). More than that, the social paradigm covers a network of influence layers, from the regional characteristic features to group distinct manifestations (family groups, ethnic groups, religious groups, professional groups – the so-called corporatist culture) and even to the individual way of referring to the contemporary realities (in the sense that each individual searches for his own cultural answers to the challenges of life): it has also been suggested that culture exists on a multitude of levels and dimensions in which nationality is only one. Furthermore, people are affected by regional, organizational, family and work group cultures in addition to national culture, and there are not always clear boundaries where the influence of one culture ends and another begins. (Sharmin, 2011, p.115)

Since along the years cultures have been defined in various ways, which stress its spiritual and material dimension defined by cultural identifiers as ideas, beliefs, rules, customs, language, eating habits etc., local culture derived from the former one collects the same meaning, but in a concise sense, because it can be understood as the essential core that preserves, enriches and carries on the ancient heritage which marks each pattern of any culture. Acknowledging the importance and the impact of culture and its derivative, local culture, provides a sense of belonging and an arena in which residents can make a difference. (Brennan et al., 2014, p.2)

The syntagm local culture is not restrained to a comprehension associated to cultural heritage (traditions, folklore, native language, ethnic features, specific adaptability patterns etc.). In fact, it encompasses concrete actions, practices or organizing resources initiatives of the individuals and collectivities as respondents to the new logic of the existence. In this respect, various definitions of the local culture include specific reference to people and groups of people: The term local culture *is* commonly used to characterize the experience of everyday life in specific, identifiable localities. It reflects ordinary people's feelings of appropriateness, comfort, and correctness - attributes that define personal preferences and changing tastes. (https://www.britannica.com/science/cultural-globalization#ref750780). The culture specific to a particular place is kept alive by people "who see themselves as a collective or a community, who share experiences, customs, and traits, and who work to preserve those traits and customs in order to claim uniqueness and to distinguish themselves from others." (https://www2.warwick.ac.uk/fac/soc/al/globalpad/openhouse/interculturalskills/global_pad_-_what_is_culture.pdf)

Administering (preserving, reinventing, restructuring, promoting) local culture as a subdivision of the cultural identity is a complex task as the "recipient", namely a group/community living in a specific place, is not an abstract organism, but an entity comprising multilayered interconnections.

One may think of how to give a concrete example, how "local" and "authentic" (as a form of "cultural resistance") the rural tourism promoted by Romanian 'peasants'- (entrepreneurs who cleverly sell and manipulate superficial folk traditions to the naive buyers) is. As Robertson stated, glocalization involves the construction of increasingly differentiated consumers, the 'invention' of 'consumer traditions' (of which tourism, arguably the biggest 'industry' of the contemporary world, is undoubtedly the most clear-cut example. (1995, p.29) Regarding the previously mentioned first audience, what they actually obtain, besides a pseudo-culture (or perhaps just because of it), is a capitalist spirit of the Romanian 'village.' This spirit is learning to grow from his previous mummified corpse; in fact, the resurrection consists precisely in selling his new aseptic and marketed body. (Vizureanu, 2013, p.75)

Attempts to redress, to reconfigure and to reshape the unstoppable and sometimes the unbearable phenomenon of globalization have been made all over the world by the decisional factors at the political, economic and cultural level. In this respect, the Romanian government legislated wage increases, raising the people's living standard, and facilitated bonuses for those who want to be hired in disadvantaged regions in order to reduce migration, to ensure better paid jobs, to revitalize the depopulated areas and to give everyone a sense of security and dignity. Being supported by refundable/nonrefundable European Union funds, there have also been developed lots of economic projects to sustain rural development, centered especially on green economy with its positive and deep effects on traditional handicraft or on agriculture reviving and animal farming. In the past few years, green economy benefited from great and genuine attention not only from the central and regional authorities, but also from the beneficiaries consisting in both urban and rural locals, interested in their well-being improvement, in reducing environmental risks and ecological deficit. Green economy is defined as the efficient and sustainable use of resources, the improvement of the individuals' social standard, the raising of private and public income, in other words, as economic growth, without relating this with energy or raw materials' consumption.

In its quite recent development variants, green economy has promoted the ancient bond between man and nature revaluing and reinterpreting old traditions by means of local culture. In the past few years, there could be noticed a growing interest in discovering the exploitation of the common cultural heritage potential, in improving quality of life in the rural or urban communities. All over the world the authorities in charge of local administration have seized the value of culture as an agent of development and endeavored to conceive local/regional cultural strategies introducing them in their communitarian development programs. Resuscitating cultural vitality of the urban and rural areas has become part of the public policies meant to foster community social, economic, environmental and cultural development. In this respect, culture is seen as a bind which contributes to the internal community cooperation implying arts activities that can play vital permissive and directly developmental roles in local development strategies by create open and co-operative environments which are important in themselves, and allow other initiatives to succeed. (Matarasso, 1999, p.7)[1]

However, the realities of the contemporary society impose an extended and a more comprehensive vision on the local administrative development policies, in the sense that the interest in the economic growth (finances, exploitation of the natural and human resources, production of goods) should be supplemented by the concern about the regional/local culture. The sectored approach based on the latest development patterns focus on unique cultural characteristics of specific geographical areas (Brennan et al., 2016, p. 2), which are meant to exploit communities' territorial specific elements. *Territorial development* includes the whole potential of local resources, territory, culture, local diversity (also manifested in groups particular contribution and individual uniqueness): such perspectives tend to include recognition of the total environment in which community development operates [...] attempt to address the interdependencies of people, the environment, and the communities within a locality. (Brennan et al., 2016, p.2)

MAIN FOCUS OF THE CHAPTER

Within the last decade, there has been a trend to implement the European development policies in Romania, being noticed a shift of accent from a large scale perspective (national oriented development policies) to the communitarian development, implying stronger connection to the geographic, economic and social data of each community; in other words, there have been attempts to configure development patterns molding on each community needs and resources. The communitarian development involves a variety of resources such as human, natural, economic, financial and infrastructural ones.

One of the challenges of implementing European development policies derives from the fact that the communitarian development varies from one region to another in Romania, taking into account the geographical position, the economic potential of the region, the social profile and the cultural capital to be exploited.

The local management mechanisms reconfigure the value of culture, which is viewed as a catalyst facilitating the intergenerational contact, and thus a better understanding of the present by means of the past values. This leads to the development of the attachment to the traditional social behavioral patterns and of a sense of belonging, a sense of social (collective) and cultural identity: Cultural activity is an infinitely diverse route to personal development in people of all ages, leading to enhance skills, confidence and creativity [...]. Cultural action builds community organizational capacity empowers local groups and nurtures active, engaged citizenship. Culture brings people together, in celebration, exploration and community, and is key factor in home and settlement. [...] culture is essential to nurturing a confident, cohesive and questioning identity. (Matarasso, 1999, p.7)

Subsidiary, culture oriented community support activities may contribute to the economic strengthening of the regions as it may guide people to the reviving of their bounds with the birth place, to the reshaping of the relationship between human and natural geography, to the revaluing of the natural wealth and outlining of the respect for the harmony of the environment.

Promoting local cultures can have a double impact on the development of a community. On the one hand, it can lead to the mobilization of the local population actively involved in the efforts of the traditional heritage reification (i.e. rehabilitation of the ethnographic specificity – traditional architecture, reanimation of the traditional crafts; rediscovery of popular festival and celebrations). Thus, being involved in activities linked to their own cultural values, members of the community are likely to become more committed to the local development efforts meant to sustain a genuine basis for social interaction and collective identity, to share the attachment to the needs, possibilities and opportunities of the community.

On the other hand, the encouragement of the local culture can have positive effects on the local economic and social development of their local areas, as they provide opportunities for tourism promotion, commercial outcomes and increased inward investment in host regions. (Stankova, Vassenka, 2015, p.120). For example, efforts focused on the promotion, preservation, dissemination of the local/regional culture can optimize the development of the tourism within a region.

We started from the assumption that concepts such as globalization, hybridization, glocalization and heterogenization can become accessible to the young generation learning in rural schools by means of different activities included in the curriculum be them compulsory or optional. In this view, the aim of the research below is to emphasize the role of the educational system in preserving, promoting and transmitting the local cultural values, as an alternative way for the survival of the local cultural identity.

Methodology

The hypothesis of our research is that the educational system has an essential role in preserving the cultural identity of the individuals and in promoting the local culture within the rural areas, since the school remains an important stronghold of the community, be it urban or rural.

In this respect, there were developed a series of case studies within the rural schools in Romania (Prahova and Buzău counties) having in view the components of the educational process which are meant to contribute to capitalizing, reevaluating and valuing the cultural local identity.

The paper aims to present the results of the study cases focused on both the formal activities (included in the study programs or in the planning of the study units: topics of discussion, study themes, optional courses etc.) and the non-formal events which involve the local community administration (which develop activities such as traditional local festivals, school feasts, religious/folk celebrations etc.), projects, workshops in which teachers and pupils take part, activities meant to preserve the local culture and to make children aware of their identity values.

The applied part of the research was based on a questionnaire distributed to a network of potential respondents. The target group was made up of teachers actively involved not only in the educational process, but also in the cultural life of the community.

The documentation envisaged not only the theoretical section of the chapter (studies, books containing clarifications of the concepts and terminology used), but also the interpretation of the results obtained during the field research (books, monographs, local stories/legends about the history and the cultural specificity of each village, community participating in the case study).

Research Instrument

The questionnaire was conceived in a flexible manner, meant to guide and to help the teachers to gather the necessary information from their respondents' network (colleagues from school, pupils, members of the community, local administration etc.) The questionnaire comprised questions detailing a series of essential points for the present research:

1. Specific cultural values recognized within the community as representative for the local identity (customs, traditions, manifestations - celebrations, festivals);
2. Activities initiated within the community in order to preserve and popularize the local specificity (fairs promoting local cuisine, festivals promoting natural products, popular celebrations, craft fairs promoting local crafts etc.);
3. Activities developed within schools in partnership with the local administration and non-governmental organizations supporting projects which had as objectives the involvement of the young generation in redescovering the local cultural values, in preserving and revitalising them;
4. The impact (participation degree, dissemination, feedback) of these activities on the participants (members of the community, teachers, pupils);

5.   Individual initiatives (monographs, optional courses, pilot studies realized by teachers in their attempt to familiarize pupils with the local cultural treasures and to integrate these values in the teaching process).

Participants

Two rural schools from two different regions were chosen as participants in the case study: one from Buzău county – Mătești (Săpoca), a small school with a capacity of around 125 pupils (elementary and secondary) and the other from Prahova county – Bărcănești (Tătărani), a rural school, with a number of approximately 250 pupils attending primary and secondary educational level. Both educational institutions initiated and developed during the years formal and non-formal activities aiming to sustain the cultural specificity of their villages.

Data Analysis and Results

Participant Number One: Mătești Secondary School (Buzău County)

Together with the administrative center (the Village Hall) and the religious center (the church) the school plays an important role in the life of a community with certain future development capacities. In this village, school (teachers, pupils and their families) actively takes part in all the manifestations conceived to promote local identity. In the last decades, this community has managed to rediscover and to reinvent itself revaluing the old traditions and initiating new ones.

In 2007, the educational staff from Mătești school started the project Reel of the Village (Hora satului)[2] meant to bring about the folk culture still preserved in their community. The project involves all the pupils of the school, one of the main objectives of the project being to reestablish the intergenerational relations by means of the folk culture heritage, especially folk music and dance and folk art. The core of the manifestation is a parade of the folk costumes specific to this region[3]. In the same time, the event is conceived as an opportunity to honor the iconic/emblematic people of the village. The old members of the community also participate in the event by telling stories about the past of the village, reconstructing the collective memory in this way.

In the last two decades, Romanian villages and towns have experienced different renewal patterns based on the capitalization and revaluation of the cultural legacy within the urban and rural areas, the so called gentrification process. (Zukin, 1995, p.39) At the same time, the reconfiguration of the geographical zone – be it urban or rural – also takes place by redirecting the resources, including the cultural ones, towards the satisfaction of the needs associated with the consumerism and entertainment. According to Lipovetsky (2007), the mechanisms of the modern consumerism involve a series of marketing strategies focused on a rebranded image, by making use of the cultural specificity and local traditions:

Regrowth of the popularity of the holiday is accompanied by a plethora of new manifestations. The 3rd stage is the witness of various types of commemorations, of a greater variety of traditional holydays of the regions and villages, of an explosion of ‹thematic› celebrations with their inevitable series of musical shows, lively streets, fireworks, epoch costumes, stalls displaying trifles, boutiques, craftworks. On the Celebration of Music, of Cinema, of water sports, of Snow Days, of Fruits Days, of Vegetarians Days, of Light days, of Flower days, of Forest Days, there are out of common celebrations during which there is a mixture between culture and game, history and tourism, tradition and trade interest [...]. Not long ago, celebrations were organized on the basis of traditional religious or political principles; or, more and more frequently, trade interest in urban and regional image marketing are those which determine an increasing inflation. By emphasizing the local and historical traits, the hypermodern order of celebration, of transforming culture into commodity, of media promotion and of mass tourism, occurs. (Lipovetsky, 2007, p.220)[4]

"Exploiting" the traditional occupations of the villagers and the natural resources – Mătești is famous for its vineyards and its vegetable cultures – the local administration tries to sustain the economy of the village and to encourage the local tourism by means of events such as:

Greengrocers' Parade, Householders' March and Grandmother's Pantry: The main reasons for organizing a festival for local products / traditions are associated with improving location's image, promoting local products and traditions and supporting tourism activities, thus raising the local cultural awareness. The exchange of experiences and culture, and entertainment were stated as benefits from holding the event. They seem to offer the possibility for socializing, finding community identity and at the same time raising community's cultural awareness. Thus, people are seeking friendly, genuine relationships, true and original experience, roots. Rural settlements are places where tourist can search, find or at least to compensate their lost identity. The image of the province as the mother of all traditions where one can find one's origin and all that honors the national character and culture in order to satisfy one's social demand for cultural identity. (Stankova, Vassenka, 2015, p.125)

Both manifestations intend to promote the local community and to make it part of the agrotouristic circuit attracting lots of participants, such as locals and people from other areas. The *Greengrocers' Parade* started in 2008 and is usually organized each year in September, on Sundays, being preceeded by a parade of wagons full of vegetables, fruits and many products from the vineyard (grapes, wine, brandy made of grapes). The wagons and the horses follow an established route between Mătești and Sapoca villages, each community being distinguished by its own flag.

The Householders' March represents another rural festivity, within which, each year, a different vegetable is declared the "queen" of the celebration. Many housewives compete against each other by making a huge variety of dishes having as a main ingredient the "queen" vegetable. The first prize is awarded to the best meal by specialists in the rural Romanian cuisine. The event also includes an exhibition, *Grandmothers' Pantry*, with traditional food products such as bakery goods, sausages, or products made of lamb (pastrami), unfermented wine, all these being prepared according to old recipes.

Together with the local artists who know how to prepare tasty food or to enchant the public with their handicrafts or their musical programs, the schools from the community promote products made of natural raw materials by the pupils. On this occasion many villagers or people born in this village who live in other places come back in Mătești to meet their relatives or their acquaintances and to participate to various games and competitions such as: knitting onion ropes, playing football with cabbages instead of balls, carrying bags full of potatoes or their wives on their shoulders.

Each year the school participates with a stand of handmade products created by the pupils (guided by teachers and their families). In this way, they are stimulated to learn about the traditions of their village and to contribute to the wellbeing of their community. At the same time, children are members of folk dance groups or actors in popular sketches. These activities may become an efficient method to make them interested in preserving the local cultural legacy and to actively participate in the cultural life of the community.

Besides the new invented celebrations, the community also revived the Harvest Day which is nowadays organized in partnership with a non-governmental organization (A.N.T.R.E.C)[5], recognized as a leader on the Romanian rural tourism market. Harvest Day takes place at the end of September, when the wagons full of harvest are directed to the barns, this celebration being considered a tribute to the people and to their work. The celebration was revived in 2008, when a vegetable salad of 500 kg was prepared by the women from Mătești and Săpoca, becoming the biggest one from Romania. Each edition is dedicated to a certain variety of vegetable specific to Buzău county (2009 - Buzău cabbage, 2010 – Buzău onion, 2011 - Buzău tomato, 2012 - Buzău green pepper, 2013 – varied vegetables of Buzău).

All these events dedicated especially to the development of the local economy and to the agricultural tourism contain a cultural component which revaluates the potential of the traditional art (the art of woodworking and the art of Romanian traditional sewing) because local festivals are considered as simultaneously ‹cultural› and ‹economic› phenomena. (Gibson & Kong, 2005; McCann, 2002). There are few similar local culture patterns and even very few solutions to shape these patterns in order to become accessible to the educational framework. Each community creates its own opportunities to protect and to advertise the rural cultural patrimony.

Participant Number Two: Secondary School Gheorghe Lazăr From Bărcănești (Tătărani)

The school is located on the national road, between Ploiești (an important industrial city of Romania) and București (the capital of Romania).

The proximity of urban centers may affect in time the preservation degree of the local culture. There are spatial differences in the richness of the local cultures, which make it difficult to configure a pattern of preserving and using local culture as a useful resource for education.

Small villages do not have the financial support to ensure the infrastructural development (cultural centers, museums, modern libraries, modern cinemas etc.) in order to bring to life their cultural uniqueness. One of the problems concerning that the Romanian educational system has to play in the trans-generational transmission of culture (local culture being included) is the accomplishment of a coherent cooperation policy to be functional at all the three levels: the mega level, the macro level and the micro level[6], so that the decisions and actions are based on a common view and an interconnection between all the stakeholders involved in the development of the community.

In this case, school provides not only the necessary framework (objectives, organizing and planning, human resources, knowledge), but also the logistic and managerial resources. Some of the activities envisaging the cultural heritage of a community are included in the formal register of the educational curriculum (in the study programs or in the planning of the study units: topics of discussion, study themes, optional courses etc.), others are topics included in the non-formal curriculum. These activities aim to innovate and diversify the educational offer in an accessible, attractive and interesting manner for the pupils. Appealing to small projects whose topics are associated with aspects of the local culture, teachers intend to familiarize children with their spiritual legacy, to equip them with a sense of belonging to a group and a collectivity. These projects develop pupils' attachment to genuine cultural values, form their positive attitudes for the community collective memory and enrich their life experiences.

In comparison with the first participant, the second participant developed activities as part of the extra-curricular education. The school located in Bărcăneşti initiated instructive programs inside their own village (in partnership with other institutions representing the local community – the church and the Village Hall), or in other locations. The contents were centered on the local traditions traditions connected with some religious holidays and the specific way in which they are celebrated in the village and on the folk art (traditional costumes and pottery) See Annex.

It is worth mentioning that besides the opportunity to enrich their knowledge by the traditional teaching methods of transfer of information (exposition, demonstration, explanation), the design of the activities contained components dedicated to the active involvement of the pupils (they were asked to draw, to manufacture objects, to sing, to dance etc.)

CONCLUSION

Under the pressure of globalization (with all its variants and stages) local culture may offer the substance and consistency a community needs in order to preserve and enrich its identity profile. Sharing the same system of values, the local residents develop a sense of solidarity, permanently reconstructing the linkage and consolidating the social balance inside the collectivity network.

On a cultural basis, the human resources of a village may be efficiently involved in the community development process. There may be noticed a trend to invest in all kinds of initiatives meant to rediscover the unique cultural values, to enhance the importance of the cultural diversity, not only because of its potential as *an economic commodity*, but also as a counterpart to the homogenization effect globalization is supposed to have. Financial mechanisms, logistics means, economic and even political strategies, managerial plans are oriented towards the support of the brands which are perceived as part of a genuine, authentic culture.

In Romania the support of local culture has become an issue of national policy or the objective of a large scale development concept. In this respect, there are private, individual initiatives, small projects developed by local institutions (for example educational institutions), governmental, non-governmental organizations or the local administration (the townhall, the prefect's office).

This is one of the reasons why in Romania the community development is very different from one region to another. Apart from the action of factors such as the history of the community, the geographical location, the socio-economic context or the cultural marks, the problem of a village growth depends to a great extent on the involvement of the members of the community, the resources being the ones available at a local level. In this respect, the solution of an educational partnership between school and community has been implemented with a considerable rate of success, the research developed in quite a lot of schools within the Romanian rural medium showing that there is a real cooperation at all levels of a local community (family, authorities, organizations, institutions, economic agents etc.). In some of the cases, school has become a meeting point, the connection platform between all the other entities interested in the well-being of the community. Education in general, and school in particular, has long ago surpassed its limited status of "knowledge provider", having to play a more prominent part within the modern society, from preparing the individuals to be actively integrated in their community (molding characters, forming abilities, endowing the individuals with different competences) in order to assure the continuity of the cultural tradition.

School has extended its role within the community, playing an important part in taking the necessary steps in the direction of improving the quality of the cultural manifestations within a region, promoting the local uniqueness on a national and even international level (by means of international projects such as Erasmus or experience exchange activities).

Through the attention given to the local culture, school has also provided an aesthetic and moral education for the children contributing to molding their character and their sense of belonging by making them to participate in different and repetitive activities in which they can perceive the benefit and the beauty of connection and the balance between old and new, tradition and modernity, local and global.

REFERENCES

Brennan, M., Kumaran, M., Cantrell, R., & Spranger, M. (2016). *The Importance of Incorporating Local Culture into Community Development*. UFIFAS Extension, University of Florida, FCS9232. Retrieved from http://edis.ifas.ufl.edu

Canclini, G. N. (2001). Consumers and Citizens: Globalization and Multicultural conflicts (G. Yúdice, Trans.). Minneapolis, MN: The University of Minnesota Press.

Fukuyama, F. (1992). *The End of History and the Last Man*. New York: Free Press.

Gibson, C., & Kong, L. (2005). Cultural economy: A critical review. *Progress in Human Geography, 29*(5), 541–561. doi:10.1191/0309132505ph567oa

Hannerz, U. (1990). Cosmopolitans and locals in world culture. *Theory, Culture & Society, 7*(2), 237–251. doi:10.1177/026327690007002014

Hassi, A., & Storti, G. (2012). Globalization and Culture: The Three H Scenarios. In Globalization-Approaches to Diversity. InTech.

Khondker, H. H. (2004). Glocalization as globalization: Evolution of a sociological concept. *Bangladesh e-Journal of Sociology, 1*(2), 1–9.

Kustyadji, G. (2014). The Influence of Local Culture on National Culture and Its Impact on Organizational Culture. *Interdisciplinary Journal of Contemporary Research in Business, 6*(5), 44–58.

Lipovetsky, G. (2007). *Fericirea paradoxală. Eseu asupra societății de hiperconsum.* Iasi: Editura Polirom.

McCann, E. (2002). The cultural politics of local economic development: Meaning-making, place-making, and the urban policy process. *Geoforum, 33*(3), 385–398. doi:10.1016/S0016-7185(02)00007-6

McGrew, A. (1990). A Global Society. In *Modernity and Its Futures* (pp. 467–499). Cambridge, UK: Polity Press.

Obanya, P. (2005). *Culture in Education and Education in Culture.* Fifth Conference of African Ministers of Culture, Nairobi, Kenya. Retrieved from www.africa-union.org

Ritzer, G. (2011). *Globalization: the essentials.* John Wiley & Sons.

Robertson, R. (1995). Glocalization: Time-space and homogeneity-heterogeneity. *Global Modernities, 2*, 25-45.

Rosenau, J. N. (1996). The dynamics of globalization: Toward an operational formulation. *Security Dialogue, 27*(3), 247–262. doi:10.1177/0967010696027003002

Roudometof, V. (2016). *Glocalization: a critical introduction.* Routledge.

Sharmin, S. (2011). Teaching |English in a Cross-Cultural Context: Challenges and Directions. *Journal of NELTA, 16*(1-2).

Stankova, M., & Vassenska, I. (2015). Raising cultural awareness of local traditions through festival tourism. *Tourism & Management Studies, 11*(1).

Vizureanu, V. (2013). Some Remarks Concerning the Concept of Glocalization. *Public Reason, 5*(1).

Zukin, S. (1995). *The cultures of cities Blackwell.* Cambridge, MA and Oxford.

ADDITIONAL READING

Archer, K., Martin Bosman, M., Mark Amen, M., & Schmidt, E. (2007). Locating globalisations and cultures. *Globalisations*, *4*(1), 1–14. doi:10.1080/14747730701245566

Aspin, D., Chapman, J., & Klenowski, V. (2001). Changing cultures in schools in Australia. In J. Cairns, D. Lawton, & R. Gardner (Eds.), *Values, culture and education. World year book of education, 2001* (pp. 122–143). London: Kogan Page Limited.

Banks, J. (2001). Multicultural education: Characteristics and goals. In J. Banks & C. A. McGee Banks (Eds.), *Multicultural education: Issues and perspectives* (4th ed., pp. 3–26). New York: Wiley.

Barnhardt, R. (1981). *Culture, community and the curriculum*. Retrieved February 9, 2005, from http:///www.ankn.uaf.edu/ccc2, Alaska Native Knowledge Network, University of Alaska Fairbanks.

Barnhardt, R., & Kawagley, A. O. (2004). *Culture, chaos and complexity: Catalysts for change in indigenous education*, https://www.culturalsurvival.org/publications/cultural-survival-quarterly/culture-chaos-complexity-catalysts-change-indigenous

Barnhardt, R., & Kawagley, A. O. (2005). Indigenous knowledge systems and Alaska Native ways of knowing. *Anthropology & Education Quarterly*, *36*(1), 8–23. doi:10.1525/aeq.2005.36.1.008

Berger, P. L. (1997). Four faces of global culture. *National Interest*, *49*, 23–29.

Bessière, J. (1998). Local development and heritage: Traditional food and cuisine as tourist attractions in rural areas. *Sociologia Ruralis*, *38*(1), 21–34. doi:10.1111/1467-9523.00061

Cerny, P. G. (1997). Paradoxes of the competition state: The dynamics of political globalization. *Government and Opposition*, *32*(2), 251–274. doi:10.1111/j.1477-7053.1997.tb00161.x

COBIANU-BĂCANU. M. (2003). Comunitățile rurale, porți deschise spre Uniunea Europeană, In Economistul, year XIV, no. 1486 (1512).

Cochran-Smith, M., & Lytle, S. L. (1992). Interrogating cultural diversity: Inquiry and action. *Journal of Teacher Education*, *43*(2), 104–115. doi:10.1177/0022487192043002004

Darie, Al., & Stanciu, F. (1997). *Educația adulților din mediul rural* [Adult education in the rural area]. Bucureşti: EDP.

Derrett, R. (2003). Making sense of how festivals demonstrate a community's sense of place. *Event Management*, *8*(1), 49–58. doi:10.3727/152599503108751694

Getz, D. (2007). *Event studies: theory, research and policy for planned events.* Oxford, UK: Elsevier.

Hazen, K. (2002). Identity and Language variation in a Rural Community. *Language*, *78*(2), 240–257. doi:10.1353/lan.2002.0089

Jeong, S., & Santos, C. (2004). Cultural politics and contested place identity. *Annals of Tourism Research*, *31*(3), 640–656. doi:10.1016/j.annals.2004.01.004

Kawagley, A. O. (1999). Alaska Native education: History and adaptation in the new millennium. *Journal of American Indian Education*, *39*(1), 31–51.

Klaic, D. (2002). *Challenges and strategies in festivals: challenges of growth, distinction, support base and internationalization.* Tartu: Department of Culture of the Tartu City Government.

Kostopoulou, S., Vagionis, N., & Kourkouridis, D. (2013). Cultural Festivals and Regional Economic Development: Perceptions of Key interest Groups. In A. Matias, P. Nijkamp, & M. Sarmento (Eds.), *Quantitative Methods in Tourism Economics* (pp. 175–194). Heidelberg: Advances in Tourism Economics Series, Physica-Verlag. A Springer Company. doi:10.1007/978-3-7908-2879-5_10

Lawrence, R. (1996). *Regulation, multilateralism and deeper integration.* Brookings Institution, Nueva York.

Lefley, H. (1982). Self-perception and primary prevention for American Indians. In S. Manson (Ed.), *New directions in prevention among American Indian and Alaska Native communities* (pp. 65–90). Portland, OR: Oregon Health Sciences University.

Louch, H., Hargittai, E. C., & Angel, M. (1999). Facing challenges, going global. *The Washington Quarterly*, *22*(2), 83. doi:10.1080/01636609909550389

O'Sullivan, D., & Jackson, M. (2002). "Festival tourism: A contributor to sustainable local economic development?". *Journal of Sustainable Tourism*, *10*(4), 325–342. doi:10.1080/09669580208667171

Pekajová, L., & Novosák, J. (2010). Local Culture in the Era of Globalisation: Focused on the Zlin Region. In *Beyond Globalisation: Exploring the Limits of Globalisation in the Regional Context.* Conference Proceedings, University of Ostrava, Czech Republic, pp.169-176.

Reyhner, J., & Jacobs, D. T. (2002). Preparing teachers of American Indian and Alaska Native students. *Action in Teacher Education*, *24*(2), 85–93. doi:10.1080/0 1626620.2002.10734422

Ritzer, G. (2007). *The Globalization of Nothing 2*. Thousand Oaks, London, New Delhi: Pine Forge Press.

Ritzer, G. (2010). *Globalization: A Basic Text*. Wiley-Blackwell.

Robertson, R. (1992). *Globalization: Social Theory and Global Culture*. London: Sage.

Ruigrok, W., & van Tulder, R. (1995). The Logic of International Restructuring. The Management of Dependencies in Rival Industrial Complexes.

Russel, C. A., & Valenzuela, A. (2005). Global consumption: (How) does culture matter? *Advances in Consumer Research. Association for Consumer Research (U. S.)*, *32*(1), 86–89.

Scholte, J. A. (1995). Globalisation and Modernity, Paper presented at the International Studies Association Convention, San Diego.

Stoian, S. (1942). *Sociologia şi ipedagogia satului* [Village sociology and pedagogy]. Bucureşti: EDP.

Sue, D. W., & Sue, D. (2003). *Counseling the culturally diverse: Theory and practice* (4th ed.). New York: Wiley & Sons.

Van de Wagen, L. (2005). *Event management: For tourism, cultural, business and sporting events* (2nd ed.). Frenchs Forest: Pearson Education Australia.

Williamson, J. G. (1996). Globalization, Convergence and History. *The Journal of Economic History*, *56*(2), 278. doi:10.1017/S0022050700016454

KEY TERMS AND DEFINITIONS

Globalization: The contact between different societies, civilizations, and cultures based on borrowing, importing, and reproducing all kind of patterns which shape the individual and collective mentalities in the contemporary world. A process through which the peculiar characteristics of the local culture are homogenized.

Glocalization: A mixture between global and local culture having as result a unique outcome in different geographical regions.

Green Economy: An efficient and sustainable use of resources, having as consequence the improvement of the individuals' social standard, the raising of private and public income, in sum the economic growth, without relating this with energy or raw materials' consumption.

Hybridization: A process in which global and local culture shape a new paradigm in which globalization is refracted through the local.

Local Culture: A derivative of culture, understood as the essential core that preserves, enriches and carries on the ancient heritage which marks each pattern of any culture.

ENDNOTES

[1]   As this chapter is focused on the role of the local cultural activities within rural communities, the term culture (arts is obviously included in this term) is used with a broader and inclusive meaning related to a rural universe preserved in modern form which *supposes [...] traditions, customs, rural life specific capitalization and their unification in a subtle dialectics with modern techniques and cultures, with science and up-to-date information.* (Palicica & al. 2008, p. 85) From this perspective the sphere of meanings should be expanded to all the actions/ projects initiated by the local government to create an operative cultural framework meant to contribute to the shaping of sustainable communities and to bring forth local vitality.

[2]   *Hora* is a Romanian popular/folk dance.

[3]   The village has its own popular costume, people wearing the traditional cloths until the First World War (1914-1918). Cf/Acc. to. Poveștile satului. Mătești – file de monografie, coord. Valentina Ștefan.

[4]   Our translation.

[5]   A.N.T.R.E.C is an abbreviation for National Association of Rural, Ecological and Cultural Tourism.

[6]   The involvement of the community, the interest of the local and central authorities in preserving, revaluing and promoting local cultures defines the mega level (the wider society environment – significant stakeholders, governments, elite class, civil society, culture professionals/ activists) - preoccupied with the well-faire of the people. In the inner side of the society it can be delineated the *the macro level of educational policy development, curricula, and other inputs into education programs* and *the micro level, at which direct action is taken to educate in schools and classrooms, as well as in the out-of-school learning situations.* (Obanya, 2005, p. 1).

APPENDIX

These are samples of activities developed by the second participant in the case study, *Secondary School Gheorghe Lazăr from Bărcănești* (Tătărani).

Figure 1. Exhibition of drawings on Christmas holiday entitled Open the door, Christian! On this occasion, the pupils from secondary level sang carols in Romanian, French and English.

Figure 2. Exhibition: Eastern Traditions organized in the Village Hall of Bărcănești; the pupils exhibited their photos, their drawings and their own handicraft.

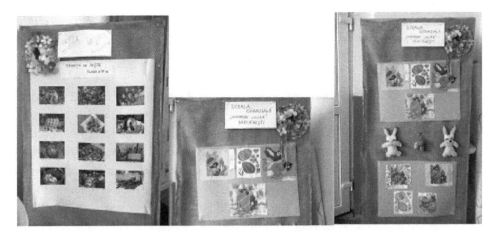

Figure 3. Visiting Townsfolk House, located in Ploieşti and dated from XVIII-XIX centuries. The pupils participated to a thematic workshop: modeling pottery objects.

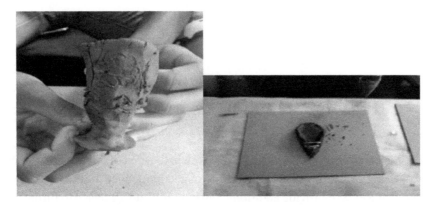

Figure 4. Romanian customs and habits: Presentation of the folk costume

Related References

To continue our tradition of advancing research in the area of environmental science and technologies, we have compiled a list of recommended IGI Global readings. These references will provide additional information and guidance to further enrich your knowledge and assist you with your own research and future publications.

Abayomi, K., de la Pena, V., Lall, U., & Levy, M. (2011). Quantifying sustainability: Methodology for and determinants of an environmental sustainability index. In Z. Luo (Ed.), *Green finance and sustainability: Environmentally-aware business models and technologies* (pp. 74–89). Hershey, PA: IGI Global. doi:10.4018/978-1-60960-531-5.ch004

Abdel Gelil, I. (2012). Globalization of the environmental issues: Response of the Arab region. In M. Tortora (Ed.), *Sustainable systems and energy management at the regional level: Comparative approaches* (pp. 147–165). Hershey, PA: IGI Global. doi:10.4018/978-1-61350-344-7.ch008

Adewumi, J., Ilemobade, A., & van Zyl, J. (2013). Application of a multi-criteria decision support tool in assessing the feasibility of implementing treated wastewater reuse. *International Journal of Decision Support System Technology*, 5(1), 1–23. doi:10.4018/jdsst.2013010101

Adeyemo, J., Adeyemo, F., & Otieno, F. (2012). Assessment of pollutant loads of runoff in Pretoria, South Africa. In E. Carayannis (Ed.), *Sustainable policy applications for social ecology and development* (pp. 115–127). Hershey, PA: IGI Global. doi:10.4018/978-1-4666-1586-1.ch009

Ahmad, A. F., & Panni, M. F. (2014). Green marketing strategy: A pedagogical view. In H. Kaufmann & M. Panni (Eds.), *Handbook of research on consumerism in business and marketing: Concepts and practices* (pp. 92–124). Hershey, PA: IGI Global. doi:10.4018/978-1-4666-5880-6.ch005

Ahmad, M. F., & Siang, A. Y. (2014). Modelling of hydrodynamics and sediment transport at Pantai Tok Jembal, Kuala Terengganu Mengabang Telipot, Terengganu, using MIKE 21. In O. Olanrewaju, A. Saharuddin, A. Ab Kader, & W. Wan Nik (Eds.), *Marine technology and sustainable development: Green innovations* (pp. 109–126). Hershey, PA: IGI Global. doi:10.4018/978-1-4666-4317-8.ch007

Ahmed Al-kerdawy, M. M. (2011). The role of environmental innovation strategy in reinforcing the impact of green managerial practices on competitive advantages of fertilizer companies in Egypt. *International Journal of Customer Relationship Marketing and Management*, 2(1), 36–54. doi:10.4018/jcrmm.2011010103

Akkaya, C., Wolf, P., & Krcmar, H. (2011). Efficient information provision for environmental and sustainability reporting. In I. Management Association (Ed.), Green technologies: Concepts, methodologies, tools and applications (pp. 1587-1609). Hershey, PA: IGI Global. doi:10.4018/978-1-60960-472-1.ch705

Al-kerdawy, M. M. (2013). The role of environmental innovation strategy in reinforcing the impact of green managerial practices on competitive advantages of fertilizer companies in Egypt. In R. Eid (Ed.), *Managing customer trust, satisfaction, and loyalty through information communication technologies* (pp. 37–53). Hershey, PA: IGI Global. doi:10.4018/978-1-4666-3631-6.ch003

Alves de Lima, A., Carvalho dos Reis, P., Branco, J. C., Danieli, R., Osawa, C. C., Winter, E., & Santos, D. A. (2013). Scenario-patent protection compared to climate change: The case of green patents. *International Journal of Social Ecology and Sustainable Development*, 4(3), 61–70. doi:10.4018/jsesd.2013070105

Ang, Z. (2011). The impact of electricity market and environmental regulation on carbon capture & storage (CCS) development in China. In Z. Luo (Ed.), *Green finance and sustainability: Environmentally-aware business models and technologies* (pp. 463–471). Hershey, PA: IGI Global. doi:10.4018/978-1-60960-531-5.ch024

Antonova, A. (2013). Green, sustainable, or clean: What type of IT/IS technologies will we need in the future? In P. Ordóñez de Pablos (Ed.), *Green technologies and business practices: An IT approach* (pp. 151–162). Hershey, PA: IGI Global. doi:10.4018/978-1-4666-1972-2.ch008

Antonova, A. (2014). Green, sustainable, or clean: What type of IT/IS technologies will we need in the future? In *Sustainable practices: Concepts, methodologies, tools and applications* (pp. 384–396). Hershey, PA: IGI Global. doi:10.4018/978-1-4666-4852-4.ch021

Appiah, D. O., & Kemausuor, F. (2012). Energy, environment and socio-economic development: Africa's triple challenge and options. In M. Tortora (Ed.), *Sustainable systems and energy management at the regional level: Comparative approaches* (pp. 166–182). Hershey, PA: IGI Global. doi:10.4018/978-1-61350-344-7.ch009

Appleby, M. R., Lambert, C. G., Rennie, A. E., & Buckley, A. B. (2011). An investigation into the environmental impact of product recovery methods to support sustainable manufacturing within small and medium-sized enterprises (SMEs). *International Journal of Manufacturing, Materials, and Mechanical Engineering, 1*(2), 1–18. doi:10.4018/ijmmme.2011040101

Appleby, M. R., Lambert, C. G., Rennie, A. E., & Buckley, A. B. (2013). An investigation into the environmental impact of product recovery methods to support sustainable manufacturing within small and medium-sized enterprises (SMEs). In J. Davim (Ed.), *Dynamic methods and process advancements in mechanical, manufacturing, and materials engineering* (pp. 73–90). Hershey, PA: IGI Global. doi:10.4018/978-1-4666-1867-1.ch004

Arora, K., Kumar, A., & Sharma, S. (2012). Energy from waste: Present scenario, challenges, and future prospects towards sustainable development. In P. Olla (Ed.), *Global sustainable development and renewable energy systems* (pp. 271–296). Hershey, PA: IGI Global. doi:10.4018/978-1-4666-1625-7.ch014

Arora, K., Kumar, A., & Sharma, S. (2014). Energy from waste: present scenario, challenges, and future prospects towards sustainable development. In *Sustainable practices: Concepts, methodologies, tools and applications* (pp. 1519–1543). Hershey, PA: IGI Global. doi:10.4018/978-1-4666-4852-4.ch085

Ashraf, G. Y. (2012). A study of eco-friendly supply chain management at cement industries of Chhattisgarh. In M. Garg & S. Gupta (Eds.), *Cases on supply chain and distribution management: Issues and principles* (pp. 146–157). Hershey, PA: IGI Global. doi:10.4018/978-1-4666-0065-2.ch007

Ashraf, G. Y. (2013). A study of eco-friendly supply chain management at cement industries of Chhattisgarh. In *Supply chain management: Concepts, methodologies, tools, and applications* (pp. 823–830). Hershey, PA: IGI Global. doi:10.4018/978-1-4666-2625-6.ch048

Asiimwe, E. N., & Åke, G. (2012). E-waste management in East African community. In K. Bwalya & S. Zulu (Eds.), *Handbook of research on e-government in emerging economies: Adoption, e-participation, and legal frameworks* (pp. 307–327). Hershey, PA: IGI Global. doi:10.4018/978-1-4666-0324-0.ch015

Aspradaki, A. A. (2013). Deliberative democracy and nanotechnologies in health. *International Journal of Technoethics*, *4*(2), 1–14. doi:10.4018/jte.2013070101

Ayadi, F. S. (2013). An empirical investigation of environmental kuznets curve in Nigeria. In K. Ganesh & S. Anbuudayasankar (Eds.), *International and interdisciplinary studies in green computing* (pp. 302–310). Hershey, PA: IGI Global. doi:10.4018/978-1-4666-2646-1.ch022

Ayuk, E. T., Fonta, W. M., & Kouame, E. B. (2014). Application of quantitative methods in natural resource management in Africa: A review. In P. Schaeffer & E. Kouassi (Eds.), *Econometric methods for analyzing economic development* (pp. 205–234). Hershey, PA: IGI Global. doi:10.4018/978-1-4666-4329-1.ch013

Bachour, N. (2012). Green IT project management: Optimizing the value of green IT projects within organizations. In W. Hu & N. Kaabouch (Eds.), *Sustainable ICTs and management systems for green computing* (pp. 146–178). Hershey, PA: IGI Global. doi:10.4018/978-1-4666-1839-8.ch007

Baginetas, K. N. (2011). Sustainable management of agricultural resources and the need for stakeholder participation for the developing of appropriate sustainability indicators: The case of soil quality. In Z. Andreopoulou, B. Manos, N. Polman, & D. Viaggi (Eds.), *Agricultural and environmental informatics, governance and management: Emerging research applications* (pp. 227–261). Hershey, PA: IGI Global. doi:10.4018/978-1-60960-621-3.ch013

Baginetas, K. N. (2012). Sustainable management of agricultural resources and the need for stakeholder participation for the developing of appropriate sustainability indicators: The case of soil quality. In *Regional development: Concepts, methodologies, tools, and applications* (pp. 632–665). Hershey, PA: IGI Global. doi:10.4018/978-1-4666-0882-5.ch401

Bailis, R., & Arabshahi, N. (2011). Voluntary emissions reduction: Are we making progress? In Z. Luo (Ed.), *Green finance and sustainability: Environmentally-aware business models and technologies* (pp. 241–273). Hershey, PA: IGI Global. doi:10.4018/978-1-60960-531-5.ch014

Banerjee, S., Sing, T. Y., Chowdhury, A. R., & Anwar, H. (2013). Motivations to adopt green ICT: A tale of two organizations. *International Journal of Green Computing*, *4*(2), 1–11. doi:10.4018/jgc.2013070101

Baptiste, A. K. (2013). Local vs. expert perception of climate change: An analysis of fishers in Trinidad and Tobago. In H. Muga & K. Thomas (Eds.), *Cases on the diffusion and adoption of sustainable development practices* (pp. 44–82). Hershey, PA: IGI Global. doi:10.4018/978-1-4666-2842-7.ch003

Bassey, K., & Chigbu, P. (2013). Optimal detection and estimation of marine oil spills through coherent pluralism. *International Journal of Operations Research and Information Systems*, 4(1), 84–111. doi:10.4018/joris.2013010105

Bata, R., & Jordão, T. C. (2011). Modeling the influences of heating fuel consumption in gaseous emissions and solid waste generation. In V. Olej, I. Obršálová, & J. Krupka (Eds.), *Environmental modeling for sustainable regional development: System approaches and advanced methods* (pp. 162–185). Hershey, PA: IGI Global. doi:10.4018/978-1-60960-156-0.ch008

Beall, A. M., & Ford, A. (2012). Reports from the field: Assessing the art and science of participatory environmental modeling. In J. Wang (Ed.), *Societal impacts on information systems development and applications* (pp. 195–213). Hershey, PA: IGI Global. doi:10.4018/978-1-4666-0927-3.ch013

Ben Brahim, H., & Duckstein, L. (2011). Descriptive methods and compromise programming for promoting agricultural reuse of treated wastewater. In H. do Prado, A. Barreto Luiz, & H. Filho (Eds.), *Computational methods for agricultural research: Advances and applications* (pp. 355–388). Hershey, PA: IGI Global. doi:10.4018/978-1-61692-871-1.ch017

Bentley, G. C., Cromley, R. G., Hanink, D. M., & Heidkamp, C. P. (2013). Forest cover change in the northeastern U.S.: A spatial assessment in the context of an environmental kuznets curve. *International Journal of Applied Geospatial Research*, 4(3), 1–18. doi:10.4018/jagr.2013070101

Berke, M. Ö., Sütlü, E., Avcioglu, B., & Gem, E. (2013). Identification of priority areas for conservation in Lake Egirdir and Lake Kovada, Turkey. In J. Papathanasiou, B. Manos, S. Arampatzis, & R. Kenward (Eds.), *Transactional environmental support system design: Global solutions* (pp. 199–202). Hershey, PA: IGI Global. doi:10.4018/978-1-4666-2824-3.ch018

Bhattarai, N., Khanal, S., Pudasaini, P. R., Pahl, S., & Romero-Urbina, D. (2011). Citrate stabilized silver nanoparticles: Study of crystallography and surface properties. *International Journal of Nanotechnology and Molecular Computation*, 3(3), 15–28. doi:10.4018/ijnmc.2011070102

Bier, A. (2012). A system dynamics approach to changing perceptions about thermal water quality trading markets. In J. Wang (Ed.), *Societal impacts on information systems development and applications* (pp. 182–194). Hershey, PA: IGI Global. doi:10.4018/978-1-4666-0927-3.ch012

Biller, D., & Sanchez-Triana, E. (2013). Enlisting markets in the conservation and sustainable use of biodiversity in South Asia's Sundarbans. *International Journal of Social Ecology and Sustainable Development*, 4(3), 71–86. doi:10.4018/jsesd.2013070106

Bonadiman, R. (2013). Sustainability: Brazilian perspectives and challenges after the first kioto's protocol period. *International Journal of Social Ecology and Sustainable Development*, 4(3), 52–60. doi:10.4018/jsesd.2013070104

Boote, K. J., Jones, J. W., Hoogenboom, G., & White, J. W. (2012). The role of crop systems simulation in agriculture and environment. In P. Papajorgji & F. Pinet (Eds.), *New technologies for constructing complex agricultural and environmental systems* (pp. 326–339). Hershey, PA: IGI Global. doi:10.4018/978-1-4666-0333-2.ch018

Boulton, A., Devriendt, L., Brunn, S. D., Derudder, B., & Witlox, F. (2014). City networks in cyberspace and time: Using Google hyperlinks to measure global economic and environmental crises. In *Crisis management: Concepts, methodologies, tools and applications* (pp. 1325–1345). Hershey, PA: IGI Global. doi:10.4018/978-1-4666-4707-7.ch067

Bradbury, M. (2012). The sustainable waterfront. In O. Ercoskun (Ed.), *Green and ecological technologies for urban planning: Creating smart cities* (pp. 274–292). Hershey, PA: IGI Global. doi:10.4018/978-1-61350-453-6.ch015

Bradbury, M. (2014). The sustainable waterfront. In *Sustainable practices: Concepts, methodologies, tools and applications* (pp. 1683–1700). Hershey, PA: IGI Global. doi:10.4018/978-1-4666-4852-4.ch093

Brimmo, A., & Emziane, M. (2014). Carbon nanotubes for photovoltaics. In M. Bououdina & J. Davim (Eds.), *Handbook of research on nanoscience, nanotechnology, and advanced materials* (pp. 268–311). Hershey, PA: IGI Global. doi:10.4018/978-1-4666-5824-0.ch012

Brister, E., Hane, E., & Korfmacher, K. (2011). Visualizing plant community change using historical records. *International Journal of Applied Geospatial Research*, 2(4), 1–18. doi:10.4018/jagr.2011100101

Buxton, G. (2013). Nanotechnology and polymer solar cells. In S. Anwar, H. Efstathiadis, & S. Qazi (Eds.), *Handbook of research on solar energy systems and technologies* (pp. 231–253). Hershey, PA: IGI Global. doi:10.4018/978-1-4666-1996-8.ch009

Buxton, G. (2014). Nanotechnology and polymer solar cells. In Nanotechnology: Concepts, methodologies, tools, and applications (pp. 384-405). Hershey, PA: IGI Global. doi:10.4018/978-1-4666-5125-8.ch015

Cadman, T., & Hume, M. (2012). Developing sustainable governance systems for regional sustainability programmes and 'green' business practices: The case of 'green' timber. In M. Tortora (Ed.), *Sustainable systems and energy management at the regional level: Comparative approaches* (pp. 365–382). Hershey, PA: IGI Global. doi:10.4018/978-1-61350-344-7.ch019

Cai, T. (2014). Artificial neural network for industrial and environmental research via air quality monitoring network. In Z. Sun & J. Yearwood (Eds.), *Handbook of research on demand-driven web services: Theory, technologies, and applications* (pp. 399–419). Hershey, PA: IGI Global. doi:10.4018/978-1-4666-5884-4.ch019

Cai, T. (2014). Geospatial technology-based e-government design for environmental protection and emergency response. In K. Bwalya (Ed.), *Technology development and platform enhancements for successful global e-government design* (pp. 157–184). Hershey, PA: IGI Global. doi:10.4018/978-1-4666-4900-2.ch009

Calipinar, H., & Ulas, D. (2013). Model suggestion for SMEs economic and environmental sustainable development. In N. Ndubisi & S. Nwankwo (Eds.), *Enterprise development in SMEs and entrepreneurial firms: Dynamic processes* (pp. 270–290). Hershey, PA: IGI Global. doi:10.4018/978-1-4666-2952-3.ch014

Carvajal-Escobar, Y., Mimi, Z., Khayat, S., Sulieman, S., Garces, W., & Cespedes, G. (2011). Application of methodologies for environmental flow determination in an andean and a Mediterranean basin: Two case studies of the Pance River (Colombia) and Wadi River (Palestine) basin. *International Journal of Social Ecology and Sustainable Development*, 2(4), 26–43. doi:10.4018/jsesd.2011100103

Carvajal-Escobar, Y., Mimi, Z., Khayat, S., Sulieman, S., Garces, W., & Cespedes, G. (2013). Application of methodologies for environmental flow determination in an andean and a Mediterranean basin: Two case studies of the Pance River (Colombia) and Wadi River (Palestine) basin. In E. Carayannis (Ed.), *Creating a sustainable ecology using technology-driven solutions* (pp. 296–314). Hershey, PA: IGI Global. doi:10.4018/978-1-4666-3613-2.ch020

Cascelli, E., Crestaz, E., & Tatangelo, F. (2013). Cartography and geovisualization in groundwater modelling. In G. Borruso, S. Bertazzon, A. Favretto, B. Murgante, & C. Torre (Eds.), *Geographic information analysis for sustainable development and economic planning: New technologies* (pp. 49–67). Hershey, PA: IGI Global. doi:10.4018/978-1-4666-1924-1.ch004

Ceccaroni, L., & Oliva, L. (2012). Ontologies for the design of ecosystems. In T. Podobnikar & M. Čeh (Eds.), *Universal ontology of geographic space: semantic enrichment for spatial data* (pp. 207–228). Hershey, PA: IGI Global. doi:10.4018/978-1-4666-0327-1.ch009

Charuvilayil, R. A. (2013). Industrial pollution and people's movement: A case study of Eloor Island Kerala, India. In H. Muga & K. Thomas (Eds.), *Cases on the diffusion and adoption of sustainable development practices* (pp. 312–351). Hershey, PA: IGI Global. doi:10.4018/978-1-4666-2842-7.ch012

Chen, E. T. (2011). Green information technology and virtualization in corporate environmental management information systems. In *Green technologies: Concepts, methodologies, tools and applications* (pp. 1421–1434). Hershey, PA: IGI Global. doi:10.4018/978-1-60960-472-1.ch605

Chen, H., & Bishop, I. D. (2013). Collaborative environmental knowledge management. *International Journal of E-Planning Research*, 2(1), 58–81. doi:10.4018/ijepr.2013010104

Chen, X. M. (2011). GIS and remote sensing in environmental risk assessment. In *Green technologies: Concepts, methodologies, tools and applications* (pp. 840–847). Hershey, PA: IGI Global. doi:10.4018/978-1-60960-472-1.ch415

Chen, Y. (2013). Generalize key requirements for designing IT-based system for green with considering stakeholder needs. *International Journal of Information Technologies and Systems Approach*, 6(1), 78–97. doi:10.4018/jitsa.2013010105

Chinchuluun, A., Xanthopoulos, P., Tomaino, V., & Pardalos, P. (2012). Data mining techniques in agricultural and environmental sciences. In P. Papajorgji & F. Pinet (Eds.), *New technologies for constructing complex agricultural and environmental systems* (pp. 311–325). Hershey, PA: IGI Global. doi:10.4018/978-1-4666-0333-2.ch017

Chitra, S. (2011). Adopting green ICT in business. In I. Management Association (Ed.), Green technologies: Concepts, methodologies, tools and applications (pp. 1145-1153). Hershey, PA: IGI Global. doi:10.4018/978-1-60960-472-1.ch501

Chiu, M. (2013). Gaps between valuing and purchasing green-technology products: Product and gender differences. *International Journal of Technology and Human Interaction*, 8(3), 54–68. doi:10.4018/jthi.2012070106

Cho, C. H., Patten, D. M., & Roberts, R. W. (2014). Environmental disclosures and impression management. In R. Hart (Ed.), *Communication and language analysis in the corporate world* (pp. 217–231). Hershey, PA: IGI Global. doi:10.4018/978-1-4666-4999-6.ch013

Christophoridis, C., Bizani, E., & Fytianos, K. (2011). Environmental quality monitoring, using GIS as a tool of visualization, management and decision-making: Applications emerging from the EU water framework directive EU 2000/60. In Z. Andreopoulou, B. Manos, N. Polman, & D. Viaggi (Eds.), *Agricultural and environmental informatics, governance and management: Emerging research applications* (pp. 397–424). Hershey, PA: IGI Global. doi:10.4018/978-1-60960-621-3.ch021

Christophoridis, C., Bizani, E., & Fytianos, K. (2013). Environmental quality monitoring, using GIS as a tool of visualization, management and decision-making: Applications emerging from the EU water framework directive EU 2000/60. In *Geographic information systems: Concepts, methodologies, tools, and applications* (pp. 1559–1586). Hershey, PA: IGI Global. doi:10.4018/978-1-4666-2038-4.ch094

Cincu, C., & Diacon, A. (2013). Hybrid solar cells: Materials and technology. In L. Fara & M. Yamaguchi (Eds.), *Advanced solar cell materials, technology, modeling, and simulation* (pp. 79–100). Hershey, PA: IGI Global. doi:10.4018/978-1-4666-1927-2.ch006

Cocozza, A., & Ficarella, A. (2013). Electrical resistivity measures in cohesive soils for the simulation of an integrated energy system between CCS and low-enthalpy geothermal. *International Journal of Measurement Technologies and Instrumentation Engineering*, 3(1), 48–68. doi:10.4018/ijmtie.2013010105

Cohen, E., & Zimmerman, T. D. (2012). Teaching the greenhouse effect with inquiry-based computer simulations: A WISE case study. In L. Lennex & K. Nettleton (Eds.), *Cases on inquiry through instructional technology in math and science* (pp. 551–580). Hershey, PA: IGI Global. doi:10.4018/978-1-4666-0068-3.ch020

Congedo, L., Baiocco, F., Brini, S., Liberti, L., & Munafò, M. (2013). Urban environment quality in the Italian spatial data infrastructure. In G. Borruso, S. Bertazzon, A. Favretto, B. Murgante, & C. Torre (Eds.), *Geographic information analysis for sustainable development and economic planning: New technologies* (pp. 179–192). Hershey, PA: IGI Global. doi:10.4018/978-1-4666-1924-1.ch012

Cosmi, C., Di Leo, S., Loperte, S., Pietrapertosa, F., Salvia, M., Macchiato, M., & Cuomo, V. (2011). Comprehensive energy systems analysis support tools for decision making. In *Green technologies: Concepts, methodologies, tools and applications* (pp. 493–514). Hershey, PA: IGI Global. doi:10.4018/978-1-60960-472-1.ch307

Cotton, M. (2012). Community opposition and public engagement with wind energy in the UK. In M. Tortora (Ed.), *Sustainable systems and energy management at the regional level: Comparative approaches* (pp. 310–327). Hershey, PA: IGI Global. doi:10.4018/978-1-61350-344-7.ch016

Cuccurullo, S., Francese, R., Passero, I., & Tortora, G. (2013). A 3D serious city building game on waste disposal. *International Journal of Distance Education Technologies*, *11*(4), 112–135. doi:10.4018/ijdet.2013100108

Cunha, M. D. (2011). Wastewater systems management at the regional level. In V. Olej, I. Obršálová, & J. Krupka (Eds.), *Environmental modeling for sustainable regional development: System approaches and advanced methods* (pp. 186–203). Hershey, PA: IGI Global. doi:10.4018/978-1-60960-156-0.ch009

Cunha, M. D. (2012). Wastewater systems management at the regional level. In *Regional development: Concepts, methodologies, tools, and applications* (pp. 1161–1177). Hershey, PA: IGI Global. doi:10.4018/978-1-4666-0882-5.ch607

Da Ronch, B., Di Maria, E., & Micelli, S. (2013). Clusters go green: Drivers of environmental sustainability in local networks of SMEs. *International Journal of Information Systems and Social Change*, *4*(1), 37–52. doi:10.4018/jissc.2013010103

Danahy, J., Wright, R., Mitchell, J., & Feick, R. (2013). Exploring ways to use 3D urban models to visualize multi-scalar climate change data and mitigation change models for e-planning. *International Journal of E-Planning Research*, *2*(2), 1–17. doi:10.4018/ijepr.2013040101

Dhal, S. (2013). Indigenous agricultural knowledge and innovation: A study of agricultural scientists in odisha. *International Journal of Information Systems and Social Change*, *4*(3), 57–71. doi:10.4018/jissc.2013070104

Dimitriou, D., Voskaki, A., & Sartzetaki, M. (2014). Airports environmental management: Results from the evaluation of European airports environmental plans. *International Journal of Information Systems and Supply Chain Management*, *7*(1), 1–14. doi:10.4018/IJISSCM.2014010101

Dizdaroglu, D., Yigitcanlar, T., & Dawes, L. (2011). Planning for sustainable urban futures. In *Green technologies: Concepts, methodologies, tools and applications* (pp. 1922–1932). Hershey, PA: IGI Global. doi:10.4018/978-1-60960-472-1.ch806

Djeflat, A. (2014). Harnessing knowledge for sustainable development: Challenges and opportunities for Arab countries. In A. Driouchi (Ed.), *Knowledge-based economic policy development in the Arab world* (pp. 229–244). Hershey, PA: IGI Global. doi:10.4018/978-1-4666-5210-1.ch009

Dolney, T. J. (2011). A GIS methodology for assessing the safety hazards of abandoned mine lands (AMLs): Application to the state of Pennsylvania. *International Journal of Applied Geospatial Research, 2*(3), 50–71. doi:10.4018/jagr.2011070104

Dubovski, S. (2014). Activities in oil and gas processing for avoiding or minimizing environmental impacts. In D. Matanovic, N. Gaurina-Medjimurec, & K. Simon (Eds.), *Risk analysis for prevention of hazardous situations in petroleum and natural gas engineering* (pp. 247–263). Hershey, PA: IGI Global. doi:10.4018/978-1-4666-4777-0.ch012

Dugas, D. P., DeMers, M. N., Greenlee, J. C., Whitford, W. G., & Klimaszewski-Patterson, A. (2011). Rapid evaluation of arid lands (REAL): A methodology. *International Journal of Applied Geospatial Research, 2*(3), 32–49. doi:10.4018/jagr.2011070103

Dusmanescu, D. (2013). Aspects regarding implementation of renewable energy sources in Romania up to 2050. *International Journal of Sustainable Economies Management, 2*(4), 1–21. doi:10.4018/ijsem.2013100101

Ehlinger, T., Tofan, L., Bucur, M., Enz, J., Carlson, J., & Shaker, R. (2011). Application of a participatory ex ante assessment model for environmental governance and visualizing sustainable redevelopment in Gorj County, Romania. In Z. Andreopoulou, B. Manos, N. Polman, & D. Viaggi (Eds.), *Agricultural and environmental informatics, governance and management: Emerging research applications* (pp. 61–86). Hershey, PA: IGI Global. doi:10.4018/978-1-60960-621-3.ch004

Ehlinger, T., Tofan, L., Bucur, M., Enz, J., Carlson, J., & Shaker, R. (2012). Application of a participatory ex ante assessment model for environmental governance and visualizing sustainable redevelopment in Gorj County, Romania. In *Regional development: Concepts, methodologies, tools, and applications* (pp. 743–768). Hershey, PA: IGI Global. doi:10.4018/978-1-4666-0882-5.ch407

Ekekwe, N. (2013). Nanotechnology and microelectronics: The science, trends and global diffusion. *International Journal of Nanotechnology and Molecular Computation, 3*(4), 1–23. doi:10.4018/ijnmc.2013100101

El Alouani, H., & Driouchi, A. (2014). The oil and gas sectors, renewable energy, and environmental performance in the Arab world. In A. Driouchi (Ed.), *Knowledge-based economic policy development in the Arab world* (pp. 172–228). Hershey, PA: IGI Global. doi:10.4018/978-1-4666-5210-1.ch008

El-Daoushy, F. (2011). Assessing environment-climate impacts in the Nile basin for decision-making. In *Green technologies: Concepts, methodologies, tools and applications* (pp. 694–712). Hershey, PA: IGI Global. doi:10.4018/978-1-60960-472-1.ch407

Elkarmi, F., & Abu Shikhah, N. (2012). Renewable energy technologies. In *Power system planning technologies and applications: Concepts, solutions and management* (pp. 121–142). Hershey, PA: IGI Global. doi:10.4018/978-1-4666-0173-4.ch008

Ene, C. (2013). Post-consumer waste: Challenges, trends and solutions. *International Journal of Sustainable Economies Management*, *2*(3), 19–31. doi:10.4018/ijsem.2013070102

Erdoğdu, M. M., & Karaca, C. (2014). A road map for a domestic wind turbine manufacturing industry in Turkey. In B. Christiansen & M. Basilgan (Eds.), *Economic behavior, game theory, and technology in emerging markets* (pp. 57–90). Hershey, PA: IGI Global. doi:10.4018/978-1-4666-4745-9.ch005

Espiritu, J. F., & Ituarte-Villarreal, C. M. (2013). Wind farm layout optimization using a viral systems algorithm. *International Journal of Applied Evolutionary Computation*, *4*(4), 27–40. doi:10.4018/ijaec.2013100102

Evangelista, P., Huge-Brodin, M., Isaksson, K., & Sweeney, E. (2013). Purchasing green transport and logistics services: Implications from the environmental sustainability attitude of 3PLs. In D. Folinas (Ed.), *Outsourcing management for supply chain operations and logistics service* (pp. 449–465). Hershey, PA: IGI Global. doi:10.4018/978-1-4666-2008-7.ch026

Evangelista, P., Huge-Brodin, M., Isaksson, K., & Sweeney, E. (2014). Purchasing green transport and logistics services: Implications from the environmental sustainability attitude of 3PLs. In *Sustainable practices: Concepts, methodologies, tools and applications* (pp. 86–102). Hershey, PA: IGI Global. doi:10.4018/978-1-4666-4852-4.ch005

Ewald, J. A., Sharp, R. J., Beja, P., & Kenward, R. (2013). Pan-European survey and database of environmental assessment factors. In J. Papathanasiou, B. Manos, S. Arampatzis, & R. Kenward (Eds.), *Transactional environmental support system design: Global solutions* (pp. 97–119). Hershey, PA: IGI Global. doi:10.4018/978-1-4666-2824-3.ch006

Fann, J., & Rakas, J. (2011). Greener transportation infrastructure: Theoretical concepts for the environmental evaluation of airports. In Z. Luo (Ed.), *Green finance and sustainability: Environmentally-aware business models and technologies* (pp. 394–421). Hershey, PA: IGI Global. doi:10.4018/978-1-60960-531-5.ch021

Fann, J., & Rakas, J. (2013). Methodology for environmental sustainability evaluation of airport development alternatives. *International Journal of Applied Logistics, 4*(4), 8–31. doi:10.4018/ijal.2013100102

Fara, L., & Yamaguchi, M. (2013). Prospects and strategy of development for advanced solar cells. In L. Fara & M. Yamaguchi (Eds.), *Advanced solar cell materials, technology, modeling, and simulation* (pp. 287–296). Hershey, PA: IGI Global. doi:10.4018/978-1-4666-1927-2.ch014

Farmani, R., Savic, D., Henriksen, H., Molina, J., Giordano, R., & Bromley, J. (2011). Evolutionary Bayesian belief networks for participatory water resources management under uncertainty. In *Green technologies: Concepts, methodologies, tools and applications* (pp. 524–539). Hershey, PA: IGI Global. doi:10.4018/978-1-60960-472-1.ch309

Fearnside, P. M. (2013). Climate change as a threat to Brazil's Amazon forest. *International Journal of Social Ecology and Sustainable Development, 4*(3), 1–12. doi:10.4018/jsesd.2013070101

Filipović, V., Roljević, S., & Bekić, B. (2014). Organic production in Serbia: The transition to green economy. In *Sustainable practices: Concepts, methodologies, tools and applications* (pp. 769–785). Hershey, PA: IGI Global. doi:10.4018/978-1-4666-4852-4.ch043

Finardi, U. (2012). Nanosciences and nanotechnologies: Evolution trajectories and disruptive features. In N. Ekekwe & N. Islam (Eds.), *Disruptive technologies, innovation and global redesign: Emerging implications* (pp. 107–126). Hershey, PA: IGI Global. doi:10.4018/978-1-4666-0134-5.ch007

Finardi, U. (2014). Nanosciences and nanotechnologies: Evolution trajectories and disruptive features. In Nanotechnology: Concepts, methodologies, tools, and applications (pp. 1-20). Hershey, PA: IGI Global. doi:10.4018/978-1-4666-5125-8.ch001

Fokaides, P. A. (2012). Towards zero energy buildings (ZEB): The role of environmental technologies. In O. Ercoskun (Ed.), *Green and ecological technologies for urban planning: Creating smart cities* (pp. 93–111). Hershey, PA: IGI Global. doi:10.4018/978-1-61350-453-6.ch006

Fokaides, P. A. (2014). Towards zero energy buildings (ZEB): The role of environmental technologies. In I. Management Association (Ed.), Sustainable practices: Concepts, methodologies, tools and applications (pp. 1742-1761). Hershey, PA: IGI Global. doi:10.4018/978-1-4666-4852-4.ch096

Gadatsch, A. (2011). Corporate environmental management information systems influence of green IT on IT management and IT controlling. In *Green technologies: Concepts, methodologies, tools and applications* (pp. 1408–1420). Hershey, PA: IGI Global. doi:10.4018/978-1-60960-472-1.ch604

Gálvez, J., Parreño, M., Pla, J., Sanchez, J., Gálvez-Llompart, M., Navarro, S., & García-Domenech, R. (2011). Application of molecular topology to the prediction of water quality indices of Alkylphenol pollutants. *International Journal of Chemoinformatics and Chemical Engineering*, *1*(1), 1–11. doi:10.4018/ijcce.2011010101

Gálvez, J., Parreño, M., Pla, J., Sanchez, J., Gálvez-Llompart, M., Navarro, S., & García-Domenech, R. (2013). Application of molecular topology to the prediction of water quality indices of Alkylphenol pollutants. In A. Haghi (Ed.), *Methodologies and applications for chemoinformatics and chemical engineering* (pp. 1–10). Hershey, PA: IGI Global. doi:10.4018/978-1-4666-4010-8.ch001

Garner, N., Lischke, M. D., Siol, A., & Eilks, I. (2014). Learning about sustainability in a non-formal laboratory context for secondary level students: A module on climate change, the ozone hole, and summer smog. In K. Thomas & H. Muga (Eds.), *Handbook of research on pedagogical innovations for sustainable development* (pp. 229–244). Hershey, PA: IGI Global. doi:10.4018/978-1-4666-5856-1.ch012

Gaurina-Medjimurec, N., & Pasic, B. (2014). CO2 underground storage and wellbore integrity. In D. Matanovic, N. Gaurina-Medjimurec, & K. Simon (Eds.), *Risk analysis for prevention of hazardous situations in petroleum and natural gas engineering* (pp. 322–357). Hershey, PA: IGI Global. doi:10.4018/978-1-4666-4777-0.ch015

Ghosh, N., & Goswami, A. (2014). Biofuels and renewables: Implications for people, planet, policies, politics. In *Sustainability science for social, economic, and environmental development* (pp. 64–87). Hershey, PA: IGI Global. doi:10.4018/978-1-4666-4995-8.ch007

Ghosh, N., & Goswami, A. (2014). Biofuel sustainability and transition pathways. In *Sustainability science for social, economic, and environmental development* (pp. 88–95). Hershey, PA: IGI Global. doi:10.4018/978-1-4666-4995-8.ch008

Ghosh, N., & Goswami, A. (2014). Economics, environmental policy, trade and sustainability. In *Sustainability science for social, economic, and environmental development* (pp. 246–268). Hershey, PA: IGI Global. doi:10.4018/978-1-4666-4995-8.ch016

Ghosh, N., & Goswami, A. (2014). Energy and emission linkages from the three wheeler autorickshaws of Kolkata: An exploratory analysis of the impact on economic, environmental, social dimensions of sustainability. In *Sustainability science for social, economic, and environmental development* (pp. 221–245). Hershey, PA: IGI Global. doi:10.4018/978-1-4666-4995-8.ch015

Ghosh, N., & Goswami, A. (2014). Labour observatories for agricultural policymaking and sustainable development. In *Sustainability science for social, economic, and environmental development* (pp. 56–63). Hershey, PA: IGI Global. doi:10.4018/978-1-4666-4995-8.ch006

Ghosh, N., & Goswami, A. (2014). On value and price of environmental resources. In *Sustainability science for social, economic, and environmental development* (pp. 24–32). Hershey, PA: IGI Global. doi:10.4018/978-1-4666-4995-8.ch002

Ghosh, N., & Goswami, A. (2014). Story of live discussion in autos of Delhi: What do they say about sustainability? In *Sustainability science for social, economic, and environmental development* (pp. 216–220). Hershey, PA: IGI Global. doi:10.4018/978-1-4666-4995-8.ch014

Ghosh, N., & Goswami, A. (2014). Two first generation biofuel (biodiesel, bioethanol) and sustainability: Some other realities for India and trade patterns. In *Sustainability science for social, economic, and environmental development* (pp. 174–208). Hershey, PA: IGI Global. doi:10.4018/978-1-4666-4995-8.ch012

Ghosh, N., & Goswami, A. (2014). Valuation and market-based pricing of economic and ecosystem services of water resources. In *Sustainability science for social, economic, and environmental development* (pp. 96–132). Hershey, PA: IGI Global. doi:10.4018/978-1-4666-4995-8.ch009

Ghosh, N., & Goswami, A. (2014). Water scarcity and conflicts: Can water futures exchange in South Asia provide the answer? In *Sustainability science for social, economic, and environmental development* (pp. 147–173). Hershey, PA: IGI Global. doi:10.4018/978-1-4666-4995-8.ch011

Gil, J., Díaz, L., Granell, C., & Huerta, J. (2013). Open source based deployment of environmental data into geospatial information infrastructures. In I. Management Association (Ed.), Geographic information systems: Concepts, methodologies, tools, and applications (pp. 952-969). Hershey, PA: IGI Global. doi:10.4018/978-1-4666-2038-4.ch059

Gill, L., Hathway, E. A., Lange, E., Morgan, E., & Romano, D. (2013). Coupling real-time 3D landscape models with microclimate simulations. *International Journal of E-Planning Research*, 2(1), 1–19. doi:10.4018/ijepr.2013010101

Giuliani, G., Ray, N., Schwarzer, S., De Bono, A., Peduzzi, P., Dao, H., ... Lehmann, A. (2011). Sharing environmental data through GEOSS. *International Journal of Applied Geospatial Research*, 2(1), 1–17. doi:10.4018/jagr.2011010101

Giuliani, G., Ray, N., Schwarzer, S., De Bono, A., Peduzzi, P., Dao, H., ... Lehmann, A. (2013). Sharing environmental data through GEOSS. In *Geographic information systems: Concepts, methodologies, tools, and applications* (pp. 1260–1275). Hershey, PA: IGI Global. doi:10.4018/978-1-4666-2038-4.ch076

Godbole, N. (2011). E-waste management: Challenges and issues. In B. Unhelkar (Ed.), *Handbook of research on green ICT: Technology, business and social perspectives* (pp. 480–505). Hershey, PA: IGI Global. doi:10.4018/978-1-61692-834-6.ch035

Goel, A., Tiwary, A., & Schmidt, H. (2011). Approaches and initiatives to green IT strategy in business. In *Green technologies: Concepts, methodologies, tools and applications* (pp. 1361–1375). Hershey, PA: IGI Global. doi:10.4018/978-1-60960-472-1.ch601

Granit, J. J., King, R. M., & Noël, R. (2013). Strategic environmental assessment as a tool to develop power in transboundary water basin settings. In E. Carayannis (Ed.), *Creating a sustainable ecology using technology-driven solutions* (pp. 269–281). Hershey, PA: IGI Global. doi:10.4018/978-1-4666-3613-2.ch018

Gräuler, M., Teuteberg, F., Mahmoud, T., & Gómez, J. M. (2013). Requirements prioritization and design considerations for the next generation of corporate environmental management information systems: A foundation for innovation. *International Journal of Information Technologies and Systems Approach*, 6(1), 98–116. doi:10.4018/jitsa.2013010106

Gräuler, M., Teuteberg, F., Mahmoud, T., & Gómez, J. M. (2013). Requirements prioritization and design considerations for the next generation of corporate environmental management information systems: A foundation for innovation. *International Journal of Information Technologies and Systems Approach*, 6(1), 98–116. doi:10.4018/jitsa.2013010106

Greenlee, B., & Daim, T. (2011). Building a sustainable regional eco system for green technologies: Case of cellulosic ethanol in Oregon. In Z. Luo (Ed.), *Green finance and sustainability: Environmentally-aware business models and technologies* (pp. 535–568). Hershey, PA: IGI Global. doi:10.4018/978-1-60960-531-5.ch028

Greenlee, B., & Daim, T. (2013). Building a sustainable regional eco system for green technologies: Case of cellulosic ethanol in Oregon. In I. Management Association (Ed.), Small and medium enterprises: Concepts, methodologies, tools, and applications (pp. 993-1025). Hershey, PA: IGI Global. doi:10.4018/978-1-4666-3886-0.ch049

Grigoroudis, E., Kouikoglou, V. S., & Phillis, Y. A. (2012). Approaches for measuring sustainability. In P. Olla (Ed.), *Global sustainable development and renewable energy systems* (pp. 101–130). Hershey, PA: IGI Global. doi:10.4018/978-1-4666-1625-7.ch006

Grigoroudis, E., Kouikoglou, V. S., & Phillis, Y. A. (2014). Approaches for measuring sustainability. In *Sustainable practices: Concepts, methodologies, tools and applications* (pp. 158–184). Hershey, PA: IGI Global. doi:10.4018/978-1-4666-4852-4.ch009

Guangming, L., & Zhaofeng, A. (2013). Empirical study on the correlations of environmental pollution, human capital, and economic growth: Based on the 1990-2007 data in Guangdong China. In P. Ordóñez de Pablos (Ed.), *Green technologies and business practices: An IT approach* (pp. 128–137). Hershey, PA: IGI Global. doi:10.4018/978-1-4666-1972-2.ch006

Gupta, A. K., Chakraborty, A., Giri, S., Subramanian, V., & Chattaraj, P. (2011). Toxicity of halogen, sulfur and chlorinated aromatic compounds: A quantitative-structure-toxicity-relationship (QSTR). *International Journal of Chemoinformatics and Chemical Engineering, 1*(1), 61–74. doi:10.4018/ijcce.2011010105

Gupta, A. K., Chakraborty, A., Giri, S., Subramanian, V., & Chattaraj, P. (2013). Toxicity of halogen, sulfur and chlorinated aromatic compounds: A quantitative-structure-toxicity-relationship (QSTR). In A. Haghi (Ed.), *Methodologies and applications for chemoinformatics and chemical engineering* (pp. 60–73). Hershey, PA: IGI Global. doi:10.4018/978-1-4666-4010-8.ch005

Habala, O., Šeleng, M., Tran, V., Šimo, B., & Hluchý, L. (2012). Mining environmental data in the ADMIRE project using new advanced methods and tools. In N. Bessis (Ed.), *Technology integration advancements in distributed systems and computing* (pp. 296–308). Hershey, PA: IGI Global. doi:10.4018/978-1-4666-0906-8.ch018

Hájek, P., & Olej, V. (2011). Air quality assessment by neural networks. In V. Olej, I. Obršálová, & J. Krupka (Eds.), *Environmental modeling for sustainable regional development: System approaches and advanced methods* (pp. 91–117). Hershey, PA: IGI Global. doi:10.4018/978-1-60960-156-0.ch005

Hall, C., Easley, R., Howard, J., & Halfhide, T. (2013). The role of authentic science research and education outreach in increasing community resilience: Case studies using informal education to address ocean acidification and healthy soils. In H. Muga & K. Thomas (Eds.), *Cases on the diffusion and adoption of sustainable development practices* (pp. 376–402). Hershey, PA: IGI Global. doi:10.4018/978-1-4666-2842-7.ch014

Hall, G. M., & Howe, J. (2013). The drivers for a sustainable chemical manufacturing industry. In *Industrial engineering: Concepts, methodologies, tools, and applications* (pp. 1659–1679). Hershey, PA: IGI Global. doi:10.4018/978-1-4666-1945-6.ch088

Hashemi, M., & O'Connell, E. (2013). Science and water policy interface: An integrated methodological framework for developing decision support systems (DSSs). In *Data mining: Concepts, methodologies, tools, and applications* (pp. 405–434). Hershey, PA: IGI Global. doi:10.4018/978-1-4666-2455-9.ch020

Heck, M., & Schmidt, G. (2013). Lot-size planning with non-linear cost functions supporting environmental sustainability. In K. Ganesh & S. Anbuudayasankar (Eds.), *International and interdisciplinary studies in green computing* (pp. 226–231). Hershey, PA: IGI Global. doi:10.4018/978-1-4666-2646-1.ch016

Herold, S., & Sawada, M. C. (2013). A review of geospatial information technology for natural disaster management in developing countries. In *Geographic information systems: Concepts, methodologies, tools, and applications* (pp. 175–215). Hershey, PA: IGI Global. doi:10.4018/978-1-4666-2038-4.ch014

Higginson, N., & Vredenburg, H. (2012). Finding the sweet spot of sustainability in the energy sector: A systems approach to managing the canadian oil sands. In M. Tortora (Ed.), *Sustainable systems and energy management at the regional level: Comparative approaches* (pp. 184–201). Hershey, PA: IGI Global. doi:10.4018/978-1-61350-344-7.ch010

Hilty, L. M. (2011). Information and communication technologies for a more sustainable world. In D. Haftor & A. Mirijamdotter (Eds.), *Information and communication technologies, society and human beings: Theory and framework (festschrift in honor of Gunilla Bradley)* (pp. 410–418). Hershey, PA: IGI Global. doi:10.4018/978-1-60960-057-0.ch033

Hin, L. T., & Subramaniam, R. (2012). Use of policy instruments to promote sustainable energy practices and implications for the environment: Experiences from Singapore. In M. Tortora (Ed.), *Sustainable systems and energy management at the regional level: Comparative approaches* (pp. 219–235). Hershey, PA: IGI Global. doi:10.4018/978-1-61350-344-7.ch012

Hrncevic, L. (2014). Petroleum industry environmental performance and risk. In D. Matanovic, N. Gaurina-Medjimurec, & K. Simon (Eds.), *Risk analysis for prevention of hazardous situations in petroleum and natural gas engineering* (pp. 358–387). Hershey, PA: IGI Global. doi:10.4018/978-1-4666-4777-0.ch016

Hsiao, S., Chen, D., Yang, C., Huang, H., Lu, Y., Huang, H., ... Lin, Y. (2013). Chemical-free and reusable cellular analysis: Electrochemical impedance spectroscopy with a transparent ITO culture chip. *International Journal of Technology and Human Interaction*, 8(3), 1–9. doi:10.4018/jthi.2012070101

Hunter, J., Becker, P., Alabri, A., van Ingen, C., & Abal, E. (2011). Using ontologies to relate resource management actions to environmental monitoring data in South East Queensland. *International Journal of Agricultural and Environmental Information Systems*, 2(1), 1–19. doi:10.4018/jaeis.2011010101

Imbrenda, V., D'Emilio, M., Lanfredi, M., Ragosta, M., & Simoniello, T. (2013). Indicators of land degradation vulnerability due to anthropic factors: Tools for an efficient planning. In G. Borruso, S. Bertazzon, A. Favretto, B. Murgante, & C. Torre (Eds.), *Geographic information analysis for sustainable development and economic planning: New technologies* (pp. 87–101). Hershey, PA: IGI Global. doi:10.4018/978-1-4666-1924-1.ch006

Imbrenda, V., D'Emilio, M., Lanfredi, M., Ragosta, M., & Simoniello, T. (2014). Indicators of land degradation vulnerability due to anthropic factors: Tools for an efficient planning. In I. Management Association (Ed.), Sustainable practices: Concepts, methodologies, tools and applications (pp. 1400-1413). Hershey, PA: IGI Global. doi:10.4018/978-1-4666-4852-4.ch078

Iojă, C., Niță, M. R., & Stupariu, I. G. (2014). Resource conservation: Key elements in sustainable rural development. In Z. Andreopoulou, V. Samathrakis, S. Louca, & M. Vlachopoulou (Eds.), *E-innovation for sustainable development of rural resources during global economic crisis* (pp. 80–97). Hershey, PA: IGI Global. doi:10.4018/978-1-4666-4550-9.ch008

Ioja, C., Rozylowicz, L., Patroescu, M., Nita, M., & Onose, D. (2011). Agriculture and conservation in the Natura 2000 network: A sustainable development approach of the European Union. In Z. Andreopoulou, B. Manos, N. Polman, & D. Viaggi (Eds.), *Agricultural and environmental informatics, governance and management: Emerging research applications* (pp. 339–358). Hershey, PA: IGI Global. doi:10.4018/978-1-60960-621-3.ch018

Ioja, C., Rozylowicz, L., Patroescu, M., Nita, M., & Onose, D. (2013). Agriculture and conservation in the Natura 2000 network: A sustainable development approach of the European Union. In *Geographic information systems: Concepts, methodologies, tools, and applications* (pp. 1276–1296). Hershey, PA: IGI Global. doi:10.4018/978-1-4666-2038-4.ch077

Ip-Soo-Ching, J. M., & Zyngier, S. (2014). The rise of "environmental sustainability knowledge" in business strategy and entrepreneurship: An IT-enabled knowledge-based view of tourism operators. In P. Ordóñez de Pablos (Ed.), International business strategy and entrepreneurship: An information technology perspective (pp. 23-40). Hershey, PA: IGI Global. doi:10.4018/978-1-4666-4753-4.ch002

Ivask, M., Aruvee, E., & Piirimäe, K. (2013). Database of environmental decision support tools. In J. Papathanasiou, B. Manos, S. Arampatzis, & R. Kenward (Eds.), *Transactional environmental support system design: Global solutions* (pp. 70–96). Hershey, PA: IGI Global. doi:10.4018/978-1-4666-2824-3.ch005

Jacobsson, M., Linde, A., & Linderoth, H. (2011). The relation between ICT and environmental management practice in a construction company. In *Green technologies: Concepts, methodologies, tools and applications* (pp. 1099–1117). Hershey, PA: IGI Global. doi:10.4018/978-1-60960-472-1.ch430

Jafari, M. (2013). Challenges in climate change and environmental crisis: Impacts of aviation industry on human, urban and natural environments. *International Journal of Space Technology Management and Innovation, 3*(2), 24–46. doi:10.4018/ijstmi.2013070102

Jain, H. (2011). Green ICT organizational implementations and workplace relationships. In B. Unhelkar (Ed.), *Handbook of research on green ICT: Technology, business and social perspectives* (pp. 146–168). Hershey, PA: IGI Global. doi:10.4018/978-1-61692-834-6.ch010

Jamous, N. (2013). Light-weight composite environmental performance indicators (LWC-EPI): A new approach for environmental management information systems (EMIS). *International Journal of Information Technologies and Systems Approach, 6*(1), 20–38. doi:10.4018/jitsa.2013010102

Jan, Y., Lin, M., Shiao, K., Wei, C., Huang, L., & Sung, Q. (2013). Development of an evaluation instrument for green building literacy among college students in Taiwan. *International Journal of Technology and Human Interaction*, 8(3), 31–45. doi:10.4018/jthi.2012070104

Jarmoszko, A., D'Onofrio, M., Lee-Partridge, J. E., & Petkova, O. (2013). Evaluating sustainability and greening methods: A conceptual model for information technology management. *International Journal of Applied Logistics*, 4(3), 1–13. doi:10.4018/jal.2013070101

Jena, R. K. (2013). Green computing to green business. In P. Ordóñez de Pablos (Ed.), *Green technologies and business practices: An IT approach* (pp. 138–150). Hershey, PA: IGI Global. doi:10.4018/978-1-4666-1972-2.ch007

Jinturkar, A. M., & Deshmukh, S. S. (2013). Sustainable development by rural energy resources allocation in India: A fuzzy goal programming approach. *International Journal of Energy Optimization and Engineering*, 2(1), 37–49. doi:10.4018/ijeoe.2013010103

Jirava, P., & Obršálová, I. (2011). Modeling the effects of the quality of the environment on the health of a selected population. In V. Olej, I. Obršálová, & J. Krupka (Eds.), *Environmental modeling for sustainable regional development: System approaches and advanced methods* (pp. 344–365). Hershey, PA: IGI Global. doi:10.4018/978-1-60960-156-0.ch017

Jonoski, A., & Evers, M. (2013). Sociotechnical framework for participatory flood risk management via collaborative modeling. *International Journal of Information Systems and Social Change*, 4(2), 1–16. doi:10.4018/jissc.2013040101

Joshi, P. K., & Priyanka, N. (2011). Geo-informatics for land use and biodiversity studies. In Y. Trisurat, R. Shrestha, & R. Alkemade (Eds.), *Land use, climate change and biodiversity modeling: Perspectives and applications* (pp. 52–77). Hershey, PA: IGI Global. doi:10.4018/978-1-60960-619-0.ch003

Joshi, P. K., & Priyanka, N. (2013). Geo-informatics for land use and biodiversity studies. In I. Management Association (Ed.), Geographic information systems: Concepts, methodologies, tools, and applications (pp. 1913-1939). Hershey, PA: IGI Global. doi:10.4018/978-1-4666-2038-4.ch114

Júnior, R., Rigitano, R., & Boesten, J. (2011). Pesticide leaching models in a Brazilian agricultural field scenario. In H. do Prado, A. Barreto Luiz, & H. Filho (Eds.), *Computational methods for agricultural research: Advances and applications* (pp. 266–295). Hershey, PA: IGI Global. doi:10.4018/978-1-61692-871-1.ch013

Kader, A. S., & Olanrewaju, O. S. (2014). River transportation master plan study for environmental enhancement. In O. Olanrewaju, A. Saharuddin, A. Ab Kader, & W. Wan Nik (Eds.), *Marine technology and sustainable development: Green innovations* (pp. 178–184). Hershey, PA: IGI Global. doi:10.4018/978-1-4666-4317-8.ch011

Kamaja, C. K., Rajaperumal, M., Boukherroub, R., & Shelke, M. V. (2014). Silicon nanostructures-graphene nanocomposites: Efficient materials for energy conversion and storage. In M. Bououdina & J. Davim (Eds.), *Handbook of research on nanoscience, nanotechnology, and advanced materials* (pp. 176–195). Hershey, PA: IGI Global. doi:10.4018/978-1-4666-5824-0.ch009

Kaplan, A. (2012). "Green infrastructure" concept as an effective medium to manipulating sustainable urban development. In O. Ercoskun (Ed.), *Green and ecological technologies for urban planning: Creating smart cities* (pp. 234–254). Hershey, PA: IGI Global. doi:10.4018/978-1-61350-453-6.ch013

Kašparová, M., & Krupka, J. (2011). Air quality modeling and metamodeling approach. In V. Olej, I. Obršálová, & J. Krupka (Eds.), *Environmental modeling for sustainable regional development: System approaches and advanced methods* (pp. 144–161). Hershey, PA: IGI Global. doi:10.4018/978-1-60960-156-0.ch007

Kenward, R., Casey, N. M., Walls, S. S., Dick, J. M., Smith, R., & Turner, S. L. ... Sharp, R. J. (2013). Pan-European analysis of environmental assessment processes. In J. Papathanasiou, B. Manos, S. Arampatzis, & R. Kenward (Eds.), Transactional environmental support system design: Global solutions (pp. 120-133). Hershey, PA: IGI Global. doi:10.4018/978-1-4666-2824-3.ch007

Kokkinakis, A., & Andreopoulou, Z. (2011). E-governance and management of inland water ecosystems using time-series analysis of fishery production. In Z. Andreopoulou, B. Manos, N. Polman, & D. Viaggi (Eds.), *Agricultural and environmental informatics, governance and management: Emerging research applications* (pp. 318–338). Hershey, PA: IGI Global. doi:10.4018/978-1-60960-621-3.ch017

Kongar, E. A., & Rosentrater, K. (2013). Data envelopment analysis approach to compare the environmental efficiency of energy utilization. In K. Ganesh & S. Anbuudayasankar (Eds.), *International and interdisciplinary studies in green computing* (pp. 273–288). Hershey, PA: IGI Global. doi:10.4018/978-1-4666-2646-1.ch020

Kosaka, M., Yabutani, T., & Zhang, Q. (2014). A value co-creation model for energy-saving service business using inverters. In M. Kosaka & K. Shirahada (Eds.), *Progressive trends in knowledge and system-based science for service innovation* (pp. 292–306). Hershey, PA: IGI Global. doi:10.4018/978-1-4666-4663-6.ch016

Kram, T., & Stehfest, E. (2011). Integrated modeling of global environmental change (IMAGE). In Y. Trisurat, R. Shrestha, & R. Alkemade (Eds.), *Land use, climate change and biodiversity modeling: Perspectives and applications* (pp. 104–118). Hershey, PA: IGI Global. doi:10.4018/978-1-60960-619-0.ch005

La Greca, P., La Rosa, D., Martinico, F., & Privitera, R. (2013). Land cover analysis for evapotranspiration assessment in Catania metropolitan region. In G. Borruso, S. Bertazzon, A. Favretto, B. Murgante, & C. Torre (Eds.), *Geographic information analysis for sustainable development and economic planning: New technologies* (pp. 102–114). Hershey, PA: IGI Global. doi:10.4018/978-1-4666-1924-1.ch007

Laike, Y., & Chun, L. (2012). China-European Union trade and global warming. In E. Carayannis (Ed.), *Sustainable policy applications for social ecology and development* (pp. 18–28). Hershey, PA: IGI Global. doi:10.4018/978-1-4666-1586-1.ch003

Laing, R., Bennadji, A., & Gray, D. (2013). Traffic control and CO2 reduction: Utilisation of virtual modelling within university estates master planning. *International Journal of E-Planning Research*, 2(1), 43–57. doi:10.4018/ijepr.2013010103

Lam, J. C., & Hills, P. (2011). Promoting technological environmental innovations: What is the role of environmental regulation? In Z. Luo (Ed.), *Green finance and sustainability: Environmentally-aware business models and technologies* (pp. 56–73). Hershey, PA: IGI Global. doi:10.4018/978-1-60960-531-5.ch003

Lam, J. C., & Hills, P. (2012). Transition to low-carbon hydrogen economy in America: The role of transition management. In Z. Luo (Ed.), *Advanced analytics for green and sustainable economic development: Supply chain models and financial technologies* (pp. 92–111). Hershey, PA: IGI Global. doi:10.4018/978-1-61350-156-6.ch007

Lam, J. C., & Hills, P. (2013). Promoting technological environmental innovations: The role of environmental regulation. In Z. Luo (Ed.), *Technological solutions for modern logistics and supply chain management* (pp. 230–247). Hershey, PA: IGI Global. doi:10.4018/978-1-4666-2773-4.ch015

Lee, S., Yigitcanlar, T., Egodawatta, P., & Goonetilleke, A. (2011). Sustainable water provision. In *Green technologies: Concepts, methodologies, tools and applications* (pp. 1768–1781). Hershey, PA: IGI Global. doi:10.4018/978-1-60960-472-1.ch714

Lee, Y. M., An, L., Liu, F., Horesh, R., Chae, Y. T., & Zhang, R. (2014). Analytics for smarter buildings. *International Journal of Business Analytics*, *1*(1), 1–15. doi:10.4018/ijban.2014010101

Leff, E. (2012). Environmental rationality: Innovation in thinking for sustainability. In F. Nobre, D. Walker, & R. Harris (Eds.), *Technological, managerial and organizational core competencies: Dynamic innovation and sustainable development* (pp. 1–17). Hershey, PA: IGI Global. doi:10.4018/978-1-61350-165-8.ch001

Leff, E. (2014). Environmental rationality: Innovation in thinking for sustainability. In *Sustainable practices: Concepts, methodologies, tools and applications* (pp. 1–17). Hershey, PA: IGI Global. doi:10.4018/978-1-4666-4852-4.ch001

Lefley, F., & Sarkis, J. (2011). A pragmatic profile approach to evaluating environmental sustainability investment decisions. In Z. Luo (Ed.), *Green finance and sustainability: Environmentally-aware business models and technologies* (pp. 321–332). Hershey, PA: IGI Global. doi:10.4018/978-1-60960-531-5.ch017

Li, H., & Zhang, X. (2012). Study on environmental tax: A case of China. In D. Ura & P. Ordóñez de Pablos (Eds.), *Advancing technologies for Asian business and economics: Information management developments* (pp. 207–219). Hershey, PA: IGI Global. doi:10.4018/978-1-4666-0276-2.ch016

Li, X., Ortiz, P., Kuczenski, B., Franklin, D., & Chong, F. T. (2012). Mitigating the environmental impact of smartphones with device reuse. In W. Hu & N. Kaabouch (Eds.), *Sustainable ICTs and management systems for green computing* (pp. 252–282). Hershey, PA: IGI Global. doi:10.4018/978-1-4666-1839-8.ch011

Li, X., Ortiz, P. J., Browne, J., Franklin, D., Oliver, J. Y., Geyer, R., ... Chong, F. T. (2012). A study of reusing smartphones to augment elementary school education. *International Journal of Handheld Computing Research*, *3*(2), 73–92. doi:10.4018/jhcr.2012040105

Lin, C., Chu, L., & Hsu, H. (2013). Study on the performance and exhaust emissions of motorcycle engine fuelled with hydrogen-gasoline compound fuel. *International Journal of Technology and Human Interaction*, *8*(3), 69–81. doi:10.4018/jthi.2012070107

Lingarchani, A. (2011). Environmental challenges in mobile services. In B. Unhelkar (Ed.), *Handbook of research on green ICT: Technology, business and social perspectives* (pp. 355–363). Hershey, PA: IGI Global. doi:10.4018/978-1-61692-834-6.ch025

Lingarchani, A. (2012). Environmental challenges in mobile services. In *Wireless technologies: Concepts, methodologies, tools and applications* (pp. 1891–1899). Hershey, PA: IGI Global. doi:10.4018/978-1-61350-101-6.ch710

Loeser, F., Erek, K., & Zarnekow, R. (2013). Green IT strategies: A conceptual framework for the alignment of information technology and corporate sustainability strategy. In P. Ordóñez de Pablos (Ed.), *Green technologies and business practices: An IT approach* (pp. 58–95). Hershey, PA: IGI Global. doi:10.4018/978-1-4666-1972-2.ch004

Loi, N. K. (2013). Sustainable land use and watershed management in response to climate change impacts: Overview and proposed research techniques. In *Geographic information systems: Concepts, methodologies, tools, and applications* (pp. 2080–2101). Hershey, PA: IGI Global. doi:10.4018/978-1-4666-2038-4.ch124

Lucignano, C., Squeo, E. A., Guglielmotti, A., & Quadrini, F. (2013). Recycling of waste epoxy-polyester powders for foam production. In J. Davim (Ed.), *Dynamic methods and process advancements in mechanical, manufacturing, and materials engineering* (pp. 91–101). Hershey, PA: IGI Global. doi:10.4018/978-1-4666-1867-1.ch005

Mahbub, P., Ayoko, G., Egodawatta, P., Yigitcanlar, T., & Goonetilleke, A. (2011). Traffic and climate change impacts on water quality. In I. Management Association (Ed.), Green technologies: Concepts, methodologies, tools and applications (pp. 1804-1823). Hershey, PA: IGI Global. doi:10.4018/978-1-60960-472-1.ch716

Maillé, E., & Espinasse, B. (2011). Pyroxene: A territorial decision support system based on spatial simulators integration for forest fire risk management. *International Journal of Agricultural and Environmental Information Systems*, 2(2), 52–72. doi:10.4018/jaeis.2011070104

Maillé, E., & Espinasse, B. (2012). Pyroxene: A territorial decision support system based on spatial simulators integration for forest fire risk management. In P. Papajorgji & F. Pinet (Eds.), *New technologies for constructing complex agricultural and environmental systems* (pp. 244–264). Hershey, PA: IGI Global. doi:10.4018/978-1-4666-0333-2.ch014

Mallios, Z. (2012). Irrigation water valuation using spatial hedonic models in GIS environment. In J. Wang (Ed.), *Societal impacts on information systems development and applications* (pp. 308–320). Hershey, PA: IGI Global. doi:10.4018/978-1-4666-0927-3.ch020

Manikas, I., Ieromonachou, P., & Bochtis, D. (2014). Environmental sustainability initiatives in the agrifood supply chain. In Z. Andreopoulou, V. Samathrakis, S. Louca, & M. Vlachopoulou (Eds.), *E-innovation for sustainable development of rural resources during global economic crisis* (pp. 221–232). Hershey, PA: IGI Global. doi:10.4018/978-1-4666-4550-9.ch016

Manou, D., & Papathanasiou, J. (2013). Exploring the development of new tourism activities in the municipality of Kerkini by using the area's natural resources sustainably, municipality of Kerkini, Greece. In J. Papathanasiou, B. Manos, S. Arampatzis, & R. Kenward (Eds.), *Transactional environmental support system design: Global solutions* (pp. 172–175). Hershey, PA: IGI Global. doi:10.4018/978-1-4666-2824-3.ch012

Maragkogianni, A., Papaefthimiou, S., & Zopounidis, C. (2013). Emissions trading schemes in the transportation sector. In A. Jean-Vasile, T. Adrian, J. Subic, & D. Dusmanescu (Eds.), *Sustainable technologies, policies, and constraints in the green economy* (pp. 269–289). Hershey, PA: IGI Global. doi:10.4018/978-1-4666-4098-6.ch015

Maragkogianni, A., Papaefthimiou, S., & Zopounidis, C. (2014). Emissions trading schemes in the transportation sector. In *Sustainable practices: Concepts, methodologies, tools and applications* (pp. 65–85). Hershey, PA: IGI Global. doi:10.4018/978-1-4666-4852-4.ch004

Marino, D. J., Castro, E. A., Massolo, L., Mueller, A., Herbarth, O., & Ronco, A. E. (2011). Characterization of polycyclic aromatic hydrocarbon profiles by multivariate statistical analysis. *International Journal of Chemoinformatics and Chemical Engineering, 1*(2), 1–14. doi:10.4018/ijcce.2011070101

Marino, D. J., Castro, E. A., Massolo, L., Mueller, A., Herbarth, O., & Ronco, A. E. (2013). Characterization of polycyclic aromatic hydrocarbon profiles by multivariate statistical analysis. In A. Haghi (Ed.), *Methodologies and applications for chemoinformatics and chemical engineering* (pp. 102–116). Hershey, PA: IGI Global. doi:10.4018/978-1-4666-4010-8.ch008

Marshall, A. (2011). The middle ground for nuclear waste management: Social and ethical aspects of shallow storage. *International Journal of Technoethics, 2*(2), 1–13. doi:10.4018/jte.2011040101

Mbzibain, A. (2013). The effect of farmer capacities, farm business resources and perceived support of family, friends and associational networks on intentions to invest in renewable energy ventures in the UK. *International Journal of Applied Behavioral Economics, 2*(3), 43–58. doi:10.4018/ijabe.2013070104

Mbzibain, A. (2014). The effect of farmer capacities, farm business resources and perceived support of family, friends and associational networks on intentions to invest in renewable energy ventures in the UK. In *Sustainable practices: Concepts, methodologies, tools and applications* (pp. 1072–1088). Hershey, PA: IGI Global. doi:10.4018/978-1-4666-4852-4.ch059

McKnight, K. P., Messina, J. P., Shortridge, A. M., Burns, M. D., & Pigozzi, B. W. (2011). Using volunteered geographic information to assess the spatial distribution of West Nile Virus in Detroit, Michigan. *International Journal of Applied Geospatial Research*, *2*(3), 72–85. doi:10.4018/jagr.2011070105

Mengel, M. A. (2011). Constructing an experience in a virtual green home. In G. Vincenti & J. Braman (Eds.), *Multi-user virtual environments for the classroom: Practical approaches to teaching in virtual worlds* (pp. 285–301). Hershey, PA: IGI Global. doi:10.4018/978-1-60960-545-2.ch018

Miidla, P. (2011). Data envelopment analysis in environmental technologies. In V. Olej, I. Obršálová, & J. Krupka (Eds.), *Environmental modeling for sustainable regional development: System approaches and advanced methods* (pp. 242–259). Hershey, PA: IGI Global. doi:10.4018/978-1-60960-156-0.ch012

Miidla, P. (2013). Data envelopment analysis in environmental technologies. In *Industrial engineering: Concepts, methodologies, tools, and applications* (pp. 625–642). Hershey, PA: IGI Global. doi:10.4018/978-1-4666-1945-6.ch036

Militano, L., Molinaro, A., Iera, A., & Petkovics, Á. (2013). A game theoretic approach to guarantee fairness in cooperation among green mobile network operators. *International Journal of Business Data Communications and Networking*, *9*(3), 1–15. doi:10.4018/jbdcn.2013070101

Miller, W., & Birkeland, J. (2011). Green energy. In *Green technologies: Concepts, methodologies, tools and applications* (pp. 1–16). Hershey, PA: IGI Global. doi:10.4018/978-1-60960-472-1.ch101

Miralles, A., Pinet, F., & Bédard, Y. (2012). Describing spatio-temporal phenomena for environmental system development: An overview of today's needs and solutions. In P. Papajorgji & F. Pinet (Eds.), *New technologies for constructing complex agricultural and environmental systems* (pp. 211–226). Hershey, PA: IGI Global. doi:10.4018/978-1-4666-0333-2.ch012

Misso, R. (2011). Sustainable governance in the integrated system "environment-agriculture–health" through ICTs. In Z. Andreopoulou, B. Manos, N. Polman, & D. Viaggi (Eds.), *Agricultural and environmental informatics, governance and management: Emerging research applications* (pp. 87–101). Hershey, PA: IGI Global. doi:10.4018/978-1-60960-621-3.ch005

Mitroi, M. R., Fara, L., & Moraru, A. G. (2013). Organic solar cells modeling and simulation. In L. Fara & M. Yamaguchi (Eds.), *Advanced solar cell materials, technology, modeling, and simulation* (pp. 120–137). Hershey, PA: IGI Global. doi:10.4018/978-1-4666-1927-2.ch008

Mochal, T., & Krasnoff, A. (2013). GreenPM®: The basic principles for applying an environmental dimension to project management. In G. Silvius & J. Tharp (Eds.), *Sustainability integration for effective project management* (pp. 39–57). Hershey, PA: IGI Global. doi:10.4018/978-1-4666-4177-8.ch003

Montgomery, M. C., & Chakraborty, J. (2013). Social vulnerability to coastal and inland flood hazards: A comparison of GIS-based spatial interpolation methods. *International Journal of Applied Geospatial Research*, *4*(3), 58–79. doi:10.4018/jagr.2013070104

Moreno, I. S., & Xu, J. (2013). Energy-efficiency in cloud computing environments: Towards energy savings without performance degradation. In S. Aljawarneh (Ed.), *Cloud computing advancements in design, implementation, and technologies* (pp. 18–36). Hershey, PA: IGI Global. doi:10.4018/978-1-4666-1879-4.ch002

Morris, J. Z., & Thomas, K. D. (2013). Implementing biosand filters in rural Honduras: A case study of his hands mission international in Copán, Honduras. In H. Muga & K. Thomas (Eds.), *Cases on the diffusion and adoption of sustainable development practices* (pp. 468–496). Hershey, PA: IGI Global. doi:10.4018/978-1-4666-2842-7.ch017

Mu, Z., Jing, L., Xiaohong, Z., Lei, T., Xiao-na, F., & Shan, C. (2011). Study on low-carbon economy model and method of Chinese tourism industry. *International Journal of Applied Logistics*, *2*(2), 69–102. doi:10.4018/jal.2011040105

Mu, Z., Jing, L., Xiaohong, Z., Lei, T., Xiao-na, F., & Shan, C. (2013). Study on low-carbon economy model and method of chinese tourism industry. In Z. Luo (Ed.), *Technological solutions for modern logistics and supply chain management* (pp. 284–317). Hershey, PA: IGI Global. doi:10.4018/978-1-4666-2773-4.ch018

Mudhoo, A., & Lin, Z. (2012). Phytoremediation of nickel: Mechanisms, application and management. In N. Ekekwe & N. Islam (Eds.), *Disruptive technologies, innovation and global redesign: Emerging implications* (pp. 173–195). Hershey, PA: IGI Global. doi:10.4018/978-1-4666-0134-5.ch010

Murugesan, S. (2011). Strategies for greening enterprise IT: Creating business value and contributing to environmental sustainability. In B. Unhelkar (Ed.), *Handbook of research on green ICT: Technology, business and social perspectives* (pp. 51–64). Hershey, PA: IGI Global. doi:10.4018/978-1-61692-834-6.ch004

Nagni, M., & Ventouras, S. (2013). Implementation of UML schema in relational databases: A case of geographic information. *International Journal of Distributed Systems and Technologies*, 4(4), 50–60. doi:10.4018/ijdst.2013100105

Nair, S. R., & Ndubisi, N. O. (2013). Entrepreneurial values, environmental marketing and customer satisfaction: Conceptualization and propositions. In N. Ndubisi & S. Nwankwo (Eds.), *Enterprise development in SMEs and entrepreneurial firms: Dynamic processes* (pp. 257–269). Hershey, PA: IGI Global. doi:10.4018/978-1-4666-2952-3.ch013

Nourani, V., Roumianfar, S., & Sharghi, E. (2013). Using hybrid ARIMAX-ANN model for simulating rainfall - runoff - sediment process case study: Aharchai Basin, Iran. *International Journal of Applied Metaheuristic Computing*, 4(2), 44–60. doi:10.4018/jamc.2013040104

Obara, S. (2011). Fuel reduction effect of the solar cell and diesel engine hybrid system with a prediction algorithm of solar power generation. In *Green technologies: Concepts, methodologies, tools and applications* (pp. 815–839). Hershey, PA: IGI Global. doi:10.4018/978-1-60960-472-1.ch414

Oktay, D. (2014). Sustainable urbanism revisited: A holistic framework based on tradition and contemporary orientations. In *Sustainable practices: Concepts, methodologies, tools and applications* (pp. 1723–1741). Hershey, PA: IGI Global. doi:10.4018/978-1-4666-4852-4.ch095

Olanrewaju, O. S. (2014). Evolving sustainable green ship technology. In O. Olanrewaju, A. Saharuddin, A. Ab Kader, & W. Wan Nik (Eds.), *Marine technology and sustainable development: Green innovations* (pp. 127–145). Hershey, PA: IGI Global. doi:10.4018/978-1-4666-4317-8.ch008

Olanrewaju, O. S. (2014). Risk requirement for multi-hybrid renewable energy for marine system. In O. Olanrewaju, A. Saharuddin, A. Ab Kader, & W. Wan Nik (Eds.), *Marine technology and sustainable development: Green innovations* (pp. 83–95). Hershey, PA: IGI Global. doi:10.4018/978-1-4666-4317-8.ch005

Olanrewaju, O. S., & Kader, A. S. (2014). Applying the safety and environmental risk and reliability model (SERM) for Malaysian Langat River collision aversion. In O. Olanrewaju, A. Saharuddin, A. Ab Kader, & W. Wan Nik (Eds.), *Marine technology and sustainable development: Green innovations* (pp. 193–225). Hershey, PA: IGI Global. doi:10.4018/978-1-4666-4317-8.ch013

Olej, V., & Hájek, P. (2011). Air quality modeling by fuzzy sets and IF-sets. In V. Olej, I. Obršálová, & J. Krupka (Eds.), *Environmental modeling for sustainable regional development: System approaches and advanced methods* (pp. 118–143). Hershey, PA: IGI Global. doi:10.4018/978-1-60960-156-0.ch006

Omer, A. M. (2012). Renewable energy and sustainable development. In P. Vasant, N. Barsoum, & J. Webb (Eds.), *Innovation in power, control, and optimization: Emerging energy technologies* (pp. 95–136). Hershey, PA: IGI Global. doi:10.4018/978-1-61350-138-2.ch003

Omer, A. M. (2014). Cooling and heating with ground source energy. In *Sustainable practices: Concepts, methodologies, tools and applications* (pp. 261–278). Hershey, PA: IGI Global. doi:10.4018/978-1-4666-4852-4.ch014

Ondieki, C. M. (2013). Hydrology and integrated water resource management for sustainable watershed management in Kenya. In H. Muga & K. Thomas (Eds.), *Cases on the diffusion and adoption of sustainable development practices* (pp. 352–375). Hershey, PA: IGI Global. doi:10.4018/978-1-4666-2842-7.ch013

Ozbakir, B. A. (2012). Urban environmental applications of GIScience: Challenges and new trends. In O. Ercoskun (Ed.), *Green and ecological technologies for urban planning: Creating smart cities* (pp. 192–211). Hershey, PA: IGI Global. doi:10.4018/978-1-61350-453-6.ch011

Ozbakir, B. A. (2014). Urban environmental applications of GIScience: Challenges and new trends. In *Sustainable practices: Concepts, methodologies, tools and applications* (pp. 602–620). Hershey, PA: IGI Global. doi:10.4018/978-1-4666-4852-4.ch034

Oztaysi, B., Isik, M., & Ercan, S. (2013). Multi-criteria decision aid for sustainable energy prioritization using fuzzy axiomatic design. *International Journal of Energy Optimization and Engineering*, 2(1), 1–20. doi:10.4018/ijeoe.2013010101

Palantzas, G., Naniopoulos, A., & Koutitas, C. (2014). Management of environmental issues in port activities: The Hellenic caste study. *International Journal of Information Systems and Supply Chain Management*, 7(1), 40–55. doi:10.4018/ijisscm.2014010103

Pang, L., & Zhao, J. (2013). An empirical study on China's regional carbon emissions of agriculture. *International Journal of Asian Business and Information Management*, *4*(4), 67–77. doi:10.4018/ijabim.2013100105

Papajorgji, P., Pinet, F., Miralles, A., Jallas, E., & Pardalos, P. (2012). Modeling: A central activity for flexible information systems development in agriculture and environment. In P. Papajorgji & F. Pinet (Eds.), *New technologies for constructing complex agricultural and environmental systems* (pp. 286–310). Hershey, PA: IGI Global. doi:10.4018/978-1-4666-0333-2.ch016

Papaspyropoulos, K. G., Christodoulou, A. S., Blioumis, V., Skordas, K. E., & Birtsas, P. K. (2011). The improvement of environmental performance in the nonprofit sector through informatics. In Z. Andreopoulou, B. Manos, N. Polman, & D. Viaggi (Eds.), *Agricultural and environmental informatics, governance and management: Emerging research applications* (pp. 359–376). Hershey, PA: IGI Global. doi:10.4018/978-1-60960-621-3.ch019

Pappis, C. P. (2011). Frameworks of policy making under climate change. In C. Pappis (Ed.), *Climate change, supply chain management and enterprise adaptation: Implications of global warming on the economy* (pp. 271–308). Hershey, PA: IGI Global. doi:10.4018/978-1-61692-800-1.ch009

Paquette, S. (2011). Applying knowledge management in the environmental and climate change sciences. In D. Schwartz & D. Te'eni (Eds.), *Encyclopedia of knowledge management* (2nd ed.; pp. 20–26). Hershey, PA: IGI Global. doi:10.4018/978-1-59904-931-1.ch003

Pechanec, V., & Vávra, A. (2013). Education portal on climate change with web GIS client. *Journal of Cases on Information Technology*, *15*(1), 51–68. doi:10.4018/jcit.2013010104

Perl-Vorbach, E. (2012). Communicating environmental information on a company and inter-organizational level. In *Regional development: Concepts, methodologies, tools, and applications* (pp. 914–932). Hershey, PA: IGI Global. doi:10.4018/978-1-4666-0882-5.ch505

Perry, J., Paas, L., Arreola, M. E., Santer, E., Sharma, N., & Bellali, J. (2011). Promoting e-governance through capacity development for the global environment. In *Green technologies: Concepts, methodologies, tools and applications* (pp. 980–1010). Hershey, PA: IGI Global. doi:10.4018/978-1-60960-472-1.ch423

Pessoa, M., Fernandes, E., Nascimento de Queiroz, S., Ferracini, V., Gomes, M., & Dornelas de Souza, M. (2011). Mathematical-modelling simulation applied to help in the decision-making process on environmental impact assessment of agriculture. In H. do Prado, A. Barreto Luiz, & H. Filho (Eds.), *Computational methods for agricultural research: Advances and applications* (pp. 199–233). Hershey, PA: IGI Global. doi:10.4018/978-1-61692-871-1.ch011

Peters, E. J. (2013). Promoting rainwater harvesting (RWH) in small island developing states (SIDS): A case in the Grenadines. In H. Muga & K. Thomas (Eds.), *Cases on the diffusion and adoption of sustainable development practices* (pp. 403–438). Hershey, PA: IGI Global. doi:10.4018/978-1-4666-2842-7.ch015

Peters, E. J. (2014). Promoting rainwater harvesting (RWH) in small island developing states (SIDS): A case in the Grenadines. In Sustainable practices: Concepts, methodologies, tools and applications (pp. 1657-1682). Hershey, PA: IGI Global. doi:10.4018/978-1-4666-4852-4.ch092

Ploberger, C. (2011). A critical assessment of environmental degeneration and climate change: A multidimensional (political, economic, social) challenge for China's future economic development. *International Journal of Applied Logistics*, *2*(2), 1–16. doi:10.4018/jal.2011040101

Ploberger, C. (2013). A critical assessment of environmental degeneration and climate change: A multidimensional (political, economic, social) challenge for China's future economic development. In Z. Luo (Ed.), *Technological solutions for modern logistics and supply chain management* (pp. 212–229). Hershey, PA: IGI Global. doi:10.4018/978-1-4666-2773-4.ch014

Ploberger, C. (2013). China's environmental issues, a domestic challenge with regional and international implications. *International Journal of Applied Logistics*, *4*(3), 47–61. doi:10.4018/jal.2013070104

Polat, E. (2012). An approach for land-use suitability assessment using decision support systems, AHP and GIS. In O. Ercoskun (Ed.), *Green and ecological technologies for urban planning: Creating smart cities* (pp. 212–233). Hershey, PA: IGI Global. doi:10.4018/978-1-61350-453-6.ch012

Polat, E. (2013). An approach for land-use suitability assessment using decision support systems, AHP and GIS. In *Data mining: Concepts, methodologies, tools, and applications* (pp. 2153–2173). Hershey, PA: IGI Global. doi:10.4018/978-1-4666-2455-9.ch110

Pülzl, H., & Wydra, D. (2013). The evaluation of the implementation of sustainability norms: An exercise for experts or citizens? In E. Carayannis (Ed.), *Creating a sustainable ecology using technology-driven solutions* (pp. 32–45). Hershey, PA: IGI Global. doi:10.4018/978-1-4666-3613-2.ch003

Pusceddu, C. (2012). Grenelle environment project: An institutional tool for building collaborative environmental policies at a national level. In M. Tortora (Ed.), *Sustainable systems and energy management at the regional level: Comparative approaches* (pp. 348–364). Hershey, PA: IGI Global. doi:10.4018/978-1-61350-344-7.ch018

Puškaric, A., Subic, J., & Bekic, B. (2013). Regionalization as a factor of agriculture development of the Republic of Serbia. *International Journal of Sustainable Economies Management*, 2(1), 46–54. doi:10.4018/ijsem.2013010105

Rafferty, J. M. (2012). Design of outdoor and environmentally integrated learning spaces. In M. Keppell, K. Souter, & M. Riddle (Eds.), *Physical and virtual learning spaces in higher education: Concepts for the modern learning environment* (pp. 51–70). Hershey, PA: IGI Global. doi:10.4018/978-1-60960-114-0.ch004

Rahim, R. E., & Rahman, A. A. (2014). Green IT capability and firm's competitive advantage. *International Journal of Innovation in the Digital Economy*, 5(1), 41–49. doi:10.4018/ijide.2014010104

Raj, P. P., & Azeez, P. A. (2012). Public on conserving an urban wetland: A case from Kerala, India. In E. Carayannis (Ed.), *Sustainable policy applications for social ecology and development* (pp. 1–7). Hershey, PA: IGI Global. doi:10.4018/978-1-4666-1586-1.ch001

Rasulev, B., Leszczynska, D., & Leszczynski, J. (2014). Nanoparticles: Towards predicting their toxicity and physico-chemical properties. In Nanotechnology: Concepts, methodologies, tools, and applications (pp. 1071-1089). Hershey, PA: IGI Global. doi:10.4018/978-1-4666-5125-8.ch049

Rene, E. R., Behera, S. K., & Park, H. S. (2012). Predicting adsorption behavior in engineered floodplain filtration system using backpropagation neural networks. In S. Kulkarni (Ed.), *Machine learning algorithms for problem solving in computational applications: Intelligent techniques* (pp. 179–194). Hershey, PA: IGI Global. doi:10.4018/978-1-4666-1833-6.ch011

Rene, E. R., López, M. E., Park, H. S., Murthy, D. V., & Swaminathan, T. (2012). ANNs for identifying shock loads in continuously operated biofilters: Application to biological waste gas treatment. In M. Khan & A. Ansari (Eds.), *Handbook of research on industrial informatics and manufacturing intelligence: Innovations and solutions* (pp. 72–103). Hershey, PA: IGI Global. doi:10.4018/978-1-4666-0294-6.ch004

Rene, E. R., López, M. E., Veiga, M. C., & Kennes, C. (2011). Artificial neural network modelling for waste: Gas and wastewater treatment applications. In B. Igelnik (Ed.), *Computational modeling and simulation of intellect: Current state and future perspectives* (pp. 224–263). Hershey, PA: IGI Global. doi:10.4018/978-1-60960-551-3.ch010

Rivas, A. A., Kahn, J. R., Freitas, C. E., Hurd, L. E., & Cooper, G. (2013). The role of payments for ecological services in the sustainable development and environmental preservation of the rainforest: A case study of Barcelos, Amazonas, BR. *International Journal of Social Ecology and Sustainable Development*, 4(3), 13–27. doi:10.4018/jsesd.2013070102

Rodrigues dos Anjos, M., & Schulz, M. (2013). Investigation of deforestation of environmental protection areas of Madeira River permanent preservation areas in Rondônia Amazon, Brazil. In E. Carayannis (Ed.), *Creating a sustainable ecology using technology-driven solutions* (pp. 335–343). Hershey, PA: IGI Global. doi:10.4018/978-1-4666-3613-2.ch023

Rojas-Mora, J., Josselin, D., Aryal, J., Mangiavillano, A., & Ellerkamp, P. (2013). The weighted fuzzy barycenter: Definition and application to forest fire control in the PACA region. *International Journal of Agricultural and Environmental Information Systems*, 4(4), 48–67. doi:10.4018/ijaeis.2013100103

Rolim da Paz, A., Uvo, C., Bravo, J., Collischonn, W., & Ribeiro da Rocha, H. (2011). Seasonal precipitation forecast based on artificial neural networks. In H. do Prado, A. Barreto Luiz, & H. Filho (Eds.), *Computational methods for agricultural research: Advances and applications* (pp. 326–354). Hershey, PA: IGI Global. doi:10.4018/978-1-61692-871-1.ch016

Romano, B., & Zullo, F. (2013). Models of urban land use in Europe: Assessment tools and criticalities. *International Journal of Agricultural and Environmental Information Systems*, 4(3), 80–97. doi:10.4018/ijaeis.2013070105

Rosen, M., Krichevsky, T., & Sharma, H. (2011). Strategies for a sustainable enterprise. In B. Unhelkar (Ed.), *Handbook of research on green ICT: Technology, business and social perspectives* (pp. 1–28). Hershey, PA: IGI Global. doi:10.4018/978-1-61692-834-6.ch001

Roussey, C., Pinet, F., & Schneider, M. (2013). Representations of topological relations between simple regions in description logics: From formalization to consistency checking. *International Journal of Agricultural and Environmental Information Systems, 4*(2), 50–69. doi:10.4018/jaeis.2013040105

Rushforth, R., & Phillips, C. F. (2012). Gathering under a green umbrella: collaborative rainwater harvesting at the University of Arizona. In E. Carayannis (Ed.), *Sustainable policy applications for social ecology and development* (pp. 139–149). Hershey, PA: IGI Global. doi:10.4018/978-1-4666-1586-1.ch011

Ruutu, J., Nurminen, J. K., & Rissanen, K. (2013). Energy efficiency of mobile device recharging. *International Journal of Handheld Computing Research, 4*(1), 59–69. doi:10.4018/jhcr.2013010104

Saïdi, S., Camara, A., Gazull, L., Passouant, M., & Soumaré, M. (2013). Lowlands mapping in forest Guinea. *International Journal of Agricultural and Environmental Information Systems, 4*(1), 20–34. doi:10.4018/jaeis.2013010102

Salewicz, K. A., Nakayama, M., & Bruch, C. (2011). Building capacity for better water decision making through internet-based decision support systems. In *Green technologies: Concepts, methodologies, tools and applications* (pp. 466–492). Hershey, PA: IGI Global. doi:10.4018/978-1-60960-472-1.ch306

Salter, S. J. (2011). When low-carbon means low-cost: Putting lessons from nature to work in our cities. *International Journal of Social Ecology and Sustainable Development, 2*(4), 12–25. doi:10.4018/jsesd.2011100102

Salter, S. J. (2013). When low-carbon means low-cost: putting lessons from nature to work in our cities. In E. Carayannis (Ed.), *Creating a sustainable ecology using technology-driven solutions* (pp. 282–295). Hershey, PA: IGI Global. doi:10.4018/978-1-4666-3613-2.ch019

Salvadó, J. A., López, J. E., & Martín de Castro, G. (2012). Social innovation, environmental innovation, and their effect on competitive advantage and firm performance. In F. Nobre, D. Walker, & R. Harris (Eds.), *Technological, managerial and organizational core competencies: Dynamic innovation and sustainable development* (pp. 89–104). Hershey, PA: IGI Global. doi:10.4018/978-1-61350-165-8.ch006

Saroar, M. M., & Routray, J. K. (2013). Desert in Bengal Delta- Changes in landscape, changes in livelihood: Can diffusion and adoption of sustainable adaptation make a difference? In H. Muga & K. Thomas (Eds.), *Cases on the diffusion and adoption of sustainable development practices* (pp. 83–117). Hershey, PA: IGI Global. doi:10.4018/978-1-4666-2842-7.ch004

Saroar, M. M., & Routray, J. K. (2014). Desert in Bengal Delta-Changes in landscape, changes in livelihood: Can diffusion and adoption of sustainable adaptation make a difference? In *Sustainable practices: Concepts, methodologies, tools and applications* (pp. 1414–1441). Hershey, PA: IGI Global. doi:10.4018/978-1-4666-4852-4.ch079

Schmehl, M., Eigner-Thiel, S., Ibendorf, J., Hesse, M., & Geldermann, J. (2012). Development of an information system for the assessment of different bioenergy concepts regarding sustainable development. In *Regional development: Concepts, methodologies, tools, and applications* (pp. 274–292). Hershey, PA: IGI Global. doi:10.4018/978-1-4666-0882-5.ch206

Schröter, M., Jakoby, O., Olbrich, R., Eichhorn, M., & Baumgärtner, S. (2011). Remote sensing of bush encroachment on commercial cattle farms in semi-arid rangelands in Namibia. In V. Olej, I. Obršálová, & J. Krupka (Eds.), *Environmental modeling for sustainable regional development: System approaches and advanced methods* (pp. 327–343). Hershey, PA: IGI Global. doi:10.4018/978-1-60960-156-0.ch016

Schultz, R. A. (2014). Environmentalism and sustainability. In *Technology versus ecology: Human superiority and the ongoing conflict with nature* (pp. 180–212). Hershey, PA: IGI Global. doi:10.4018/978-1-4666-4586-8.ch010

Schultz, R. A. (2014). More about modern technology. In *Technology versus ecology: Human superiority and the ongoing conflict with nature* (pp. 145–158). Hershey, PA: IGI Global. doi:10.4018/978-1-4666-4586-8.ch008

Schultz, R. A. (2014). The role of science and technology. In *Technology versus ecology: Human superiority and the ongoing conflict with nature* (pp. 213–230). Hershey, PA: IGI Global. doi:10.4018/978-1-4666-4586-8.ch011

Sdrali, D., Galanis, N., Goussia-Rizou, M., & Abeliotis, K. (2014). Are Greek high school students environmental citizens? A cluster analysis approach. *International Journal of Information Systems and Social Change*, 5(1), 16–29. doi:10.4018/ijissc.2014010102

Selmaoui-Folcher, N., Flouvat, F., Gay, D., & Rouet, I. (2012). Spatial pattern mining for soil erosion characterization. In P. Papajorgji & F. Pinet (Eds.), *New technologies for constructing complex agricultural and environmental systems* (pp. 190–210). Hershey, PA: IGI Global. doi:10.4018/978-1-4666-0333-2.ch011

Shahid, M., Mishra, H., Mishra, H. K., Tripathi, T., Khan, H. M., Sobia, F., & Singh, A. (2012). Pharmaco-ecomicrobiology and its potential role in medical and environmental sciences. In T. Gasmelseid (Ed.), *Pharmacoinformatics and drug discovery technologies: Theories and applications* (pp. 291–302). Hershey, PA: IGI Global. doi:10.4018/978-1-4666-0309-7.ch018

Shakir, I., Ali, Z., Rana, U. A., Nafady, A., Sarfraz, M., Al-Nashef, I., ... Kang, D. (2014). Nanostructured materials for the realization of electrochemical energy storage and conversion devices: Status and prospects. In M. Bououdina & J. Davim (Eds.), *Handbook of research on nanoscience, nanotechnology, and advanced materials* (pp. 376–413). Hershey, PA: IGI Global. doi:10.4018/978-1-4666-5824-0.ch015

Sharma, P., Hussain, N., Das, M. R., Deshmukh, A. B., Shelke, M. V., Szunerits, S., & Boukherroub, R. (2014). Metal oxide-graphene nanocomposites: Synthesis to applications. In M. Bououdina & J. Davim (Eds.), *Handbook of research on nanoscience, nanotechnology, and advanced materials* (pp. 196–225). Hershey, PA: IGI Global. doi:10.4018/978-1-4666-5824-0.ch010

Sidorov, E., & Ritschelová, I. (2011). Economic performance and environmental quality at the regional level an approach to modeling depletion adjusted macro aggregates for the Czech coal mining regions. In V. Olej, I. Obršálová, & J. Krupka (Eds.), *Environmental modeling for sustainable regional development: System approaches and advanced methods* (pp. 281–302). Hershey, PA: IGI Global. doi:10.4018/978-1-60960-156-0.ch014

Silva, M. R., & McLellan, S. L. (2012). Environmental and social impact of stormwater outfalls at Lake Michigan beaches. In E. Carayannis (Ed.), *Sustainable policy applications for social ecology and development* (pp. 150–165). Hershey, PA: IGI Global. doi:10.4018/978-1-4666-1586-1.ch012

Snyder, A. (2014). Environmental protection agency. In J. Krueger (Ed.), *Cases on electronic records and resource management implementation in diverse environments* (pp. 363–377). Hershey, PA: IGI Global. doi:10.4018/978-1-4666-4466-3.ch022

Somavat, P., & Namboodiri, V. (2012). Information and communication technology revolution and global warming. In W. Hu & N. Kaabouch (Eds.), *Sustainable ICTs and management systems for green computing* (pp. 23–44). Hershey, PA: IGI Global. doi:10.4018/978-1-4666-1839-8.ch002

Spanu, V., & McCall, M. K. (2013). Eliciting local spatial knowledge for community-based disaster risk management: Working with cybertracker in Georgian caucasus. *International Journal of E-Planning Research, 2*(2), 45–59. doi:10.4018/ijepr.2013040104

Stewart, A. W. (2014). Integrating sustainability within higher education. In K. Thomas & H. Muga (Eds.), *Handbook of research on pedagogical innovations for sustainable development* (pp. 369–382). Hershey, PA: IGI Global. doi:10.4018/978-1-4666-5856-1.ch017

Stewart, C. O., & Rhodes, C. (2014). Global warming as a socioscientific controversy. In R. Hart (Ed.), *Communication and language analysis in the public sphere* (pp. 276–289). Hershey, PA: IGI Global. doi:10.4018/978-1-4666-5003-9.ch016

Suaire, R., Durickovic, I., Simonnot, M., & Marchetti, M. (2013). Monitoring of road deicers in a retention pond. *International Journal of Measurement Technologies and Instrumentation Engineering*, *3*(1), 39–47. doi:10.4018/ijmtie.2013010104

Subic, J., & Jelocnik, M. (2013). Economic and environmental aspects of controlled vegetable production within the region of Danube basin. In A. Jean-Vasile, T. Adrian, J. Subic, & D. Dusmanescu (Eds.), *Sustainable technologies, policies, and constraints in the green economy* (pp. 39–62). Hershey, PA: IGI Global. doi:10.4018/978-1-4666-4098-6.ch003

Tabrizi, A., & Sanguinetti, P. (2013). Case study: Evaluation of renewable energy strategies using building information modeling and energy simulation. *International Journal of 3-D Information Modeling, 2*(4), 25-37. doi:10.4018/ij3dim.2013100103

Taylor, R., Barron, E., & Eames, K. A. (2014). Embedding sustainability learning: Robustness in changing circumstances - Perspectives from a United Kingdom (UK) higher education institution (HEI). In K. Thomas & H. Muga (Eds.), *Handbook of research on pedagogical innovations for sustainable development* (pp. 641–671). Hershey, PA: IGI Global. doi:10.4018/978-1-4666-5856-1.ch033

Thiell, M., & Zuluaga, J. P. (2013). Is it feasible to implement green logistics in emerging markets? *International Journal of Applied Logistics*, *4*(1), 1–13. doi:10.4018/jal.2013010101

Thongmak, M. (2013). A systematic framework for sustainable ICTs in developing countries. *International Journal of Information Technologies and Systems Approach*, *6*(1), 1–19. doi:10.4018/jitsa.2013010101

Torrens, F., & Castellano, G. (2012). Cluster origin of solvent features of fullerenes, single-wall carbon nanotubes, nanocones, and nanohorns. In E. Castro & A. Haghi (Eds.), *Nanoscience and advancing computational methods in chemistry: Research progress* (pp. 1–57). Hershey, PA: IGI Global. doi:10.4018/978-1-4666-1607-3.ch001

Torrens, F., & Castellano, G. (2014). Cluster origin of solvent features of fullerenes, single-wall carbon nanotubes, nanocones, and nanohorns. In I. Management Association (Ed.), Nanotechnology: Concepts, methodologies, tools, and applications (pp. 262-318). Hershey, PA: IGI Global. doi:10.4018/978-1-4666-5125-8.ch011

Touza, L. L., & López-Gunn, E. (2012). Climate change policies—Mitigation and adaptation at the local level: The case of the city of Madrid (Spain). In M. Tortora (Ed.), *Sustainable systems and energy management at the regional level: Comparative approaches* (pp. 261–287). Hershey, PA: IGI Global. doi:10.4018/978-1-61350-344-7.ch014

Trautmann, N. M., & McLinn, C. M. (2012). Using online data for student investigations in biology and ecology. In A. Olofsson & J. Lindberg (Eds.), *Informed design of educational technologies in higher education: Enhanced learning and teaching* (pp. 80–100). Hershey, PA: IGI Global. doi:10.4018/978-1-61350-080-4.ch005

Trisurat, Y., Shrestha, R. P., & Alkemade, R. (2011). Linkage between biodiversity, land use informatics and climate change. In Y. Trisurat, R. Shrestha, & R. Alkemade (Eds.), *Land use, climate change and biodiversity modeling: Perspectives and applications* (pp. 1–22). Hershey, PA: IGI Global. doi:10.4018/978-1-60960-619-0.ch001

Trivedi, B. (2011). Developing environmentally responsible business strategies: A research perspective. *International Journal of Green Computing*, 2(1), 47–57. doi:10.4018/jgc.2011010105

Trivedi, B. (2013). Developing environmentally responsible business strategies: A research perspective. In K. Ganesh & S. Anbuudayasankar (Eds.), *International and interdisciplinary studies in green computing* (pp. 47–57). Hershey, PA: IGI Global. doi:10.4018/978-1-4666-2646-1.ch005

Tsalapata, H., Alimsi, R., & Heidmann, O. (2012). Environmental education through envkids didactical framework and ICT tools. In Z. Lu (Ed.), *Learning with mobile technologies, handheld devices, and smart phones: Innovative methods* (pp. 147–161). Hershey, PA: IGI Global. doi:10.4018/978-1-4666-0936-5.ch009

Tsalapata, H., Alimsi, R., & Heidmann, O. (2014). Environmental education through envkids didactical framework and ICT tools. In *Sustainable practices: Concepts, methodologies, tools and applications* (pp. 1492–1504). Hershey, PA: IGI Global. doi:10.4018/978-1-4666-4852-4.ch083

Turek, A. (2013). Sustainable agriculture: between sustainable development and economic competitiveness. In A. Jean-Vasile, T. Adrian, J. Subic, & D. Dusmanescu (Eds.), *Sustainable technologies, policies, and constraints in the green economy* (pp. 219–235). Hershey, PA: IGI Global. doi:10.4018/978-1-4666-4098-6.ch012

Turgut, E. T., & Rosen, M. A. (2012). Emission assessment of aviation. In E. Abu-Taieh, A. El Sheikh, & M. Jafari (Eds.), *Technology engineering and management in aviation: Advancements and discoveries* (pp. 20–72). Hershey, PA: IGI Global. doi:10.4018/978-1-60960-887-3.ch002

Twesigye, C. K. (2011). Application of remote sensing technologies and geographical information systems in monitoring environmental degradation in the Lake Victoria watershed, East Africa. In *Green technologies: Concepts, methodologies, tools and applications* (pp. 653–677). Hershey, PA: IGI Global. doi:10.4018/978-1-60960-472-1.ch405

Uchida, S., Hayashi, K., Sato, M., & Hokazono, S. (2011). Construction of agri-environmental data using computational methods: The case of life cycle inventories for agricultural production systems. In H. do Prado, A. Barreto Luiz, & H. Filho (Eds.), *Computational methods for agricultural research: advances and applications* (pp. 412–433). Hershey, PA: IGI Global. doi:10.4018/978-1-61692-871-1.ch019

Unhelkar, B. (2011). Green enterprise architecture using environmental intelligence. *International Journal of Green Computing*, 2(1), 58–65. doi:10.4018/jgc.2011010106

Unhelkar, B., & Trivedi, B. (2011). A framework for environmentally responsible business strategies. In B. Unhelkar (Ed.), *Handbook of research on green ICT: Technology, business and social perspectives* (pp. 214–232). Hershey, PA: IGI Global. doi:10.4018/978-1-61692-834-6.ch014

Urban, M. J., Marker, E., & Falvo, D. A. (2012). An interdisciplinary exploration of the climate change issue and implications for teaching STEM through inquiry. In L. Lennex & K. Nettleton (Eds.), *Cases on inquiry through instructional technology in math and science* (pp. 523–550). Hershey, PA: IGI Global. doi:10.4018/978-1-4666-0068-3.ch019

Urooj, S., Hussain, A., & Srivastava, N. (2013). Biodiesel production from algal blooms: A step towards renewable energy generation & measurement. *International Journal of Measurement Technologies and Instrumentation Engineering*, 2(3), 60–71. doi:10.4018/ijmtie.2012070106

Uyttersprot, I., & Vermeir, I. (2014). Should I recycle or not? Effects of attitude strength and social pressure. In A. Kapoor & C. Kulshrestha (Eds.), *Dynamics of competitive advantage and consumer perception in social marketing* (pp. 292–308). Hershey, PA: IGI Global. doi:10.4018/978-1-4666-4430-4.ch012

Varga, L., Camci, F., Boxall, J., Toossi, A., Machell, J., Blythe, P. T., & Taylor, C. (2013). Transforming critical infrastructure: Matching the complexity of the environment to policy. *International Journal of E-Planning Research*, 2(3), 38–49. doi:10.4018/ijepr.2013070104

Viaggi, D., & Raggi, M. (2011). Estimation of irrigation water demand on a regional scale combining positive mathematical programming and cluster analysis in model calibration. In V. Olej, I. Obršálová, & J. Krupka (Eds.), *Environmental modeling for sustainable regional development: System approaches and advanced methods* (pp. 204–220). Hershey, PA: IGI Global. doi:10.4018/978-1-60960-156-0.ch010

Wang, H. (2011). GHG emissions from the international goods movement by ships and the adaptation funding distribution. In Z. Luo (Ed.), *Green finance and sustainability: Environmentally-aware business models and technologies* (pp. 274–290). Hershey, PA: IGI Global. doi:10.4018/978-1-60960-531-5.ch015

Wang, H., & Ghose, A. K. (2011). Green strategic alignment: Aligning business strategies with sustainability objectives. In B. Unhelkar (Ed.), *Handbook of research on green ICT: Technology, business and social perspectives* (pp. 29–41). Hershey, PA: IGI Global. doi:10.4018/978-1-61692-834-6.ch002

Wang, S., Ku, C., & Chu, C. (2013). Sustainable campus project: Potential for energy conservation and carbon reduction education in Taiwan. *International Journal of Technology and Human Interaction*, 8(3), 19–30. doi:10.4018/jthi.2012070103

Wang, Y. (2014). Texted environmental campaign in China: A case study of new media communication. In J. Pelet & P. Papadopoulou (Eds.), *User behavior in ubiquitous online environments* (pp. 19–43). Hershey, PA: IGI Global. doi:10.4018/978-1-4666-4566-0.ch002

Wani, A. H., Amin, M., Shahnaz, M., & Shah, M. A. (2012). Antimycotic activity of nanoparticles of MgO, FeO and ZnO on some pathogenic fungi. *International Journal of Manufacturing, Materials, and Mechanical Engineering*, 2(4), 59–70. doi:10.4018/ijmmme.2012100105

Wani, A. H., Amin, M., Shahnaz, M., & Shah, M. A. (2014). Antimycotic activity of nanoparticles of MgO, FeO and ZnO on some pathogenic fungi. In Nanotechnology: Concepts, methodologies, tools, and applications (pp. 1289-1299). Hershey, PA: IGI Global. doi:10.4018/978-1-4666-5125-8.ch059

Wati, Y., & Koo, C. (2011). A new recommendation for green IT strategies: A resource-based perspective. In Z. Luo (Ed.), *Green finance and sustainability: Environmentally-aware business models and technologies* (pp. 153–175). Hershey, PA: IGI Global. doi:10.4018/978-1-60960-531-5.ch008

Williamson, T. B., Hauer, G. K., & Luckert, M. K. (2011). Economic concepts, methods, and tools for risk analysis in forestry under climate change. In V. Olej, I. Obršálová, & J. Krupka (Eds.), *Environmental modeling for sustainable regional development: System approaches and advanced methods* (pp. 303–326). Hershey, PA: IGI Global. doi:10.4018/978-1-60960-156-0.ch015

Wong, Y. M. (2014). Fair share of supply chain responsibility for low carbon manufacturing. In Z. Luo (Ed.), *Smart manufacturing innovation and transformation: interconnection and intelligence* (pp. 303–332). Hershey, PA: IGI Global. doi:10.4018/978-1-4666-5836-3.ch012

Wu, J., & Haasis, H. (2013). Integration of knowledge management approach to the planning stage of freight villages: Towards sustainable development. *International Journal of Applied Logistics*, *4*(2), 46–65. doi:10.4018/jal.2013040104

Yamaguchi, M., & Fara, L. (2013). New trends in solar cells. In L. Fara & M. Yamaguchi (Eds.), *Advanced solar cell materials, technology, modeling, and simulation* (pp. 1–21). Hershey, PA: IGI Global. doi:10.4018/978-1-4666-1927-2.ch001

Yi, L. (2011). E-business/ICT and carbon emissions. In O. Bak & N. Stair (Eds.), *Impact of e-business technologies on public and private organizations: Industry comparisons and perspectives* (pp. 214–232). Hershey, PA: IGI Global. doi:10.4018/978-1-60960-501-8.ch013

Yi, L. (2013). E-business/ICT and carbon emissions. In *Industrial engineering: Concepts, methodologies, tools, and applications* (pp. 1833–1852). Hershey, PA: IGI Global. doi:10.4018/978-1-4666-1945-6.ch098

Younessi, D. (2011). Sustainable business value. In B. Unhelkar (Ed.), *Handbook of research on green ICT: Technology, business and social perspectives* (pp. 98–115). Hershey, PA: IGI Global. doi:10.4018/978-1-61692-834-6.ch007

Yu, T., Lenzen, M., & Dey, C. (2011). Large-scale computational modeling for environmental impact assessment. In V. Olej, I. Obršálová, & J. Krupka (Eds.), *Environmental modeling for sustainable regional development: system approaches and advanced methods* (pp. 1–17). Hershey, PA: IGI Global. doi:10.4018/978-1-60960-156-0.ch001

Zhu, Y., & Heath, T. (2012). Technologies in urban design practice: Integrating environmental design considerations. In O. Ercoskun (Ed.), *Green and ecological technologies for urban planning: Creating smart cities* (pp. 133–152). Hershey, PA: IGI Global. doi:10.4018/978-1-61350-453-6.ch008

Zoltáni, T. A. (2013). Carbon as an emerging tool for risk management. *International Journal of Applied Logistics*, *4*(4), 51–69. doi:10.4018/ijal.2013100104

Compilation of References

Aarhus University. (2016). Animal Nutrition and Environment, Department of Animal Science. *Project partners.* Retrieved from http://anis.au.dk/forskning/projekter/nometmet/project-partners

Abuajah, C. I., Ogbonna, A. C., & Osuji, C. M. (2015). Functional components and medicinal properties of food: A review. *Journal of Food Science and Technology, 52*(5), 2522–2529. doi:10.1007/s13197-014-1396-5 PMID:25892752

Adams, D. C., & Salois, M. J. (2010). Local versus organic: A turn in consumer preferences and willingness-to-pay. *Renewable Agriculture and Food Systems, 25*(4), 331–341. doi:10.1017/S1742170510000219

Agnihotri, M. K., Verma, A. K., & Rajkumar, V. (2012). *Sustainable animal products production for food security.* Paper presented at the National Seminar on Vet for Health; Vet for Food; Vet for the planet, New Delhi, India.

Agnihotri, M. K., Rajkumar, V., & Dutta, T. K. (2006). Effect of feeding complete rations with variable protein and energy levels prepared using by-products of pulses and oilseeds on carcass characteristics, meat and meat ball quality of goats. *Asian-Australasian Journal of Animal Sciences, 19*(10), 1437–1449. doi:10.5713/ajas.2006.1437

Aguinis, H., & Glavas, A. (2012). What we know and don't know about corporate social responsibility: A review and research agenda. *Journal of Management, 38*(4), 932–968. doi:10.1177/0149206311436079

Ahmad, H., Shah, I. A., & Ahmad, K. (2009). Factors in environmental advertising influencing consumer's purchase intention. *Cell, 333*, 5339752.

Akaah, I. P. (1990). Attitudes of marketing professionals toward ethics in marketing research: A cross-national comparison. *Journal of Business Ethics, 9*(1), 45–53. doi:10.1007/BF00382563

Al Pop, N. (2000). *Marketing Strategic.* Editura Economică.

Al Stanciu, O. (2008). *Dimensiuni ale comportamentului consumatorului produselor ecologice pe piata romaneasca in viziunea marketingului modern* (Unpublished doctoral dissertation). The Bucharest University of Economic Studies.

Alnıaçık, Ü., Yılmaz, C., & Alnıaçık, E. (2010). Reklamlarda Çevreci İddalar ve Reklam Etkililiği:Başarılı Reklamlar Üzerine Deneysel Bir Araştırma. *Anadolu Üniversitesi Sosyal Bilimler Dergisi, 10*(1), 85–106.

Alves, H., & Raposo, M. (2010). The Influence of University Image on Student Behaviour. *International Journal of Educational Management, 24*(1), 73–85. doi:10.1108/09513541011013060

AMAP website, Associations pour le maintien d'une agriculture paysanne. (n.d.). Retrieved July 23, 2016, from http://www.reseau-amap.org/

Analysis of budget support to the development of rural tourism in Serbia and the diversification of economic activities in the countryside. (2009). Retrieved from Ministry of Agriculture, Forestry and Water Management of the Republic of Serbia - Sector for Rural Development, Direction for National referent laboratories, MAEP, 2015: http://www.dnrl.minpolj.gov.rs/o_nama/organska.html

Arriaga, H. (2010). *Cattle nutrition as a strategy to mitigate gaseous nitrogen losses from dairy farming* (Doctoral Thesis). University of Barcelona, Spain.

Arvanitoyannis, I. S., & Krystallis, A. (2004). *Current state of the art of legislation and marketing trends of organic foods worldwide.* World Scientific.

Azak, S., & Miran, B. (2015). *Turk Tuketicilerin Organik Pazara ve Organik Urunlere Yonelik Davranislarinin Analizi: Izmir Ornegi.* Retrieved July 23, 2016 from http://www.eto.org.tr/?p=1341

Bae, J., & Cameron, G. T. (2006). Conditioning effect of prior reputation on perception of corporate giving. *Public Relations Review, 32*(2), 144–150. doi:10.1016/j.pubrev.2006.02.007

Banerjee, S., Gulas, C. S., & Iyer, E. (1995). Shades of green: A multidimensional analysis of environmental advertising. *Journal of Advertising, 24*(2), 21–31. doi:10.1080/00913367.1995.10673473

Baran, T., & Popescu, C. (2016). Generation Z Attitudes Toward Green Marketing: A Cross Country Study. *3th Information Society and Sustainable Development International Symposium.*

Barney, J. (1993). Firm resources and sustained competitive advantage. *Journal of Management, 17*(1), 99–120. doi:10.1177/014920639101700108

Bauer, T. N., & Aiman-Smith, L. (1996). Green Career Choices: The Influence of Ecological Stance on Recruiting. *Journal of Business and Psychology, 10*(4), 445–458. doi:10.1007/BF02251780

Benchaar, C., Calsamiglia, S., Chaves, A. V., Fraser, G. R., Colombatto, D., McAllister, T. A., & Beauchemin, K. A. (2008). A review of plant-derived essential oils in ruminant nutrition and production. *Animal Feed Science and Technology, 145*(1-4), 209–228. doi:10.1016/j.anifeedsci.2007.04.014

Bhattacharya, C. B., & Sen, S. (2001). Does doing good always lead to doing better? Consumer reactions to corporate social responsibility. *JMR, Journal of Marketing Research, 38*(2), 225–243. doi:10.1509/jmkr.38.2.225.18838

Birhala, B., & Mollers, J. (2014, August). *Community Supported Agriculture in Romania: Solidarity partnerships as viable innovations for small farms?* Paper presented at the EAAE 2014 Congress 'Agri-Food and Rural Innovations for Healthier Societies'. Ljubljana.

Birth, G., Illia, L., Lurati, F., & Zamparini, A. (2008). Communicating CSR: Practices among Switzerland's top 300 companies. *Corporate Communications, 13*(2), 182–196. doi:10.1108/13563280810869604

Bögel, P. M. (2015). Processing of CSR communication: Insights from the ELM. *Corporate Communications, 20*(2), 128–143. doi:10.1108/CCIJ-11-2013-0095

Bonny, S. P. F., Pethick, D. W., Legrand, I., Wierzbicki, J., Allen, P., Farmer, L. J., ... Gardner, G. E. (2016). European conformation and fat scores have no relationship with eating quality. *Animal, 10*(6), 1–11. doi:10.1017/S1751731115002839 PMID:26755183

Bougherara, D., Grolleau, G., & Mzoughi, N. (2009). Buy local, pollute less: What drives households to join a community supported farm? *Ecological Economics, 68*(5), 1488–1495. doi:10.1016/j.ecolecon.2008.10.009

Bravo, R., Montaner, T., & Pina, J. M. (2009). The Role of Bank Image for Customers Versus Non-Customers. *International Journal of Bank Marketing, 27*(4), 315–334. doi:10.1108/02652320910968377

Brennan, M., Kumaran, M., Cantrell, R., & Spranger, M. (2016). *The Importance of Incorporating Local Culture into Community Development.* UFIFAS Extension, University of Florida, FCS9232. Retrieved from http://edis.ifas.ufl.edu

Brown, D. M., & Laverick, S. (1994). Measuring Corporate Performance. *Long Range Planning, 27*(4), 89–98. doi:10.1016/0024-6301(94)90059-0

BUKOOP website. (n.d.). Retrieved July 26, 2016, from http://www.bukoop.org

Burcă-Voicu, M. (2012). The Evolution of the Organic Food Market in Romania-Trends, Opportunities and Threats in the Current International Economic Context. Romanian Review of International Studies, 4(2).

Burton, B. K., Farh, J. L., & Hegarty, W. H. (2000). A cross-cultural comparison of corporate social responsibility orientation: Hong Kong vs. United States students. *Teaching Business Ethics, 4*(2), 151–167. doi:10.1023/A:1009862130160

Campbell, B. L., Mhlanga, S., & Lesschaeve, I. (2013). Perception versus reality: Canadian consumer views of local and organic. *Canadian Journal of Agricultural Economics, 61*(4), 531–558. doi:10.1111/j.1744-7976.2012.01267.x

C. L. Campbell (Ed.). (2015). Marketing in Transition: Scarcity, Globalism, & Sustainability. In *Proceedings of the 2009 World Marketing Congress.* Springer.

Canan, A. Y., & Ecevit, Z. (2005). Çevre Bilinçli Tüketiciler. *Akdeniz University Faculty of Economics & Administrative Sciences Faculty Journal/Akdeniz Universitesi Iktisadi ve Idari Bilimler Fakultesi Dergisi, 5*(10).

Canclini, G. N. (2001). Consumers and Citizens: Globalization and Multicultural conflicts (G. Yúdice, Trans.). Minneapolis, MN: The University of Minnesota Press.

Capper, J. L. (2012). Is the Grass Always Greener? Comparing the Environmental Impact of Conventional, Natural and Grass-Fed Beef Production Systems. *Animals (Basel), 2*(2), 127–143. doi:10.3390/ani2020127 PMID:26486913

Capper, J. L., & Hayes, D. J. (2012). The environmental and economic impact of removing growth-enhancing technologies from U.S. beef production. *Journal of Animal Science, 90*(10), 3527–3537. doi:10.2527/jas.2011-4870 PMID:22665660

Carlson, L., Grove, S. J., Kangun, N., & Polonsky, M. J. (1996). An international comparison of environmental advertising: Substantive versus associative claims. *Journal of Macromarketing, 16*(2), 57–68. doi:10.1177/027614679601600205

Castro, F. (2013). *Overview of Participatory Guarantee Systems in 2012*. The World of Organic Agriculture and Emerging Trends 2013. Retrieved July 28, 2016, from https://shop.fibl.org/fileadmin/documents/shop/1606-organic-world-2013.pdf

Cătoiu, I., & Teodorescu, N. (2001). Comportamentul consumatorului. Abordare instrumentală. *Editura Uranus, Bucureşti, 2001*, 130.

Cătoiu, I., & Teodorescu, N. (2004). *Comportamentul consumatorului. Teorie şi practică*. Bucureşti: Editura Economică.

CAYEK website. (n.d.). Retrieved July 26, 2016, from http://www.cayek.org, https://www.facebook.com/groups/cayekcanakkale/

Celik, S. (2013). Kimler, neden organik gida satin aliyor? Bir alan arastirmasi. *Selcuk University Journal of Institute of Social Sciences, 30*, 93–108.

Cerci, A. (2015, June). *Gida Hakkı ve Gida Topluluklari*. Paper presented at 3rd Ankara Ecological Society and Living Days, Ankara.

Chan, K., & Fan, F. (2015). How consumers perceive environmental advertising in the banking context. *Asian Journal of Business Research, 5*(1), 69.

Chan, R. Y. (2000). The effectiveness of environmental advertising: The role of claim type and the source country green image. *International Journal of Advertising, 19*(3), 349–375. doi:10.1080/02650487.2000.11104806

Charanza, A. D. (2011). *Consumers' dependency on media for information about food safety incidents related to the beef industry* (Master's thesis). Texas A&M University.

Choi, I., Nisbett, R. E., & Norenzayan, A. (1999). Causal attribution across cultures: Variation and universality. *Psychological Bulletin, 125*(1), 47–63. doi:10.1037/0033-2909.125.1.47

Choudhury, P. K., Salem, A. Z. M., Jena, R., Kumar, S., Singh, R., & Puniya, A. K. (2015). Rumen Microbiology: An Overview. In A. K. Puniya, R. Singh, & D. N. Kamra (Eds.), *Rumen Microbiology: From Evolution to Revolution* (pp. 3–16). New Delhi: Springer India; doi:10.1007/978-81-322-2401-3_1

Christensen, L. T., & Askegaard, S. (2001). Corporate Identity and Corporate Image Revisited – A Semiotics Perspective. *European Journal of Marketing, 35*(3/4), 292–315. doi:10.1108/03090560110381814

Christie, P. M. J., Kwon, I. W. G., Stoeberl, P. A., & Baumhart, R. (2003). A cross-cultural comparison of ethical attitudes of business managers: India Korea and the United States. *Journal of Business Ethics, 46*(3), 263–287. doi:10.1023/A:1025501426590

Cifric, I., (2000). Bioetika i ekologija. *Socijalna ekologija: casopis za ekolosku misao i sociologijska istrazivanja okoline, 9*(1-2), 143-146.

Çiftçioğlu, B. A. (2009). *Kurumsal İtibar Yönetimi*. Bursa: Dora.

Circular Academy. (2017). *How can we bridge the circularity gap?* Retrieved from http://www.circular.academy/circular-economy-critics-and-challenges/

Cirkularna ekonomija kao šansa za razvoj Srbije. (2017). Retrieved from http://aarhusns.rs/aarhus/wp-content/uploads/2016/12/Cirkularna-ekonomija-Web.pdf

Cohen, J. R., Pant, L. W., & Sharp, D. J. (1996). A methodological note on cross-cultural accounting ethics research. *The International Journal of Accounting, 31*(1), 55–66. doi:10.1016/S0020-7063(96)90013-8

Collins, J. M. (2005). *Preventing Identity Theft in Your Business – How to Protect Your Business, Customers, and Employees*. Hoboken, NJ: John Wiley & Sons, Inc.

Costanigro, M., Kroll, S., Thilmany, D., & Bunning, M. (2014). Is it love for local/organic or hate for conventional? Asymmetric effects of information and taste on label preferences in an experimental auction. *Food Quality and Preference, 31*, 94–105. doi:10.1016/j.foodqual.2013.08.008

Cowan, C. (1998). Irish and European consumer views on food safety. *Journal of Food Safety, 18*(4), 275–295. doi:10.1111/j.1745-4565.1998.tb00221.x

Cronin, J. J. Jr, Smith, J. S., Gleim, M. R., Ramirez, E., & Martinez, J. D. (2011). Green marketing strategies: An examination of stakeholders and the opportunities they present. *Journal of the Academy of Marketing Science, 39*(1), 158–174. doi:10.1007/s11747-010-0227-0

Cross, F. B. (1990). The weaning of the green: Environmentalism comes of age in the 1990s. *Business Horizons, 33*(5), 40–46. doi:10.1016/0007-6813(90)90026-8

Cui, Y., Trent, E. S., Sullivan, P. M., & Matiru, G. N. (2003). Cause-related marketing: How generation Y responds. *International Journal of Retail & Distribution Management*, *31*(6), 310–320. doi:10.1108/09590550310476012

Cullen, J. B., Parboteeah, K. P., & Victor, B. (2003). The effects of ethical climates on organizational commitment: A two-study analysis. *Journal of Business Ethics*, *46*(2), 127–141. doi:10.1023/A:1025089819456

Cutait, M. S. (2013). Letter from the Chairman. In International Feed Industry Federation Annual Report 2012/13 (p. 5). International Feed Industry Federation.

D'Souza, C., & Taghian, M. (2005). Green advertising effects on attitude and choice of advertising themes. *Asia Pacific Journal of Marketing and Logistics*, *17*(3), 51–66. doi:10.1108/13555850510672386

Dahlsrud, A. (2008). How corporate social responsibility is defined: An analysis of 37 definitions. *Corporate Social Responsibility and Environmental Management*, *15*(1), 1–13. doi:10.1002/csr.132

Dalli, C. M. (2015, June). *Kentte Alternatif bir Örgütlenme Modeli: BuKoop*. Paper presented at 3rd Ankara Ecological Society and Living Days, Ankara.

Davis, A. (2006). *Halkla ilişkilerin ABC'si. Ümit Şendilek (çev)*. İstanbul: Kapital Medya Hizmetleri AŞ.

Davis, S. (1984). *Managing Corporate Culture*. Harper & Row Publishers.

DBB website, Dogal Besin, Bilincli Beslenme. (n.d.). Retrieved July 26, 2016, from https://ankaradbb.wordpress.com/

De Athayde, A. (2015). Towards Sustainable Feed & Food – Working Together at International Level. *International Animal Health Journal*, *2*(2), 28–30.

De Boer, I. J. M., Cederberg, C., Eady, S., Gollnow, S., Kristensen, T., Macleod, M., ... Zonderland-Thomassen, M. A. (2011). Greenhouse gas mitigation in animal production: Towards an integrated life cycle sustainability assessment. *Current Opinion in Environmental Sustainability*, *3*(5), 423–431. doi:10.1016/j.cosust.2011.08.007

De Vries, M., & De Boer, I. J. M. (2010). Comparing environmental impacts for livestock products: A review of life cycle assessments. *Livestock Science*, *128*(1-3), 1–11. doi:10.1016/j.livsci.2009.11.007

Delmas, M. A., & Burbano, V. C. (2011). The drivers of greenwashing. *California Management Review*, *54*(1), 64–87. doi:10.1525/cmr.2011.54.1.64

Demetrescu, M. C. (1971). *Metode cantitative în marketing*. Bucureşti: Editura Ştiinţifică.

Demirtaş, M. (2010). Örgütsel Iletişimin Verimlilik ve Etkinliğinde Yararlanılan Iletişim Araçlari Ve Halkla Ilişkiler Filmleri Örneği. *Marmara Üniversitesi İİBF Dergisi*, *28*(1), 411–444.

Den Hertog-Meischke, M. J. A., van Laack, R. J. L. M., & Smulders, F. J. M. (1997). The water-holding capacity of fresh meat. *The Veterinary Quarterly*, *19*(4), 175–181. doi:10.1080/016521 76.1997.9694767 PMID:9413116

Dichter, E. (1985). What's an Image? *Journal of Consumer Marketing*, *2*, 75–81.

Do Paço, A. M. F., & Reis, R. (2012). Factors affecting skepticism toward green advertising. *Journal of Advertising*, *41*(4), 147–155. doi:10.1080/00913367.2012.10672463

Donaton, S., & Fitzgerald, K. (1992). Polls show ecological concern is strong. *Advertising Age*, *63*(3), 19–23.

Donella, C., H., Meadows, D.L., Randers, J., & Behrens III, V.W. (1974). *Granice rasta*. Zagreb: Stvarnost.

Drljaca, M. (2015). Koncept kruzne ekonomije. *Kvalitet & izvrsnost, 4*(9-10), 18-22.

Dschaak, C. M. (2012). *Rumen modifiers to manipulate ruminal fermentation and improve nutrient utilization and lactational performance of dairy cows* (Doctoral Thesis). Utah State University, Logan, UT.

Du, S., Bhattacharya, C. B., & Sen, S. (2010). Maximizing business returns to corporate social responsibility (CSR): The role of CSR communication. *International Journal of Management Reviews*, *12*(1), 8–19. doi:10.1111/j.1468-2370.2009.00276.x

Dutton, J. E., & Dukerich, J. M. (1991). Keeping an Eye on The Mirror: Image and Identity in Organizational Adaptation. *Academy of Management Journal*, *34*(3), 517–554. doi:10.2307/256405

Dutton, J. E., Dukerich, J. M., & Harquail, C. V. (1994). Organizational Images and Member Identification. *Administrative Science Quarterly*, *39*(2), 239–263. doi:10.2307/2393235

Ellen MacArthur Foundation. (2012). *Towards the Circular Economy: Vol. 1. An economic and business rationale for an accelerated transition*. Retrieved from https://www.ellenmacarthurfoundation.org/publications/towards-the-circular-economy-vol-1-an-economic-and-business-rationale-for-an-accelerated-transition

Ellen MacArthur Foundation. (2013). *Towards the Circular Economy: Vol. 2. Opportunities for the consumer goods sector*. Retrieved from https://www.ellenmacarthurfoundation.org/publications/towards-the-circular-economy-vol-2-opportunities-for-the-consumer-goods-sector

Ellen MacArthur Foundation. (2014). *Towards the Circular Economy: Vol. 3. Accelerating the scale-up across global supply chains*. Retrieved from https://www.ellenmacarthurfoundation.org/publications/towards-the-circular-economy-vol-3-accelerating-the-scale-up-across-global-supply-chains

Ellen MacArthur Foundation. (2015). *Growth Within: a circular economy vision for a competitive Europe*. Retrieved from https://www.ellenmacarthurfoundation.org/publications/growth-within-a-circular-economy-vision-for-a-competitive-europe

Ellen MacArthur Foundation. (2016). *Intelligent Assets: Unlocking the circular economy potential.* Retrieved from https://www.ellenmacarthurfoundation.org/publications/intelligent-assets

Ellen MacArthur Foundation. (2017). *Achieving "Growth Within".* Retrieved from https://www.ellenmacarthurfoundation.org/assets/downloads/publications/Achieving-Growth-Within-20-01-17.pdf

Ellen, P. S., Webb, D. J., & Mohr, L. A. (2006). Building corporate associations: Consumer attributions for corporate socially responsible programs. *Journal of the Academy of Marketing Science, 34*(2), 147–157. doi:10.1177/0092070305284976

Ercoskun, O. Y., Gokmen, A., & Gokmen, I. (2010). Can We Create Networks For Sustainable Living In Our Cities and Villages? In *Proceedings of International Conference on Organic Farming In Scope of Environmental Problems* (pp.181-190). Gazi Magosa, the Turkish Republic of Northern Cyprus: EMCC Press.

Ercoskun, O. Y. (2015). Creating Resilient Communities: Local Currencies and Time. In A. J. Vasile, I. R. Andrea, & T. R. Adrian (Eds.), *Green Economic Structures in Modern Business and Society* (pp. 1–19). Hershey, PA: Information Science Publishing. doi:10.4018/978-1-4666-8219-1.ch001

Escribano, A. J. (2016a). Organic Livestock Farming: Challenges, Perspectives, And Strategies to Increase its Contribution to the Agrifood System's Sustainability – A Review. In P. Konvalina (Ed.), *Organic Farming - A Promising Way of Food Production* (pp. 229–260). InTech. doi:10.5772/61272

Escribano, A. J. (2016b). Beef Cattle Farms' Conversion to the Organic System. Recommendations for Success in the Face of Future Changes in a Global Context. *Sustainability, 8*(6), 572. doi:10.3390/su8060572

Escribano, A. J., Gaspar, P., Mesías, F. J., & Escribano, M. (2016). The role of the level of intensification, productive orientation and self-reliance in extensive beef cattle farms. *Livestock Science, 193*, 8–19. doi:10.1016/j.livsci.2016.09.006

Escribano, A. J., Gaspar, P., Mesías, F. J., Escribano, M., & Pulido, F. (2015). Comparative Sustainability Assessment of Extensive Beef Cattle Farms in a High Nature Value Agroforestry System. In V. R. Squires (Ed.), *Rangeland Ecology, Management and Conservation Benefits* (pp. 65–85). New York, NY: Nova Science Publishers, Inc.

Escribano, A. J., Gaspar, P., Mesías, F. J., Pulido, A. F., & Escribano, M. (2014). A sustainability assessment of organic and conventional beef cattle farms in agroforestry systems: The case of the 'dehesa' rangelands. *ITEA. Información Técnica Económica Agraria, 110*(4), 343–367. doi:10.12706/itea.2014.022

European Feed Manufacturers' Federation (FEFAC). (2014). *The Feed Chain in Action Animal Nutrition –the key to animal performance, health & welfare.* Bruxelles, Belgium: Fefac.

EUROSTAT. (n.d.). Retrieved from http://ec.europa.eu/eurostat/statistics-explained/index.php/Organic_farming_statistics

306

Fang, T. (2003). A critique of Hofstede's fifth national culture dimension. *International Journal of Cross Cultural Management*, *3*(3), 347–368. doi:10.1177/1470595803003003006

FAO (Food and Agriculture Organization of the United Nations). (1983). World Food Security: a Reappraisal of the Concepts and Approaches. Director General's Report. Rome, Italy: FAO.

FAO. (2006). Global Perspective Studies Unit: Food and Agriculture Organization of the United Nations. World agriculture: towards 2030/2050. Interim Report. Prospects for food, nutrition, agriculture and major commodity groups. Rome, Italy: FAO.

FAO. (2014). Towards a concept of sustainable animal diets. FAO Animal Production and Health Report. No. 7. Rome, Italy: FAO.

FAO. (n.d.). *Why is organic food more expensive than conventional food?* Available at http://www.fao.org/organicag/oa-faq/oa-faq5/en/?ncid=txtlnkusaolp00000618

Fatt, J. P. T., Wei, M., Yuen, S., & Suan, W. (2000). Enhancing Corporate Image in Organizations. *Management Research News*, *23*(7), 28–54. doi:10.1108/01409170010782037

Field, A. P. (2009). *Discovering statistics using SPSS*. Thousand Oaks, CA: SAGE Publications.

Fisher, A. B. (1990). What consumers want in the 1990s. *Fortune*, *121*(3), 108–112.

Fisk, G. (1973). Criteria for a theory of responsible consumption. *Journal of Marketing*, *37*(2), 24–31. doi:10.2307/1250047

Flavian, C., Guinaliu, M., & Torres, E. (2005). The Influence of Corporate Image on Consumer Trust. *Internet Research*, *15*(4), 447–470. doi:10.1108/10662240510615191

Flora, C. B., & Bregendahl, C. (2012). Collaborative community-supported agriculture: Balancing community capitals for producers and consumers. *Int. Jrnl. of Soc. of Agr. & Food*, *19*(3), 329–346.

Folkes, V. S. (1988). Recent attribution research in consumer behaviour: A review and new directions. *The Journal of Consumer Research*, *14*(4), 548–565. doi:10.1086/209135

Food Marketing Institute (FMI). (1998). Trends in the United States: Consumer attitudes and the supermarket. Washington, DC: Research Department, Food Marketing Institute.

Forehand, M. R., & Grier, S. (2003). When is honesty the best policy? The effect of stated company intent on consumer skepticism. *Journal of Consumer Psychology*, *13*(3), 349–356. doi:10.1207/S15327663JCP1303_15

Fowler, A. R. III, & Close, A. G. (2012). It ain't easy being green: Macro, meso, and micro green advertising agendas. *Journal of Advertising*, *41*(4), 119–132. doi:10.1080/00913367.2012.10672461

Franke, G. R., & Nadler, S. S. (2008). Culture, economic development, and national ethical attitudes. *Journal of Business Research*, *61*(3), 254–264. doi:10.1016/j.jbusres.2007.06.005

Freeman, R. E., & Liedtka, J. (1991). Corporate Social Responsibility: A Critical Approach. *Business Horizons*, *34*(4), 92–98. doi:10.1016/0007-6813(91)90012-K

Friestad, M., & Wright, P. (1994). The persuasion knowledge model: How people cope with persuasion attempts. *The Journal of Consumer Research*, *21*(1), 1–31. doi:10.1086/209380

Fukuyama, F. (1992). *The End of History and the Last Man*. New York: Free Press.

Fukuyama, F. (1995). *Trust: The social virtues and the creation of prosperity*. New York: Free Press Paperbacks.

Furlow, N. E. (2010). Greenwashing in the New Millennium. *Journal of Applied Business & Economics*, *10*(6), 22–25.

Galtung, J. (1986). *Towards a new economics: On the theory and practice of self-reliance. In The Living Economy: A New Economics in the Making*. London: Routledge.

Gao, Y. (2009). Corporate social performance in China: Evidence from large companies. *Journal of Business Ethics*, *89*(1), 23–35. doi:10.1007/s10551-008-9982-y

Gerber, P. J., Steinfeld, H., Henderson, B., Mottet, A., Opio, C., Dijkman, J., & Tempio, G. (2013). *Tackling climate change through livestock: A global assessment of emissions and mitigation opportunities*. Rome: FAO.

Gibson, C., & Kong, L. (2005). Cultural economy: A critical review. *Progress in Human Geography*, *29*(5), 541–561. doi:10.1191/0309132505ph567oa

Gidatopluluklari website. (n.d.). Retrieved July 28, 2016, from http://gidatopluluklari.org/

Gilbert, D. T., & Malone, P. S. (1995). The correspondence bias. *Psychological Bulletin*, *117*(1), 21–38. doi:10.1037/0033-2909.117.1.21 PMID:7870861

Gill, M., Smith, P., & Wilkinson, J. M. (2010). Mitigating climate change: The role of domestic livestock. *Animal*, *4*(03), 323–333. doi:10.1017/S1751731109004662 PMID:22443938

Ginsberg, J. M., & Bloom, P. N. (2004). Choosing the right green-marketing strategy. *MIT Sloan Management Review*, *46*(1), 79.

Gjølberg, M. (2009). Measuring the immeasurable?: Constructing an index of CSR practices and CSR performance in 20 countries. *Scandinavian Journal of Management*, *25*(1), 10–22. doi:10.1016/j.scaman.2008.10.003

GlobeScan SustainAbility Sustainabiliy Leaders Survey. (2014). Retrieved on August 13, 2017 from http://www.globescan.com/component/edocman/?view=document&id=103&Itemid=591

Globescan. (2012). Credibility gap persists around companies' CSR communications. *Featured Findings*. Retrieved on 13 August, 2017 from http://www.globescan.com/commentary-and-analysis/featured-findings/entry/credibility-gap-persists-around-companies-csr-communications.html

Godfrey, K. B. (1996). Towards sustainability? Tourism in the Republic of Cyprus. *Practicing responsible tourism: International case studies in tourism planning, policy and development*, 58-79.

Golusin, M., MunitlakIvanovic, O., Domazet, S., Dodic, S., & Vucurovic, D. (2011). Assessment of the effectiveness of policy implementation for sustainable energy development in South East Europe. *Journal of Renewable and Sustainable Energy, 3.*

Gracia, A., Barreiro-Hurlé, J., & López-Galán, B. (2014). Are Local and Organic Claims Complements or Substitutes? A Consumer Preferences Study for Eggs. *Journal of Agricultural Economics*, *65*(1), 49–67. doi:10.1111/1477-9552.12036

Gray, E. R., & Balmer, J. M. T. (1998). Managing Corporate Image and Corporate Reputation. *Long Range Planning*, *31*(5), 695–702. doi:10.1016/S0024-6301(98)00074-0

Griffin, R. W. (1990). *Management* (7th ed.). Mifflin Co.

Grunert, K. G. (2006). Future trends and consumer lifestyles with regard to meat consumption. *Meat Science*, *74*(1), 149–160. doi:10.1016/j.meatsci.2006.04.016 PMID:22062724

Grunert, K. G., Larsen, H. H., Madsen, T. K., & Baadsgaard, A. (1996). *Market orientation in food and agriculture*. Norwell, MA: Springer US. doi:10.1007/978-1-4613-1301-4

Grunert, K. G., Skytte, H., Esbjerg, L., & Hviid, M. (2002). *Dokumenteret kødkvalitet. MAPP project paper*. Aarhus: The Aarhus School of Business.

Hall, D., Roberts, L., & Mitchell, M. (2003). *New directions in rural tourism*. Ashgate Publishing Ltd.

Hannerz, U. (1990). Cosmopolitans and locals in world culture. *Theory, Culture & Society*, *7*(2), 237–251. doi:10.1177/026327690007002014

Harrison, R. (1987). *Organization Culture and Quality of Service*. London: The Association for Management Education and Development.

Hart, K. J., Yáñez-Ruiz, D. R., Duval, S. M., McEwan, N. R., & Newbold, C. J. (2008). Plant extracts to manipulate rumen fermentation. *Animal Feed Science and Technology*, *147*(1-3), 8–35. doi:10.1016/j.anifeedsci.2007.09.007

Haslam, S. A., Eggins, R. A., & Reynolds, K. J. (2003). The ASPIRe Model: Actualizing Social and Personal Identity Resources to Enhance Organizational Outcomes. *Journal of Occupational and Organizational Psychology*, *76*(1), 83–113. doi:10.1348/096317903321208907

Hassi, A., & Storti, G. (2012). Globalization and Culture: The Three H Scenarios. In Globalization-Approaches to Diversity. InTech.

Haytko, D. L., & Matulich, E. (2008). Green advertising and environmentally responsible consumer behaviors: Linkages examined. *Journal of Management and Marketing Research*, *1*(1), 5–14.

Henderson, E. (2010, February). *The World of Community Supported Agriculture*. Paper presented at Urgenci Kobe Conference. Retrieved July 28, 2016, from http://www.chelseagreen.com/blogs/elizabeth-henderson-the-world-of-community-supported-agriculture/

Henson, S., & Northern, J. (2000). Consumer Assessment of the Safety of Beef at the Point of Purchase: A Pan-European Study. *Journal of Agricultural Economics*, *51*(1), 90–105. doi:10.1111/j.1477-9552.2000.tb01211.x

Hoffman, J., & Hoffman, M. (2009). What is Greenwashing? *Scientific American*, 1.

Hofstede, G. (1980). Motivation, leadership, and organization: Do American theories apply abroad? *Organizational Dynamics*, *9*(1), 42–63. doi:10.1016/0090-2616(80)90013-3

Hofstede, G. (2001). *Culture's consequences: Comparing values, behaviors, institutions, and organizations across cultures* (2nd ed.). London: Sage.

Hofstede, G. H. (1984). *Culture's consequences: International differences in work-related values* (2nd ed.). Beverly Hills, CA: Sage Publications.

Hofstede, G. H., & Hofstede, G. (2001). *Culture's consequences: Comparing values, behaviors, institutions and organizations across nations* (2nd ed.). Thousand Oaks, CA: Sage Publications.

Hofstede, G., Hofstede, G. J., & Minkov, M. (2010). *Cultures and Organizations: Software of the Mind. Revised and Expanded* (3rd ed.). New York: McGraw-Hill.

Hofstede, G., & Minkov, M. (2010). Hofstede's fifth dimension: New evidence from the World Values Survey. *Journal of Cross-Cultural Psychology*.

Hofstede, G., & Ochiană, G. (1996). *Managementul structurilor multiculturale: Software-ul gândirii*. Bucureşti: Editura Economică.

Holbrook, M. B. (1999). *Consumer Value: A Framework for Analysis and Research*. London: Routledge. doi:10.4324/9780203010679

Hood, D. E., & Mead, G. C. (1993). Modified atmosphere storage of fresh meat and poultry. In R. T. Parry (Ed.), *Principles and applications of modified atmosphere packaging of food* (pp. 269–298). London: Blackie Academic and Professional. doi:10.1007/978-1-4615-2137-2_11

Howard, M. L. (2015). *The Effect of Social Media on Consumer Perceptions of the Beef Industry* (Master's Thesis). University of Tennessee. Retrieved from http://trace.tennessee.edu/utk_gradthes/3373

Hughner, R. S., McDonagh, P., Prothero, A., Shultz, C. J., & Stanton, J. (2007). Who are organic food consumers? A compilation and review of why people purchase organic food. *Journal of Consumer Behaviour*, *6*(2-3), 94–110. doi:10.1002/cb.210

Huţu, C. A. (1999). *Cultură organizaţională şi transfer de tehnologie*. Bucureşti: Editura Economică.

IFIF (International Feed Industry Federation). (2013). *The International Feed Industry Federation Annual Report 2012/13*. Retrieved from http://ifif.org/uploadImage/2013/10/1/c838a3d3dbb286acb4685f331c1b70241380656385.pdf

IFOAM website. (n.d.). Retrieved May 29, 2016, from http://www.ifoam.bio/en/organic-policy-guarantee/participatory-guarantee-systems-pgs

Index, G. (2009). *About greenwashing: What is greenwashing? It's whitewashing, but with a green brush*. Academic Press.

Ivy, J. (2001). Higher Education Institution Image: A Correspondence Analysis Approach. *V. International Journal of Educational Management*, *15*(6), 276–282. doi:10.1108/09513540110401484

Iyer, E., & Banerjee, B. (1993). Anatomy of green advertising. *Advances in Consumer Research. Association for Consumer Research (U. S.)*, *20*.

Jackson, T. (2015). A New Philosophical Approach to Social Transformation for a "Green Economy" in Technology and Innovation for Sustainable Development. New York: Bloomsbury Academic.

Javidan, M., House, R. J., Dorfman, P. W., Hanges, P. J., & De Luque, M. S. (2006). Conceptualizing and measuring cultures and their consequences: A comparative review of GLOBE's and Hofstede's approaches. *Journal of International Business Studies*, *37*(6), 897–914. doi:10.1057/palgrave.jibs.8400234

Joel, J. D. (1992). Ethics and Green Marketing. *Journal of Business Ethics*, *11*(2), 81–87. doi:10.1007/BF00872314

Johnston, J. (2001). Consuming social justice: Shopping for fair-trade chic. *Arena Magazine*, *51*, 42–47.

Jones, A. P., & James, L. R. (1979). Psychological climate: Dimensions and relationships of individual and aggregated work environment perceptions. *Organizational Behavior and Human Performance*, *23*(2), 201–250. doi:10.1016/0030-5073(79)90056-4

Jost, F. A. (1996). *Sustainable Development: The Roles of Science and Ethics*. London, UK: Edvard Elgar.

Jouany, J. P., & Morgavi, D. P. (2007). Use of 'natural' products as alternatives to antibiotic feed additives in ruminant production. *Animal*, *1*(10), 1443–1466. doi:10.1017/S1751731107000742 PMID:22444918

Jovanovic, M., & Eskinja, I. (2008). Neki aspekti neoliberalizma u svetskom gospodarstvu. *Zbornik Pravnog Fakulteta Sveucilista u Rijeci*, *29*(2), 941–985.

Kalafatis, S. P., Pollard, M., East, R., & Tsogas, M. H. (1999). Green marketing and Ajzen's theory of planned behaviour: A cross-market examination. *Journal of Consumer Marketing*, *16*(5), 441–460. doi:10.1108/07363769910289550

Kallas, Z., Realini, C., & Gil, J. M. (2014). Health information impact on the relative importance of beef attributes including its enrichment with polyunsaturated fatty acids (omega-3 and conjugated linoleic acid). *Meat Science, 97*(4), 497–503. doi:10.1016/j.meatsci.2014.03.015 PMID:24769150

Kan, C. A., & Meijer, G. A. L. (2007). The risk of contamination of food with toxic substances present in animal feed. *Animal Feed Science and Technology, 133*(1-2), 84–108. doi:10.1016/j.anifeedsci.2006.08.005

Kangun, N., Carlson, L., & Grove, S. J. (1991). Environmental advertising claims: A preliminary investigation. *Journal of Public Policy & Marketing*, 47–58.

Karakoc, U., & Baykan, B. G. (2009). *Turkiye'de Organik Tarım Gelisiyor*. BETAM Research Note, 35, Bahcesehir Uni., Istanbul.

Karna, J., Juslin, H., Ahonen, V., & Hansen, E. (2001). Green advertising: greenwash or a true reflection of marketing strategies? *Greener Management International*, 59-71.

Kartal Municipality website. (n.d.). Retrieved July 26, 2016, from http://en.kartal.bel.tr/content/projects-ecological-market.aspx

Katz, J. P., Swanson, D. L., & Nelson, L. K. (2001). Culture-based expectations of corporate citizenship: A propositional framework and comparison of four cultures. *The International Journal of Organizational Analysis, 9*(2), 149–171. doi:10.1108/eb028931

Kauffman, R. G., & Marsh, B. B. (1987). Quality characteristics of muscle as food. In J. F. Price & B. S. Schweigert (Eds.), *The science of meat and meat products* (3rd ed.; pp. 349–369). Westport, CT: Food and Nutrition Press, Inc.

Keegan, W. J., & Seringhaus, F. H. R. (1996). *Global Marketing Management* (5th ed.). Scarborough, Canada: Prentice-Hall Canada Inc.

Keith, D., & Blomstrom, R. L. (1975). *Business and society: Environment and responsibility*. New York: McGraw-Hill.

Keller, G. M. (1987). Industry and the Environment: Toward a New Philosophy. *Vital Speeches, 54*(5), 154–157.

Khondker, H. H. (2004). Glocalization as globalization: Evolution of a sociological concept. *Bangladesh e-Journal of Sociology, 1*(2), 1–9.

Kim, Y., & Kim, S.-Y. (2010). The Influence of Cultural Values on Perceptions of Corporate Social Responsibility: Application of Hofstede's Dimensions to Korean Public Relations Practitioners. *Journal of Business Ethics, 91*(4), 485–500. doi:10.1007/s10551-009-0095-z

King, A. W., & Zeithaml, C. P. (2001). Competencies and Firm Performance: Examining the Causal Ambiguity Paradox. *Strategic Management Journal, 22*(1), 75–99. doi:10.1002/1097-0266(200101)22:1<75::AID-SMJ145>3.0.CO;2-I

Kirchner, C. (2014, October) *Participatory Guarantee Systems (PGS) Practitioners.* Paper presented at IFOAM Organic World Congress, Istanbul.

Kirkman, B. L., Lowe, K. B., & Gibson, C. B. (2006). A quarter century of culture's consequences: A review of empirical research incorporating Hofstede's cultural values framework. *Journal of International Business Studies, 37*(3), 285–320. doi:10.1057/palgrave.jibs.8400202

Korzen, S., & Lassen, J. (2010). Meat in context. On the relation between perceptions and contexts. *Appetite, 54*(2), 274–281. doi:10.1016/j.appet.2009.11.011 PMID:19944122

Koster, E. P., & Mojet, J. (2007). Theories of food choice development. In L. Frewer & H. van Trijp (Eds.), *Understanding consumers of food products* (pp. 93–124). Cambridge: Woodhead. doi:10.1533/9781845692506.1.93

Kotler, P. (2011). Reinventing marketing to manage the environmental imperative. *Journal of Marketing, 75*(4), 132–135. doi:10.1509/jmkg.75.4.132

Kotler, P., & Andreasen, A. R. (1996). *Positioning the Organisation: Strategic Marketig for Non-Profit Organisation.* Toronto: Prentice-Hall.

Kotler, Ph., & Keller, K. (2008). *Managementul Marketingului.* Bucureşti: Editura Teora.

Kotler, Ph., Saunders, J., Armstrong, G., & Wong, V. (2008). *Principiile Marketingului.* Bucureşti: Editura Teora.

Krivokapic, Z., Vujovic, A., & Jovanovic, J. (2014*). Ekoloska inovativnost u funkcji drustvene odgovornosit.* Paper presented at the 41. Nacionalna konferencija o kvalitetu, 9. Nacionalna konferencija o kvalitetu zivota, 5. Konferencija studenata industrijskog inzenjerstva i menadzmenta, Fakultet inzenjerskih nauka, Kragujevac.

Krystallis, A., Arvanitoyannis, I., & Chryssohoidis, G. (2006). Is there a real difference between conventional and organic meat? Investigating consumers' attitudes towards both meat types as an indicator of organic meat's market potential. *Journal of Food Products Marketing, 12*(2), 47–78. doi:10.1300/J038v12n02_04

Kustyadji, G. (2014). The Influence of Local Culture on National Culture and Its Impact on Organizational Culture. *Interdisciplinary Journal of Contemporary Research in Business, 6*(5), 44–58.

Lacy, P., & Rutqvist, J. (2015). *Waste to Wealth, The Circular Economy Advantage.* Palgrave Macmillan.

Lamb, G. (1994). Community supported agriculture. *Threefold Review, 11*, 39–43.

Landes, D. (1999). *The Wealth and Poverty of Nations: Why Some Are So Rich and Some So Poor.* New York: W.W. Norton & Company.

Lane, B. (1994). What is rural tourism? *Journal of Sustainable Tourism, 2*(1-2), 7–21. doi:10.1080/09669589409510680

Leonidou, C. N., & Leonidou, L. C. (2011). Research into environmental marketing/management: A bibliographic analysis. *European Journal of Marketing*, *45*(1/2), 68–103. doi:10.1108/03090561111095603

Leonidou, L. C., Leonidou, C. N., & Kvasova, O. (2010). Antecedents and outcomes of consumer environmentally friendly attitudes and behaviour. *Journal of Marketing Management*, *26*(13-14), 1319–1344. doi:10.1080/0267257X.2010.523710

Leonidou, L. C., Leonidou, C. N., Palihawadana, D., & Hultman, M. (2011). Evaluating the green advertising practices of international firms: A trend analysis. *International Marketing Review*, *28*(1), 6–33. doi:10.1108/02651331111107080

Leung, K., Bhagat, R. S., Buchan, N. R., Erez, M., & Gibson, C. B. (2005). Culture and international business: Recent advances and their implications for future research. *Journal of International Business Studies*, *36*(4), 357–378. doi:10.1057/palgrave.jibs.8400150

Lipovetsky, G. (2007). *Fericirea paradoxală. Eseu asupra societății de hiperconsum*. Iasi: Editura Polirom.

Lull, J. (2001). *Medya, İletişim, Kültür*. Ankara: Vadi Yayınları.

Lyon, T. P., & Maxwell, J. W. (2011). Greenwash: Corporate environmental disclosure under threat of audit. *Journal of Economics & Management Strategy*, *20*(1), 3–41. doi:10.1111/j.1530-9134.2010.00282.x

Maignan, I. (2001). Consumers' perceptions of corporate social responsibilities: A cross-cultural comparison. *Journal of Business Ethics*, *30*(1), 57–72. doi:10.1023/A:1006433928640

Makkar, H. P. S., Tran, G., Heuzé, V., Giger-Reverdin, S., Lessire, M., Lebas, F., & Ankers, P. (2015). Seaweeds for livestock diets: A review. *Animal Feed Science and Technology*, *212*, 1–17. doi:10.1016/j.anifeedsci.2015.09.018

Malthus, T. J. (n.d.). *An Essay on the Principle of Population*. Available from http://www.esp.org/books/malthus/population/malthus.pdf

Mangleberg, T. F., & Terry, B. (1998). Socialization and Adolescents' Skepticism Toward Advertising. *Journal of Advertising*, *27*(Fall), 11–21. doi:10.1080/00913367.1998.10673559

Marín, L., Cuestas, P. J., & Román, S. (2016). Determinants of consumer attributions of corporate social responsibility. *Journal of Business Ethics*, *138*(2), 247–260. doi:10.1007/s10551-015-2578-4

Markwick, N., & Fill, C. (1997). Towards A Framework for Managing Corporate Identity. *European Journal of Marketing*, *31*(5/6), 396–409. doi:10.1108/eb060639

Matten, D., & Moon, J. (2008). "Implicit" and "Explicit" CSR: A Conceptual Framework for a Comparative Understanding of Corporate Social Responsibility. *Academy of Management Review*, *33*(2), 404–424. doi:10.5465/AMR.2008.31193458

Max-Neef, M., Elizalde, A., & Hopenhayn, M. (1989). Human Scale Development: An Option for Future Development. *Dialogue*, 5–80.

McCann, E. (2002). The cultural politics of local economic development: Meaning-making, place-making, and the urban policy process. *Geoforum*, *33*(3), 385–398. doi:10.1016/S0016-7185(02)00007-6

McGrew, A. (1990). A Global Society. In *Modernity and Its Futures* (pp. 467–499). Cambridge, UK: Polity Press.

Medlock, K. (2017, January 1). This Japanese town will produce absolutely zero waste by 2020 [Web log comment]. Retrieved from http://inhabitat.com/this-japanese-town-will-produce-absolutely-zero-waste-by-2020/

Melewar, T. C. (2003). Determinants of Corporate Identity Construct: A Review of The Literature. *Journal of Marketing Communications*, *9*(4), 195–220. doi:10.1080/1352726032000119161

Menon, S., & Kahn, B. E. (2003). Corporate sponsorships of philanthropic activities: When do they impact perception of sponsor brand? *Journal of Consumer Psychology*, *13*(3), 316–327. doi:10.1207/S15327663JCP1303_12

Meroni, A. (2007). *Creative Communities: People inventing sustainable ways of living.* Milan: Edizioni Poli.Design.

Mesías, F. J., Escribano, M., Gaspar, P., & Pulido, F. (2008). Consumers' attitudes towards organic, PGI and conventional meats in Extremadura (Spain). *Archivos de Zootecnia*, *57*, 139–146.

Mesías, F. J., Martínez-Carrasco Pleite, F., Martínez-Paz, J. M., & Gaspar, P. (2011). Functional and Organic Eggs as an Alternative to Conventional Production: A Conjoint Analysis of Consumers' preferences. *Journal of the Science of Food and Agriculture*, *91*(3), 532–538. doi:10.1002/jsfa.4217 PMID:21218489

Meyer, J. P., & Allen, N. J. (1997). *Commitment in the Workplace: Theory, Research, and Application.* Thousand Oaks, CA: Sage Publications.

Meznar, M. B., & Nigh, D. (1995). Buffer or bridge? Environmental and organizational determinants of public affairs activities in American firms. *Academy of Management Journal*, *38*(4), 975–996. doi:10.2307/256617

Milanovic, C.Z., Radovic, S., & Vucic, V. (2002). *Otpad nije smece.* Zagreb, Republika Hrvatska: Gospodarstvo i okolis.

Miller, E. (2010). Solidarity Economy: Key Concepts and Issues. In E. Kawano, T. Masterson, & J. Teller-Ellsberg (Eds.), *Solidarity Economy I: Building Alternatives for People and Planet* (pp. 1–12). Amherst, MA: Center for Popular Economics.

Miller, R. K. (2002). Factors affecting the quality of raw meat. In J. P. Kerry, J. F. Kerry, & D. Ledward (Eds.), *Meat processing—Improving quality* (pp. 27–63). Cambridge, UK: Woodhead Publishing Co. doi:10.1533/9781855736665.1.27

Miroshnik, V. (2002). Culture and international management: A review. *Journal of Management Development, 21*(7), 521–544. doi:10.1108/02621710210434647

Mitic, P., Munitlak Ivanovic, O., & Zdravkovic, A. (2017). A Cointegration Analysis of Real GDP and CO2 Emissions in Transitional Countries. *Sustainability, 9*(4), 1–18. doi:10.3390/su9040568

Mohr, L. A., Webb, D. J., & Harris, K. E. (2001). Do consumers expect companies to be socially responsible? The impact of corporate social responsibility on buying behavior. *The Journal of Consumer Affairs, 35*(1), 45–72. doi:10.1111/j.1745-6606.2001.tb00102.x

Mollison, B., Slay, R. M., Girard, J. L., Bourgignon, C., & Bourguignon, L. (1991). *Introduction to permaculture*. Tyalgum, Australia: Tagari Publications.

Montoro, R. (2006). Improving attitudes toward brands with environmental associations: An experimental approach. *Journal of Consumer Marketing, 23*(1), 26–33. doi:10.1108/07363760610641136

Morales, A. (2011). Marketplaces: Prospects for social, economic, and political development. *Journal of Planning Literature, 26*(1), 3–17. doi:10.1177/0885412210388040

Morsing, M., & Schultz, M. (2006). Corporate social responsibility communication: Stakeholder information, response and involvement strategies. *Business Ethics (Oxford, England), 15*(4), 323–338. doi:10.1111/j.1467-8608.2006.00460.x

Munitlak Ivanovic O., Mitic, P., & Popovic, S. (2015). Globalizacija i tehnicko-tehnoloske promene – savremenije drustvo i/ili globalna ekoloska propast. *Poslovna ekonomija, 16*(9), 263-276.

Munitlak Ivanovic, O. (2007). Uloga drzave u primeni ekonomskih instrumenata u funkciji realizacije koncepta odrzivog razvoja. *Poslovna ekonomija, 1*(1), 135-149.

Munitlak Ivanovic, O. (2009). Ekoloski menadzment kao model upravljanja rizikom. *Poslovna ekonomija, 3*(4), 155-160.

MunitlakIvanovic, O. (2017, April). *Pokusaji redukcije emisija CO2 analizom Kuznetzovekrive i medjunarodnih protokola –instrumenti za realizaciju odrzivog razvoja*. Paper presented on Medjunarodna naucna konferencija: Ciljevi odrzivog razvoja u III milenijumu, knjiga apstrakata, Beograd, Srbija.

MunitlakIvanovic, O., & Zubovic, J. (2017). From the Millennium Development Goals to the Resilience Concept – Theoretical Similarities and Differences. In The State and the Market in Economic Development: In Pursuit of Milennium Development Goals (pp. 7-29). The IIDS Australia Inc.

Murthy, R. S., Mazumdar, P., Rani, M., Tabassum, S., & Chandra, K. (2014). Rapid Growth of Eco-friendly Low Cost Sustainable Organic Agriculture Production Systems in the World. In P. K. Shetty, C. Alvares, & A. K. Yadav (Eds.), *Organic Farming and Sustainability* (pp. 249–258). Bangalore: NIAS Books and Special Publications.

Mutlu, N. (2007). *Consumer attitude and behavior towards organic food: Cross-cultural study of Turkey and Germany* (Unpublished master thesis). Institute for Agricultural Policy and Markets, Universitat Hohenheim, Germany.

Myers, T. A. (2011). Goodbye, listwise deletion: Presenting hot deck imputation as an easy and effective tool for handling missing data. *Communication Methods and Measures*, *5*(4), 297–310. doi:10.1080/19312458.2011.624490

Nance, G. A. (2012). Organic Farming in Turkey and the Contribution of Bugday to the Sector's Development. *The World of Organic Agriculture 2012, Europe Country Report: Turkey* (pp. 221-225). Retrieved July 26, 2016, from http://www.organic-world.net/fileadmin/documents/ yearbook/2012/altin-2012-turkey-221-225.pdf

National Action Plan on Organic Agriculture 2013-2016, Turkey. (n.d.). Retrieved July 26, 2016, from http://www.tarim.gov.tr/BUGEM/Belgeler/Bitkisel%20%C3%9Cretim/Organik%20 Tar%C4%B1m/UlusalEylemPlan-2013-2016.pdf

Newell, S. J., Goldsmith, R. E., & Banzhaf, E. J. (1998). The effect of misleading environmental claims on consumer perceptions of advertisements. *Journal of Marketing Theory and Practice*, *6*(2), 48–60. doi:10.1080/10696679.1998.11501795

Nguyen, N., & LeBlanc, G. (2001). Image and Reputation of Higher Education Institutions in Students' Retention Decisions. *International Journal of Educational Management*, *15*(6), 303–311. doi:10.1108/EUM0000000005909

Nguyen, N., & Leblanc, G. (2002). Contact Personnel, Physical Environment and The Perceived Corporate Image of Intangible Services by New Clients. *International Journal of Service Industry Management*, *13*(3), 242–262. doi:10.1108/09564230210431965

Nyilasy, G., Gangadharbatla, H., & Paladino, A. (2014). Perceived greenwashing: The interactive effects of green advertising and corporate environmental performance on consumer reactions. *Journal of Business Ethics*, *125*(4), 693–707. doi:10.1007/s10551-013-1944-3

O'Brien, D., Capper, J. L., Garnsworthy, P. C., Grainger, C., & Shalloo, L. (2014). A case study of the carbon footprint of milk from high-performing confinement and grass-based dairy farms. *Journal of Dairy Science*, *97*(3), 1835–1851. doi:10.3168/jds.2013-7174 PMID:24440256

Obanya, P. (2005). *Culture in Education and Education in Culture*. Fifth Conference of African Ministers of Culture, Nairobi, Kenya. Retrieved from www.africa-union.org

OECD. (1994), *Tourism Strategies and Rural Development*. General Distribution, OECD/GD (94)49, 9-10. Retrieved from http://www.oecd.org/dataoecd/31/27/2755218.pdf

Oldenburg, R. (1989). *The Great Good Place: Cafes, Coffee Shops, Community Centers, Beauty Parlors, General Stores, Bars, Hangouts and How They Get Through The Day*. New York: Paragon House.

Olivas, R., Díaz, M., & Bernabeu, R. (2013). Structural Equation Modeling of lifestyles and consumer attitudes towards organic food by income: A Spanish case study. *Ciencia e Investigación Agraria, 40*(2), 265–277. doi:10.4067/S0718-16202013000200003

Olmedilla-Alonso, B., Jiménez-Colmenero, F., & Sánchez-Muniz, F. J. (2013). Development and assessment of healthy properties of meat and meat products designed as functional foods. *Meat Science, 95*(4), 919–930. doi:10.1016/j.meatsci.2013.03.030 PMID:23623320

Oltjen, J. W., Kebreab, E., & Lapierre, H. (Eds.). (2013). *Energy and protein metabolism and nutrition in sustainable animal production* (Vol. 134). Wageningen Academic Publishers. doi:10.3920/978-90-8686-781-3

Orboi, M. D. (2013). Aspects regarding the evolution the organic food market in the world. *Research Journal of Agricultural Science, 45*(2), 201–209.

Orecchini, F., Valitutti, V., & Vitali, G. (2012). Industry and academia for a transition towards sustainability: Advancing sustainability science through university–business collaborations. *Sustainability Science, 7*(S1), 57–73. doi:10.1007/s11625-011-0151-3

Orlowski, D. (1982). *Die internationale Wetthewerbsf.* Göttingen: Vanderhoeck und Ruprecht.

Ozesmi, U. (2016). *TEDxReset Talks Prosumer Economy for a Future.* Retrieved June 13, 2016, from, https://www.youtube.com/watch?v=8ceCiWie0lM&feature=share

Özkaya, B. (2010). İşletmelerin Sosyal Sorumluluk Anlayışının Uzantısı Olarak Yeşil Pazarlama Bağlamında Yeşil Reklamlar. *Öneri, 9*(34), 247-258.

Parguel, B., Benoît-Moreau, F., & Larceneux, F. (2011). How sustainability ratings might deter 'greenwashing': A closer look at ethical corporate communication. *Journal of Business Ethics, 102*(1), 15–28. doi:10.1007/s10551-011-0901-2

Pearce, J. (2003). *Social Enterprise in Any Town.* Calouste Gulbenkian Foundation.

Peattie, K. (2001). Golden goose or wild goose? The hunt for the green consumer. *Business Strategy and the Environment, 10*(4), 187–199. doi:10.1002/bse.292

Peri, C. (2006). The universe of food quality. *Food Quality and Preference, 17*(1-2), 3–8. doi:10.1016/j.foodqual.2005.03.002

Peters, T. J., Waterman, R. H., & Jones, I. (1982). *In search of excellence: Lessons from America's best-run companies.* Academic Press.

Pettigrew, A. M. (1979). On studying organizational cultures. *Administrative Science Quarterly, 24*(4), 570–581.

Pfanner, E. (2008, July 18). Cooling off on dubious eco-friendly claims. *The New York Times,* p. C3.

Pfau, M., Haigh, M. M., Sims, J., & Wigley, S. (2008). The influence of corporate social responsibility campaigns on public opinion. *Corporate Reputation Review, 11*(2), 145–154. doi:10.1057/crr.2008.14

Polonsky, M. J. (1994). An introduction to green marketing. *Electronic Green Journal*, *1*(2).

Polonsky, M. J., & Rosenberger, P. J. III. (2001). Reevaluating green marketing: A strategic approach. *Business Horizons*, *44*(5), 21–30. doi:10.1016/S0007-6813(01)80057-4

Polonsky, M. J., Rosenberger, P. J. III, & Ottman, J. (1998). Developing green products: Learning from stakeholders. *Asia Pacific Journal of Marketing and Logistics*, *10*(1), 22–43. doi:10.1108/13555859810764454

Pomering, A., & Dolnicar, S. (2009). Assessing the Prerequisite of Successful CSR Implementation: Are Consumers Aware of CSR Initiatives? *Journal of Business Ethics*, *85*(S2), 285–301. doi:10.1007/s10551-008-9729-9

Poon, A. (2003). Competitive strategies for a 'new tourism'. *Classic reviews in tourism*, 130-142.

Poon, A. (2007). Local Involvment in Tourism. In *Proceedings of Meeting on the Trade and Development Implications of Tourism Services for Developing Countries*. UNCTAD XII pre-event.

Poon, A. (1990). Flexible specialization and small size: The case of Caribbean tourism. *World Development*, *18*(1), 109–123. doi:10.1016/0305-750X(90)90106-8

Poon, A. (1993). *Tourism, technology and competitive strategies*. CAB international.

Poon, A. (1994). The 'new tourism'revolution. *Tourism Management*, *15*(2), 91–92. doi:10.1016/0261-5177(94)90001-9

Porter, M. E., & Kramer, M. R. (2006). The link between competitive advantage and corporate social responsibility. *Harvard Business Review*, *84*(12), 78–92. PMID:17183795

Porter, S. S., & Claycomb, C. (1997). The Influence of Brand Recognition on Retail Store Image. *Journal of Product and Brand Management*, *16*(6), 373–387. doi:10.1108/10610429710190414

Prahalad, C. K., & Hamel, G. (1990). The Core Competence of The Corporation. *Harvard Business Review*, *68*(3), 79–81.

Provenza, F. D., Meuret, M., & Gregorini, P. (2015). Our landscapes, our livestock, ourselves: Restoring broken linkages among plants, herbivores, and humans with diets that nourish and satiate. *Appetite*, *95*, 500–519. doi:10.1016/j.appet.2015.08.004 PMID:26247703

Pugliese, P., Zanasi, C., Atallah, O., & Cosimo, R. (2013). Investigating the interaction between organic and local foods in the Mediterranean: The Lebanese organic consumer's perspective. *Food Policy*, *39*, 1–12. doi:10.1016/j.foodpol.2012.12.009

Puniya, A. K., Singh, R., & Kamra, D. N. (Eds.). (2015). *Rumen Microbiology: From Evolution to Revolution*. New Delhi, India: Springer India. doi:10.1007/978-81-322-2401-3

Quazi, A. M., & O'Brien, D. (2000). An empirical test of a cross-national model of corporate social responsibility. *Journal of Business Ethics*, *25*(1), 33–51. doi:10.1023/A:1006305111122

Rallapalli, K. C., Vitell, S. J., Wiebe, F. A., & Barnes, J. H. (1994). Consumer ethical beliefs and personality traits: An exploratory analysis. *Journal of Business Ethics, 13*(7), 487–495. doi:10.1007/BF00881294

Ramasamy, B., & Yeung, M. (2009). Chinese consumers' perception of corporate social responsibility (CSR). *Journal of Business Ethics, 88*(1), 119–132. doi:10.1007/s10551-008-9825-x

Realini, C. E., Kallas, Z., Perez-Juan, M., Gomez, I., Olleta, J. L., Beriain, M. J., ... Sañudo, C. (2014). Relative importance of cues underlying Spanish consumers' beef choice and segmentation, and consumer liking of beef enriched with n-3 and CLA fatty acids. *Food Quality and Preference, 33*, 74–85. doi:10.1016/j.foodqual.2013.11.007

Realini, C., Font, I., Furnols, M., Sañudo, C., Montossi, F., Oliver, M. A., & Guerrero, L. (2013). Spanish, French and British consumers' acceptability of Uruguayan beef, and consumers' beef choice associated with country of origin, finishing diet and meat price. *Meat Science, 95*(1), 14–21. doi:10.1016/j.meatsci.2013.04.004 PMID:23644048

Restakis, J. (2006). *Defining the Social Economy-the BC context.* Prepared for BC Social Economy Roundtable. Retrieved November 23, 2016, from, http://bcca.coop/sites/bcca.coop/files/u2/Defining_Social_Economy.pdf

Rikkonen, P., Kotro, J., Koistinen, L., Penttilä, K., & Kauriinoja, H. (2013). Opportunities for local food suppliers to use locality as a competitive advantage – a mixed survey methods approach. *Acta Agriculturae Scandinavica, Section B — Soil & Plant Science, 63*, 29–37. doi:10.1080/09064710.783620

Riordan, C., Gatewood, R. D., & Bill, J. B. (1997). Corporate Image: Employee Reactions and Implications for Managing Corporate Social Performance. *Journal of Business Ethics, 16*(4), 401–412. doi:10.1023/A:1017989205184

Ritzer, G. (2011). *Globalization: the essentials.* John Wiley & Sons.

Robertson, R. (1995). Glocalization: Time-space and homogeneity-heterogeneity. *Global Modernities, 2*, 25-45.

Robins, K. (1999). *İmaj Görmenin Kültür ve Politikası.* İstanbul: Ayrıntı Yayınları.

Roljević, S. (2014). *Productivity of alternative small grains in the organic farming system* (Doctoral dissertation). Faculty of Agriculture, University of Belgrade, UDC 631.147: 633.11 (043.3)).

Roljević, S., Grujić, B., & Sarić, R. (2012). *Organic agriculture in terms of sustainable development and rural areas development.* Academic Press.

Rosenau, J. N. (1996). The dynamics of globalization: Toward an operational formulation. *Security Dialogue, 27*(3), 247–262. doi:10.1177/0967010696027003002

Roudometof, V. (2016). *Glocalization: a critical introduction.* Routledge.

Roulet, T. J., & Touboul, S. (2015). The intentions with which the road is paved: Attitudes to liberalism as determinants of greenwashing. *Journal of Business Ethics, 128*(2), 305–320. doi:10.1007/s10551-014-2097-8

Russell, B. A. (2009). *The Basic Writings of Bertrand Russell.* London, UK: Routledge.

Ružić, P. (2009). *Rural Tourism.* Pula: Institute for Agriculture and Tourism Porec.

Sabuncuoğlu, Z., & Tuz, M. (1998). Örgütsel Psikoloji. Alfa Yayınevi, 3.

Sachs, J. A. (2015). *The Age of Sustainable Development.* New York: Columbia University Press. doi:10.7312/sach17314

Samovar, L., Porter, R., McDaniel, E., & Roy, C. (2014). *Inter-cultural communication: A reader.* Boston: Cengage Learning.

Sariatli, F. (2017). Linear economy versus Circular economy: A comparative and analyzer study for optimization of Economy for Sustainability. *Visegrad Journal of Bioeconomy and Sustainable Development, 1*, 31–34.

Saunders, M., Lewis, P., & Thornhill, A. (2009). *Research methods for business students* (5th ed.). Harlow, MA: Pearson Education.

Schein, E. H. (1985). *Organizational Culture and Leadership.* San Francisco: Jossey Bass.

Schleenbecker, R., & Hamm, U. (2013). Consumers' perception of organic product characteristics. A review. *Appetite, 71*, 420–429. doi:10.1016/j.appet.2013.08.020 PMID:24012637

Scholtens, B., & Dam, L. (2007). Cultural values and international differences in business ethics. *Journal of Business Ethics, 75*(3), 273–284. doi:10.1007/s10551-006-9252-9

Schukies, G. (1998). *Halkla İlişkilerde Müşteri Memnuniyetine Dönük Kalite.* İstanbul: Rota Yayınları.

Schultz, M. (2007). *Organizational Image. International Encyclopedia of Organization Studies.* Sage Publications.

Sciabalabba, N. E. H., & Williamson, D. (2004). *The scope of organic agriculture, sustainable forest management and ecoforestry in protected area management.* Food and Agriculture Organization of the United Nations. Retrieved from ftp://ftp.fao.org/docrep/fao/007/y5558e/y5558e00.pdf

Seele, P., & Gatti, L. (2015). Greenwashing Revisited: In Search of a Typology and Accusation-Based Definition Incorporating Legitimacy Strategies. Business Strategy and the Environment.

Sehirlioglu, B. (2015). *%100 Ekolojik Pazar.* Retrieved March 24, 2016, from http://ekolojikpazar.org/author/batur/page/2/

SERI. (n.d.). Retrieved from http://www.seri.de/home/themes/resource-efficiency-and-demateralisation/

Seyfang, G. (2005). Shopping for sustainability: Can sustainable consumption promote ecological citizenship? *Environmental Politics*, *14*(2), 290–306. doi:10.1080/09644010500055209

Sharmin, S. (2011). Teaching |English in a Cross-Cultural Context: Challenges and Directions. *Journal of NELTA*, *16*(1-2).

Sharpley, R. (2003). Rural Tourism and Sustainability - A Critique. In New Directions in Rural Tourism. Academic Press.

Shaw, P. (2006). *The Four Vs of Leadership – Vision, Values, Value- Added, Vitality*. Chichester, UK: Capstone Publishing Ltd.

Shetty, P. K., Alvares, C., & Yadav, A. K. (Eds.). (2014). Organic Farming and Sustainability. National Institute of Advanced Studies, Bangalore, India.

Shrum, L. J., McCarty, J. A., & Lowrey, T. M. (1995). Buyer characteristics of the green consumer and their implications for advertising strategy. *Journal of Advertising*, *24*(2), 71–82. doi:10.10 80/00913367.1995.10673477

Simga-Mugan, C., Daly, B. A., Onkal, D., & Kavut, L. (2005). The influence of nationality and gender on ethical sensitivity: An application of the issue-contingent model. *Journal of Business Ethics*, *57*(2), 139–159. doi:10.1007/s10551-004-4601-z

Si, S. X., & Hitit, M. A. (2003). A Study of Organizational Image Resulting from International Joint Ventures in Transitional Economies. *Journal of Business Research*, 1–8.

Soares, A. M., Farhangmehr, M., & Shoham, A. (2007). Hofstede's dimensions of culture in international marketing studies. *Journal of Business Research*, *60*(3), 277–284. doi:10.1016/j. jbusres.2006.10.018

Soil Association website. (n.d.). Retrieved July 26, 2016, from https://www.soilassociation.org/

Soil Association. (2011). *The impact of community supported agriculture*. Retrieved July 26, 2016, from http://www.communitysupportedagriculture.org.uk/wp-content/uploads/2015/03/The-impact-of-community-supported-agriculture.pdf

Stankova, M., & Vassenska, I. (2015). Raising cultural awareness of local traditions through festival tourism. *Tourism & Management Studies*, *11*(1).

State, O. (2004). *Cultura organizaţiei şi managementul*. Bucureşti: Editura ASE.

Stevanovic, B. (2003). Cvrsti i opasni otpad. In EnciklopedijaZivotnasredina i odrzivirazvoj (pp. 239-249). Beograd, RepublikaSrbija: Ecolibri.

Stiglitz, J. (2004). *Ekonomija javnog sektora*. Beograd, Republika Srbija: Ekonomski fakultet u Beogradu.

Stroudco Food Hub website. (n.d.). Retrieved July 20, 2016, from http://www.stroudco.org.uk/how-it-works/

Szulanski, G. (1996). Exploring internal stickiness: Impediments to the transfer of best practice within the firm. *Strategic Management Journal, 17*(S2), 27–43. doi:10.1002/smj.4250171105

Tamminga, S. A., Bannink, A., Dijkstra, J., & Zom, R. (2007). *Feeding strategies to reduce methane loss in cattle.* Report 34. Animal Sciences Group, Wageningen UR Livestock Research: Lelystad.

Taylor, C. R. (2005). Moving international advertising research forward: A new research agenda. *Journal of Advertising, 34*(1), 7–16. doi:10.1080/00913367.2005.10639187

Temurcu, C. (2015, June). *DBB- Ankara'da bir aracisiz dogal urun orgutlenmesi/ katilimci onay sistemi modeli.* Paper presented at 3rd Ankara Ecological Society and Living Days, Ankara.

Temurcu, C. (2016). *Turkey. Mapping Local and Solidarity-Based Partnerships Between Producers and Consumers In The Mediterranean Basin.* Retrieved July 26, 2016, from http://urgenci.net/wp-content/uploads/2016/03/UR_Med-MAPPING_RESULTS-0416.pdf

The International Fund for Agricultural Development. (n.d.). *Rural Development Report 2016.* Available at https://www.ifad.org/documents/30600024/8f07f4f9-6a91-496a-89c1-d1b120f8de8b

The Master Plan for Sustainable Rural Tourism Development in Serbia. (2011). Ministry of finance and economy of the Republic of Serbia.

Thøgersen, J. (2010). Country differences in sustainable consumption: The case of organic food. *Journal of Macromarketing, 30*(2), 171–185. doi:10.1177/0276146710361926

Thomassen, M. A., Dolman, M. A., Van Calker, K. J., & De Boer, I. J. M. (2009). Relating life cycle assessment indicators to gross value added for Dutch dairy farms. *Ecological Economics, 68*(8-9), 2278–2284. doi:10.1016/j.ecolecon.2009.02.011

Tiwari, R., & Rana, C. S. (2015). Plant secondary metabolites: A review. *International Journal of Engineering Research and General Science, 3*(5), 661–670.

TOBB. (2013). *Turkey Agriculture Sector Report.* Retrieved July 25 2016, from http://www.tobb.org.tr/Documents/yayinlar/2014/turkiye_tarim_meclisi_sektor_raporu_2013_int.pdf

Todorović, M., & Bjeljac, Ž. (2009). Rural tourism in Serbia as a way of development in undeveloped regions. *Acta Geographica Slovenica, 49*(2), 453–473. doi:10.3986/AGS49208

Todorović, M., & Stetic, S. (2009). *Rural tourism.* Belgrade: University of Belgrade, Faculty of Geography.

Triandis, H. C. (1989). The self and social behavior in differing cultural contexts. *Psychological Review, 96*(3), 506–520. doi:10.1037/0033-295X.96.3.506

Triandis, H. C. (1993). Collectivism and individualism as cultural syndromes. *Cross-Cultural Research, 27*(3), 155–180. doi:10.1177/106939719302700301

Troy, D. J., & Kerry, J. P. (2010). Consumer perception and the role of science in the meat industry. *Meat Science, 86*(1), 214–226. doi:10.1016/j.meatsci.2010.05.009 PMID:20579814

Udo, H. M. J., Aklilu, H. A., Phong, L. T., Bosma, R. H., Budisatria, I. G. S., Patil, B. R., ... Bebe, B. O. (2011). Impact of intensification of different types of livestock production in smallholder crop-livestock systems. *Livestock Science, 139*(1-2), 22–29. doi:10.1016/j.livsci.2011.03.020

UN WTO. (2003). Rural Tourism in Europe: Experiences, Development and Perspectives. In *Proceeding of Seminars* (pp. 115-121). UNWTO.

UNEP. (2012). Tourism in the green economy–background report. UNWTO.

UNWTO. (2004). Rural Tourism in Europe: Experiences, Development and Perspectives. In *Proceeding from Seminars* (pp. 27-31). UNWTO. Retrieved from http://www.idestur.org.br/download/20120219145557.pdf

UNWTO. (2007). *A Practical Guide to Tourism Destination Management*. Retrieved from http://pub.unwto.org/WebRoot/Store/Shops/Infoshop/4745/8BCE/AD9A/ECA8/048B/C0A8/0164/0B7A/071115_practical_guide_destination_management_excerpt.pdf

URGENCI website. (n.d.). Retrieved July 26, 2016, from http://urgenci.net/the-network/

URGENCI. (2016). *Mapping Local and Solidarity-Based Partnerships Between Producers and Consumers In The Mediterranean Basin*. Retrieved July 26, 2016, from http://urgenci.net/wp-content/uploads/2016/03/UR_Med-MAPPING_RESULTS-0416.pdf

Van der Leeuw, S., Wiek, A., Harlow, J., & Buizer, J. (2012). How much time do we have? Urgency and rhetoric in sustainability science. *Sustainability Science, 7*(S1), 115–120. doi:10.1007/s11625-011-0153-1

Van Riel, C. B., & Fomburn, C. J. (2007). *Essentials of Corporate Communications: Implementing Practices for Effective Reputation Management*. New York: Routledge Publishing. doi:10.4324/9780203390931

Van Wezemael, L., Verbeke, W., de Barcellos, M. D., Scholderer, J., & Perez-Cueto, F. (2010). Consumer perceptions of beef healthiness: Results from a qualitative study in four European countries. *BMC Public Health, 10*(1), 342. doi:10.1186/1471-2458-10-342 PMID:20550647

Vanhamme, J., & Grobben, B. (2009). "Too good to be true!". The effectiveness of CSR history in countering negative publicity. *Journal of Business Ethics, 85*(2), 273–283. doi:10.1007/s10551-008-9731-2

Vigoda-Gadot, E., Vinarski-Peretz, H., & Ben-Zion, E. (2003). Politics and Image in The Organizational Landscape: An Empirical Examination Amongst Public Sector Employees. *Journal of Managerial Psychology, 18*(8), 764–787. doi:10.1108/02683940310511872

Viscusi, K. A. (1983). *Risk by Choice: Regulating Gealth and Safety in Workplace*. Harvard University Press. doi:10.4159/harvard.9780674186217

Visser, W., & Tolhurst, N. (Eds.). (2010). *The world guide to CSR: A country-by-country analysis of corporate sustainability and responsibility.* Sheffield, UK: Greenleaf Publishing.

Vitell, S. J., & Festervand, T. A. (1987). Business ethics: Conflicts, practices and beliefs of industrial executives. *Journal of Business Ethics, 6*(2), 111–122. doi:10.1007/BF00382024

Vitell, S. J., & Paolillo, J. G. (2004). A cross-cultural study of the antecedents of the perceived role of ethics and social responsibility. *Business Ethics (Oxford, England), 13*(2-3), 185–199. doi:10.1111/j.1467-8608.2004.00362.x

Vitell, S. J., Paolillo, J. G., & Thomas, J. L. (2003). The perceived role of ethics and social responsibility: A study of marketing professionals. *Business Ethics Quarterly, 13*(01), 63–86. doi:10.5840/beq20031315

Vizureanu, V. (2013). Some Remarks Concerning the Concept of Glocalization. *Public Reason, 5*(1).

Vlachos, P. A., Tsamakos, A., Vrechopoulos, A. P., & Avramidis, P. K. (2009). Corporate social responsibility: Attributions, loyalty, and the mediating role of trust. *Journal of the Academy of Marketing Science, 37*(2), 170–180. doi:10.1007/s11747-008-0117-x

Von Bertalanffy, L. (1972). The history and status of general systems theory. *Academy of Management Journal, 15*(4), 407–426. doi:10.2307/255139

Vuković, P., Čavlin, G., & Čavlin, M. (2015). Komplementarnost u razvoju ruralnog sa banjskim, spa i wellness turizmom. *Ekonomika Poljoprivrede, 62*(1), 259–270. doi:10.5937/ekoPolj1501259V

Walsh, B. J., Rydzak, F., Palazzo, A., Kraxner, F., Herrero, M., Schenk, P. M., ... Obersteiner, M. (2015). New feed sources key to ambitious climate targets. *Carbon Balance and Management, 10*(26), 1–8. doi:10.1186/s13021-015-0040-7 PMID:26661066

Wanapat, M., Cherdthong, A., Phesatcha, K., & Kang, S. (2015). Dietary sources and their effects on animal production and environmental sustainability. *Animal Nutrition, 1*(3), 96–103. doi:10.1016/j.aninu.2015.07.004

Wanderley, L. S. O., Lucian, R., Farache, F., & de Sousa Filho, J. M. (2008). CSR information disclosure on the web: A context-based approach analysing the influence of country of origin and industry sector. *Journal of Business Ethics, 82*(2), 369–378. doi:10.1007/s10551-008-9892-z

Watson, S. (2009). The Magic of the Marketplace: Sociality in a Neglected Public Space. *Urban Studies (Edinburgh, Scotland), 46*(8), 1577–1591. doi:10.1177/0042098009105506

Watson, S., & Studdert, D. (2006). *Markets as sites for social interaction.* Bristol: The Policy Press.

Webb, D. J., & Mohr, L. A. (1998). A typology of consumer responses to cause-related marketing: From skeptics to socially concerned. *Journal of Public Policy & Marketing,* 226–238.

White, R. R., & Brady, M. (2014). Can consumers' willingness to pay incentivize adoption of environmental impact reducing technologies in meat animal production? *Food Policy, 49*(Part 1), 41–49. doi:10.1016/j.foodpol.2014.06.007

White, R. R., Brady, M., Capper, J. L., & Johnson, K. A. (2014). Optimizing diet and pasture management to improve sustainability of U.S. beef production. *Agricultural Systems, 130*, 1–12. doi:10.1016/j.agsy.2014.06.004

White, R. R., Brady, M., Capper, J. L., McNamara, J. P., & Johnson, K. A. (2015). Cow–calf reproductive, genetic, and nutritional management to improve the sustainability of whole beef production systems. *Journal of Animal Science, 93*(6), 3197–3211. doi:10.2527/jas.2014-8800 PMID:26115306

White, R. R., & Capper, J. L. (2013). An environmental, economic, and social assessment of improving cattle finishing weight or average daily gain within U.S. beef production. *Journal of Animal Science, 91*(12), 5801–5812. doi:10.2527/jas.2013-6632 PMID:24146151

White, R. R., & Capper, J. L. (2014). Precision diet formulation to improve performance and profitability across various climates: Modeling the implications of increasing the formulation frequency of dairy cattle diets. *Journal of Dairy Science, 97*(3), 1563–1577. doi:10.3168/jds.2013-6859 PMID:24393175

Wilson, N. J. (2009). *What is Greenwashing? Don't let the truth-stretchers pull the wool over your eyes.* Academic Press.

Wilson, R. M., & Gilligan, C. (2012). *Strategic marketing management.* Routledge.

World Commission on Environment and Development. (1987). *Our common future.* New York: Oxford University Press.

Yáñez-Ruiz, D. R., Abecia, L., & Newbold, C. (2015). Manipulating rumen microbiome and fermentation through interventions during early life: A review. *Frontiers in Microbiology, 6*, 1133. doi:10.3389/fmicb.2015.01133 PMID:26528276

Yildirim, A. E. (2015). *Organik Pazar Arastirmasi.* Retrieved July 22, 2016, from http://www.tarimdunyasi.net/2015/07/22/organik-pazar-arastirmasi/

Yoon, Y., Gürhan-Canli, Z., & Schwarz, N. (2006). The effect of corporate social responsibility activities on companies with bad reputations. *Journal of Consumer Psychology, 16*(4), 377–390. doi:10.1207/s15327663jcp1604_9

Zdorov, A. B. (2009). Comprehensive development of tourism in the countryside. *Studies on Russian Economic Development, 20*(4), 453–455. doi:10.1134/S107570070904011X

Zhang, Y., & Gelb, B. D. (1996). Matching advertising appeals to culture: The influence of products' use conditions. *Journal of Advertising, 25*(3), 29–46. doi:10.1080/00913367.1996.10673505

Zinkhan, G. M. (1994). International Advertising: *A Research Agenda. Journal of Advertising, 23*(1), 11–15. doi:10.1080/00913367.1994.10673427

Zinkhan, G. M., & Carlson, L. (1995). Green advertising and the reluctant consumer. *Journal of Advertising, 24*(2), 1–6. doi:10.1080/00913367.1995.10673471

Zorleţan, T., Burduş, E., & Căprărescu, G. (1995). *Managementul tranziţiei.* Bucureşti: Editura Holding Reporter.

Zsolnai, L., & Podmaniczky, L. (2010). Community-supported agriculture. In The Collaborative Enterprise: Creating Values for a Sustainable World (pp. 137-150). Oxford, UK: Peter Land Academic.

Zukin, S. (1995). *The cultures of cities Blackwell.* Cambridge, MA and Oxford.

About the Contributors

Violeta Sima holds the position of Associate Professor in the Department of Business Administration, Faculty of Economics, Petroleum-Gas University of Ploiesti Romania. She obtained a Ph.D. in Economic Cybernetics and Statistics from Bucharest University of Economic Studies. She has published about 55 international papers in outstanding journals, 5 book chapters in edited books and 3 authored books. Her research and teaching interests encompass Customer Relationship Management, Marketing Research, Business to Business Marketing, Green Marketing, and Social Responsibility. She has participated in research projects in the field of Marketing and Human Resources Development.

* * *

Tamer Baran was born in Van, Turkey. He completed his undergraduate at Dumlupinar University. MBA degree at Pamukkale University. He has contiuned his PhD at Pamukkale University. He worked at Celal Bayar University 2009-2011 and he has worked at Pamukkale University since 2011 as a Lecturer in the Tourism and Travel Agency department. His researches interest branding, consumer behaviour, retailing, marketing research and green marketing.

Mitu Augustin Constantin, Ph.D. in Economic Sciences, Specialist in marketing research, market analysis, consumer behavior and promotional programs implementation. ESOMAR member since 2004. Project manager of research project CIVITAS II, SUCCESS (2005-2009) - European research project (contract TREN / 04 / FP6EN / S07.39573 / 513 785) and Manager of local evaluation within the same project, in partnership with the Ploiesti's local Administration, Public Transport Operator Ploiesti and local governments of cities Preston (UK) and Larochelle (France) for the implementation of innovative measures on urban transport and recreational areas to improve urban environment and quality of life. Director of research projects carried out in partnership with local business community and member in the implementation of several projects of human resource development (HRD). 5 books published in the marketing field over 40 paperwork published during the 20 years of experience in this field.

Ozge Ercoskun is an associate professor in the City and Regional Planning Department of the Gazi University, Ankara, Turkey. She graduated from the City and Regional Planning Department of the Istanbul Technical University in 1998. She completed her master's studies in the Geodetic and Geographic Information Technologies Department of the METU in 2002. She got her Ph.D. degree from the City and Regional Planning Department of the Gazi University in 2007. She has attended several national and international congresses; summer schools and workshops related to ecological urban planning and geographic information systems. She has written 4 books and more than 50 papers on sustainable urban design and ecological and smart urban planning, geographic information systems and information technologies. She worked as a researcher in many national and institutional projects. She has awards about sustainability and urban growth, sustainable tourism. She has written a chapter named 'Green Urban Planning and Design for Smarter Communities' in 2010 published by Information Science Publishing. She has published an edited book named 'Green and Ecological Technologies for Urban Planning: Creating Smart Cities' from the same publisher in 2012.She has written chapters named 'Creating Resilient Communities: Local Currencies and Time Banks in Green Economy' in 2015 and 'Smart Technologies for Sustainable Mobility' in 2016 and Sustainable Parking Planning for Smart Growth of Metropolitan Cities in 2017 by Information Science Publishing.

Alfredo J. Escribano finished his Veterinary Sciences Degree on 2008. From the, he has hold diiferent positions within the animal production sector/field of knowledge. Since 2009, he has been analyzing different aspects of livestock farms (including economics and sustainability) as well as researching on consumers' behaviour towards products of animal origin. From 2014, he has been combining his activity in the private sector (feed industry) with the abovementioned research topics. He also participates as trainer-professor in courses for professionals related to animal production.

Cristina Gafu is an associate professor in the Philology Department of Petroleum and Gas University of Ploiesti, Romania. She holds a Ph.D. in Ethnology and Folklore from the University of Bucharest. She teaches Ethnology and Folklore for undergraduate students and Romanian Culture and Civilization for the international students. Her interests include storytelling phenomenon, contemporary narratives, and didactics, having published more than 50 studies on these topics and three books dealing mainly with narratives in the urban environment and aspects of the urban ethnologic research. Some of her representative studies are Family narratives in the urban milieu, Narration, and narrativity in the contemporary folk media, Aspects of the ethnological research in the Romanian urban milieu, The importance of a multicultural approach in teaching Romanian Culture and Civilization to international students written in association with Mihaela Iancu, The role of particular types of exercises in remedial teaching. A case study, Cultural integration of foreign students by means of Romanian Culture and Civilization classes, both articles written in association with Cristina Iridon and Mihaela Badea, A case study on using xeroxlore in teaching English at academic level, Advantages and Disadvantages of Storytelling in Teaching English at Academic Level: A Case Study in the University of Ploiesti, Romania, both studies written in association with Mihaela Badea, The dynamic of the musical repertoire of the Istroromans from Croatia. Preserving and revaluating dimensions, and Islands of preserving ethnical identity. Istroromans, both articles written in association with MihaelaNurbert-Chetan.

Cristina Iridon is an associate professor in the Philology Department of Petroleum and Gas University of Ploiesti, Romania. She holds a Ph.D. in Classical Languages and Literature from the University of Bucharest. She teaches Latin, History of the Romanian Language and Comparative Literature to undergraduate students. She carries out research into issues related to classical studies, didactics, and literature. She published the Latin Language. Morphology in 2009, Latin Language. Syntax in 2010, Latin Language. Theory and Exercises in 2014, Comparative Literature. Antiquity in 2014 and Modernity Elements of the Ancient Novel in 2015. She also wrote more than 50 articles on the topics mentioned above. Some of the representative ones are: The significance of the text of the short stories in the context of Roman novels, Traditional patterns and symbols in Breban's novel Animale bolnave, A few considerations on names in Apuleius' Metamorphoses, (Dis)similarities in Gilgamesh and Arjunas' journey, Civitas ante naturam, A study on Satyricon and its ancient approach to education, Zahlen in Petronius and I.L. Caragiale, The role of certain types of exercises in remedial teaching. A case study, written in association with Cristina Gafu and Mihaela Badea, Cultural integration of foreign students by means of Romanian Culture and Civilization classes, written in association with Cristina Gafu and Mihaela Badea, Students' evaluation of a Romanian language textbook, written in association with Mihaela Badea.

Olja Munitlak Ivanovic as the youngest participant in the project, she was given an award for the youngest project participant and leader in the field of sustainable development. The project was funded and supported by the Environmental Ambassadors and Ambassade van het Koninkrijk der Nederland, Project: Identification of Sustainable Development and Environmental Leaders for Tomorrow, Belgrade,

May 2007, – Acknowledgement of Edukons University for encouragement and development of research activities at the University, 25 May 2011, – Jubilee Award of Edukons University on the basis of the decision of the Senate of Edukons University, No. R. dated 24 May 2011, – Andrejević Foundation Charter for cooperation in pursuing its founding goals and contribution to development of scientific creativity, Belgrade, 2014, – Serbian Society for the Environmental Protection, ECOLOGICA, HONOURARY AWARD is presented to Prof. dr Olja Munitlak Ivanović, In proud recognition of her outstanding contribution to science in the field of the environmental protection and the development of international cooperation, Belgrade April 2015.

Mehmet Kiziloglu was born in Denizli, Turkey. He studied in Istanbul at the Yeditepe University: a B.A. in Economics. As a scholar he continued for another degree, in master studies at Gaziantep University and Ph.D. in Management and Organization at Pamukkale University. His Phd Dissertation is: "Relationship Between Organizational Culture And Organizational Power In The Contex Of Denison Organizational Culture Model". Dr. Mehmet Kiziloglu is an Lecturer in Business Management Department in Pamukkale University.

Raluca Georgiana Ladaru is Lecturer at The Bucharest University of Economic Studies, Department of Agrifood and Environmental Economics. Her main areas of expertise are: agro marketing and research market techniques.

Lars Moratis is professor of Sustainable Business at the NHTV University of Applied Sciences and professor and academic director of the Competence Center Corporate Responsibility at Antwerp Management School. His research interests are responsible management education, sustainability-drive business modelling, the credibility of corporate CSR claims, and CSR standards. He is also founder of Impact Academy.

Daniela Rojas, Colombian, Economist and Master in Business Administration of the University of Amsterdam. Passionate about creating a fairer food system. In her work as sustainability advisor at a global fruit merchant and as an academicus of the Slow Food Youth Network Academy she was confronted with the challenges of the current food system. She is convinced that agriculture is crucial in our path towards sustainable development and that it is very important that all the voices involved are heard to come up with effective solutions.

Svetlana Roljević-Nikolić graduated 2008 on the Faculty of Agriculture, University of Belgrade. Doctoral thesis: "Productivity of alternative small grains in the organic system" degree 2014 at the Faculty of Agriculture, University of Belgrade, and gained title a Ph.D. He has been working in the Institute of Agricultural Economics, Belgrade since 2008. Svetlana is member of following professional bodies: Balkan Scientific Association of Agricultural Economists (B.S.A.A.E); Serbian Association of Agricultural Economists.

Predrag Vuković graduated 2003 on the Faculty of Economics, University of Belgrade. There he completed postgraduate specialist studies 2006 and Master's degree in management at tourism 2008. Master's thesis: "Evaluation competitiveness of tourist destination, example shown at the City of Novi Sad" degree 2010. Doctoral thesis: "Management model to increase the competitiveness of rural tourist destinations in Serbia" degree 2016 at the Faculty of Economics, University of Kragujevac, and gained title a Ph.D. of Economic Sciences. He has been working in the Institute of Agricultural Economics, Belgrade since 2004. Since he started to work, he has been involved actively in numerous projects of the Institute. Membership in professional associations: European Association of Agricultural Economists (E.A.A.E); Balkan Scientific Association of Agricultural Economists (B.S.A.A.E); Serbian Association of Agricultural Economist (S.A.A.E.).

Index

A

Advertising Research 103
Agricultural Economics 167, 180
animal nutrition 190, 192, 194, 199-200
animal production 147, 171, 189, 191, 194, 198
Attribution Theory 26, 57

B

Business Performance Measurement Systems 131

C

circular economy 1-3, 6, 8-10, 12-14, 20
Community-Supported Agriculture 137-139, 143, 145, 149, 166
competitive advantage 60, 63, 68, 116, 125, 131, 221, 226
consumption of organic products 176, 180
cooperation 13, 33, 58, 113, 142, 159, 216, 239, 246, 248
Corporate Social Responsibility (CSR) 22, 24, 57, 80, 183
CSR 21-33, 37-40, 42, 45-48, 57, 183, 197
culture 6, 21, 23-24, 28-32, 34-36, 42, 44-45, 47-48, 57-59, 62, 68-69, 71, 104-114, 116, 118-127, 131-132, 136, 138-140, 142, 168, 211, 223, 232-244, 246-248, 252-253

D

Demand for organic products 176, 180

E

Eco-Friendly Advertising 79, 103
ecological responsibility 1-3, 5, 13-15, 20, 142

F

food community 137, 139, 145, 147, 166
food security 138, 181-182
food system 147, 159, 181, 209
formal 108, 131, 149, 157, 233, 242-243, 246

G

globalization 23, 28, 234-237, 239, 241, 247, 252-253
GMO 138, 166
green advertisement 24, 26, 29, 31, 34-36, 42, 47-48, 77
green economy 137-140, 210, 222-224, 239, 253
greenwashing 22, 25-26, 58-60, 64-71, 77

H

heterogenization 236-237, 241
Hofstede 28-34, 36-37, 39-41, 48, 107, 109, 237
homogenization 234-237, 247
hybridization 236-237, 241, 253

I

Impact Measurement of the Promotional Campaign 103

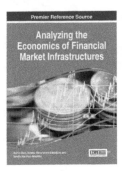

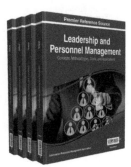

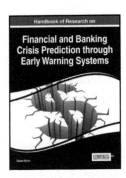

Stay Current on the Latest Emerging Research Developments

Become an IGI Global Reviewer for Authored Book Projects

Premier Reference Source

Emerging GIS Applications for Emergency and Disaster Management

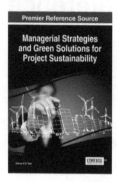

Premier Reference Source

Managerial Strategies and Green Solutions for Project Sustainability

Premier Reference Source

Comparative Approaches to Using R and Python for Statistical Data Analysis

Premier Reference Source

Solutions for High-Touch Communications in a High-Tech World

The overall success of an authored book project is dependent on quality and timely reviews.

In this competitive age of scholarly publishing, constructive and timely feedback significantly decreases the turnaround time of manuscripts from submission to acceptance, allowing the publication and discovery of progressive research at a much more expeditious rate. Several IGI Global authored book projects are currently seeking highly qualified experts in the field to fill vacancies on their respective editorial review boards:

Applications may be sent to:
development@igi-global.com

Applicants must have a doctorate (or an equivalent degree) as well as publishing and reviewing experience. Reviewers are asked to write reviews in a timely, collegial, and constructive manner. All reviewers will begin their role on an ad-hoc basis for a period of one year, and upon successful completion of this term can be considered for full editorial review board status, with the potential for a subsequent promotion to Associate Editor.

If you have a colleague that may be interested in this opportunity, we encourage you to share this information with them.

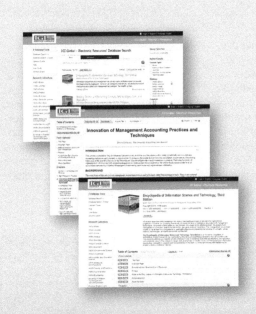

Lightning Source UK Ltd.
Milton Keynes UK
UKHW050744211218
334270UK00003B/38/P